Chinese Documentaries

In China, unlike in Western cinema, documentary film, rather than fiction film, has been the dominant mode since 1949. In recent years, documentary TV programmes have experienced a meteoric rise. This book discusses various types of Chinese documentaries, under both the planned and the market economy. It discusses especially the relationship between documentaries and society, showing how, under the market economy, although the government continues to use the genre as propaganda to promote its ideologies and policies, documentaries are being increasingly used as a medium where public concerns and alternative voices can be heard. It argues that there is a gradual process of 'democratisation' in the media, in which documentaries play a significant role.

Yingchi Chu is a Senior Lecturer in Media Studies and Research Fellow of Asia Research Centre at Murdoch University, Western Australia. She has published journal articles and book chapters on Chinese media, and is the author of *Hong Kong Cinema: Coloniser, Motherland and Self* (2003).

Routledge Media, Culture and Social Change in Asia
Series Editor
Stephanie Hemelryk Donald
Institute for International Studies, University of Technology, Sydney

The aim of this series is to publish original, high-quality work by both new and established scholars in the West and the East, on all aspects of media, culture and social change in Asia.

Chinese Documentaries
From dogma to polyphony

Yingchi Chu

 Routledge
Taylor & Francis Group

LONDON AND NEW YORK

First published 2007
by Routledge
2 Park Square, Milton Park, Abingdon, Oxon OX14 4RN

Simultaneously published in the USA and Canada
by Routledge
270 Madison Ave, New York, NY 10016

Routledge is an imprint of the Taylor & Francis Group, an informa business

© 2007 Yingchi Chu

British Library Cataloguing in Publication Data
A catalogue record for this book is available from the British Library

Library of Congress Cataloging in Publication Data
Chu, Yingchi.
  Chinese documentaries : from dogma to polyphony / Yingchi Chu.
    p. cm. — (Routledge media, culture and social change in Asia
series ; 8)
  Filmography: p.
  Includes bibliographical references and index.
  1. Documentary films—China—History and criticism.
  2. Documentary films—Social aspects—China. I. Title.
PN1995.9.D6C48 2007
070.1'8—dc22
                                        2006039265

ISBN10: 0-415-37570-3 (hbk)
ISBN10: 0-203-09967-2 (ebk)

ISBN13: 978-0-415-37570-2 (hbk)
ISBN13: 978-0-203-09967-4 (ebk)

For My Parents
Huang Ziqin (黄子琴) and Zhu Wei (朱未)

Contents

Acknowledgements

I wish to acknowledge my appreciation of the help I have been given by a large number of colleagues, friends, and students, as well as institutions, during the writing of this book.

My first thanks go to Peter Sowden, my editor at Routledge, who introduced me to the press; his kind patience has been exceptional. Thanks also to Professor Stephanie Hemelryk Donald for years of encouragement and her input as series editor for this book. Professor Tim Wright will always be appreciated as a first-rate scholar and generous mentor over many years. I thank him for his early critical comments on my application for an Australian Discovery Grant and his critical reading of some of the chapters of the book, his valuable research advice, and his improvements on my pinyin (any remaining mistakes are surely mine). I would also like to acknowledge the fact that part of Chapter 5 'Documenting the law' appeared as a contribution to the volume *Chinese Citizenship: Views from the Margins* (2006), edited by Vanessa L. Fong and Rachel Murphy. I thank Routledge for permission to include the material in *Chinese Documentaries*.

For research input in China, I want to thank the following persons: Dr Kang Ning (President, CETV), who has proved an inspirational source of knowledge; Chen Hong (director and producer, CETV), Zhang Zhaojun (Head of Research, CETV), and Calvin Qin Cheng (CETV) for making my stays in Beijing such pleasurable experiences; Tong Ning (executive producer, Channel Ten CCTV), Liu Xiaoli and Han Yali (China Television Documentary Association); Chen Jinliang and San Wanli (Beijing Film Archive); Professor Meng Jian (Director, Centre for Visual Research, Fudan University), Professor Lü Xinyu (Centre for Visual Research, Fudan University); President Xiong Shuxin (Minorities Research Centre, Yunnan), Professor Guo Jing and He Yuan (Yunnan Academy of Social Sciences), Zhou Yuejun (Film Director, Yunnan TV Station); and Li Dehua (Director, China News, Urumqi). I would also like to thank many research assistants for their input in arranging my stay in China and collecting archival data for me.

The research for this book was made possible by a number of awards, an Australian national ARC Discovery Grant, two REGS grants from the

Humanities and one REGS grant from the Asia Research Centre at Murdoch University, Western Australia. I also wish to acknowledge the generous research leave, including one OSP, I have received from Murdoch University, which provided the indispensable span of time without which the data collection for this book could not have been accomplished. To Dr Martin Mhando and MED333 Documentary students at Murdoch University between 2003–2006, thank you for allowing me to present my arguments in lectures and tutorials.

Finally, I wish to thank my husband, Professor Horst Ruthrof, for his critical reading of the manuscript and his devotion to making me a better scholar.

Yingchi Chu

Introduction

Writing about Chinese documentaries

The current popularity of Chinese cinema in the West has been sparked in the main by the fiction films of such directors as Zhang Yimuo, Chen Kaige, Feng Xiaoning, Zhang Yang or Feng Xiaogang. However, their movies constitute only the tip of the iceberg of a much larger volume of Chinese cinema the vast bulk of which is made up of documentary films. Relatively little has been written in English about Chinese documentary cinema in any comprehensive sense. This is a gap which I wish to fill at least partially in presenting *Chinese Documentaries* to the reading public. In China, on the other hand, there is now a burgeoning industry of critical literature on documentary film and television programmes. A secondary aim then is to bring some of that literature to the attention of the Anglophone readership. A third aim is to redress an imbalance in many Western analyses of contemporary Chinese media. I have been struck by a certain asymmetry in at least some of that literature where a relatively small body of data serves as illustrative material for the exposition of approaches informed by a lively theoretical debate in such fields as politics, media research, and film studies. Useful as many of these theories are in lending the debate about the current state of the media in China a higher degree of precision, when the data are overwhelmed by theorisation what we are able to learn about China can be jeopardised. Accordingly, my investigation is informed foremost by a respect for the data as much as has been possible, without falling into the trap of assuming that data can stand on their own or that they contain their own theorisation. With this caution in mind I propose a modest kind of conceptualisation throughout the book, looking at documentary cinema from the 1920s to the present from the perspective of a loosely conceived spectrum stretching between the poles of highly constrained and dogmatic film making at one end of the scale and a multi-voiced or polyphonic form of cinema, at the other. I will return to these terms for clarification in Chapter 1.

Why documentary film? To film buffs the question would be superfluous since for them any branch of cinema since its invention by the Lumière brothers in Lyon in December of 1895 is intriguing in itself. From the perspective of a film theorist the reasons for turning to documentary television programmes and to documentary film in China are more specific.

Documentaries, more than fiction films, are a record of the way a society typically represents and so understands itself and others. This moves documentary cinema into the vicinity of historiography and ethnography. At the same time, documentary techniques often inform and supplement visual news reporting in the sense of providing details that go beyond the narrow confines of news genres. As such, documentary can, to a certain extent, claim to be able to function as a mirror of social, cultural and political change. This is why I have focused throughout the book on films addressing social issues, leaving scientific and other instructional documentaries to other investigators. With this proviso in mind, a detailed generic delimitation of documentary film with reference to the relevant literature will be attempted in Chapter 1.

And why Chinese documentaries? Unlike documentary cinema in the West, which has played a secondary role and is now clearly in the shadow of the fiction film, in China this relation is reversed. Here documentary film production has outpaced its fictional relation by a very long shot. Yet it is not only the sheer quantity that makes Chinese documentary films an attractive target of scholarship; collectively, documentary cinema constitutes a unique archive of China's cultural and political fortunes that would otherwise remain largely hidden from the rest of the world – especially that showing Mao's reign and its decline during the years of the Cultural Revolution – documentary film and archival footage is proving a unique and largely untapped resource. If we wish to understand what is going on in the Chinese media scene today, critical reflection on that period is a *sine qua non*. Chapter 3 is dedicated to offering such a reflection. Likewise, there are not many better ways of trying to come to grips with the social changes in China today than having a careful look at the television documentaries that make up a hefty portion of the programmes screened daily by China's 314 television stations. This is why in Chapters 4 to 7, in Part II of the book, I offer a number of perspectives on contemporary television documentaries.

The commitment to a sound database required extensive travelling and fieldwork in China. Several trips over three years and a three months research stay in China in 2005 allowed me to collect a substantial corpus of policy documents, industrial statistics, statements by film directors, producers, and television management, as well as a large body of documentary films and television programmes. In addition, a satellite dish permitting reception of some 25 Chinese television channels has provided new materials on a continuing basis right up to the final drafting of the manuscript. As a result of sifting and analysing these materials, several observations have forced themselves to the forefront of my research. I sum them up in the following six sections.

First, because of its prominence in China throughout the period from the 1920s to the present, documentary cinema has played a privileged role in reflecting social and political aspirations, their transformations and effects, and so provides important insights into the lay of China's political and social landscapes. I am deliberately speaking here of cinema rather than film since cinema includes film policy, production, film text, distribution, film culture and film criticism, all of which have been profoundly affected by the political events during that period.

Second, the differences between documentary cinema during the Mao era and that of today could not be starker. This, in spite of the fact that the government under Mao, as does the Chinese government under the leadership of Hu Jingtao, referred to itself as Communist. In this context, it is well worth taking note of Henry Kissinger's answer in an interview in June 2006 conducted by a prominent journalist, Ruan Cishan, in *Fengyun duihua / Dialogue* at 7.30pm on Sunday on the Hong Kong based Phoenix TV. Asked by Ruan how he compared his impression of the Chinese government in the 1970s with that of today Kissinger said, 'the only thing that has remained the same is the label Communist'. While this difference is readily recognised in economic terms, there is a widely held view amongst media analysts in the West that underneath the obvious accommodation of global market pressures the Communist government has continued to exert its iron grip on Chinese society (C. Lee 2000; 1994; Y. Zhao 1998). While this is undoubtedly the case in certain respects, control over the Chinese media management, media policy and programming has undergone significant changes. This transformation will be part of the argument informing Chapters 4 to 7.

Third, it would be starry eyed to assume that whatever relaxation of government control over the media in China can be observed is primarily the result of spontaneous or organised democratic pressure. The irony here is that many of the changes that are occurring now are a direct result of new government policies themselves. Two political factors in particular have played a prominent role in bringing about this shift: the debates following the Tiananmen Square demonstration of 1989 and the conclusions drawn by the Communist leadership from Deng Xiaoping's visit to China's south in 1992. The students had been inspired by the six part documentary series *He Shang / River Elegy* portraying the Yellow River catastrophes and advocating Western-style reforms on the advice of Party General Secretary Zhao Ziyang. The Tiananmen Square student demands for more radical reforms and especially free elections can be read as an extension of precisely the reform agenda initiated by Zhao Ziyang. When talks between the students and Li Peng, the Soviet trained Premier and Party ideologue, as well as with General Secretary Zhao Ziyang, failed, the government embarked on its ill-fated termination of the protest. In the wake of the crackdown, between 1989 and 1992, the ensuing struggle between ideologues and pragmatists put a temporary halt on the reform policies introduced by Deng Xiaoping in 1978. It was only in 1992, after Deng's inspection tour of South China's Special Economic Zone of Shenzhen, Guangzhou, Zhuhai and Shanghai that his arguments in favour of the compatibility of socialism and market economy finally won through. Once that had happened, media policies were reviewed and from a very different perspective: the demands of the market.

Fourth, three market forces have been instrumental in bringing about the kind of changes we are witnessing today: advertising, ratings and the demand for audience participation in order to achieve higher rating. As far as advertising is concerned, in a very short period of time China has become the third largest advertiser of commodities in the world, after the US and Japan. This transformation of the Chinese media is not simply a consequence of the broad government directive to become market oriented; rather, it is a result of new policies specifically requiring that television stations become financially self-sufficient. Indeed, 90 per cent of all media income now comes from advertising, affording television stations a certain degree of freedom in decision making, while government retains ownership and a 10 per cent funding obligation to secure what they regard as sufficient control. This change has had a powerful impact on the management and production of the media, and especially of television. At the same time, quite another market force has made its appearance: ratings. To gauge the popularity of their programmes, television stations have had to adopt Western style ratings mechanisms, by establishing their own ratings departments or outsourcing the task to specialised ratings companies. As a consequence, television audiences nationwide have become active players in the mix of programmes on offer. But not only programme content is being affected by this shift towards audience preferences. There is also an increasing demand for slicker presentational modes, partly in response to programmes entering mainland China from the Hong Kong based and Rupert Murdoch owned television station Phoenix. A third market force, related to the second, is the growing, active participation of audiences in the programmes themselves, as well as the demands by the audience for a greater variety in programming. We can today observe an explosion of audience participation in Chinese television, a phenomenon which has likewise prompted a transformation of what is being produced and consumed. In turn, the new participatory horizon of expectations amongst television viewers is having feed-back effects on programming to a degree that is just now beginning to be understood.

Fifth, two advances in film technology have exerted a significant influence on the way documentary filming is now able to record perceptual reality and how footage is collected and edited. One is the introduction in 1979 of cordless cameras with inbuilt battery packs and the technology of recording location sound. This not only allowed virtually unlimited access to remote areas and places where it was difficult to film, but also introduced a much greater sense of immediacy to documentary cinema by giving the film viewer direct access to the ambient sounds that are part of the documented scene. Some 20 years after its introduction in the West, China had finally caught up with the technology of location sound, which has fundamentally transformed the experience of documentary cinema. The second important technological innovation we need to take seriously into account as a factor in the evolution of Chinese documentary is the more recent invention, and fast spreading use, of digital video (DV) in the early 1990s. Without this new user-friendly technology there would not have occurred the explosion of semi-independent and independent filmmakers that we are witnessing in China today. Not only is this expansion of the range of available camera technology responsible for a rapid increase in the documentary films being produced, it has also encouraged a new variety of ways of looking at China's social world. The most recent innovation has been the advent of mobile phone video technology since 2005, marked in China by Chen Liaoyu at the Beijing Film Academy who uploaded his mobile phone films, such as *Pingguo / Apple*, on to his webpage. At least partly as a result of such new technologies, we can now observe the emergence of an alternative and critical film culture in addition to the official documentary channels.

Sixth, and last, throughout this book we should keep in mind that there are a few major differences between the way documentary film has developed in China compared with its evolution in Western cultures. One is the Chinese traditional view that art forms should have an educational function. Chinese documentary cinema has been profoundly affected by this perspective from its beginnings to the present. This is also at least partly responsible for another difference, the fact that the Chinese documentary tradition is characterised by a certain sense of seriousness barring such frivolities as mock documentaries in the style, say, of *Forgotten Silver* (Jackson and Botes, 1992). This is perhaps also the reason behind the absence so far of any self-reflexive presentational mode. It is not so surprising then that one of the self-reflexive features of Western documentary cinema, film ethics, has been slow to develop in China. While there are some media laws and regulations in place to protect people with regard to their rights when they are being filmed, documentary film practice has been somewhat lagging behind the law.

A realistic comprehension of what is occurring in today's Chinese media market requires, I suggest, the broader picture of visual representation and self-representation since the early twentieth century. An investigation of documentary film and, more recently, documentary television programmes, is I believe a sound gauge by which to assemble such a larger picture. To hold my selection of materials together I have followed a research hunch to the effect that we can observe an evolutionary trajectory of Chinese documentaries from promising beginnings in the 1920s through a period of dogmatic, ideological domination under Mao Zedong's leadership, a period of tentative relaxation of government control in the 1980s, to the present state of documentary diversity. With this tentative plan in mind, I have divided the book into two parts, Part I consisting of a chapter on the generic features of documentary and two historical chapters covering the period from the 1920s to the end of the Cultural Revolution in 1977, with a concluding section of the all important transition period to 1993, and Part II which addresses documentary film making and documentary television programmes from 1993 to the present. The chapters of Part II are not arranged in chronological order; rather, each chapter offers a different perspective on recent and current documentaries. The rationale of the chapter order in Part II is informed by the relationship between television, film, and digital video (DV) production. Chapters 4 and 5 focus on television, its production policies and documentary programming to reflect the fact that since 1993 television has become the leading medium for documentary. Chapter 4 begins with television reform, and ends with a detailed discussion of the China Education Television (CETV) in terms of its policy reform and documentary programming and the introduction of audience participation. Chapter 5 sharpens the focus further by singling out a particular documentary programme and its role in citizenship education. As from 1999 onwards DV has become increasingly popular in documentary filmmaking, Chapter 6 looks at the documentary representation in film, television and DV. The concluding chapter, Chapter 7, deals mainly with television and DV production after 1999. In so doing, Chapters 6 and 7 offer critical insights into documentary social representations of minorities and the Han majority in rural and urban environments. The focus on documentary in relation to television is essential also because of the double function of television stations as producers of both documentary film and documentary programmes and as the main exhibition site of film and DV in the documentary mode. In the following sections I identify and sum up the core arguments of each chapter.

Chapter 1 'The documentary genres and Chinese documentaries' situates Chinese documentaries in the wider frame of international documentary cinema and the principles that govern documentary film as a genre. The chapter has two intertwined aims. One is to identify those features in documentaries in general that permit us to recognise a documentary film for what it is and especially to be able to distinguish it from fiction film. Here the chapter offers the reader a shortcut view of the theorisation of the documentary genre in Western literature, notably with reference to the work of Bill Nichols, as well as that of other theoreticians, in order to demonstrate the current, dominant discourse on documentary film texts. The second aim is to alert the reader to some important differences between Chinese documentaries and the documentary film tradition in the West. The two aims are then connected in the sense that these differences make it necessary to enlarge the scale of generic expectations in standard Western accounts to be able to accommodate the range of Chinese documentaries to be dealt with in this book. Specifically the broadly accepted generic scale from expository to self-reflexive documentaries has to be expanded at the expository end in order to cater for what I call the 'dogmatic mode' of documentary presentation. Such an analysis of course presupposes the completed research, but I believe it is necessary to flag from the outset where standard theorisation of documentary film is insufficient for a comprehensive description of the evolution of Chinese documentary.

Chapter 2 'Nationalism and the birth of Chinese documentary' introduces the reader to the fate of documentary film making in China at the hands of commercial film producers, the Guomindang and the Communists before 1949. In that period, my argument goes, the promise of a generously conceived documentary film culture was stifled by specific historical circumstances: a firmly engrained and limiting Chinese aesthetic, Guomindang propagandist fervour and a Communist agenda, suddenly brought into sharp relief by the Japanese invasion of China. Thus the seeds of a multi-voiced or polyphonic kind of documentary cinema open to a broad range of subject matter, experimentation with a rich potential of representational styles, and a forum for many different voices and positions to be seen and heard, were unable to sprout. Instead, we observe a narrowing of themes, styles, and voice in China's early documentary cinema that was to be further constrained after the Communist 'liberation' in 1949.

Chapter 3 'The dogmatic formula' traces the trajectory of documentary cinema during Mao Zedong's reign in terms of film policy, industry, film texts, distribution, film viewing and film criticism. What we find, the chapter argues, is a tightly knit web of political prescriptions, control of studios, ideologically driven film and subject plan, meticulously supervised film crews, narrowly circumscribed scripts and footage, heavily censored film texts, well organised, compulsory mass film viewings, and rigorously curtailed film criticism. Whatever the specific details of film policies during that time, they all adhere to the Lenin inspired notion that documentary is to be employed as visual propaganda. This motto, combined with Mao's adaptation of the traditional Chinese aesthetic formula of *wen yi zai dao* (the function of literature is to convey the *Dao*, the Confucian philosophical and moral principles) into a tool of political pedagogy resulted, the chapter shows, in a documentary cinema characterised by a 'dogmatic formula'. The chapter ends with a section on the 'period of transition' between 1978 and 1993, when the political and economic pragmatism introduced by Deng Xiaoping resulted also in a radical transformation of the media and documentary film. The section highlights the seminal impulses we need to remember from this period if we are to understand the development of documentary film and its televisual relations from 1993 to the present.

Chapter 4 'Media reform, documentary programming and the new citizen' opens with an overview of the government's media policies after 1993 before turning the reader's attention to a single television station, the only nationwide provider of televisual education, the CETV. In this chapter, I investigate the process of restructuring television management and programming in the wake of China's adoption of a market oriented economy. The chapter traces the relevant changes in government media policies and the subsequent internal responses at management level at the CETV, as well as the impact of those changes on documentary programme production. At the same time, I am trying to show how the reforms in management policy are steering a path between significantly reduced government directives and the demands of the market. Since the CETV, and most other television stations, are now required to look after much of their own funding by making themselves more attractive to viewers, ratings have become a new and crucial factor in television programming. In this respect, an increased demand for audience participation is one of the striking features of the media market, reflecting as it does the hitherto untapped wishes of the viewing public. As a consequence, I argue, documentary television programmes have begun to change to accommodate this particular form of market pressure. With reference to a number of selected documentary programmes, I demonstrate how an increase in audience participation is gradually transforming not only programme content, but also the dominant presentational modes in the direction of a more polyphonic style.

Chapter 5 'Documenting the law' shrinks the focus of analysis to a specific, though representative, example: the documentary television series *Jinri shuofa / Legal Report*, screened to around 900 million viewers every day at lunch prime time for half an hour. With over one thousand episodes of this series already broadcast, the programme is shown to depend for its success on an entirely new phenomenon in Chinese television, the inclusion in each episode of a number of clearly differentiated and often opposing voices, opinions, and speaking positions: investigative reporters, victims of a crime, alleged perpetrators of misdemeanours, felonies or fraud, witnesses on both sides, experts providing legal and other relevant advice, as well as the voices of the viewing public participating via email, phone-in, SMS, letters, and other feedback mechanisms. The polyphonic, 'enunciative modalities', in Foucault's sense, of the *Legal Report* draw on a broad social configuration, including the peasantry and the urban middle class, and address such matters as corruption amongst lower and middle level government officials.

Chapter 6 'Documenting the minorities' looks at the way the Chinese minorities are typically represented in documentary film and television documentary. I have chosen this perspective to describe the change from a monological and authoritarian style of film making to a new documentary style characteristic of the Chinese market economy, in which increasingly multi-voiced or polyphonic presentational modes are beginning to take hold. The focus on minorities, I suggest, is particularly helpful in this respect as here official or government sponsored programme and film production initially still dominates the documentary film market, with an increasing number of television productions, semi-independent and independent filmmakers contesting the dominant visual discourse.

Chapter 7 'The many voices of Chinese documentary' brings the reader up to date with a critical overview of the documentary scene in present-day China. As in some previous chapters, the argument once more proceeds from a discussion of media policies to an analysis of the media industry and interpretations of selected film texts. In doing so, the chapter shows how each of these domains has undergone visible transformations and, as a consequence, has contributed to the production of what is now available in China. The preceding chapters all lead up to this concluding argument, either historically or by way of contemporary perspectives, in which the original hypothesis is cashed in: Chinese documentaries have evolved from an initial failure to develop their generic potential before 1949, through a phase of monological, dogmatic style, to a polyphonic diversity in terms of subject matter, presentational mode, and speaking positions in today's media market. I briefly review the different notions of 'voice' in documentary representations before I turn, in the main body of the chapter, to a reading of a series of films and DV productions. The films, I suggest, strongly support the argument that we can observe in the documentaries of the last few years a demonstrable increase in polyphonic heterogeneity. In this section I mix close analysis with summary readings of recent documentaries, ending the chapter with a few in-depth analyses of documentaries in a socially critical mode suggestive of the rise of a new critical discourse in China.

The Conclusion 'Documentaries as critical discourse' opens by briefly linking the book with the current debate on media and democracy in China, before reviewing the argument advanced in the various chapters from a bird's eye perspective. The Conclusion ends with the suggestion that what we are witnessing in the documentary film and programme scene in China today amounts to a rehearsal of democracy by means other than the obviously political and that Chinese documentaries have at least the potential of ushering in a new critical discourse as a precondition for a broadly based kind of democratisation.

Finally, a word concerning the reading of this book. Chinese culture is fond of speaking of the 'harmonious society' (*hexie shehui*). While this is no doubt a worthwhile ideal to strive for, it is certainly not an accurate description of China or any other society at any stage of their histories. If the slogan means that every social act, including writing, is to be harmoniously balanced, this would amount to celebrating the status quo and change would be difficult to achieve. No doubt, some of my Chinese readers will find the book overly critical, just as many of my Western readers will probably find its critique too mild. But such is the fate of a cultural broker, a position between cultures that I believe affords me a special perspective. I hope it has allowed me to present a picture of Chinese documentary cinema not readily available to either culture.

Part I

1 The documentary genre and Chinese documentaries

Introduction

Documentary film and television documentary programmes make up a substantial share of the overall film and television productions of China today. From its inception in early 1910s, documentary filmmaking has occupied a much more prominent place in the cinema in China than it has in the West. Today Chinese documentary productions of all kinds are flourishing in a rapidly expanding media market. Why this is so and how this came about are questions to be addressed in the course of the argument of this book. Above all else, this book seeks to understand how documentary film in China has changed since its beginnings in the 1910s to the present, from an imitation of the Western tradition, to a highly authoritarian mode of presentation in the Mao era, and to today's more polyphonic and, as I will argue in the second part of the book, a more 'democratic' and critical style. Documentary film has also played a highly prominent role in the visual culture and politics of China since 1949. It is the main genre addressing the official, elite, popular and 'underground' (unofficial, marginal, illegitimate) film culture in China. The government has used documentary film to promote its political ideologies and policies, while the intellectuals increasingly use it to test, debate and communicate their new theories and perspectives. Outside the official system, marginal views are now about to be circulated through independent, semi-independent or community driven documentary filmmaking. This is partly why documentary film is the most produced, as well as one of the most widely consumed, genres in China today. The Central China Television Station (CCTV) alone produced over 1,000 documentaries per year before the end of the last century (Ren 1997: 24). Today that figure is significantly higher. Nor is the CCTV the only television station to engage in this kind of production. The development of the Chinese documentary film from dogmatic modes in the planned economy to polyphonic styles in the market economy can also be argued to reflect, as well as promote, the complex process of preparing for 'democratisation' in China.

However, before we address Chinese documentary film production in detail, a few preliminary general remarks about this intriguing form of cinema are necessary. This is so, I suggest, because much of the discussion to follow rests on the double perspective of the advanced practices and theorisation of documentary film in Western countries and of the quite different history and political constraints within which documentary film has emerged in China. Few writers and film viewers support the claim that documentary film is primarily a technical, optical replication of social and physical reality. Yet nobody doubts that in some way documentary does provide a visual record of what is actually occurring, even if such a record is always already qualified by a range of complications to be addressed later. Certainly, documentary film makes claims about how we think the world is and how we think we are able to know about the world. We could call these the ontological and epistemological functions of documentary cinema. No matter how distorted the documented reality may appear to us, this double function is never completely buried under the multiple ways in which fictional, subjective, religious, political, and ideological commitments colour a documentary film. This has surfaced in film practice, criticism and film theory under the deceptively simple and ultimately misleading heading of 'truth'. Indeed, the discussion of documentary film in the literature on film in the West has for a long time been occupied with the question of how accurately documentary film can and typically does (re)present physical and social reality. In China this topic has been approached in a somewhat different manner, as we shall see. The big problem here, as elsewhere in the study of culture, is that everything we look at appears to us through some form of *mediation*. Nothing is directly given, not even in human perception. It should not come as a surprise then that in documentary, which is always a complex transformation of *perceptual actuality*, mediation plays a fundamental role.

In this context, we notice a number of major relations that make 'pure' film documentation unlikely. Leaving aside the philosophical problematic of how objects are constituted in the human brain, we can sum up the main reasons for this suspicion as (1) the complex relations between world (perceptual actuality) and screen; (2) relations within the production process; (3) relations of screen and film viewing, including film criticism; and (4) relations between documentary film and film industry. First, then, there are unavoidable constraints in the relations between our perceptual actuality and screen. Our perception of the world is culturally over-determined, and even the machines we use always reflect the cultural paradigm to which they belong. Pictures produced from a camera in the nineteenth century are markedly different from those of a digital camera in the twenty-first century. Hence all documentary representation carries with it the cultural mediation of its age. Furthermore, all documentary films show a 'slice of world' chosen by filmmakers who are always already embedded in specific historical ideological situations.

Second, we note specific constraints owing to the production process. The choice of film stock already carries with it a modification of perceptual actuality. How does a black and white representation affect documentation?

Do various kinds of colour technologies produce different visual documentation? Does a moving camera document the world as it is more accurately than a camera that is stationary? Does the moving camera introduce an element of fictionalisation? There is likewise the question whether short takes increase fictionalisation in documentary films? Are long takes more faithful to the documented phenomena? Does the number of cameras have an effect on the degree of documentation? Does the large number of cameras increase the 'reality effect' of documentation in the *Big Brother* series? Do more cameras mean more observation and hence more 'truth'? Or is the opposite the case? How do camera angles affect the degree of documentation? Are hand held cameras more likely to give the impression of human documentation? Does the use of filters introduce an additional 'unreality' effect and hence an additional degree of fictionalisation? When is lighting no longer 'natural' lighting? Or does location sound guarantee documentary accuracy? In addition, there are questions concerning the directing of documentary film. After all, directors are always more or less present in documentary film. At what degree of intervention could one say that the documentary 'contract' is broken? As to the editing process, we may ask whether the selection of shots before us can be regarded as documentary. Likewise, there is a question about sequencing. When Shot A is followed by Shot B, can we say that this is how the world is? How much is the documentable world distorted by those decisions? Extradiegetic sound poses a similar problem: is non-location sound another way by which fictionalisation and subjectification intrude into documentary film? How far are such non-diegetic texts as titles, intertitles, and captions documentary and what is their potential for fictionalisation and subjective intrusion? Lastly, and most importantly, how does the editorial process, especially in ethnographic accounts and propaganda films, affect the documentary character of a film? After all, the ethnographic documentary tends to run the risk of exaggerating the differences between us and the filmed Other, while the propaganda film by definition serves ideological purposes rather than the ideal of accurate historical portrayal. At the level of documentary film production, then, even when the documentary function of objectivities is maintained, that is, where persons and objects are presented as themselves, such objectivities can never be 'purely' represented. This situation is aggravated by the fact that the presence of the camera and the realisation by subjects that they are being filmed introduce a significant shift of consciousness.

Third, as far as the relations between screen and film viewing are concerned, they too undermine the ideal of documentary representation. What a film actually 'is' can best be described as the virtual effects of screen images on film viewers and the consequent construction of cinematic meaning by the viewers. Films do not 'contain' their interpretations, no matter how much interpretive guidance has been inserted in the image chain. Rather, the differences in the perception of actuality amongst individuals are multiplied in the process of meaning construction in the situation of film viewing.

Moreover, since the 'horizon of expectations' amongst viewers differs widely, so do the constructions of filmic realities. Film criticism also plays a role as part of the process of consumption. To a certain degree, film reviews channel viewer expectations in certain directions. This is particularly so in circumstances where documentary filmmaking is a function of the state apparatus.

Lastly, the relations between documentary film and the documentary film industry also play a role in making documentary a complex phenomenon, a fact that further undermines any straightforward notion of documentary 'truth'. Institutional documentaries, that is, films that are produced from within a specific institutional framework, such as a government sponsored or owned television station, tend to share recognizable features that are not primarily dictated by any documented perceptual actuality. Likewise, distribution networks and funding bodies exert an indirect, sometimes even a direct, influence on what a documentary should look like. Needless to say, policies of government and television institutions and especially various kinds of censorship add to the forces that make an ideally 'truthful' documentary a practical impossibility. There is no such thing then as a 'pure' documentary film. For a 'pure' documentary film would be one in which not only the perceived actuality is fully reproduced but also a film in which all the cinematic features of the film text and its production are employed with 'neutral' transparency. Given these multi-faceted constraints under which filmmakers generate documentary films, it seems all too obvious that there is no such animal as a documentary without fictionalising or subjectifying elements. Nevertheless, and this is an important point to make, in spite of all these difficulties, we do recognise a documentary film when we see one and accordingly distinguish it from the fiction film. It is only in the border area of documentary films which include a large dose of fictionalisation, and fiction films which include a large amount of documented material, that we find it difficult to decide.

From this position, documentary film can be regarded as a second order mediation, a filmic complication of what we are able to experience with our human scale senses and their interpretive complexities in the mind. Now the question arises how this second order mediation differs typically from the fiction film. Broadly speaking, we can say that fiction film is a fantasy variation on the actualities of culture, or a third order mediation of what we perceive. More precisely, fiction film is free to play with visual evidence in a way documentary is not. This is not to say that aspects of fictionalisation do not appear in documentary film. They do, but when they do they tend to undermine the documented filmic world and raise questions about the director's motives. The most obvious difference between the two genres, fiction film and documentary, can be seen in the way they (re)present the filmed *objectivities*. The actors in a fiction film typically do not (re)present themselves, but somebody else, a character. (There are a few exceptions to this general rule.) In other words, the (re)presentational function of the body, an actual *objectivity*, is split in the fiction film. The same applies to many other filmed objectivities, such as houses and landscapes that often (re)present other, fictional houses and fictive landscapes rather than their originals. This however does not deny that fiction film is also free to include as much documented actuality in its fictional world as the director wishes to draw on without in any way weakening its generic conventions.

Importantly, in documentary film the *(re)presentational split* does not occur as a rule. The documented objectivities, persons, animals, plants, objects, landscape and cities are filmed to (re)present themselves. There are however, many specific ways by which a degree of *fictionalisation* enters documentary filmmaking. To sketch this problematic let us distinguish between intra-image relations (what goes on inside the documented images; mise-en-scene; mise-en-shot; location sound; long takes; deep focus; filters; angles; etc.), inter-image relations (continuous editing; montage); and extra-image relations (voice over; other extra-diegetic sound; etc.). Fictional intervention can happen in all three domains. The most obvious forms of fictionalisation however occur in the inter-image relations, the selection of footage and the way the image sequence is determined in the editing process. Voice over, an extra-image feature, also has played a powerful role in documentary filmmaking and it is here that the viewer is most dependent on the more or less authoritarian, as well as more or less fictionalising guidance by the filmmaker. Perhaps the most used and abused devices of fictionalisation are *re-enactment* and *staging*, two favourites of the dogmatic film culture in China during the period between 1949 and 1977. In documentaries, re-enactment is expected to be declared as such in the film text; its concealed use is regarded as unethical. As to staging, if the depiction of social actuality is to be the core criterion of documentary cinema, then the device must be regarded as a form of deception.

Documentary as genre

No study of film can avoid the question of *genre*. Perhaps the most important point about genre is that it must not be confused with such things as category, class, formal set, or drawers and boxes into which we can throw individual films to distinguish them from another group of films. This proviso is absolutely crucial. Genre is set apart from these classificatory terms by the absence of clearly marked boundaries. And this is precisely why genre is such a useful term for organising complex objects such as novels, legends, the Western, biography, or films in the documentary mode. For none of these artefacts have features that would permit their strict definition. One useful way of accommodating this fuzziness is the use of Ludwig Wittgenstein's idea of 'family resemblance', according to which in a photograph depicting a large family the members only share a limited number of features with some others but not all other members of the same family. Likewise, documentary films can be grouped together under the loose principle of 'family resemblance' (Wittgenstein 1986: 32). Another way of escaping the definitional logic of class, set, and category is the phenomenological approach to complex entities via typification and type. The main difference between, say, class and type in the phenomenological sense is that while class is determined from the outside, its definitional boundary, typification and type are defined by their centres. A type in this sense is an ideal construct, for example, the idealised type of documentary film that 'faithfully' portrays a minority culture, as in the ideal of the ethnographic film. Such a film does of course not exist, hence the term idealised type. What then is the advantage here? The advantage is that we can use the ideal type as interpretive base on which to compare documentaries of a similar kind. As long as we do not confuse the ideal type so stipulated with actual films, this approach is useful precisely because it avoids definitional classification. Actual Westerns are always more or less typical of the stipulated definition of the Western. A third, more recent approach, can be derived from Jacques Derrida's influential paper 'The Law of Genre', in which the author goes to subtle lengths to demonstrate the impossibility of complex objects *belonging* to a genre, strictly conceived. As Derrida observes, 'a text would not belong to any genre. Every text participates in one or several genres, there is no genreless text, there is always a genre and genres, yet such participation never amounts to belonging' (Derrida 1980: 230). Derrida's law of genre then is 'a sort of participating without belonging – a taking part in without being part of, without having membership of a set' (Derrida 1980: 227). So, instead of a law of purity, we could speak of 'a law of impurity or a principle of contamination' (Derrida 1980: 225). What is different in this approach to genre from the two previous ones is that Derrida has it both ways. Genres are inescapable. Every work, including films, are to a certain extent always already associated with one or several genres; yet at the same time no work such as a film could be said to be a component of a genre in the way we speak of a component of a fully defined set. A looser but by no means ineffectual relationship therefore exists between work and generic constraints.

The last word so far on genre can be found in the book *Genre* by John Frow, a concise and up to date summary and critical extension of scholarly insights, with special reference to literature and other written and spoken as well as visual texts. Frow's genre is 'a set of conventional and highly organised constraints on the production and interpretation of meaning'. Genre is seen here to have 'structuring effects' that produce meaning. Genre, in this sense, becomes a 'basic condition' for meaning, both enabling and constraining it. For Frow genre 'is central to human meaning-making and to the social struggle over meanings' (Frow 2006: 10). Nothing we do in social symbolic interaction escapes the network of generic constraints. If this is so, then it is not only useful but necessary in the study of meaning-making by cinematic means to investigate the role of genre. As Frow writes about the material conditions that inform generic constraints in film, 'for the documentary, the medium of film involves not only the film stock but also the optical capacities of cameras and editing suites, the apparatus of sound recording, the set-up of a studio, the costs of production, and the possible screening outlets. All these inform and constrain the representational possibilities available to the filmmaker, and thus the ways in which he or she can address a viewer' (Frow 2006: 73). Contrary to genre theories that are based primarily on the text, such as documentary film, Frow's contribution is important in its insistence that the entire process of production, as well as the conditions under which both production and consumption take place, are captured in the notion of genre. This has proved fruitful in the description of Chinese documentaries, which are uniquely shaped by the larger frame of political and economic constraints. It is from this broader perspective that I now look at two dominant discourses characteristic of documentary theorisation in the West, the discourse of documentary representation of reality and the discourse of documentary classification.

Documentary between 'truth' and fiction

A vast number of bytes have been used up in the debate about the question as to how close to the 'truth' cinematic documentation is able to get. Because this is a question that has been raised in a very different manner in the tradition of Chinese documentary cinema, I sum up some of the more recent positions in this debate. Let me begin by sketching the extreme poles of this theorisation. On the one hand we have Bill Nichols who in the opening of his book *Introduction to Documentary* claims that 'every film is a documentary'. For Nichols there exist two kinds film only: 'documentaries of wish-fulfilment' and 'documentaries of social representation'. His reason for calling what we normally regard as fiction film 'documentaries of wish-fulfilment' is that they 'give tangible expression to our wishes and dreams, our nightmares and dreads' and so in a way document our imagination (Nichols 2001: 1). As we shall see, Nichols has qualified this radical opposition in some of his other writings. The opposite position is well exemplified by Trinh T. Minh-ha who, in a chapter entitled 'The Totalising Quest of Meaning', argues that 'there is no such thing as documentary – whether the term designates a category of material, a genre, an approach, or a set of techniques. This assertion – as old and as fundamental as the antagonism between names and reality – needs incessantly to be restated despite the very visible existence of a documentary tradition' (1993: 90). Her reason for this stark claim is that since 'reality runs away, reality denies reality' and so filmmaking cannot be anything but a 'framing' of reality on the run. (1993: 101) The 'irreality' of the assumption that documentary films could ever aspire to a faithful representation 'manifests itself in the need to require that visual and verbal constructs yield meaning down to their last detail' (1993: 107). In opposition to such a positivist view of the world, all we can hope for in film is 'a form of ordering and closing' such that 'each closure can defy its only closure, opening onto other closures, thereby emphasising the interval between apertures and creating a space in which meaning remains fascinated by what escapes and exceeds it' (1993: 105). Between Nichols's documentary imperialism and Trinh T. Minh-ha's Derridean anti-totalising stance we find a host of arguments that qualify truth claims for non-fiction film while nevertheless acknowledging the status of documentary film as a recognizable genre.

Michael Renov, in the Introduction to *Theorizing Documentary*, accommodates fictionalisation in documentaries as, 'moments at which a presumably objective representation of the world encounters the necessity of creative intervention'. (Renov 1993: 2) This includes the 'construction of character', the 'use of poetic language, narration, or musical accompaniment to heighten emotional impact or the creation of suspense via the agency of embedded narratives . . . the use of high or low camera angles . . . close-ups which trade emotional resonance for spatial integrity, the use of telephoto or wide-angle lenses which squeeze or distort space, the use of editing to make time contract, expand or become rhythmic' (1993: 2–3). This is so, says Renov. because documentary film fundamentally 'shares the status of all discursive forms with regard to its tropic or figurative character' (1993: 3). Given this position, is Renov then able to distinguish at all between documentaries and their fictional counterparts? The difference, he says, lies in 'the extent to which the referent of the documentary sign may be considered as a piece of the world plucked from its everyday context rather than fabricated for the screen' (1993: 7). Thus documentary film is seen as 'the more or less artful reshaping of the historical world' (1993: 11). This reshaping, as Renov argues in a chapter of his collection, displays itself in the guise of four documentary 'modalities' which inform one another in a relation of 'paradoxical mutuality' (Renov 1993: 28). The four modalities are (1) to record, reveal, or preserve; (2) to persuade or promote; (3) to analyse or interrogate; (4) to express (Renov 1993: 21–35). In the first modality the emphasis is on the replication of the historical real, the creation of a 'second-order reality cut to the measure of our desire'; to defy the passing of time and insist on the 'fabled ability of the moving image form to preserve the fleeting moment' (1993: 26). Renov's second modality, to persuade and promote, is part of the 'documentary "truth claim"' and as such 'the baseline of persuasion for all of nonfiction, from propaganda to rock documentary' (1993: 30). In the third modality, to analyse and interrogate, Renov acknowledges Clifford Geertz's observation that cultural analysis is of necessity 'incomplete' and that 'the more deeply it goes the less complete it is'. Hence documentary filmmaking needs to recognise that 'mediational structures are formative rather than mere embellishments' (30f.). Analysis is crucial also for Renov in the Brechtian sense that consumerism is in need of critical intervention (1993: 32). Lastly, the expressive modality of documentary is inevitable, even if, in Renov's view, it has been notoriously undervalued. For 'the documenting eye is necessarily transformational in a thousand ways'

(1993: 33). As a result, 'expressive variability' remains part and parcel of filmic non-fiction and so 'the aesthetic function can never be wholly divorced from the didactic one insofar as the aim remains "pleasurable learning"' (1993: 35).

With reference to Bruno Latour's characterisation of scientific instruments as 'inscription devices', Brian Winston argues in 'Documentary as Scientific Inscription' that the scientific basis of image production as a guarantee of objectivity is an illusion (1993: 41). Winston challenges the assumed 'mimetic status of the photographic image', especially now that digital technology is mocking the realist assumption of the 'fixity of the relationship' between image and reality (55–6). This alleged instability of documentary signification is qualified by Philip Rosen's 'Document and Documentary: On the Persistence of Historical Concepts' which points to the crucial role of narrativity as a principle in historiography as well as documentary film. While the majority of film theorists tend to align narrative with fiction film, Rosen argues, correctly in my view, that documentary, as well as other nonfiction genres, relies on narrative techniques, the sequencing of documentable materials (Rosen 1993: 58–89). Leaning towards the other camp, Susan Schreiber offers an argument in favour of seeing documentary film as a visual 'performative'. In doing so, she critiques the Austinian notion of performative speech act from a Derridean perspective by sharpening the force of the performative over the referent. In 'Constantly Performing the Documentary: the Seductive Promise of Lightening Over Water' Schreiber argues that once we recognise documentary film as primarily a performative discourse, its assumed constative, the represented real, is relegated to the margin. Documentary film 'seduces us with the promise of the constative, the promise of a plenitude of meaning embodied in a referent', which however turns out to be no more than an 'impossible dream' (1993: 149).

For Bill Nichols, the impossible dream of visual 'authentication' is not so much a failure but rather the combined result of 'the surrounding frames, contexts, narrative structures, televisual forms, viewer assumptions, and expectations' which together establish 'a social arena devoted to interpretive struggle' (1993: 190). Beyond Nichols, Brian Winston insists on the world of fact which, he quips, 'need only be dusted off and reported' (Winston 1995: 19). On the other side of the divide in this debate are theorists who address the complication introduced by reflexive and self-reflexive documentary strategies. Jay Ruby for one emphasises that the impression in the audience's minds that they are dealing with a coherent whole consisting of 'producer, the process of making, and the product' as 'necessary' knowledge. As Ruby observes in 'The Image Mirrored: Reflexivity and the Documentary Film', 'to be reflexive is to reveal that films – all films, whether they are labelled fiction, documentary, or art – are created, structured articulations of the filmmaker and not authentic, truthful, objective records' (2005: 44). This diminished form of visual documentation is rescued by Linda Williams as the recording of truth as a 'receding goal'. In 'Mirrors Without Memories: Truth, History, and the New Documentary' she argues that this is not a choice 'between two entirely separate regimes of truth and fiction'. The choice, rather, lies in 'strategies of fiction for the approach to relative truths'. Contrary to Trinh T. Minh-ha, Williams objects to conflating documentary with fiction, but concedes that it 'should use all the strategies of fictional construction to get at truths' (2005: 72). Which leaves at abeyance what precisely we mean by the term 'truth', a problem that seems to lie at the heart of this kind of debate and suggests that the term itself is perhaps best avoided in the description of documentary film. This ambivalence has failed, however, to stop film theorists and critics in the West as in China to continue to invoke the signifier 'truth' in their analyses.

A more promising avenue for distinguishing documentary and fiction film seems to me to focus on specific, concrete features of filmmaking. In this respect, the central feature of documentary film is the evidential representation of actual objectivities. In other words, documentary is typically recognised by the absence of the splitting of the representational function, as discussed in the Introduction to this chapter, and the declaration of re-enactment as such whenever it occurs. Another way of getting a grip on the slippery nature of documentary film is to distinguish amongst its typical, different presentational modes.

The documentary spectrum

No serious critic or theorist of documentary film can avoid addressing the manner in which Bill Nichols has over several years crystallised the main presentational modes of documentary cinema. Yet while he defines each mode in its own right, he concedes that in practice they typically appear as *mixed modes*, with one of them usually dominating the others. Ever since his chapter 'Documentary Modes of Representation' in *Representing Reality: Issues and Concepts in Documentary* (1991) which distinguishes four different modes of presentation, Bill Nichols has developed and refined his spectrum. In *Introduction to Documentary* (2001) Nichols discusses six modes: expository, observational, participatory (now including the earlier interactive mode), performative, poetic, and reflexive. I have rearranged his sequence to better match the argument of the present book.

(1) Expository mode

In this mode, the viewer is directly addressed, 'with titles or voices that advance an argument about the historical world' (Nichols 1991: 34). The dominant mode for films conveying information since around the 1920s, its main structural components are commentary addressed to the film viewer, with the image chain functioning as supporting evidence. Sound is mainly 'nonsynchronous' rather than 'location sound', location sound being an addition of the early sixties (34f.). Rhetorical continuity overrides the continuities of perceptual actuality (35). In spite of this emphasis on persuasion, 'the expository mode emphasises the impression of objectivity and of well-substantiated judgment' (35). Hence the prominence of 'an unseen "voice of God" or an on-camera voice of authority who speaks on behalf of the text' (37). Highlighting a problem, puzzle or newsworthy event, the expository mode, says Nichols, is central to documentary filmmaking and appears, in diminished form, in the other representational modes discussed below.

(2) Observational mode

Nichols' observational mode is what is also known as cinema verité or direct cinema. The main difference between this and other modes is that here the emphasis is on the 'nonintervention of the filmmaker' (Nichols 1991: 38). To achieve this style, the observational mode tends to avoid 'voice-over commentary', extra-diegetic music, 'intertitles, re-enactments, and even interviews' (38). Sensitive to questions of film ethics, the observational mode struggles with the problem of intrusion into the lives of persons being documented. The focus of the observational mode is the portrayal of everyday life, the assumption being that realist documentation can be best achieved via careful observation. So it is not surprising that the observational mode is strongly associated with ethnographic filmmaking where both ethical questions and a commitment to realism are indispensable tools. As a result, the fact of cinematic mediation, so crucial to all filmic representation, tends to be somewhat concealed, as if we were able to grasp the world in the way an ideal observer would. This, of course, is an illusion which it is the task of documentary film to expose.

(3) Performative mode

In *Introduction to Documentary* (2001) Nichols adds three further representational modes: the poetic, the performative, and the participatory. According to Nichols, 'performative documentary underscores the complexity of our knowledge of the world by emphasising its subjective and affective dimensions' (Nichols 2001: 131). As such, the performative mode undermines the idea of factual recording by an emphasis on subjectivity and such domains as memory and personal experience. In films in which the performative mode is dominant, says Nichols, we encounter fascinating combinations of perceptual actuality and imagination. Our sensitivity and responsiveness to the presented world are stimulated by affect and affinity rather than by logic and intellect. It is no mere coincidence that typical topics in the performative mode are 'underrepresented, or misrepresented' subjects, 'women and ethnic minorities, gays and lesbians'. Here, evocative emphasis and subjective expression go hand in hand with moral issues, sensitising us to the plight of people rather than arguing their case (Nichols 2001: 133).

(4) Poetic mode

As the term suggests, the filmmaker who chooses this mode does so in order to add a lyrical touch to the raw presentation of social and physical phenomena. In the words of Nichols, the 'poetic mode is particularly adept at opening up the possibility of alternative forms of knowledge to the straightforward transfer of information, the prosecution of a particular argument or point of view, or the presentation of reasoned propositions about problems in need of solution'. Above all else this mode, in Nichols's schema, foregrounds 'mood, tone, and affect' rather than social facts. We note the prominence of 'subjective impressions, incoherent acts, and loose associations', as well as the fragmentation of time and space into 'multiple perspectives' (Nichols 2001: 103). One of the reasons that the 'poetic mode' is relevant to our study is that in China documentary filmmakers used it for a while because it promised an escape from the dogmatic constraints of film production during Mao's era. I will return to this point in Chapter 3.

(5) Interactive and participatory mode

The interactive mode of documentary filmmaking has its origins in the 1920s *Kino-Pravda*, but began to flourish only from the 1950s when portable equipment encouraged experiments with synchronous location sound. This allowed the expansion of postproduction sound editing from the studio to the arena of social interaction. According to Nichols, the potential of the interactive mode is considerable. 'The possibilities of serving as mentor, participant, prosecutor, or provocateur in relation to the social actors recruited to the film are far greater than the observational mode would suggest' (44). The viewer is given the impression of local immediacy and the dramatic sense of interaction between filmmaker and social actors. As a result, the tenor of the interactive mode tends to emphasise less the cohesion of an objective world than the dynamics of dialogue between filmmaker and documented persons. Spatial and temporal relations tend to be sacrificed to the logic of symbolic interaction. Nichols makes a special note with respect to the question of documentary ethics. How far, he asks, should this kind of participation go? How are the limits of interaction to be negotiated? What tactics should be permitted in the interrogation of documented social reality? These questions affect all the typical ingredients of the interactive mode, such as dialogue, interview, questions and answers, accusation and defence, as well as non-verbal interaction by way of gestures, glances, smiles, and other non-verbal signification. Perhaps the overarching impression granted by the interactive mode is a sense of compelling immediacy and specificity, and the articulate self-presenting of the documented social world.

We talk of a participatory mode of documentary representation rather than an interactive mode, when the voices of documented subjects come to the fore in their own right. Contrary to the interactive mode, in participatory documentaries the final cinematic outcome can be as much determined by the filmed subjects as by the initial conception of the filmmaker (Nichols 2001: 117). Nichols discusses a number of films in which the personal encounter between filmmakers and subjects is the driving force of what we see on the screen. In this sense the encounter between filmmaker and subject transcends that between director and documented person to one of co-creation. As a consequence of the intimate relation between filming and what is filmed, a variety of interview techniques are prominent. Interviews in the participatory style often tend to have the appearance of a confession, which suggests a certain degree of trust by the subject in the integrity of the filmmaker. The implications for professional ethics are obvious. The social world that emerges from such situations is neither 'objective' (expository) nor subjective (poetic), but intersubjective, giving the film viewer a 'sense that we are witness to a form of dialogue between filmmaker and subject that stresses situated engagement, negotiated interaction, and emotion-laden encounter' (Nichols 2001: 123).

(6) Reflexive mode

This mode highlights the filmmaker's thoughts about the process of representation themselves. Here the filmmaker takes a step back from the social scene to comment on the problematic of its representation and the role that the filmmaking plays in the process. This amounts to a reflection as to 'how we talk about the historical world' (Nichols 1991: 57). Reflexive documentaries then strike us as 'self-conscious not only about form and style', as poetic films do, but also as to their 'strategy, structure, conventions, expectations, and effects' (57). At their best, documentaries in the reflexive mode challenge orthodox procedures of filmmaking, as well as cinematic realism itself. An important point made by Nichols is that 'the reflexive mode of representation gives emphasis to the encounter between filmmaker and viewer rather than filmmaker and subject' (60). As such, reflexive documentary can be regarded as a highly advanced form of filmmaking, functioning as it does as an interrogation of the very possibilities of cinematic representation. Thus, reflexive documentaries tend to train their audiences by undermining naïve viewing attitudes, revealing the philosophical potential of film as a tool with which to ask questions of epistemology, the way we think we know about the world, including ourselves. Reflexive documentary is relevant to the Chinese situation mainly because so far it hardly exists. One rare example I have noticed is Tian Zhuangzhuang's *Chama gudao/Chama Road* (2004).

Currently, we witness a rapid expansion of the participatory mode of representation in China, where documentary filmmaking appears to be filling a political vacuum of public and private expression. The participatory mode with its emphasis on polyphonic rather than monological presentation appears particularly well suited to giving expression to otherwise unheard positions, experiences, complaints, ambitions, hopes, and a sense of being able to voice individual opinions and convictions. As I shall argue later, beyond personal expressions and within certain fundamental political constraints, participatory film and television programmes in China seems to point to the emergence of a public media sphere as a forum for rehearsing more broadly democratic concerns.

I want to conclude this taxonomic section with two criticisms of Nichols. First, from the perspective of Chinese documentaries, what is missing in the spectrum of Nichols' presentational modes of documentary film is a classification that can account for the strictly circumscribed way in which documentaries were produced in the period between 1949 and 1977. As I will argue in Chapter 3, a special presentational mode needs to be identified to cater for this branch of documentary cinema. I have called this mode the dogmatic mode of documentary film. My second objection is methodological. It concerns Nichols' generic approach via the film text itself. As Frow points out, and as any viewing of Chinese documentary drives home, without reference to the political frame, the available technology, and the conditions of production and consumption, we hardly get a sense of why a film strikes us the way it does. Its generic constraints must therefore be seen from a broader perspective than a focus on the film text alone.

From dogma to polyphony

The metaphor 'from dogma to polyphony' functions as a guiding thread throughout this book, providing a certain orientation for the reader with respect to the documentary materials discussed. 'From dogma to polyphony', thus acts as an ordering principle and a way of identifying an overall trend from the beginnings of documentary in the Mao era to its diversification in today's China. I use the signifier 'dogma' to indicate an all-embracing, top–down, unitary, monological voice by which official doctrine, authoritative and authoritarian government declarations, deceptions and formulations constitute an official political ideology. In documentary film and other documentary modes, dogma, in this sense, typically appears as a 'voice of God' style, as well as in non-verbal modes of presentation that do not invite alternative viewpoints. Whilst 'dogma' is the dominant presentational mode in the documentaries of the Mao period, the 'dogmatic' style can be observed to this day, although now a much reduced form, as 'remnants of dogma'. It is a central thesis of this book that 'dogma' in the sense described, has gradually given way, in China's current market oriented media, to an increasingly polyphonic style of documentation.

The signifier 'polyphony' draws on several historical uses, such as Bach's counterpoint innovation in music, according to which several independent melodies interact with one another. In recent Chinese documentaries the polyphonic interaction of different presentations and self-presentations likewise produce effects that stand in marked structural contrast to monological modes. Yet another source of the notion of polyphony as used in this book is the idea of a 'polyphony of aesthetic value qualities' expounded by the Polish phenomenologist Roman Ingarden. According to Ingarden, 'aesthetic value qualities' in the literary work of art are made to interact by the reader such that they produce an overall aesthetic value in the performance of the act of reading, the reader's 'concretisation' of the work. The viewers of the documentary film are in a similar position in that they too assemble the various speaking positions, as well as non-verbal presentations, into an overall cinematic effect. Lastly, the term 'polyphony' also refers to Mikhael Bakhtin's well-known usage in describing the polyphonic novel in which the author's voice is distributed across a spectrum of speakers holding not only different opinions but also differing ideological positions. This is especially useful for the present study since the gradual replacement of the dogmatic style in Chinese documentaries by disseminated viewing positions and speech attitudes in itself constitutes an ideological shift. While a large number of voices alone does not hold any liberating potential at all – they may constitute no more than a Fascist chorus – polyphony as a juxtaposition of many alternative voices does indeed, I suggest, herald for China the emerging conditions for a media based public sphere, in a broadened sense. Throughout this book, then, polyphony will refer to all forms of personal, political and cultural self-presentation in the documentary visual media. Such self-presentation ranges from self-referential images and statements of the directors to letting members of the public present themselves and their views. Documentary polyphony, I claim, can be observed today in the selection of subject matter, presentational modes, and actual speaking positions and their 'enunciative modalities', in Foucault's sense. The more a documentary disperses its filmic authority amongst the documented subjects, including members of the public, who are now taking on the tasks of directing and filming, the more appropriate is the signifier 'participatory'. Thus the metaphor from 'dogma to polyphony' also indicates a tendency from authoritarian and exclusive to inclusive and participatory documentation.

I draw once more on Nichols in clarifying what I mean by multi-voice or polyphonic documentary filmmaking and what he has termed the 'voice' of documentary. In a recent chapter entitled 'The Voice of Documentary' Nichols defines 'voice' as 'that which conveys to us a sense of a text's social point of view, of how it is speaking to us and how it is organising the materials it is presenting to us'. Thus, 'voice' acts as something like the overall social and political statement a documentary film makes for the viewer. It is in this sense that Nichols complains that 'far too many contemporary filmmakers appear to have lost their voice' (2005: 19). While this use of the term is useful for broad descriptions of what a documentary is about, for my purposes in this book I need to retain the potential of differentiation implied in the specific voices that we encounter in film. I also want to go further and suggest that subject matter as well as modes of presentation speak to us as viewers and so metaphorically constitute 'voices' in competition with one another. I will elaborate these notions in the final chapter of the book. With these introductory remarks on the theorisation of documentary film in the West completed, I must now attend to the documentary scene in China.

Documentary cinema in China

Documentary cinema in China has played a role somewhat different from that in the Anglosphere and in Europe. From early propagandist forms to their recent transformations in the market economy, documentary film has been a mainstay in the government's project of nation building and national education. While documentary film outside China comes a clear second when compared with the prominence of fiction feature films, in the evolution of Chinese cinema the relation is reversed: the documentary has been the leading film genre in China after 1949. Because of the central role that documentary films have occupied in politics as well as in the imagination of a vast viewing audience, any investigation into the topic needs to be sensitive to the specific Chinese varieties of the genre as well as cautious when it comes to applying existing critical frameworks, their terminology and theoretical implications. Many of the tools in the universalist armoury of documentary film theory will of course prove useful. Nevertheless, the specific historical, political, economic and technological processes that have characterised China since the first half of the last century have moulded Chinese documentary cinema into a recognizable film form in need of specific investigation and recognition.

As I hope to be able to demonstrate, the very forms of documentary films in China reflect the political climate, economic trends, technological stage of development, and social aspirations of the country. For example, the transition from ideologist to reformist government policies finds its filmic expression in documentaries replacing the idealised Communist hero by the depiction of local people in ordinary circumstances. In both domains we can observe how Marxist dogma is replaced by Deng Xiaoping's pragmatist credo 'seeking truth from facts' or 'making practice the sole criterion of truth'. Yet, the new pragmatism did not only manifest itself in the economic reforms of 1980s; it began to usher in an entirely new socio-political climate. At the same time, digital technologies spread through China, with profound consequences for the televisual industries and their regulatory policies. Under the double pressure of new cinematic technologies and popular demand for locally relevant programmes, the government in 1993 disseminated the central role of the Central News Documentary Film Studio (*Zhongyang xinwen jilu dianying zhipian chang*) in Beijing to the CCTV nationwide. As a result, television documentary began to flourish, with significant shifts in the formal structure of today's documentaries.

The heuristic polarities of dogmatic and polyphonic tendencies will be shown to be useful not only for the analysis of individual documentary films, but also to have historical relevance in that the entire evolution of documentary cinema in China, *cum grano salis*, can be viewed from within this schema. One might assume that at least theoretically any subject can be treated dogmatically or in a polyphonic fashion; in practice, this is not the case. For example, the spread of subjects in the history of documentary filmmaking in China avoided the European emphasis on ethnographic and anthropological representation. In doing so, it also avoided some of the typical pitfalls of such films, such as the accusation of manipulation and exploitation. Instead of showing 'the poorest of the poor', the miserable and naked people of the world, Chinese documentaries began by focusing on the heroism of its soldiers and peasants. In practice, then, the presentational mode and choice of subject matter appear to go hand in hand with questions of political control and ideological commitments. The transformations which we are able to observe in Chinese documentary film and television programmes are not merely conceived in this book as changes in style, but more profound shifts that reveal substantial modifications in the attitude of the Chinese government towards the media under market pressure, as well as in the face of radical changes in the horizon of viewing expectations amongst China's mass media audiences. These changes, I suggest, are indicators of a society in the process towards 'democratisation' and regime modification, a process in which the media are playing an increasingly significant role. This may look like an exaggerated claim, but there seems to me sufficient evidence to suggest that current documentary film and television programme practice in China constitutes an emerging public media sphere in which heterogeneous positions are increasingly being debated, even if this so far excludes a range of well-understood hot political topics.

Given traditional aesthetics with its emphasis on moral messages (*wen yi zai dao*) and the creation of imaginary worlds (*yijin*), documentary film was not a natural genre in China. *Wen yi zai dao* requires morality as a story ingredient, which is difficult to achieve in the documentary mode without fictionalisation. *Yijin* emphasises the invention of an imaginary world and meanings that are generated and communicated through that world, which in a profound way undermines the realist principles of documentary film. Nonetheless, under the influence of Soviet cultural policy, and especially Lenin's view that film is the most powerful tool for mass education and that documentary film is a forceful form of visualised political argument, documentary film became hugely important in China (Situ 2001: 188). Since the 1950s, documentary in China has been understood as a genre somewhere between cinematic newsreel and the longer and later version of cinematic 'newsreel', embracing national achievements, political unity, and the celebration of particular historical moments, as well as Communist and other national heroes. Essay style, lyrical script, and voice-of-God narration are dominant in both, with staged events, easily recognised as such. In addition, since 1980 *zhuanti pian* (special topics) emerged, a television documentary series on one particular topic. The majority of these also inherited some of the characteristics of Communist documentary film: attention to the composition of well-framed images, meticulous description of details with close-ups, studio lighting, fragmented images that illustrate words, and the separation of sound from images. We also find staged performance and ample use of music to foreground political themes, while the cinematic events are ideologically controlled by the filmmaker. Not surprisingly then, the majority of the Chinese documentary films before the early 1990s did not pay attention to ordinary individuals, but rather portrayed individualised heroic principles.

It was only in early 1990s that Chinese filmmakers and critics were in a position to re-define and theorise the documentary film genre from a cinematic perspective. There are several reasons for this transformation: the market began to reject the propaganda content of the political documentary; communication with the West increased sharply and with it acquaintance with a broad range of documentary cinematic options; a need to produce Chinese documentary films for the Western markets; an explosion of scholarly, critical reassessments of the Chinese cinematic tradition, and the weakening of the long-standing and rigid association of documentary filmmaking with the political leadership. In turn, the redefinition of documentary film had a feedback influence on the redirection of documentary film production in China. The main landmark in this evolution was the 1993 transference of the China News Documentary Film Studio to the CCTV, which made documentary film a part of television. The reasons for this act were that film proved to be too expensive and that documentary film was deemed to be too important to be left to elitist aesthetics and should instead continue to function as an essential element of mass culture, the television. Certainly, documentary filmmaking since the 1990s has found its own momentum, encouraging the right to some public expression of opinions and the display of individual perceptions of society. Filmmakers now work inside as well as outside the system. Increasingly questions are being raised by filmmakers, producers, film theorists and film critics that address not only the generic mechanisms of documentary film but transcend the boundaries of cinema (Situ 2001: 191; Lü 2003: 253–78). What kind of relation between Party, government and ordinary people should be reflected? Should documentaries continue to remain the tool of government doctrine? Should ordinary people be encouraged to participate in documentary film and documentary filmmaking? What are the new aesthetic confines of documentary film?

In light of the history of documentary cinema, to be addressed in detail in Chapters 2 and 3, and the political constraints under which it evolved, it should not be surprising that the theorisation of the genre was not able to develop as freely as it did in Europe and the Anglosphere. Nevertheless, there is now a fast growing body of writings in China dedicated to the description of documentary film and its potential. The approach to documentary film and television programmes that emerges from this literature can be divided roughly according to the following emphases: documentary as mouthpiece of the Party; documentary during the transition period from

1980 to 1993; documentary and 'truth'; documentary in China and the West; and documentaries in China today.

Chinese film critics now look back at the period between 1957 and 1977 as the 'dark ages' of documentary cinema, commonly referred to as the 'twin of the Party newspaper' (Gao 2003: 131; Fang 2003: 205; San 2005: 354). Documentary film before 1980 is now identified by its 'narrow range of subject matters', 'organised directorial interference', as well as such technical matters as the 'separation of sound and image' (Lu and Zhao 2002: 238). Whatever the specific observations about that period, suffice it to say here that there is hardly any disagreement amongst Chinese film critics today that documentary cinema has come a long way since then. I will discuss this period of filmmaking in depth in Chapter 3 under the heading of the 'dogmatic formula'. An intriguing historical transition in Chinese documentary cinema is the time between the 1980s and the early 1990s when the Chinese government wavered between maintaining its traditional control over the media and loosening the vice grip of its media policies. The dominant form of documentary during the transition period, the *zhuanti pian* (special topics), is typically composed of a few episodes organised around a grand theme, such as Chinese culture, the Great Wall, the Yellow River, Silk Road, Grand Canal or the Economic Reform. We also note a certain degree of toning down of narration, a highlighting of human concerns, a diminished political tenor, and an emphasis on interview and location sound. In spite of these tendencies, however, '*xuan chuan*' (propaganda) is still seen as the fundamental principle informing *zhuanti pian* (Situ 2001: 189). It took the screening of *Dongfang shikong / Oriental Horizon* by the CCTV in 1993 to usher in a more liberated media climate. This means that now *putong ren*, ordinary people without financial or political privilege, increasingly appear on the screen as documented subjects.

One of the favourite topics in the theorisation of this new kind of documentary is its relation to *zhen shi* (truth). The novel emphasis on 'interviews in the documentaries of the 1990s has come about', writes Zhu Qinjiang, 'because in the past we had faced too many lies. So what we want to do is to seek the truth to understand what really happened'. He applauds the slogan of the new generation of independent filmmakers, 'our camera doesn't lie' because our only 'aim is to find the truth' (Zhu 2004: 18). Jin Xiumin sees the main task of the documentary mode to be the use of sound and visual language to exclude fictionalisation. Documentary is to employ a process of 'describing or reconstructing' real life and, above all, 'must contain the idea of truth' (Jin 2005: 7). This sense of truth is echoed also in the question 'What is the documentary spirit?' to which Tao Tao gives three answers: first, the recording of history; second, the truthful representation of actuality; and third, to encourage society to form critical judgements (Tao 2004: 36). This is exciting, I think, because the notion of critical discourse is largely absent in the Chinese tradition. To attribute to documentary this critical dimension is a timely intervention in the theorisation of the genre and one that will resurface as a theme in Part II of this book. The three goals, says Tao, depend in no small measure on two basic conditions: one, documentary is a moving picture which depends significantly on modern industry and technology; and two, a crucial criterion of documentary is 'raw footage of actuality' (Tao 2004: 35–6). The spirit of presenting the truth of the actual world as meticulously as possible also informs the observation made by Xiao Ping that 'documentary is not a creative treatment of actuality' but rather an attempt at 'recording an action or event that cannot be repeated'. Hence, in a way, documentary attempts to 'return to the most primitive way of showing' (Xiao 2003: 1). Not all Chinese film critics share the trust in 'truth' however; Zhong Danian for one suggests that what we call 'true' and 'truth' in the domain of documentary film 'is a myth about actuality'. And even if we were to concede that 'truth' can be regarded as a foundation for documenting, as far as filmmakers are concerned we should replace the term by 'sincerity'. In fact, says, Zhong Danian, to reflect reality 'truthfully' is not really the purpose of documentary at all; rather, documentary film is about making value judgements with respect to life (Zhong 2003: 44–50).

Closely related to the notion of documentary truth is the Chinese pre-occupation with the 'social real' and with 'social realism' (*jishi zhuyi*). Zhong Danian explains why it has been so difficult for Chinese documentary to achieve a proper form of socially oriented realism in spite of the socialist agenda of successive Communist governments since 1949. He argues that three distinct idealist traditions have hampered the emergence of *jishi zhuyi* in documentary film: the 'illustration of political theory'; the 'beautification' of actual life; and the ideal of education (Zhong 2003: 35–8). What is needed now, most Chinese film critics agree, is the representation of ordinary people in ordinary circumstances. This is echoed in the writing of Situ Zhaodun who believes that documentaries should only film real people and real events rather than abstract ideas and concepts; documentaries in his view can only show individuals, not general principles. The foundation of documentary film is the image rather than narration and so documentaries can only present the 'now', and what is 'happening now' and cannot express the 'forever' (Situ 2001: 193). No longer can documentary film be equated with visualised political theory, nor is it any longer a news film, nor even a television art film: documentary is now firmly defined as a genre with real people and real events at its centre. As Ren writes:

> Documentary is non-fiction film or a video product which reports and records accordingly on political, economic, cultural, military and his-torical events. Documentary film directly represents real people and real events, made-up fictional events are not permissible. The main narrative reporting includes interview and film location. This means the use of selection, waiting for and catching the right moment for recording real people, real events, in real environments and real time. This for 'real' is the life of documentary.

> (Ren 1997: 3)

Another intriguing discussion concerns the perceived differences between Chinese documentaries and the documentary film tradition in the West. As in many other such sweeping comparisons, Chinese film critics emphasise the contrast between Confucian philosophy (*wen yi zai dao*) and Christian culture (Zheng Wei 1997: 174; Luo Yijun 1992: 7–13). When Zheng Wei ties Western scientific thought to Christianity she fails to note that documentary film in the West emerged out of the secular tradition of the European Enlightenment rather than from European religiosity. What is at stake here is perhaps summed up most succinctly in Kant's observation in the *Critique of Pure Reason* that what characterises the new enlightened thinking is that 'everything must submit to critique'. In the absence of a critical discourse in the Chinese tradition, it is understandable why this important point tends to be missed. Zheng Wei further distinguishes the two traditions by stressing the Soviet ideological influence on Chinese documentary cinema, as against the Western preoccupation with scientific observation. Second, she sharpens the distinction between the Chinese penchant for documentary education and the Western predilection for the display of conflict between individual and society, nature and culture, life and death. Third, Zheng Wei observes a deep difference in the ways Chinese and Western documentaries tell their stories. While the former celebrates detail and narrative continuity, Western styles prefer discontinuities, leaps, and fragmentation (Zheng Wei 1997: 196–204). These principles are very much supported in the work of Ren and Peng who focus on four major differences: Western understanding of documentary foregrounds the real where the Chinese emphasise educational benefits; the West highlights individual values where the Chinese filmmaker emphasises an ideal of social morality; in terms of narrative strategies, Western documentaries often celebrate fragmentation while the Chinese prefer narrative closure; lastly, the main difference as to the filmic image lies in the Western preference for dynamic presentation as against the careful framing of the photographic still in Chinese documentaries (Ren and Peng 1999: 12–17). In spite of indisputable Western influences, both industrial and cinematographic, Chinese documentary filmmakers and theorists postulate a generic format somewhat different from the conventions that have evolved in traditions outside China.

The 'New Documentary Movement' since the early 1990s has been characterised as paying attention to the poor, the marginal, and ordinary people and their often trivial lives. There is a shift towards independent and semi-independent films, with the emergence of individual styles, with a realistic, bottom-up rather than top–down description of Chinese society. As such, writes Lü Xinyu, the 'New Documentary Movement' is the 'opposite to *zhuanti pian* with its "grand themes"'. As Lü observes,

> We should not understand the term '*jilu pian*' (documentary film) in the context of the West. In the West, the development of documentary film has various schools and streams, which are generated from the different historical contexts of different societies. In China, the term

'documentary film' gained its significance in the 1980s and 90s from the understanding of the term as resistance to the term *zhuanti pian* (special topics).

(Lü 2003: 13)

Here, Lü is defining documentary as a genre that has emerged as a form of resistance to the kind of government propaganda characteristic of *zhuanti pian*. What we need instead is a telling of 'history that is able to inform the future' (Lü 2003: 37). For 'if you completely identify with mainstream discourse, there is no need to make a documentary' (Lü 2003: 39).

China has only very recently emerged from a strictly controlled media scene. As a result, there has been little time for a full theorisation of documentary to unfold. Nonetheless, a growing number of film critics and cultural theorists are now addressing the complexities of the genre. An intriguing perspective on the documentary genre is offered by Ren who describes it as 'the art of discovery'; 'the art of the interview'; and 'the art of editing' (Ren 1997: 11–14). Zhang Yaxin sums up the debate well when she locates documentary film in China today at the intersection of four pairs of oppositions: historical past vs. present actuality; fictionalisation vs. knowledge; lighthearted presentation vs. serious content; and national culture vs. globalisation (Zhang 1999: 274). At the same time, documentary film policies and studio practices have undergone significant changes. This is borne out by the words of Professor Lin Qidong of the Beijing Broadcasting University who observes that 'since 1993 all influential documentaries have been produced in the format of a consensus between independent filmmakers and television producers', even if such 'documentary films are made within the system' (Zhu and Bin 2004: 9). No doubt, semi-independent and independent filmmakers are coming to the fore within and outside the system. This trend, writes Zhu Qinjiang, is largely the result of the need for independent filmmakers to acquire legitimacy, a case of 'having no choice' and of sheer 'survival instinct' (Zhu and Bin 2004: 7). While the CCTV documentary filmmaker is able to claim 'I film for the people: I am the voice of the people', his and her independent counterpart is often confronted with the question 'who gave you the right to film in the first place?' This, says Zhu Qinjiang, means that 'the identity of the documentary filmmaker to a large extent determines his or her film subject', adding that 'we are walking on a no-hope road with great hope' (Zhu and Bin 2004: 5–10).

Today, documentary film and documentary television programmes are a major industry in China. Almost all television stations now produce a variety of documentary styles, and the stature of television stations is being judged by the standard of their documentary programmes (Ren 1997: 24). A style of documenting 'real', ordinary people, people on the margin, and work-a-day stories as they happen around us is now the dominant mode. As Li notes, three major changes characterise Chinese documentary films today: 'a change of media channels from film to television; a change from "single voice narration" to "multi-voice narration and location sound"; and from seeking the "truth" and the "no-me" stage to the "me" stage' that emphasises a personal style (Li 2002: 260–71). Another three transformations are observed by Li Cunli, from 'lecturing' to 'allowing reality to talk'; from 'heroism' to the 'consciousness of ordinary people'; and from literary expression or 'expressionism' to 'documenting the human', the 'documentary of the heart' (Li Cunli 1999: 290–3). However, this does not signal the disappearance of *zhuanti pian*, government sponsored documentaries in the service of visualised political theory. Such films are still being produced but now in a much toned down propagandist mode and very much in competition with market driven documentary production.

Increasingly, public awareness of the power of media, as well as their willingness to participate, makes the cinematic construction of the 'real' an inevitable evolution. Perhaps the most important observation here is the emphasis on an emerging *participatory mode*. As documentary film producer Chen Hanyuan observes,

> Nowadays ordinary people appear very natural in front of the camera. They are not shy at all. Some discuss the fees we should pay for filming them, some even remark on our right to use their images. They are actively engaging with us on what our films are about, raising interesting questions. Their narrations are smooth and their ideas are differentiated, sometimes opinionated. All this could hardly be imagined in the 1980s. Even more surprisingly, people from the country, the unemployed, or even monks, have gradually not only attracted our cameras, but also become central characters in our documentary films.
>
> (Chen 2001: 677)

In addition to the new principle of *participation*, 'real people' here means largely 'ordinary people' and especially people at the margins of society, a special mode of cinematic 'individualisation'. According to Lü, 'this is the most important contribution by contemporary Chinese documentary filmmakers. Their documentary film movement is about 'poor people in the city, country migrants, the disabled, cancer sufferers, orphans, ethnic minorities, and stories in poverty areas' (Lü 2003: 691). Given the focus on this kind of subject matter and the realist techniques developed to do it justice, it should perhaps not be surprising to find that some Chinese observers of documentary film have taken the important step to claim publicly that 'the emphasis on objectivity and truth in documentary filmmaking inevitably links with the idea of democracy, an open society and the freedom of speech' (Situ 2001: 186). That this turn to social realism is not a natural event is supported by Liu's observation that 'the reason why our films appeared untrue is not so much because of what we filmed is not real, but because that *we filmed the real into the unreal!* Or because the real thing becomes unreal after being filmed' (Liu, Deyuan 2001: 814). That this should be so was the result of, for example, the absence of words spoken by documented subjects, the absence of interviews and location sound, and the dominance of perfectly framed images with studio lighting, exaggerated theme music and the authoritarian mode of the voice of God narration serving ideological dogma. That documentary film should be free of ideological messages and political doctrine is however only one way of realising the genre's democratic potential. There are other avenues, such the new focus on the presentation of actual social reality, the break with traditional aesthetics, and the reduction of editorial manipulation. As Andrew Basin once observed, editing is the enemy of the 'perception of democracy'. But perhaps the most promising path towards bringing out the democratic potential in documentary film genre is the introduction of participatory strategies, and in particular increased audience participation. This can take many forms, but, as Ren rightly notes, 'directing by the audience itself is the highest level of participation' (Ren 1997: 246).

As defined, political dogma tends to be a monological discourse, a one way communication hostile to democratic processes. In all its forms, democracy is heavily dependent on the interplay of many and opposing voices, in short, *heterogeneous polyphonic negotiation*. Bakhtin described polyphony in Dostoevsky's works as a dialogic interplay of multiple voices replacing authoritarian monologism by allowing different and oppositional voices to compete with one another. In Dostoevsky's work, he argues, we are dealing with a 'fully realised dialogical position which confirms the hero's independence, inner freedom, unfinalisedness and indeterminacy' (1973: 51). The linguistic-semiotic principles at work here can be taken as an analogue to actual socio-political situations, as well as the specifics of media discourse. When we consider the history of documentary film in China, even a summary view strongly suggests that we are dealing with the evolution of a genre from monological towards polyphonic modes of presentation, from authoritarian to participatory cinematic conventions. However, not all monological films are of necessity authoritarian, just as not all participatory documentaries could be called 'democratic'. Other factors have to be considered. Nonetheless, as I will show, there is ample evidence for arguing that there is an increase in 'democratic films and filmmaking'. This does not mean that authoritarian styles have disappeared. Even after the introduction of interviews into documentary film in the mid-1980s (the first attempt at using interviews on television was *Heshang / River Elegy* in 1986), authoritarian styles have been associated with government propaganda, no matter whether what is presented can be said to be 'real' or not. Authoritarian modes are generated not only by a dogmatic voice of God narration, ideological editing and fragmented images, but also when a film, in spite of its artistic use of a range of cinematic strategies, largely reflects the single voice of the Party.

What we are looking for, then, is a combination of cinematographic features that produce a polyphonic assemblage of heterogeneous voices, in the broad sense of including the non-verbal aspects of film. Nor should we be satisfied with a merely quantitative measure of such an assemblage. The number of participants, the amount of feedback, the number of interviews, the mere quantity of data of perceptual actuality alone by no means guarantee the exploration of the 'democratic' potential of documentary film. What seems to be essential here, in the Bakhtinian sense of polyphony, is that the many-voiced film offers a rich diversity of *opposing* positions which the film viewer must negotiate in order to constitute a socially realistic picture. Whenever I speak of *documentary cinema* rather than documentary *film*, I have chosen a broader perspective of analysis that includes such things as the documentary industry with its branches of funding, production, distribution and exhibition, as well as the history of documentaries in different societies. In particular, the socio-political and cultural contexts are of importance in order to show how different traditions of documentary filmmaking have emerged. In this respect, Chinese documentary is a telling case in point, since its evolution, as well as its aesthetic, political, and commercial status differs markedly from the development of documentary filmmaking in the West.

Conclusion

This book will show that the 'democratic' potential of documentary film and television programmes is beginning to be realised in China in a variety of ways. At the level of programme content we can observe a shift towards ordinary subjects under ordinary and not so ordinary circumstances, a decline in dogma and ideological abstraction and a foregrounding of the events of social life, with often unpredictable incidents, and a new focus on the hitherto concealed margins of society. This has led also to making public criticism of the specific failings of individual government agencies and officials as well as of the system as a whole, a permissible or at least tolerated topic.

At the level of media discourse and presentational mode, we have noted a decline in the prominence of monological, authoritarian guidance and the emergence of polyphonic styles, the reduction in doctrinal voice-of-God narration, and a diminishing of message controlled editing in favour of long takes, long shots, hand-held camera technique, and an increase in the use of interviews, as well as non-scripted filming. While the government sponsored, authoritarian documentary is by no means dead, it is now challenged by the growing presence of a variety of new documentary film styles, permitting the democratic potential of the genre to come to the fore. While none of these presentational innovations can be argued to guarantee by themselves a more democratic form of filmmaking, in combination they do suggest that China is on the way towards embracing more open and self-critical ways of viewing the world. The rise of semi-dependent and independent filmmakers and production companies adds significantly to this trend.

Finally, participatory strategies in a variety of television programmes, and especially in documentaries, are undoubtedly on the increase, strengthening such claims. We are now witnessing the powerful and so far unhindered public approval via television ratings of a polyphony of opposing voices in certain programmes, a sign, the book will argue, that one of the necessary ingredients of an emerging public sphere, the public expression of opinion 'in an unrestricted fashion', that is, free from domination, is beginning to announce itself (Habermas [1964] 1974: 49). Certainly, my argument goes, Chinese documentary film and television programmes are beginning to realise the democratic potential of *polyphonic heterogeneity*. We could speak of a rehearsal of democracy by means other than the obviously political.

2 Nationalism and the birth of Chinese documentary

Introduction

Just as documentary film as a genre is inseparable from politics, so too is the evolution of documentary film in China inextricably tied to the changes in the political landscape. Film came to China in 1896, a time period when China was close to the end of Imperial rule and the rise of a Chinese Republic. As a mass medium, Western film technology inevitably became a vehicle for Chinese artists, political supporters and revolutionaries promoting Chinese nationalism and various competing political ideologies in China. From the very first Chinese film made in Beijing in 1905, *Ding Jun Shan*, which recorded a Beijing opera, to about 15 newsreels recording about Japan's attack on Shanghai in 1932, the early Chinese silent documentaries are, on the one hand, imitations of European and American films, and on the other hand, show nationalists using film for nation-building after the collapse of the Qing dynasty in 1911. The Japanese invasion in the early 1930s reinforced the idea of film as a mass educational tool, so much so that both the *Guomindang* government and the Chinese Communist Party used film to call for the nation to participate in the anti-Japanese war effort. Between 1937 and 1945 during the anti-Japanese struggle, and the subsequent conflict between the *Guomindang* and the Communists from 1947 to 1949, newsreels and documentaries provided powerful images for gathering support inside and outside China.

In the first half of the twentieth century, the Chinese documentary film developed from imitating Western films and became at first a nationalist political tool, and then increasingly influenced by the two political parties the *Guomindang* and the Communists, both in terms of content and production. Although a few different voices appeared in this period amongst private filmmakers, the *Guomindang*, and the Communists, it would be far fetched to say that this constituted a polyphonic period, for private documentary filmmaking almost terminated in the late 1930s, and neither the *Guomindang* nor the Communists screened films produced by the opposing political parties in their controlled territories.

The close relationship between film and Chinese politics is due partly to the Chinese traditional aesthetics, the *Huaxia meixue*, according to which art should serve the educational purpose of teaching *lunli* (Confucian ethics) (Li 2001: 64), and partly to the varying political landscape in China, influenced in large measure by global politics. Since film was primarily regarded as art in China before 1949, ways of making film and film criticism were directed by traditional aesthetics, in which the Confucian *liyue xingzheng* (using ritual and music to govern the nation) is the core. According to Confucianism, *Yue cong he* (music should pay attention to harmony) and *shi zhi yan* (poetry should articulate philosophical and political views) summarise the relationship between art and politics. Since music, according to *Yue cong he*, has the ability to emotionally impact on humans, it can be used as a tool to train people to be civilised and to achieve harmonious social relations. *Shi zhi yan* adds to this that poetry should be used to articulate philosophy, history, and political views. In this ideology, morality (*lunli* ethics) is the main foundation – imposing its value system on the way subjects typically view the object world and the symbolic interaction amongst people. The highest value of art therefore is its ability to embrace morality. philosophy and political views which can then fulfil their educational function. In other words, ideational, and hence also ideological, content is seen superior to creativity in art. This is why *wen yi zai dao* (art must convey a moral message), had been a leading motto for Chinese writers and artists. Such a morally and politically driven aesthetics pays less attention to individual psychology, generalised social analysis, or self-reflexive explorations of art itself.

Western film technology attracted not only Chinese artists with traditional aesthetic convictions, but also cultural critics and the *Guomindang* government who likewise shared the view of the pedagogical function of cinema. Furthermore, for the Chinese, filmmaking and film viewing was to make a novel and major contribution to the reconstruction of Chinese identity in modern history. Given the context that film as a mass medium meant for the Chinese a tool for mass education, 'educational' here does not refer as much to disciplinary knowledge as to citizenship education. The idea of *yishu ji jiaoyu* (art as education) in film was shared by all the early Chinese filmmakers, regardless of the differences in education amongst traditionally educated and/or overseas trained Chinese (Hong 1996: 7–8). Their common starting points for making films were to 'change society' (*gaishan shehui*), 'supplement insufficient education' (*buzhu jiaoyu*) and 'guide the masses' (*zhidao minzhong*). For instance, film director Cheng Bugao (Cheng 1996: 615) pleaded for an increase in news documentaries in order to 'complement insufficient education' in 1925, and film critic Shi Heng described film as 'an efficient textbook for citizenship in society, as it is capable of gradually changing social customs' in 1927 (Shi 1996: 745). In a similar vein, the Left-Wing Film Movement from 1933 to 1935 argued and demonstrated in its film practice that cinema should be used for political, educational purposes in contradistinction to the entertainment style of Hollywood filmmaking. Their call found a strong echo in the entire film industry two years later after Japan attacked China, which found itself divided by the three competing ideologies of international capitalism, nationalism and communism.

As for documentary filmmakers, from the first Chinese film made in 1905 to the birth of the People's Republic of China in 1949, three dominant groups can be identified: the private filmmakers, including intellectuals, opera or theatre artists and republican supporters, and the two political groups, the Republican Government led by the *Guomindang*, and the Communists led by the Chinese Communist Party. The private filmmakers were the pioneers of the Chinese documentary, while the two political groups were relative latecomers. In the first two decades of the twentieth century, the private filmmakers started a small, but viable film industry in Shanghai and Hong Kong. The industry followed in the footsteps of European and American films, producing newsreels, landscape films, educational films, and sports documentaries, as well as feature films in the traditions of slapstick, melodrama, and detective mode as in the case of the non-fiction film *Shangwu yinshu guan fang gong / Workers leaving the Commercial Press* (1917), a close imitation of Lumière's *Workers leaving the Lumière Factory* (1896). However, there are certain sub-genres of non-fiction films that did not prove popular in China: as for instance the travelogue cinema of Europe, or the American ethnographic film best represented by Robert Flaherty's *Nanook of the North* (1923). Instead, the early Chinese scenery documentaries focused on well-known Chinese historical sites, and were usually produced in opposition to the images produced in non-Chinese and especially American documentaries. As a consequence of the moral emphasis in film criticism, exploration of film in the non-fiction mode was also discouraged. So it is not so surprising that European avant-garde documentaries of an experimental, abstract, poetic and robotic kind, such as Alberto Cavalcanti *Nothing but Time* (1926), Walther Ruttmann's *Berlin: the Symphony of the Great City* (1927), and Joris Ivens's *Rain* (1929) failed to capture the Chinese filmmakers' imagination in the 1920s and 1930s. It makes sense then that the theorisation of documentary, as in Dziga Vertov's notion of 'kino-eye' according to which the new filmic construction 'is far more revealing than the life it represents' (Barsam 1992: 71), likewise failed to occupy centre stage in the discussions by Chinese filmmakers and critics (Na 1996: 493). Newsreels and documentaries were regarded by film distributors and exhibitionists as attachments to feature films in exhibition. Documentary film was held to have 'no independent commercial value'; given the 'regulation for a two hour feature film, documentary films are screened mainly for filling in the absent time' (Gong 1968: 142). In the face of such an inconspicuous start, it is ironic that documentary film should nevertheless begin to flourish to the point where it began to overshadow its fiction rival. It is against this background that we should view the relative success of the Chinese documentary till the end of the first half of the twentieth century.

The private filmmakers

Private filmmakers did not begin with the idea of promoting Chinese nationalism, but rather saw films as business ventures and were probably curious about Western film technology. This period of documentary filmmaking, however, was significantly qualified by non-commercial interests. The reason for this should be seen in the fact that early Chinese filmmaking coincides with a period of transition from the Imperial system to the new Republic, and so the Chinese filmmakers were sensitive to the opportunity of making films that would contribute positive images to the nascent Republic (Cheng 1966: 71–2, 90). Two other major factors also play a role here. First, the Chinese filmmakers needed to develop films that were 'uniquely Chinese' to prevent Hollywood films dominating the domestic market. Second, this idea of a uniquely Chinese film culture was shaped and directed by the proponents of the dominant moralist art criticism that so strongly emphasised pedagogical values and a progressive nationalist look. The anti-Japanese war in the mid-1930s eventually turned the potentially diverse Chinese commercial film culture and industry into a single-voice enterprise.

After nine years of watching French and American documentaries from 1896 to 1905, the Chinese began to try their luck in indigenous film production. As the initial uptake of Western film technology was by way of *yingxi* (shadow play or shadow drama), it is not surprising that film did not, at least initially, draw the attention of any other professionals such as doctors, scientists, or teachers, but people in show business. Fengtai Photograph in Beijing made the first Chinese documentary in 1905 by recording the Chinese opera *Ding Jun Shan*. Shanghai acrobat and magician Zhu Liankui made *Wuhai zhanzheng / Wuhan War* (1911) by filming a few battles in the 1911 republican revolution, a movie that was screened as part of his acrobat show. Two years later, a similar attempt, resulting in the film *Shanghai zhanzheng / Shanghai War* (1913), was made by a Beijing opera troupe in Shanghai. The context of these very early documentaries shows that the initial interest in film rested mainly on its commercial value. And any commercial success of the Chinese films, the Chinese filmmakers soon realised, lay in making Western technology relevant to Chinese culture, artistic and otherwise.

Three years later a leading Chinese publisher, Commercial Press (*Shangwu yinshu guan*) in Shanghai recognised the potential of film for education. Building on its success in the publication of educational materials, Commercial Press established a film production unit in 1918, aiming at producing five types of films, *shishi* (current affairs or news), *fengjin* (landscape), *jiaoyu* (educational films), *guju* (Chinese opera) and *xinju* (comedies, slapsticks, and dramas). Against the background of the New Cultural Movement of anti-Confucianism in 1913–19, Commercial Press aimed to use film medium to construct a modern Chinese identity that countered French and American films that thrived on a colonial portrayal of China. In the eyes of Chinese nationalists and intellectuals, Western films were *qingbo xianzha* ('cheap, sinister and crafty') and *chiqu woguo xiadeng shehui qingkuang, yi zhi chaoxiao* ('they select to film the lowest social spectrum in Chinese society for their amusement and contempt') (Cheng 1966: 39). In contrast, the Commercial Press intended to make films that would dignify China for both domestic and international markets.

Such ideas for filmmaking reveal the desire of Chinese intellectuals to see screen images of China as a modern republican nation. One can easily recognise the historical reasons for this attitude, in the accumulations of feelings of 'humiliation' since the Opium War in 1839, as well as in the impact of seeing derogatory Chinese images portrayed in Western films. Opposed to encouraging a cinematic voyeurism of the exotic, Chinese filmmakers were driven to portraying Chinese society in a dignified manner. Unlike the travelogue films of the Lumière Brothers bringing Africa, Asia and South America to the French domestic market, the early Chinese landscape documentaries are focused on China itself, consciously correcting negative portrayals of China. These films,[1] mostly depicting well-known historical sites and cities in China, show the 'beautiful landscape of our motherland, her civilised customs, a civilisation with a long history, and architecture' (Cheng 1966: 31–2). To a certain extent, these films also promote patriotism by association with political events. For instance, the documentary *Jinan mingsheng / Famous Places in Jinan* explains the Japanese attack on and occupation of Qingdao (Cheng 1966: 32).

In its documentaries on current affairs, Commercial Press focused on social and political events in Shanghai, foregrounding the theme of a progressive republic. These films include opium burning in *Shanghai Fenhui chuntu / Burning Opium in Shanghai* (1918); European war victory celebrations in *Ouzhan zhusheng youxing / Celebration European Victory of War* (1918); the launch of a fleet in *Junjian xiashui / Fleet Launch* (1918) and the filming of a National Congress in *Guomin dahui / National Congress* (1923).[2] At the same time, the Commercial Press showed an interest in presenting sports events, once again as a symbol of a strong nation in the early twentieth century. The sports documentaries cover a university carnival in *Dongfang liu daxue yundong hui / Sports Carnival of Six Oriental Universities* (1918), the Far East sports carnival in *Diwuci yuan dong yundong hui / The Fifth Far East Sports Carnival* (1921), and promote awareness of sport, as for instance women's sports in *Nüzi tiyu guan / Women's Attitudes towards Sports* (1920).

Educational documentaries by Commercial Press were mostly made in response to their publication of educational materials, school education and social campaigns at the time. These films include special education, *Mangtong jiaoyu / Blind Children's Education* (1920), *Cishan jiaoyu / Charitable Education* (1921), *Yangzhen youzi yuan / Yangzhen Kindergarten* (1921), *Jiji daguan / Skills Show* (1921), and hygiene, *Qumie wenyin / Eradicating Mosquitoes and Flies* (1923). One can also include here their recordings of famous Chinese opera performances by opera master Mei Lanfang.

Commercial Press ended its nine year film production in 1926. One of the main reasons for the closure was the largely negative review of their fiction films by critics (Fang 2003: 28). From 1920, it seems that the company ceased all non-fiction productions, but increased its comedy, slapstick and drama productions, assuring the company's commercial profits. Within five years from 1920 to 1926, the company produced about 23 fiction films. Following American slapstick and cop shows, these films[3] were seen as 'vulgar', 'meaningless' and devoid of educational values. Some of their dramas were interpreted as promoting traditional feudal ideals. The strong criticism of Chinese imitations of American comedies and of Chinese portrayals of traditional ideologies testify to the difficulties and challenges facing the Chinese filmmakers in the 1920s as they were trying to create a screen identity for China: the cinematic construction of a dignified republic proud of its long civilisation. As a serious publisher, in the face of such criticism Commercial Press felt it had to distance itself from its film production. The end of Commercial Press's film production shows a conflict between on the one hand, the idea of commercial films, driven by Western imitations, and by attempts at creating Chinese genres for the domestic market to compete with imported films, and on the other, the idea of the didactical function of films, driven by nationalism. By implication, the incident also suggests that documentaries were regarded as a more 'meaningful' genre than that of fiction films.

The 1920s was the era of documentary exploration worldwide. Americans turned travelogues into ethnographic documentaries and European painters, musicians, writers and architects explored film technology to produce avant-garde non-fiction films. Excluding Hong Kong, Macau, and Taiwan, of about 150 registered film companies in 1925, no more than 20 companies engaged in documentary production, producing around one hundred newsreels and documentaries (San 2005: 16). Their subject matter was limited to such areas as landscape,[4] political and social events,[5] sports activities,[6] warlords or celebrities' funerals or activities,[7] police[8] and fire brigades.[9] In terms of mode of presentation, most of these films can be read as imitations of French and American early documentaries, depicting royal funerals and rituals, sports, and spectacular displays of the activities of rescue and law and order agencies.

Yet the most documented event in the 1920s in China by far was Dr Sun Yat-sen's second revolution. There were many documentaries and newsreels on Dr Sun Yat-sen,[10] the most prominent documentarist who followed Dr Sun from his 1921 resumption of the presidentship in Guangzhou to his death in Beijing in 1925, and made two major compilation films on Dr Sun, was the Hong Kong filmmaker Li Minwei. Li Minwei was perhaps, the most important documentary filmmaker in the 1920s, not only for the quantity of films he made about Dr Sun, but because he, rather than the Chinese Communist Party, or the *Guomindang*, initiated the idea that film should be subject to politics: his famous motto was 'film saves the nation' (San 2005: 17).

Li Minwei was a republican supporter who was born in Japan into a family of Hong Kong rice dealers. Less than two decades after the first Chinese film was produced in Beijing in 1905, Li Minwei recognised the pedagogic potential of film in Hong Kong. He argued that film could, and so should, be used both to educate people domestically, by changing negative social behaviour in China, and internationally by promoting positive images of the nation (Yu 1985: 43). Li aimed his films at Europe and America, with images of China representing 'ideas held aloof from the world, pure morality and innocent social custom',[11] not unlike those promoted by Commercial Press in Shanghai. After he had made the first Chinese film in the British colony in 1913, Li Minwei pioneered a promising film industry. He established a film production studio, a cinema, and opened a training centre for film talent. From 1923 Li started documentary filmmaking. He produced the first Chinese documentary film in Hong Kong, recording Chinese sportsmen attending the Sixth Far East Sports Festival in Japan in 1923.[12] In the early 1920s he followed Dr Sun Yat-sen to China to record political and social events for the Party.[13] During the 1920s Li Minwei shot abundant footage of Dr Sun Yat-sen and his *Guomindang* activities including documenting the *Zhongguo guomindang quanguo daibiao dahui / The Chinese National Guomindang Conference* (1924), *Sun Zhongshan xiansheng wei Dianjun ganbu xuexiao juxing kaimu li / Dr Sun's Attendance of the Opening Ceremony of Yunnan Army Cadre School* (1925), *Sun Zhongshan xiansheng beishang / Dr Sun Marches North, Sun dayuan shuai jianyue Guangdong quansheng jingwei jun, wuzhuang jingcha ji shangtuan / General Sun's Inspection of Military, Police and the Business Community of Guangdong Province;* and *Sun dayuan shuai chuxun Guangdong dongbei jiang ji / General Sun's Inspection of the North River in Guangdong* (1925), as well as Dr Sun's Funeral in 1925,[14] and Dr Sun's Memorial Foundation Ceremony in 1926.[15] Based on his footage of Dr Sun Yat-sen and *Guomindang* Party activities, Li Minwei made two compilation films, *Guomindang gemingjun hai, lu, kong dazhan ji / Battles of the Navy, Land and Air Forces of the Nationalist Revolutionary Army* (1927) and *Xunye qianqiu / Great Achievement Forever.* In 1941, he produced another compilation film, *Jianguo shi de yiye / A Page on the Establishment of the Nation* (1941).[16]

The Japanese invasion of Manchuria in 1931 only reinforced the relevance of Li Minwei's motto 'film saves the nation'. From 18 September 1931 onwards, when Japan attacked Manchuria, and especially after Japan's assault on Shanghai on 28 January 1932, images of bombed cities, burned villages, collapsed temples, corpses, raped women, crying children, as well as Chinese fighting against the Japanese became dominant images in the Chinese news documentaries,[17] a trend that continued after the Japanese surrendered to the Allies. These films were screened internationally as well as domestically, especially in the Chinese communities, in Hong Kong, Macau, and Southeast Asia. They were produced not only because they were newsworthy or for their dramatic violence, but also for nationalist conscious-raising aiming and in order to gather moral and financial support from overseas Chinese. Li Minwei's slogan had proved highly effective.

Apart from the mainstream war newsreels during the Japanese invasion, the 1930s is indeed an era of documentary film expansion in the world. In Europe and America, the use of documentary film as a major tool to inform and promote ideologies attracted the attention of the ruling class. The British documentary movement, the German Nazi Party and the American President's support for documentary film are examples. In China, the *Guomindang* government established its own film studio in Nanjing, and the Chinese Communist Party likewise participated actively in film production, initially through commercial film companies and film criticism. New technology enabled documentary filmmakers to record sound while filming Chinese operas. Sports documentaries continued to be popular,[18] with extended series, as for instance the four part documentary of *Diliuci quanguo yundong dahui / The Sixth National Sports Carnival* (1935). Increasingly, films on celebrities such as warlords and actors, including their activities and funerals were produced.[19] A greater variety of news was now being produced than during the 1920s, including such documentaries as *Taifeng erci xi hu / Twice Typhoon hits Shanghai* (1933), *Beiping geyong dui / Beijing Chore* (1933). A new documentary subject was Chinese industry, for instance the textile industry depicted in *Zhonghua zhi sichou / Chinese Silk* (1932), *Zhanghua nirong chang / Zhanghua Wool Fabric Factory* (1933), or communication, as in *Yuehan tielu zhushao duan gongcheng / Yuehan Railway Project* (1935), and *Jiaoji lu kehuo yunshu shebe ji yanxian fengjing / Scenery along Jiaoji Road Transportation* (1935), as well as urban construction, as for example in *Xin Guangzhou / New Guangzhou* (1934). The 1930s also witnessed the emergence of family documentaries such as *Shisheyingji de ren / The Man with the Movie Camera* (1933–34) by the famous film critic, writer and scriptwriter, Liu Naou, who fought against leftist criticism. Like many Chinese filmmakers, Liu was initially influenced by foreign films. But although Liu's *The Man with the Movie Camera* took Dziga Vertov's title, the film differs markedly in content from Vertov's film. What distinguishes Liu's documentary is the focus on family lifestyle, activities and landscape scenery in Taiwan, Guangdong, and Tokyo.[20]

Following in the footsteps of travel and exploration cinema in Europe and America in the 1920s, the Chinese documentaries of landscape in the 1930s[21] began to cover more extended and remote areas, as illustrated by *Jinxiu heshan / Beautiful Landscape of Sichuan* (1935) or the depiction of southeast Asia in *Nanyang daguan / Views of Southeast Asia* (1932). The documentary *Huang Zhuanshi feng lin ru Zang zhi ji Dala Lama / Special Envoy Huang Visits Tibet to Attend Dalai Lama's Funeral* (1935) records the *Guomindang* emissary Commissar Huang attending the funeral of the fourteenth Dalai Lama. In the same year, *Shengmi de xizang / Mysterious Tibet* was produced. Although no records of their films have survived, Chinese anthropologists, Dr Lin Chunshe and his team from The Central

Social Sciences Academy in Beijing conducted a number of field trips in the southwest to film the Miao, Li, and Yao minorities (San 2005: 31). In 1930 tertiary institutions started to use film as a teaching tool. In 1934 Jingling University (former Nanjing University) began producing documentary films for teaching purposes, with films covering topics in geography, defence, natural science, industry and agriculture. Amongst these films, *Nongren zhi chun / Spring for Farmers* (1937), depicting country scenes and lifestyles in the southern Yangzi River in spring, won China's first international award, the third prize in the category of documentary country film at a film festival in Belgium. The Chinese film industry received a deadly blow when, on 13 August 1937, Japanese bombs destroyed the entire Shanghai film production facility. A large number of filmmakers left Shanghai to join the Hong Kong film industry or joined the *Guomindang* in the west, or the Communists in the north. Even so, the *Guomindang* government had become a major and internationally recognised producer of newsreels and documentary films: a situation not unlike that during the Second World War in Europe when governments produced anti-enemy propaganda films.

The *Guomindang*

By the late 1920s, the *Guomindang*, like other nationalist groups, had firmly grasped the value of cinema as a function of education and propaganda. Unlike the Chinese Communist Party, which began their film business through film criticism, the *Guomindang* government started with censorship. In 1930 the government established Film and Theatre Censorship to regulate and censor films. In 1932, owing to the popularity of the left-wing films in Shanghai, the *Guomindang* strengthened their censorship, prohibiting films on the grounds that they were 'harming the dignity of the state and the nation, in violation of the *Guomindang*'s Three Principles, and causing disturbance of public order' (Du 1986: 123). The regulations especially targeted left-wing films promoting the Communist emphasis on class struggle and branding the government as capitalists and feudalists. In the same year, the *Guomindang* established the China Educational Film Association (*Zhongguo jiaoyu dianying xiehui*) with the mission of 'promoting nationalism, encouraging production, and constructing morality' (Du 1986: 124) through annual film publication and awards. During the same period, the *Guomindang's* film criticism supported a 'nationalist film movement' and in opposed anti-imperialist, left-wing cinema.

Yet the *Guomindang* were soon made to realise that censorship, film awards and film criticism alone were not sufficient to control film content. Through film scripts and post-production intervention, the leftwing filmmakers often managed to insert their Communist messages, which the commercial film studios appeared too 'weak' to eradicate. In 1935 the government established the Central Film Studio (*Zhongyang dianying sheying chang*) in Nanjing with the official function of promoting state 'culture and education' (Du

1986: 128). Allowing films as mere entertainment, to be produced by commercial filmmakers alone, was declared to be irresponsible. As the government's propaganda and information agency, the studio produced and distributed news documentaries for both domestic and international audiences, with the express aim of 'facilitating education and cultural development', 'making suitable films for the nation, promoting government policies, and assisting non-commercial films in fostering education and culture' (Du 1986: 126–8). And faithful to traditional Chinese aesthetics, 'the films of the Central Film Studio' emphasised education rather than merely 'entertaining the masses' (Fang 2003: 81).

With its emphasis on education and information, the Studio's documentaries were categorised as news, education, *guonan* (tragedies of the nation, or the nation is suffering), and *jiaofei* (catching the Communist bandits). In the first year of its establishment the studio produced about 200 newsreels and documentaries. From 1934 to 1937, the studio launched 53 series of *Zhongguo xinwen / News of China* and military educational films. Not surprisingly, these films were governmental propaganda, and generally anti-Communist. In 1937, after the Japanese bombed Shanghai, there were hardly any commercial film companies left able to produce documentaries.[22] In the same year, the Communist and the *Guomindang* joined forces to form the Second United Front to oppose the Japanese invaders, and so anti-Japanese messages became the key themes in the cinema. *News of China* reported the Chinese war effort in the non-Japanese occupied areas, and the new *Kangzhan shilu / Record of the Opposition to the Japanese* showed the Chinese army fighting the Japanese at the frontier. As an important consequence of the formation of the Second United Front between the Communists and the *Guomindang*, the China Film Studio (*Zhongguo Dianying Zhipian Chang*) established a branch office with a small Guomindang film crew in Hankou to where the *Guomindang* was able to withdraw when the Japanese attacked Nanjing. Apart from producing three anti-Japanese narrative films,[23] the Studio also published a series of newsreels, *Kangzhan teji / Special Report for the Anti-Japanese War, Kangzhan haowai / Special Reports on the Anti-Japanese War*, and *Dianying xinwen / News on Film*. With this abundance of documentary footage, a number of themed compilation films were produced, such as *Women de Nanjing / Our Nanjing* (1938); *Huoyao de xixian / Western Frontier* (1938); *Nanjing Zhuan hao / The Fall of Nanjing* (1938); *Tianzhu jiao da misa / Catholics Pray for Victory in the Anti-Japanese Battle* (1938) and *Jingzhong baoguo / Loyality to the Nation* (1938).

In spite of all this turmoil, the Chinese minorities were not forgotten during the anti-Japanese war period. The *Guomindang* Central Film Studio brought to the screen such documentaries as *Fenyi Chenjishihan lingjiu / Moving Ghengis Kahn's Grave* (1939), *Xizang xunli / Inspection of Tibet* (1940) documenting the Commissioner Wu attending the ceremony of the fourteenth Dalai Lama, and *Xinjiang fengguang / Sceneries of Xinjiang* (1940). At the same time the China Film Studio produced *Minzu wansui / Long Live the Chinese United Nation* (1940). This two hour documentary presented the Mongol, Tibetan, Hui, Miao and Yi minorities as they participated in the anti-Japanese war. The film contains images of the Hui, the Chinese Muslims and Tibetans praying in mosques and temples for the ending of the conflict, and included footage of minorities donating food for the Chinese soldiers, as well as Miao workers constructing roads for the Chinese army. Three years in the making, this film captures the landscapes of the Chinese West, with a mixture of narration, dialogue and self-reflection. Because of both its artistic achievement and its political correctness it is not surprising that this documentary charmed the critics of the time.

After the Japanese surrender in 1945 and the breakdown of the Second United Front, the *Guomindang* Government in Nanjing continued for a while to produce weekly newsreels, such as *News of China*, as well as documentaries, including *Guomin dahui / National Congress; Lingxiu wansui / Long Live Our Leaders; Ji Kong / Paying Respect to Confucius;* the anti-Communist *Tie / Iron; Gongfei huoguo ji / Records of the Communists Damaging the Country; Gongfei Baoxing shilu / True Records of the Communists Violence. / Who damaged the Railway?* The rift between the political right and left showed itself in the refusal by the *Guomindang* to report any Communist news, as well as in their eagerness to ban Communist films altogether. In 1947 civil war broke out between the *Guomindang* and Communists, with the Jiang Jieshi Government leaving the mainland for Taiwan two years later, an event that signalled the end of *Guomindang* film production on the mainland.

The Communists

In comparison, Communist film production was a latecomer, in spite of the fact that the Communists were the major force behind the Left-Wing Film Movement in the years between 1933 and 1935.[24] The Communists had learned from their Soviet colleagues to appreciate the potential power of film. In the late 1920s, the Communists had successfully influenced Chinese film through film reviews and scripts for commercial film production. In the early 1930s, they produced a number of classic films successfully in terms of both profitability and critical acclaim. Their films present a China of the unprivileged and the unemployed, of women, peasants and the urban proletariat exploited by the ruling class of imperialists, feudalists, the *Guomindang*, landlords and capitalists. Their Marxist approach to class analysis proved highly successful in fiction films, so it is surprising then that left-wing film criticism hardly addressed documentary filmmaking (Wu Chen 1993: 66–74).

The CCP's own first film production team, the Yan'an Dianying Tuan (Yan'an Film Brigade), was established in 1938, incidentally two years before the Yan'an Communist Radio. Officially, the purpose of CCP film production was 'to unite and encourage people to attack the enemies' (Cheng 1966: 341: Vol. 2). In particular, it aimed 'to encourage the whole Chinese people to participate in the anti-Japanese war by showing the facts of bloody battles against the Japanese' and to 'show the International communities how Chinese people are bravely fighting against the Japanese, using the living facts to gain Chinese sympathy and support' (San 2005: 81). This initial formula for film production: 'to unite and encourage people to attack the enemies', was to remain official Communist film policy from 1938 to the end of the Cultural Revolution, even if the concept 'people' (*renmin*) and 'enemy' (*diren*) changed over time to include or exclude different political and social groups in different historical periods. Paying attention to the varying definitions of 'people' (*renmin*) and 'enemy' (*diren*) is crucial to understanding not only Communist literature and art but the entire Communist ideological edifice (San 2005: 81). In the anti-Japanese war from 1937 to 1945, 'people' (*renmin*) referred to all Chinese opposing the Japanese, including the *Guomindang*. After the surrender of Japan to the US in 1945, the same signifier changed to refer to those who were prepared to fight imperialism, bureaucratic-capitalism, and landlords. Since the *Guomindang* Party was seen as the representative of imperialists, capitalists and landlords, the concept of *renmin* excluded the *Guomindang* government from 1945. More precisely, the term *renmin* was now reserved for those who actively supported the leadership of the Communist Party. What remained constant from 1938 onwards was the central aim of their films to portray images of the Chinese Communist Party and to promote Communist ideology. This was deemed legitimate by the Communists since *Guomindang* propaganda had either projected negative images about the Communists as 'bandits', or blocked information issued by Communist sources.

We should also remember that Communist filmmaking developed during a period of war when conditions for filmmaking were anything but comfortable. So it is only to be expected that news and documentaries were the main genres, with the promotion of Communist activities as their sole purpose. From 1938 to 1945, the Yan'an Film Brigade produced nine newsreels, three documentaries, and seven other collections of footage, mostly recording events and activities in the Communist controlled areas, including conferences, funerals and agricultural production (Cheng 1966: 497–8). Although it was lost in the Soviet Union in 1940 during the post-production phase, the first Communist documentary, *Yan'an yu Balu jun / Yan'an and the Eighth Route Army* by Yuan Muzhi, recorded 'the intellectual youth who gathered at Yan'an to overcome many difficulties and barriers set up by the *Guomindang*' (Qian and Gao 1981: 143). In many ways, this film can be said to have provided the foundations for later production methods and a model for Communist documentaries in technique as much as in terms of political content. (Fang 2003: 8). The film reiterates that it is the Communists who are *the* army fighting the Japanese, and *the* only legitimate army for the people of China. The first completed Communist documentary is *Shengchan yu zhandou jiehe qilai: Nanni wan / Production and Fighting Combine: Nanniwan* (1942), showing Communist life in Yan'an under the embargo imposed by the *Guomindang*. It reveals the spirit of Mao's famous article on Art in Yan'an in 1942 in its ideological documentation of 'revolutionary soldiers as the masters of the nation' (Qian and Gao 1981: 143). The film was a record of a 'new' era, and a 'new' life, which glorified the People's Liberation Army. It represented 'truthfully' and 'vividly', as Qian and Gao put it, the Liberation War in the northeast of China where 'no difficulties could not be overcome, and no war could not be won'.

After the anti-Japanese war, Communist filmmaking expanded extensively from 1946 to 1949. In 1946 Yan'an Film Brigade spawned the Yan'an Film Studio, with the brief to embark on feature film production. However, due to the breakdown of the only available camera and an urgent need to continue the production of documentaries reporting on progress in the war against the *Guomindang*, the first effort in feature film production, *Bianqu laodong yingxiong / Labour Heroes in Bianqu – the Communist area* had to be terminated. In 1947 when the *Guomindang* launched a military attack on the Communist held territory, the Yan'an Film Studio produced *Baowei Yan'an he baowei Shaanganning bianqu / Protect Yan'an, Protect Shaanxi, Gansu and Ningxia* (1947). After this production, the Party split the Yan'an Film Studio into two groups, one of which marched to Manchuria to take over the Japanese Film Studio, while the other was to follow the Liberation Army south. The first group established the Northeast Film Studio on 1 October in Changchun after taking over a Japanese film studio. The new studio's aims were similar to those of the Yan'an Film Studio, namely 'to use film to attack the enemies by educating the people'. Again, news documentaries made up the main genre. From 1947 to 1949, the studio produced about 17 issues of a newsreel titled *Minzhu de Dongbei / Democratic Northeast*. The series is divided into two sections, the war fronts, reporting on the liberation armies in the north and south fighting against the *Guomindang*, and events on the home front in Manchuria, showing the nation-building process under the Communists after the war, as well as documenting political, economic and social relations.

In 1946, the second group, the North China Film Brigade (*Huabei dianying dui*) followed the Communist army south to Shijiazhuang, where the Huabei Film Studio was established. The studio then produced two series, *Huabei xinwen / Huabei News* – mostly reporting the PLA's military progress – and the documentary *Jiefang Shijiazhuang / Liberating Shijiazhuang* (1947). In 1949 the film production crew moved to Beijing to take over the *Guomindang* Film Studio (*Beiping Dianying Zhipian Chang*). Again one main instruction was 'making news documentary first, then feature films'. A number of documentaries were produced under this banner, such as *Mao zhuxi Zhu zong siling beiping yue bing / Chairman Mao and General Zhu Inspecting the Army* (1949); *Xin zhengzhi xieshang huiyi choubei hui chengli / Preparatory Meeting for New Political Consultative Conference* (1949); *Qiyi zai Beiping / July First in Beijing* (1949); *Jiefang Taiyuan / Liberating Taiyuan; Huaihai zhanbao / Achievements of the Huaihai Campaign* and *Jianbao / News Brief* which recorded celebrations of the new China in Beijing, Shanghai, Tianjin, and other major cities. Also recorded were women's conferences, youth conferences, the establishment of the China and Soviet Union Friendship Association, the return of the Welcome Peace Delegation, the PLA crossing the Yangzi and Yellow Rivers, the liberation of Wuhan, 300,000 Shanghai people celebrating Shanghai's liberation, and the achievements at the Steel Factory in Tianjin. The Studio also made the long documentary film *Baiwan xiongshi xia jiangnan / Hundreds of Thousands PLA Soldiers Cross the Yangzi River*. Within twelve years, the Communist film production had grown from the three member team of the Yan'an Film Team in 1938 to controlling three film production studios, the Northeast, Beijing, and company in 1949 after the founding of the People's Republic.

The *Guomindang* left the mainland for Taiwan Island in 1949. Yet in spite of the often stark political differences between the two governments, they continued to produce documentaries in a very similar vein over the next four decades. And in spite of their diametrically opposed directives in terms of content, documentary cinema had become a mainstay of propaganda for both. In terms of presentational mode, both governments tended to use an easily identifiable cinematic formula. Both *Guomindang* and Communist filmmakers excluded rival voices from their productions after the breakdown of the Second United Front, and both censored or prevented opposing views from being heard in the areas they each controlled. This mutual exclusion of each other's position inevitably was to lead to a distinct mode of filmmaking, one that favoured a univocal representation of the politics of the nation. Documentary film was ideally suited to be shaped in this way as it was easy to control subject matter, representational techniques and editing. Given the increasing isolation of China in world affairs from 1949 to the end of the Mao period in 1976, it was only to be expected that in the People's Republic of China documentary film was to become a strictly censored carrier of political dogma. The next chapter will discuss the dogmatic formula of Chinese documentary filmmaking that was to characterise the period from 1949 to the early 1990s.

3 The dogmatic formula

Introduction

The relationships that had existed for a while amongst the three bodies of film production: commercial or private feature filmmakers, the Communists in the north, and the *Goumindang* in the south, changed dramatically in 1949 when the Chinese Communist Party established the People's Republic on the mainland. Defeated by the Communists in 1949, the *Guomindang* withdrew to Taiwan, while private studio ownership and production sharply declined and finally ended altogether in 1952 when the Communist government embarked on its first five year plan under its Socialist policy. After 17 years of war, the new government faced poverty, a high percentage of illiteracy, and a huge nation-building task. In those early days of Communist China, news and documentary films proved to be the most economic. direct and efficient way of disseminating information, challenging the print media and radio, as well as feature films. In 1953 the state established a centrally controlled film studio specialising in news and documentary film production: the Central News Documentary Film Studio (*Zhongyang xinwen jilu dianying zhipian chang*) in Beijing. In addition, the state also founded another two non-fiction film studios aiming to lift the general educational level of the nation: the Shanghai Science and Education Film Studio (*Shanghai kexue jiaoyu dianying zhipian chang*) in 1953 and China Agriculture Film Studio (*Zhongguo nongye dianying zhipian chang*) in 1954.

Like all film production in the planned economy from 1949 to early 1990s, the government funded, supervised and controlled the entire industry from scripting to filming, editing, distribution and exhibition. This meant a marked increase in the number of news and documentary films produced after 1949. Furthermore, the government expanded the exhibition sector to bring films to the rural and remote areas. At the same time however, the government's dogmatic attitude with respect to political ideology restricted the subject matter and artistic creativity. The influence of Lenin's view of news and documentary film as the 'visualisation of political ideology', and Mao Zedong's conviction that 'revolutionary art' should primarily serve workers, peasants and soldiers, meant that during those years Chinese film evolved within tightly monitored parameters, resulting in a cinematic style that is best described as a 'dogmatic formula'.

Whereas the European and American documentary filmmakers, film theorists and critics of the 1960s were able to question and explore the genre from its modes of expression to the philosophical level of the relationship between perception and actuality, reality, truth, and cinematic truth – Chinese documentary filmmakers and critics were bogged down in the turmoil of the Cultural Revolution. Narrowly conceived content rather than explorations of generic form dominated the critical discourse in China. This was made worse by the convictions of the policy makers and their denial of the commercial value of film production for the national economy. Thus news and documentary films in the dogmatic mode thrived. In Europe and America, from 1950 to the end of the 1970s, the popularity of television, new technologies in sound and camera, and independent documentary production systems enabled a variety of social subjects and cinematic styles to flourish in documentary filmmaking. In the same period in China, where television remained an élite medium, and sound and cinematic technologies had hardly progressed, the total control over the industry, further tightened by the Government's closed door policy, resulted in a large collection of monotonously dogmatic, documentary films. Although new technologies were introduced in the early 1980s, and media reform was launched and cultural exchange with the West began to have an impact on the media sector, it is only after Deng Xiaoping's inspection of the south in 1992 that we can observe a certain pluralism in the media.

In this chapter I want to describe the emergence and development of the Chinese dogmatic formula in news and documentary film in the period from 1949 to 1990. The chapter aims to address three questions. First, what caused the Chinese film industry to produce dogmatic and monological documentaries? Second, how were these films produced, and exhibited? And last, how does the monological and dogmatic style in these films affect subject matter and representational technique? These questions require the chapter to examine what I have termed the 'dogmatic formula' in three major areas of documentary film culture: ideology and policy, industrial practice and criticism, and subject content and cinematic style. The chapter then provides a synthesis of my observations in the form of a definitional description of the 'dogmatic formula' before concluding with a section on the all-important transition period from the early 1980s to 1993.

Ideology and film policy

Chinese film production between 1950 and the mid-1980s was *strictly* subject to film policies written from Communist perspectives on art: mainly those of Lenin and Mao Zedong. News and documentary films did not escape these constraints. Film policies referred to the official documents of instructions and regulations issued by the Chinese Communist Party, the

State Council, the Party's Central Propaganda Department, Ministry of Culture, Film Bureau, as well as other related government departments. Film policies were also included in speeches and talks on film production by high ranking government officials. Film policies guided the political directions of Chinese cinema, from the selection of film narratives, matters of censorship, planning and production, management in distribution and exhibition, to the creation of suitable cinematic styles. As film was regarded as a tool for mass education, film policies were made with the clear purpose of accomplishing national political and economic agendas.

As discussed in the previous chapter, the Chinese Communist Party used film to call on the nation to fight against the *Guomindang* and the Japanese military from 1935 until the eve of the establishment of the People's Republic. The perception of film as one of the most powerful weapons in the fight against the enemy, however, remained alive well after 1949 when China entered a period of nation-building. From the anti-rightist movement in 1956 to the end of the Cultural Revolution in 1977, the film industry created a series of cinematic enemies in response to the government's political agenda. Externally this applied to the Japanese, the *Goumindang*, and the two superpowers: the USA and the Soviet Union after the mid-1960s; internally, the cinematic foes were the landlords, the rightists, the intellectuals, the counter-revolutionaries, the 'capitalists' and the 'revisionists' inside the Party during the Cultural Revolution. Regarded as part of the ideological apparatus, filmmaking and writing about films became a battleground for political ideologies. Given this context, it is perhaps not surprising that the government was blind to such other contributions by the cinematic medium as the commercial value of film for the national economy, the artistic value of cinema in Chinese art, the cinematic features and cinematic genres of film, as well as the technological value of the media for social communication.

The Chinese understanding of film as a tool for political mass education in nation-building had specific foundations. Lenin's famous dictum that film is the most powerful amongst all arts, and especially his definition of news and documentary film as a 'visual illustration of political ideology' were the main guidelines for news and documentary filmmaking. Lenin's speech and dialogue on film, *The Party's View on Film*, was a must-read textbook for filmmakers in China. His argument that 'films should be full of the Communist spirit; reflect the reality of the Soviet Union; present images appropriate to the visualisation of political theories; follow the policies and lines of the Soviet newspapers, and be characteristic of proletarian news' functioned as a foundation for Chinese Communist filmmakers (Fang 2003: 205). Following Lenin's view that making news and documentary films should be like publishing the Party's newspaper (Gao 2003: 131; Fang 2003: 205; San 2005: 354) the Soviet Union's media policies and instructions for the print media also played a role in the ideological foundations of Chinese film production. The *People's Daily* published about 30 articles on Lenin and Stalin's talks and speeches on the print media from 4 January to December

1950, which the CCP expected media workers to absorb. Editorials admonished its media staff to 'use a big quantity' of the Soviet Union's 'rich experiences' to facilitate 'the beginning of our people's news industry' (Ding 2003: 405–6). In 1950, collections of these articles were published as books, such as *A Handbook for Journalists, How to Run a Party Newspaper*, or *Reflection of Mass Perspectives in Editorials*.

Lenin's talk on news and documentary film reveals a view that is quite different from those of the Soviet film theoreticians and practitioners Serge Eisenstein and Dziga Vertov. Where Eisenstein's film theory highlights montage and audience response to a series of images, and Vertov's 'Kino-eye' celebrates the accuracy and recording ability of a camera that is superior to the human eye, as well as new meanings emerging from the editing process. Lenin insists on a close link between print media and film, on content rather than media form, so that film followed the policies and formulations of official newspapers. Lenin equated documentary film with news, regarding film as supplementary, because his main purpose was to target the large number of illiterates in his country. Perhaps it seemed natural that in China, with an even larger underprivileged rural population than Russia, Eisenstein's montage theory of film form and Vertov's 'Kino-eye' should be viewed as less important than Lenin's statements about film content. This was not only because Lenin was generally admired as the paramount Communist leader, but also because the Chinese traditional aesthetic of *wen yi zai dao* favoured content-driven arguments over questions of film form. This is only one illustration of the fact that for Chinese policy-makers in the arts it was easier to grapple with film content than with representational style. Moreover, it is precisely this unfamiliarity with cinematic forms which paved the way for politics to override so easily the generic potential of documentary film.

Mao Zedong's *Talks at the Yan'an Forum on Literature and Art* in 1942 further consolidated the political, theoretical foundations of Chinese cinema. In his talk Mao proposed the idea of *geming wenyi* (revolutionary art) which should serve the workers, peasants, soldiers, the urban bourgeoisie and intellectuals. His inclusion of the last two does not mean that Mao supported the view that China should produce films to meet the tastes of the urban bourgeoisie. What he had in mind was that the bourgeois intelligentsia needed to be educated by way of revolutionary art. In particular, film was to teach them about the massive participation of workers, peasants and soldiers in the revolution under the leadership of the Communists. Above all else, films of revolutionary art were to be produced with the principal aim of accessibility to workers, peasants and soldiers. To achieve this in practice, Mao Zedong recommended that artists and filmmakers share the lives of workers, peasants and soldiers. Only in this way, Mao believed, could true and accessible revolutionary art be accomplished. From 1942, Mao's conception of revolutionary art inspired Communist filmmakers to develop new cinematic aesthetics that would be different from the traditional cinematic genres of Chinese opera and martial arts developed from the late 1920s, Shanghai urban bourgeois cinema in the 1930s and 1940s, as well as Hollywood and European films. Indeed, in 1946 his revolutionary cinema began to show signs of success. News and documentaries produced by the Communists in the Northeast Film Studio became increasingly popular. Their films on war and social change in the northwest's transition from Japanese controlled territory to its Communist liberation and reconstruction drew large crowds. And since these films were organised and actively promoted by the CCP, they competed well with the commercial distribution system and exhibitions at the time and so began to appeal to larger and larger audiences.

In the firm belief that the new China needed a new film culture, the Communist filmmakers were determined to continue their success in documentary filmmaking after 1949. They felt that they had found a political, theoretical and film generic foundation for the creation of a new kind of revolutionary art (Ding 1998: 138–58). They developed a principle in scriptwriting that narratives in fiction films should be based on events and people in documentaries (Ding 1998: 145). Filmmakers were encouraged to use the documentary film genre as the model to follow, which meant in the first instance that cameras were to look at workers, peasants and soldiers, instead of wild fantasies, traditions, folk culture, and the legends of the past. Using the genres of news and documentary film for revolutionary art was also practical. After 17 years of war China was in no position to support any sophisticated cinematic technologies. At the same time, the social reality in China, the change of government, the new political and economic systems, together provided ample material for cinematic dramatisation. Guided by Mao's thoughts on revolutionary art, the Communists filmmakers continued in the Yan'an spirit of self-sufficient cinematic art. According to the principles of representing the workers, peasants and soldiers, the Party instructed its filmmakers that they were to follow the Chinese traditional ways of storytelling in order to reach as wide as possible an audience in the rural areas. This conservative policy was neatly spelt out in 1952 by Premier Zhou Enlai: 'our films must have a beginning and ending; plots must be clear; patterns should not be as fast as foreign films. Because we are people from a semi-agriculture society, we can't catch up if it is too fast' (Qian and Gao 1981: 148). Furthermore, this revolutionary cinema demanded the filmmaker document the workers, peasants and soldiers as seen from amongst them rather than from a bourgeois distance. It required the filmmakers to edit footage as a true believer would without guilt, pity or shame for being 'subjective' or 'manipulative'. This revolutionary cinema insisted that filmmakers had to be highly conscious of their political purpose of educating the masses. Films were to communicate with the masses, in dialogue with the masses, enabling mass audiences to identify with heroes and political statements that were backed up by such rudimentary cinematic techniques as camera angles, editing, music and narration. Though news and documentary films were showing events of past and present, they also had to be able to project the right kind of future.

The exclusion of bourgeois and intellectual gratification, together with the political elimination of commercial considerations and profit making, assisted in the survival of this revolutionary cinema for more than three decades. In spite of this political protectionism however, the development of China's revolutionary film culture, including documentary film, in this period was far from smooth. Tensions began to appear over the dogmatic treatment of Lenin's 'visual illustration of political ideologies' and Mao's revolutionary emphasis on the representation of workers, peasants and soldiers. The foremost question to be raised was whether the principles of the new documentary film were to be loyal to actuality or to the slogan of 'visual illustration of political ideologies'. When the actual world contradicted the world of policy, which one was to be the master? More probing questions followed. For instance, should the new cinema document the realities of the most devastating famine in Chinese history and unravel its causes in the incompetence of the Party leadership and the policy of the Great Leap Forward? Should workers, peasants and soldiers be portrayed as always in agreement with the Communist representations? Should such portrayals remain restricted to Communist self-representations? Do the workers, peasants and soldiers celebrate only one type of film taste in spite of China's diversity of cultures? While such questions could not be openly aired before the 'Hundred Flowers Campaign', after 1956 they increasingly began to exercise the minds of film directors as well as policy makers. Needless to say, during the Anti-Rightist Campaign in 1957 many of the people who uttered such doubts were severely punished.

From its initial meeting deciding on the establishment of the Central News Documentary Film Studio in 1952 to the early 1990s the government's concerns about news documentary films had to do mainly with the relationship between the educational function and the representation of actuality. The government was worried about the contradictions it saw between the Party's educational intentions and images of social actuality in China. This is why from the time of the founding of the Central News Documentary Film Studio in 1953 to the transfer of the studio to the CCTV in 1993, the majority of policies and other official instructions concerning news and documentary film related to the extent and the kind of actualities to be shown. And since news and documentary film were to be based on actuality, questions of 'true', 'real', 'authenticity' and 'truth' were unavoidable. Answers to these questions were mostly driven by political ideologies rather than by any serious exploration of film genre and the cinematic problematic of the relation between perception and film, actuality and cinematic truth, or the systems and methods of production.

Discussions of *zhenshi* (real, actual, true, truthfulness) typically ranged between two poles: the actuality of represented events and people on the one hand, and, on the other, how such actualities could be filmed so they were believable, or how to achieve the purpose of effective persuasion. At the First Conference on News Documentary Filmmaking from December 1953 to January 1954, after declaring that the purpose of documentary filmmaking was 'to educate the masses about Socialism', and to 'lift the degree of Socialist consciousness of the masses', and that films 'should portray models in Socialist construction', the Deputy Minister of the Central Propaganda Department and Ministry of Culture, Zhou Yang, stressed that the uniqueness of the genre lay in its cinematic representation of actuality,

> The question of *zhenshi* in news documentary film is different from that in other arts. Based on actuality, other arts can use the imagination to describe and expand. But news documentary films must show the things as they exist and events as they happen. That is what is special about documentary film, as its events can't be fictional. Otherwise, news documentary would lose its credibility.
>
> (Gao 2003: 136)

The Minister elaborated by saying that *zhenshi* expressed itself in three ways, as 'an actual event', as 'truthful perspectives in the selection of materials', and as 'truthful methods in dealing with materials', adding that 'we are against those who manufacture events, while at the same time, we are also against a naturalism that offers footage without editing'. His views were endorsed by the following comments from the Deputy Head of the Film Bureau, Chen Huangmei:

> News documentary films can express only what has already happened or is in the process of happening. Typical events and people are what we discovered, selected in real life, not what we created. We must oppose all fictional things in news documentary: real people in false events; false people in real events; or false people in false events. ... We must refrain from adding shots to fill narrative gaps and from re-shooting, though this depends on the situation. But the thought that we can rely on re-shooting after the events is wrong.
>
> (Fang 2003: 197)

Chen Huangmei also emphasised that the only acceptable method of making news documentaries was to 'show life truthfully, as long as it achieved at the same time the goal of education in the Socialist spirit'.

The Conference reached consensus on three principles, in spite of the complexities involved in trying to balance documentary filmmaking between educational purpose and a faithful depiction of actuality. These principles remained at the centre of news and documentary filmmaking throughout the Anti-Rightist Movement, the breakdown of the Sino–Soviet Union relations and the Great Leap Forward in 1958 until the beginning of the Cultural Revolution in 1966. The three principles were, first, the conference confirmed, that news and documentary films should be understood exclusively in terms of Lenin's definition as the 'visual illustration of political ideologies'. Accordingly, making news documentary films was to follow the way of publishing a Communist Party newspaper, and cameramen were to be regarded as the 'journalists' of film. Second, *zhenshi* (actuality and truthfulness) was the essence of news documentary. Fiction in news documentaries was held to lead to a loss of political credibility. Third, scripting and directing in news and documentary filmmaking were deemed necessary. News documentary films should be planned and scripted before shooting. Directors should also participate in the post production process to ensure the quality of artistic expression of the films. Above all, news and documentary films are to be used by the Party to present national achievements in order to encourage workers, peasants and soldiers to participate in the socialist reconstruction of the country. (Gao 2003; Fang 2003)

In 1956 Mao Zedong launched the 'One Hundred Flowers' campaign to stimulate diversity in Chinese art. In turn, the Party called on the nation's artists to follow Mao's instructions. In cinema circles, some filmmakers and scholars broke their silence to ask if Lenin's notion of documentary as 'visual illustration of political ideologies' was now no longer to be regarded as the only legitimate definition of Chinese documentary. Some film directors pointed out that Lenin's prescription was not able to cover wholly what the documentary film genre does. Hence, documentary filmmakers should be allowed also to make films other than to illustrate political ideologies. Criticism followed that watching Chinese documentaries was not unlike 'attending political lectures', that subject matters were 'narrow and thin', and cinematic expression 'boring and repetitive' (Gao 2003: 162). Some also questioned whether the workers, peasants and soldiers perhaps liked to watch screen images other than representations of themselves. In the wake of Mao's 'One Hundred Flowers', a number of documentaries were indeed produced that differed markedly from the 'illustration of political theories'.[1] Predictably, these films were praised for 'using images instead of words, showing instead of narrating, and using daily images to replace blunt political education' (Gao 2003: 160). Sadly, Mao's flowers were soon to whither.

In the following year, in 1957, Mao felt compelled to embark on his 'Anti-Rightist Movement' as a penalty for those who began to question Lenin and Mao's guidelines on film, as well as for those who contributed too literally to the diversity of artistic expression. They were executed, sent to jail or some remote exile. The documentaries of that brief period of political thaw were now declared bourgeois films hostile to workers, peasants and soldiers. For instance, *Xinghua chunyu Jiangnan / Jiangnan in Spring* (1956) portrays the tranquility of South of the Yangzi River in a poetic and lyrical mode, introducing a modicum of cinematic variety in camera angle, colour, lighting, frame and sound. Now the film was criticised for presenting the peasants in the new China from a 'capitalist and bourgeois' perspective, because it failed to show the peasants as 'participating passionately and actively in the construction of the Socialist nation' (Gao 2003: 161). This criticism suggests a fear of the breach of the declared educational function of film. Far from being a 'visual illustration of political ideological theory', the film presents a romantic, poetic, and tranquil rural world and so falls foul of the political message the workers, peasants and soldiers are meant to grasp.

Like print and broadcasting, news and documentary film had lost much of their credibility, of objectivity, during the period of the Great Leap Forward in 1958 to 1959. Rallying to Mao's call for accelerating the national economy in order to accomplish the promised Communist society at a faster rate, every province except Tibet established a film studio, with most of them producing news and documentary films. It is therefore not surprising that the output of film production during 1958 and 1959 was higher than the total of films made between 1949 and 1957. In order to demonstrate news and documentary film as 'cinematic illustration of political ideologies' for mass education, the studios mass produced images and stories of factories, communities, soldiers and urban work units 'creating' and 'discovering' new technologies under the leadership of Party Secretaries. In this way, documentary film was commandeered to assist in achieving Mao's declared goal of radically advancing the national steel industry and delivering a superior Communist lifestyle that would rival that of Britain and America in fifteen years. Images of the masses working hard day and night following their Party leaders, against the background of red flags, drums, and banners with slogans, underpinned by passionate narration were typical of the documentaries of the time. Since there were no films showing the tragedies caused by the Great Leap Forward, especially the largest famine in Chinese history during which an estimated 17 million people starved to death in 1960 to 63, a false picture of China was created by directorial interference, staging, exaggeration, concealment, and radically one-sided views. This kind of falsification was of course not limited to documentary filmmaking; it applied equally to the print media and radio, as well as to other channels of public communication.

So drastic was the distortion of facts in the media that the government that had instigated the trend, felt it necessary to issue a document in June 1961 to the effect that 'news documentary films must strictly abide by the principle of total *zhenshi* (actuality and truthfulness); it must represent real persons and real events'. If it violated this principle 'news and documentary films will definitely lose their value'. At the same time, between 1960 and 1964, the total number of films was sharply reduced owing to the national financial crisis. Three factors were responsible for this situation: the failure of industrial production, the famine, and the breakdown of the Sino–Soviet relations and subsequent repayment of debts to the Soviet Union. Film production in general and especially documentary filmmaking were at an all-time low. To remedy the situation, the Film Bureau proposed a reform in 1964. Its goal was to improve both the quality and quantity of film production. Unfortunately, with the onset of the Cultural Revolution in 1966 news and documentary film production relapsed to the standard of the period of the Great Leap Forward, at least in terms of quality. From 1966 to the death of Mao Zedong in 1976, Jiang Qing, Mao's wife and a key figure in the Cultural Revolutionary Committee on art and media, declared that documentary film had to follow the principles of 'facts serve politics' (*shishi yao wei zhengzhi fuwu*) and 'truthfulness serve politics' (*Zhenshi yao wei zhengzhi fuwu*). This amounted to no less than a political definition of truth, even if the philosophical implications of the Gang of Four ruling remained unexamined. Certainly, under her leadership, documentaries, once again, documented only what the Party or the particular group of Party leaders felt was worthy of public consumption. During this period, when fiction films were close to absent, news and documentary films constituted the mainstream cinema. These films show Mao in meetings with the representatives of the Red Guards, the workers, peasants, soldiers and minorities. The documentaries also show the nation's celebration of his new policies, the founding of Revolutionary Committees, mass meetings denouncing counter-revolutionaries, and youths following Mao's call for the extension of national re-education to the rural areas. No alternative, different, critical, or contradictory perspectives and voices could be found in the news and documentary films. On screen, the nation, the minorities, industry, agriculture, the army, hospitals and universities, are presented in a monological and unifying voice, shoring up whatever new movements the Party initiated. Mao's theory of revolutionary art as an art about and for the workers, peasants and soldiers had turned out to be fundamentally a tool for Communist Party politics. As the News Documentary Film Studio was a branch directly responsible to the Propaganda Department it was unable to present voices other than those of the Party policies of the time.

In the years of 1976 and 1978 the political scene in China changed dramatically. Mao's death, the arrest and trial of the Gang of Four, the announcement of the end of the Cultural Revolution and its chaotic implementation of class struggle theory, and above all the return of Deng Xiaoping have all had a major influence not only on China's general political climate but also specifically on news and documentary filmmaking. The media were now no longer solely about and for the workers, peasants and soldiers. In the words of Deng Xiaoping, 'our arts belong to the people', *renmin*, a term that once again included all Chinese citizens. In 1978 Deng Xiaoping added to this an important pragmatic observation to the effect that practice (*shi jian*) was to be the only criterion of truth, that is, seeking truth from facts. Compared with Lenin's conception of documentary truth as visualized political theory, Mao's notion of documentary revolutionary art and Jiang Qing's definition of cinematic truth as determined by political need, Deng Xiaoping's pragmatics heralded a fundamental shift in policy and film aesthetics, a shift however that took another decade to be realised on screen.

At the same time, Deng Xiaoping's national agenda of the Four Modernisations likewise had tangible effects on the media and documentary film. Socialist art was now to celebrate the creators and pioneers of the Four

Modernisations, which meant that scientists and professionals were to be rehabilitated as unsung heroes, instead of workers, peasants and soldiers exclusively. Though news and documentary film remained one of the Party's main propaganda tools, it was no longer restricted to the singular purpose of 'visual illustration of political theories'. Now its function included artistic expression and the dissemination of knowledge. No surprise then that the 'One Hundred Flowers' was likewise rehabilitated and encouraged. Under this new direction, the subject matter of cinema began to broaden. Throughout the 1980s, documentaries flourished that were critical of the disasters of the Cultural Revolution, and they often described the incorrect accusations of politicians, scientists and writers. Films were produced that praised those who were contributing to the agenda of the Four Modernisations and especially to economic reform. Documentaries appeared on screen in which Western countries were introduced, often in a poetic and lyrical style that contrasted sharply with the dogmatic mode of film as 'illustration of political ideologies'. All these films, then, continued to reflect the government's policies in the 1980s: denouncing the Cultural Revolution, promoting Economic Reform, and legitimating the new Open Door policy. Amongst these, it was Deng Xiaoping's Open Door policy that brought about a more profound transformation of Chinese documentary film than all the Party's policies had achieved during the period from 1949 to the early 1980s. Nor should this be too surprising since the opening to the West was responsible for the explosive popularity of television in China, the availability of non-Chinese films to filmmakers and consumers, the socialist market competition at an international level, and access to new film technology.

Film industry and critical practice

The dogmatic cinema of news and documentary film in the period from 1949 to the early 1990s was not only strictly ideologically driven, but also systemically controlled by government in terms of production, distribution and exhibition, including the organisation of film viewers on a large scale. Four months before Mao Zedong announced the founding of the People's Republic in Tiananmen Square on 1 October 1949, the Central Film Bureau had been established under the control of the Party's Central Propaganda Department and Ministry of Culture. The Party was to supervise the political content of film, whereas the Ministry of Culture was responsible for the overall administration and management of film culture. Since political content could be effected anywhere in the filmmaking process, the Central Film Bureau was in charge of all areas relating to film production, distribution and exhibition. The Bureau made an overall annual budget plan for production, and distributed production tasks to film studios. According to the policies of the day, the Bureau also decided on a film's subject theme, scripts, as well as the kind and proportion of subjects in the national film productions. After completion of the tasks left to the film studio, the Bureau arranged for various official representatives to discuss the films. Because China did not have either censorship laws or media regulations until the mid-1990s, the views of individual leaders and Party representatives could decide the fate of any film. Furthermore, after private ownership of production, distribution and exhibition were terminated in 1952 the entire process was standardised, routinised and controlled by the government.

Such a centrally controlled model was bound to prove neither artistically productive, nor economically efficient, though of course that was not the Party's primary intention. In 1956, *Wenhui Daily* revealed that 70 per cent of films made between 1953 and 1956 failed to recover their production costs. The documentary *Xingfu de ertong* / *Happy Children*, for example, did not even recoup its advertising fees (Zhong 1956).[2] In the wake of Mao's 'One Hundred Flowers' agenda in 1956, the Film Bureau proposed a system of director-centered production units. The system envisaged the Bureau's continuing role in the control of the overall budget plan, film content and allocation of production to each studio. At the same time, the system encouraged film directors to choose a script from already approved film scripts, organise production teams and look after production budgets and take responsibility for any economic losses. Film studios were to be responsible for political censorship and artistic standards, as well as for guaranteeing the completion of film production and distribution. Although approved by the Central Bureau of the Party in early 1957, the Anti-Rightist Movement in late 1957 denounced the proposal as a rightist attempt to deny the Party leadership in film production. In 1961 an attempt was made to find a balance between political doctrine and economic efficiency by instituting a system of director and scriptwriter centered production units that rendered the Party's leadership in production unchallengeable.

The Party's control of film production was most visible in its decisive role in determining the subjects to be addressed in news and documentary film. The Propaganda Department and Ministry of Culture issued plans on film subjects, encouraging films showing Communist history, revolutionary activities under Communist leadership, socialist construction projects in industry and agriculture, the People's Liberation Army defending the nation, the good deeds of policy officers, scientists, teachers and children, Chinese history and landscape, the promotion of patriotism and the idea of the unified China. The proportion of each subject would vary according to the political agenda of the time. For instance, during the Land Reform period, more documentaries were produced addressing achievements in rural areas. During the Korean War, the majority of documentaries featured the military under Communist leadership. As a rule of thumb, 70 per cent of content was reserved for the representation of workers, peasants and soldiers (Hu 1995: 34–5). In 1965, in response to a request by the Party, the political content of films was strengthened in the three areas presenting the good deeds of workers and peasants during the Great Leap Forward; war and revolutionary history, Mao Zedong's thoughts on war, the participation of the masses in war; and the struggle between Communism and Capitalism (Hu 1995: 39). A perhaps not so obvious observation to make here is that the film subject plans of the time contain hints of the kind of political struggles that occurred behind closed Party doors. The film plan for 1965, for instance, clearly foreshadows the events of the following year when Mao Zedong embarked on the Cultural Revolution. The Party's instructions on documentary film subject matter and the highly selective and uniform nature of its film policies had turned Chinese film of the period into an easily identifiable type: a cinematic illustration of state policy.

In news and documentary film in particular, the Party plans that governed subject matter resulted in a singularly one-sided kind of cinema. Before 1949, owing to the war situation and the fact that the Communist army was constantly on the move, documentaries were made mostly by editing footage shot by a number of different cinematographers. To a large extent, this meant that cinematic ideas were restricted by what kinds of film images were available. This situation changed when, after the first conference on news and documentary filmmaking in 1952, approval for detailed proposals and scripts were required by the Party before shooting. This new procedure fundamentally altered the way documentaries were produced. The filmmaking process was virtually reversed by declaring the political message the framework for filming. Thus restricted, filmmakers could do no more than follow an already approved proposal, a narration to suit and then look for images likely to illustrate the prescription. In the end, the editing process was once more strictly curtailed by a political message. This, however, did not mean that the Party prohibited collection of actual footage. In fact, the Chinese film archives during that time accumulated a very large number of such unscripted filmic records of official gatherings, Party Congresses, speeches by major political figures, as well as private footage of Mao Zedong and his immediate circle. Only very selected and small proportions of such genuine documentary records were however made available to the public. Why was this kind of footage then collected so studiously? The answer to this question lies in a policy document that specifies as one of the key tasks of the Central News Documentary Film Studio and the August First Studio to record various kinds of 'realities' for usage other than political mass education.

For instance, in 1955, Mao instructed film studios to produce a documentary record of the lifestyles of the minorities before they disappeared. Likewise, during the Cultural Revolution, the Central News Documentary Film Studio, following instructions by the Party, recorded 'actual' activities of the Red Guard divisions fighting with one another, sometimes encouraged and even joined by workers and peasants (Fang 2003: 275–6). Raw footage of the lifestyles of the prominent leaders inside the Forbidden City were likewise assembled and stored by the Studio. Only a small group of insiders such as Party leaders and specially selected Party members were privileged to inspect those cinematic documents. A large amount of footage was taken for historical records, sometimes with the intention to turn it into films for public consumption when the time was right. Vice versa, sometimes political events caused the cancellation of a film that had already been earmarked for public screening. A well-known example is a documentary shot at Premier Zhou Enlai's funeral. The eulogy was read by Deng Xiaoping who, however, had suddenly become a *persona non grata*. So the film was mothballed, only to become available to the public in 1979, after Deng's return to political leadership.

Film distribution and exhibition were run strictly according to the edicts of political education. In spite of this cumbersome management style, the number of film studios increased markedly during the decade from 1952 to 1962. In 1952 there were three studios: the Beijing Film Studio, the Northeast and Shanghai Studios, then four new specialised film study centres were opened: the Central News and Documentary Film Studio, the August First Studio serving the People's Liberation Army, the Science Education Film Studio, as well as the Agriculture Film Studio of 1952–3. By 1958 the number of production studios had exploded, of which eleven were continued after the purge of 1962. Chinese film exhibition statistics could claim even more impressive records. In 1949 there were approximately 600 cinemas catering for 47.3 million viewers. By 1958, there were about 300 million viewers, serviced by more than ten thousand mobile exhibition teams in rural areas (Hu 1995: 59). These numbers should however not be misread as an indication of the profitability of Chinese revolutionary cinema, since the foremost motive for the government was how widely and effectively the Chinese masses could be educated using film. To a large extent, viewers were not expected to pay to attend the film viewing events. Nor did the state care whether the film viewers felt entertained or bored by what they saw. Films were made primarily for political rather than aesthetic purposes. Viewing was compulsory, while audiences were organised in their work units to ensure a full house.

Such draconian control over cinema culture was certainly in need of some kind of justification. In a speech addressing the heads of the film studios on 13 November 1953, the Deputy Minister of the Propaganda Department Zhou Yang explained:

(We know that) the urban population doesn't like our documentary films, but we can't follow their wishes. We need to find ways to lead them. We should educate them, and let them know that the action of refusing to watch documentary films testifies to backwardness in political ideology. When we moved into the cities, the residents didn't like to read our newspaper at the beginning either. What has happened now? They are getting used to it. We should use our socialist thoughts and feelings to get rid of those unsocialist thoughts and feelings within the population at large.

(Hu 1995: 15)

Accordingly, in order to expand the influence of news and documentary film, China's 26 major cities established the New Monthly Film Exhibition. Cinemas were not only places where news and documentary films were screened, they also served as a training ground for new viewing habits (Fang 2003: 177). Arrangements for film screening neatly reflected political topicality. For example, during the Great Leap Forward, mobile screening teams showed such documentaries as *Nongcun zai dayao jin / The Country-side in the Great Leap Forward* or *Yishan zhaohai / Moving Mountains and Building an Ocean.* Party records tell us that 'by the second day the peasants had learnt a new construction technique from the film. They imitated the film and made soil machines and worked without lifting equipment by using sticks. As a result, efficiency increased three fold' (*Film Exhibition* 1959, Issue 18). When the People's Commune was founded, the Party screened *Renmin gongshe haochu duo / Many Good Aspects of the People's Communes.*

An important shift in the Chinese film industry occurred with the advent of television. Though this was not immediately obvious and it took a while for the new technology to take hold, we cannot overestimate its impact. The birth of Chinese television on 1 May 1958, announces the end of an era, in spite of the fact that television was to remain an élite institution until the late 1970s. In 1958, when China was hardly able to manufacture its own television sets, the introduction of television was aimed mainly at providing a channel for China to present itself to the world, and for the rest of the world to be able to access information about China during the Cold War (He 2005: 8). In the year following the founding of the Beijing TV Station in 1958, the Soviet Union donated 500 television sets for distribution amongst the leaders of the Party and the government in Beijing. By the end of 1975, the total number of television sets had increased to 500,000 (He 2005: 9). But given the limited hours and coverage of broadcasting, television at that stage was not able to make major inroads into the structure of Chinese society at large.

In the period from the Great Leap Forward in 1958 to the end of the Cultural Revolution in 1977 when media, propaganda and politics were combined into one package, there was not much difference between televisual and film content. At the initial stage, the main difference was that television used 16mm film while documentaries for the cinema used 35mm films. Otherwise, the two media remained closely associated. The majority of television producers were transferred from the Central News Documentary Film Studio, and televisual production methods very much resembled those of film production. Television journalists were expected to complete two pieces of extended coverage and eight pieces of news per month (He 2005: 6–7). Similar to the practice at the Central News Documentary Film Studio, the task for the television journalists was to strictly follow Party policies, reporting the nation's major political events and achievements of socialist construction. Much like the documentaries, TV programmes were to cover major political meetings, conferences, leaders visiting overseas, with a few documentaries on geography and scenery.

It was only in the early 1980s that television in China changed from an elite media to a mass media. We witness a rapid increase of television stations from 260 to over 3,000 by end of the 1980s, including stations on the county level. At the same time, the number of television sets available to the public soared to the millions. Television had arrived as the leading media in China. The News and Documentary Film Studio had lost its leading function of producing newsreels, while it continued to offer documentary films until 1993 when it was fully transferred to the CCTV. This also marks an important moment for documentary film itself, because it became institutionalised as a televisual product. I will return to this topic in Chapters 3 and 4.

Another facet of the media industry in Mao's China was film criticism. As I emphasised earlier, in China, art criticism was traditionally content or morality driven rather than by innovative techniques of artistic expression. The left-wing film criticism in Shanghai in 1935 had been premised on political content, which was no more than a political modification of the traditional Chinese *wen yi zai dao*, the belief that art was to convey moral messages in aesthetically acceptable forms. So the period from 1949 to 1976 did not constitute a radical change, except in the sense that film criticism was now more poignantly constrained by politics. What is new is first the degree to which Communist film policy tried to make sure that no mis-readings of political morality was likely to occur and, second, the not so obvious fact that the evaluation of films provided opportunities for redirecting politics itself. Mao Zedong's film criticism, such as critics about films *Wu Xun zhuan / Wuxun Biography*, and *Hai Rui baguan / Hai Rui Dismissed from Office*, was intimately linked to a number of political movements, including the Anti-Rightist Movement and the Cultural Revolution. Critics whose views on films differed from those of the Party often paid for their deviance with their political careers, some of them even with their lives. Vice versa, those who supported the Party's views on film were rewarded with political promotions. Given this situation, it is not surprising to see that the manner of conducting film criticism was intimately associated with political struggle. Not only were documentaries themselves the carriers of political messages, film reviews were likewise a platform for political indoctrination. Alternative voices were silenced as effectively in film criticism as they were in film.

Film texts: content and style

From 1949 to the mid-1980s, the distinction between news and documentary film was not sharply drawn. For a long period, the Chinese regarded documentary film as not much more than a somewhat extended, later version of news; both were about actualities, and the approach to actualities of social and political life was predominantly a certain style of reporting. The name of the Central News Documentary Film Studio is *xinwen jilu*, 'news documentary film', which neatly reflects this conflation. In 1954, on his return from a four months training stint in the Soviet Union, the Deputy President of the Central News Documentary Film Studio, Qian Xiaozhang, reiterated the important link between techniques employed in newspapers and documentaries. He instructed the Studio to 'work hard to lift the standard of news documentary film to the standard of the Party's newspaper'. For 'only news documentaries with a clear political perspective, a high degree of true reporting, immediacy and variety, and an effort of lifting the standard of artistic expression, can be regarded as 'visual illustration of political theories'. Nor did Qian draw any generic distinctions between news and documentaries. The only difference he acknowledged was that of length. 'News film is the first task of the Studio', and 'it is necessary to make a documentary film where there is a big and complex topic, as we need films that tackle both specific and general matters.' In terms of production, the emphasis was on 'paying attention to scripts, plot outlines and direction'. (Fang 2003: 206) an approach indistinguishable from non-cinematic modes.

As discussed, documentary films in this period are mainly a cinematic illustration of governmental policies. Here I ask what kind of effects this subservience of documentary cinema had on its content and style. The Film Bureau, Propaganda Department and Ministry of Culture regularly issued *ticai guihua* (film subject plans), and in turn each film studio began to look for events that might be suitable to the broad ideology of the government as well as meet the specific demands of the film subject plan. We must draw a distinction at this point between a film subject plan and a genre plan. Briefly, genre plans target commercial profits, subject plans guarantee specific kinds of propaganda. Not surprisingly then, genre plans hardly played a role in the period of the dogmatic formula, while documentary film content and presentational style were inextricably tied up with the notion of the subject plan. As a result, during such political movements as the Great Leap Forward, or the Cultural Revolution, there is no distance, let alone any critical distance, between film and policy. Whatever the political agenda, we find it mirrored in documentary film content and style. More specifically, news and documentary films since 1949 fall into two broad categories, films illustrating governmental policies, and films showing the people's applause of such policies. In this kind of web of instruction, production and screenings, oppositional or even mildly critical views can hardly be expected. A single voice is orchestrated and received. The fact that documentary film requires at least a modicum of social reality proved no obstacle to the Party. In spite of some leaders emphasising 'actuality', whenever a policy failed to be supported by the facts, they were manufactured and staged.

Notwithstanding this monotony, we are able to distinguish three documentary genres: scripted documentary, compilation film, and newsreel. In the scripted documentary, two modes are dominant, expository and poetic presentation, however the former is more obvious. Compilation documentaries are produced from archival footage, while the newsreel documentaries are recognisable by their day-to-day relevance and relative brevity. Within these limited genres and representational modes, films typically dealt with one or two of the following areas of subject matter approved by the state: (1) significant national political events; (2) socialist construction projects in industry, agriculture, defence, science and technology; (3) the military; (4) minorities; (5) foreign affairs; (6) culture and art; and finally (7) sport.

Significant political events

Reporting political events was the priority for the Central News Documentary Film Studio before television became popular in late 1970s. Political events refer to Party Congresses and National People's Congresses, as well as various meetings announcing new political and economic tasks. National Day Celebrations, the Anniversary of the Founding of the Party and May Day are to be included here because celebrations are good opportunities for promoting achievements. Perhaps the most significant film in this category is *Xin Zhongguo de dansheng / The Birth of the New China* (1950). The film presents the nation's celebration of the establishment of Communist China. We see Mao Zedong in Tiananmen Square, announcing the founding of the People's Republic and the first Political Consultative Conference, attended by representatives from various parties, classes, minorities, and overseas Chinese communities. The documentary celebrates the rejoicing crowds, by day and night, in urban and rural settings, on trains, in the grassland and remote villages, east to the islands off Fujian, west to Xinjiang, north to Inner Mongolia, and south to Guangzhou. Images suggesting difficulties, concerns or even just doubts are glaringly absent. Nor does the narration suggest anything but victory, glory and success. The monological voice of the Party is also dominant in *Liu yi renmin de yizhi / The Will of Six Hundred Million People* (1954) presenting the unified and universal support for the Communist Leadership by the Chinese during the First National People's Congress.

This cinematic voice was systematically strengthened over the years through the Anti-Rightist Movement, the Great Leap Forward, and the Cultural Revolution. As such, the documentary, dogmatic voice of the Party amounts to a monstrous denial of human suffering and the death of millions in the Communist cause. Never in the history of humankind has cinematic propaganda been able to drown out dissent on such a massive scale. And when any alternative views were shown, they were presented as the voice of the 'enemy', of those intent on the destruction of the new China.

Many of Mao Zedong's activities were also significant events worthy of cinematic documentation. *Zhuhe / Congratulations* records Mao's last overseas trip and his delegation to Moscow, celebrating the fortieth birthday of the Soviet Union in 1957. Other documentaries, for example during the Cultural Revolution, present Mao inspecting the Red Guards, swimming, meeting foreigners, attending domestic political meetings, and meeting model workers, peasants and soldiers. Likewise, the nation's response to Mao's political initiatives and achievements in national construction were typically deemed worthy of celebratory documentation. These included marches in honour of Mao's announcements, the establishment of revolutionary committees, the launching of satellites, the hydrogen bomb, the introduction of nuclear power and successes in the ship building industry.

Socialist construction in industry, agriculture, defence, science and technology

Socialist construction or nation-building is another major category embraced in newsreels and documentary films. Peaks in film production can be noticed during the first five-year economic plan of 1953, the Great Leap Forward, and the economic reform after the Cultural Revolution. These documentaries are designed to broadcast the Party's forever renewed call for the economic construction of the nation. In line with the government's film subject plans, most films in this category fall into the four major areas: industry, agriculture, defence, and science and technology. Two messages are being reiterated in those films: the Party's responsible supervision of projects and the voluntary support for the Party by the people. Documentaries during the first three years of Communist rule, from 1950 to 1953, show the massive repair work to be done during and after the war. Such footage is given additional, emotional support by the filming of workers cheering on the Party and celebrating the great dream of a Communist China. In this mode, *Shengli zhi lu / The Road to Victory* (1950) presents a hardworking labour force repairing the railways for the Liberation Army during the Communists battles against the Nationalists. *Huanghai yümin / Fishermen in the Yellow Sea* (1950) documents the happy life of fishermen after the Communist Eight Route Army had come to their rescue in 1949. Before their liberation, the fishermen had suffered cruel exploitation at the hands of the Nationalists, the local landlords, and the Japanese. The film also shows the government's support for the fishermen in the reconstruction of their villages and a new and better life. Responding to Mao's 'We Must Control the Huai River', the documentary *Yiding yao ba Huaihe zhi hao / We Must Control the Huai River* (1952) records the people on both sides of the Huai River participating in fortifications of the river banks to minimise future natural disasters. Nor does the documentary miss the chance of telling the viewer that only under Communist leadership will the nation be able to fight large-scale catastrophes.

One of the documentaries dedicated to the first national five-year economic plan, *Diyi liang qiche / The First Vehicle* (1955) offers the Chinese public a glimpse of the building of the first car manufacturing plant in Changchun between 1953 and 1955. Acknowledging the assistance of the Soviet Union, the film praises the hard work of retired soldiers to be recognised as Communist heroes both in the battlefields against the Japanese and in the construction of the new China. *Gangtie zai jianshe zhong / We are Making Steel* (1955) shows one of China's largest steel factories, originally built by the Japanese in Anshan, and rebuilt after 1949 with the help of a significantly expanded contribution by the Soviet Union. The documentary shows training programmes, the absorption of an increasing number of workers, and major construction projects. In a similar vein, *Changjiang daqiao / The Yangzi River Bridge* is a eulogy of the workers, their determination and hard work, in building the first ever bridge across the Yangzi River, a feat the film's narration informs us could be achieved only in the new China.

Weida de tudi gaige / The Great Land Reform (1953) presents the Communist Party's policies on land reform. The documentary argues that land reform was the only way to assist peasants and so reduce the gap between rich and poor. Reviewing the Communist policies on land reforms, the film shows the exploitation of the peasants by unscrupulous landlords, and the unbridgeable divide between the two classes. A set of striking symbolic images of beds is used in the film, the broken bed of the peasants, the luxurious bed of the landlord, and a new bed given to the peasants after the land reform. Encouraged by Mao's praise of a report about three peasant households as 'the direction five hundred million peasants should follow', *Women de wuyi nongmin de fangxiang / The Direction of Our Five Hundred Million Peasants* (1955) uses 're-enactment' (not declared as such in the film) to demonstrate how the three peasant families working together are able to achieve higher yields and superior production. The film was shot in support of Mao's launch of the collectivisation programme leading up to the People's Commune in 1958. Another such documentary, *Wanxiang gengxin / New Society* (1955) praises the people's wholehearted support of the Party's state ownership programme and the termination of private ownership in 1954 and 1955.

As the Party requested more films on the promotion of the Great Leap Forward, 31 film studios geared up to produce news and documentaries in praise of the passionate effort of the entire nation embracing Mao's infamous steel making programme and the disastrous People's Commune. The majority of these films were later criticised for false reporting. During the period however, no such accusations could be raised. *Zai shengchan gaochao zhong / At the High Tide of Production* (1958) and *Zai zong luxian guanghui zhaoyao xia / Under the Light of the Great Policies* (1958) are cinematic hyperboles in the presentation of vast masses of people putting their shoulders to the wheel of the Great Leap Forward. *Renmin gongshe hao / The People's Commune is Good, Shenghuo de kaige / Victory of Life, Richan baiwan dun / A Hundred Tons Production a Day, Yibu kuaguo jiuchongtian / A Big Jump over Jiuchongtian* boast entirely unrealistic achievements in steel making and agriculture. *Laodong wansui / Long Live Work* and *Lingxiu he women tong laodong / Leaders Working with Us* show Mao Zedong, Liu Shaoqi, Zhou Enlai, and Deng Xiaoping join Beijing residents in the construction of the Shisanlin reservoir. All of the grand projects undertaken during the Great Leap Forward were documented on film. In *Huanghe jubian* / *Great Changes of the Yellow River* we witness the Sanmen Xia irrigation project, and in *Yuanzheng shamo* / *Overcoming the Desert* (1958) we are introduced to scientists conducting research into how to improve plantations in Inner Mongolia. What is lacking in these films are the voices of rational economic analysis, or of concern over the neglect of traditional seeding for the following year. Instead, the monological voice of the Party drones on, celebrating a planned economy that was doomed to fail.

The self-sufficiency and heroism of peasants and workers is at the heart of the documentary films of the Cultural Revolution in later 1960s and early 1970s *Hongqi qu* / *Red Flag Canal, Dazhai Ren* / *Dazhai People, Daqing Ren* / *Daqing People, Daqing hongqi* / *Daqing Red Flag, Tieren Wang Jinxi* / *The Ironman Wang Jinxi, Shengli youtian* / *Victory Oil Field* and many others. They testify to the hard work and determination of the peasants and workers following the Party's orders, their selflessness, their often brief lives in the harsh and dangerous environment, having to rely on primitive tools, hammers, axes, picks and the precarious use of explosives. The film viewer learns about the difficulties needed to be overcome in the construction of the Red Flag canal, the Dazhai terraces and oil fields in winter. Every one of these projects is shown to produce a dead or a disabled hero, Lei Feng, Ouyang Hai, Wang Jie, and many others who had to give their lives in the construction of the new China. One common feature in these documentaries is the nation's reliance on Chairman Mao's thoughts in solving difficulties and problems in the Herculean task of bringing China up to international speed. Unsurprisingly, the success of nuclear weapons development and China's rocket research loom large in documentary cinema. Films on such topics include *Mao Zedong sixiang de weida shengli* / *Great Victory of Mao Zedong Thoughts, Huanhu woguo fashe daodan hewuqi shiyan chenggong* / *Welcome the Success of Our Country's Nuclear Weapon*, and *Woguo diyike renzao diqiu weixing fashe chengong* / *Success of Our nation's First Satellite Rocket.*

In response to the government's call for economic reform in the late 1970s, the documentary *Tamen shi zeyang fu qilai de* / *How They Got Rich* (1980) shows how a brigade in Shandong, a commune in Zhejiang and a county in Guangdong were able to increase their production and significantly improve their lifestyles especially in the final years of the economic reform. *Chunfeng cong zheli chuiqi* / *Spring Starts Here* (1983) and *Laizi nongcun de baogao* / *Report from the Countryside* (1984) document economic changes, the abundance of food in the town market and the achievements of the 'household responsibility system' (*bao chan dao hu*) in the Anhui rural area. From a somewhat different angle, *Nongcun zhuanye hu fang Riben* / *Rich Peasants Visiting Japan* (1986) showcases a select group of well-to-do peasants in China who are able to visit Japan in order to study advanced agricultural methods.

In order to broadcast the government's determination to continue with its Economic Reforms in earnest, a large number of documentaries were produced throughout the 1980s and 1990s in celebration of economic advances. *Zhongguo mianxiang weilai / China Faces Its Future* (1987), *Jueding mingyun de shike / The Moment Deciding Destiny* (1988) and *Gaige kaifang de Zhongguo / China in the era of Economic Reform and Open Door Policy* (1989) all reiterate the message that the Party was on the right track in continuing its economic reforms and the new open door policy. *Xiwang de chuangkou / Window of the Hope* (1984) and *Yanhai shisi cheng / Fourteen Cities along the Coast Line* (1985) document trade and economic development in a number of the Special Economic Zones along the coast. *Shekou minzou qu / Shekou Singing* (1988) and *Lishi de xuanzhe / Historical Choice* (1992) are exclusively about Shekou and Shenzhen, China's first economic zones near Hong Kong, marking the successful transition to the market economy. Other areas of economic development are likewise targeted by documentary representations, such as *Pudong xin / Walking in the Shanghai Pudong District* (1993), *Xibu zai zhaohuan / Calling from the West* (1992), *Kaifang zhong de beifang chuangkou / North China Under the Open Door Policy* (1993), the latter focusing on the economic development of Helongjiang and *Lishi xinfei yue / New Leap in History* (1993), which is about the economy of Hainan Island.

A number of documentaries were made in order to put on screen the principles and practice of Deng Xiaoping's Four Modernisations Programme. We note an important shift here from the exclusive representation of workers, peasants and soldiers to a sudden foregrounding of technical staff and scientists. In this vein, *Yongpan keji gaofeng / Bravely Climbing the Mountain of Science* (1978) presents the 1978 Conference on the national planning of major natural science projects. *Cuiren fenfa de shiye / Inspiring Careers* (1983), *Anshan he Anshan ren / Anshan and Anshan People* (1984), *Daqing fangwen ji / Visiting Daqing* and *Kaituo zhe you huanle / Happiness of the Pioneers* (1984) address reforms on state-owned enterprises, while *Nanji Women laile / Here We Come, Antarctic* (1985) lets us witness a group of Chinese explorers at the Antarctic. *Chongxiang taikong / Flying towards the Universe* (1990) is a proud record of the success of the third satellite rocket launch. *Zhongguo hangtian cheng / The City of Chinese Astronomy* (1989) introduces the viewer to the development of astronomical technology in China, while *Keji de chun tian / Spring for Science and Technology* (1989) shows why China needs to advance science and technology, justifying the Party's new modernisation programmes and open door policy.

The topic of national unification had returned to the political agenda in 1979. As a result, a wave of documentaries about Taiwan, Hong Kong and Macau swamped the screens in the 1980s and 1990s. Films such as *Ya, Taiwan / Ah, Taiwan, Aiguo yi jia / Nation as One Family, Zai Ahzhu de gutu / On the Grandpa's Homeland, Siqing qu / Homesick, Huansong huiTai / Farewell the Nationalist Soldiers Returning to Taiwan, Haixia qingsi /*

Feelings Across the Taiwan Strait, Xianggang yibai tian / One Hundred Days in Hong Kong (1984), and *Aomen cangshang / Suffering Macau* (1986) elaborate on the theme of a 400 year history of humiliation about to come to an end.

The military and defence

The military is the oldest subject matter in Chinese Communist documentary filmmaking. In the 1950s military documentaries were almost exclusively based on the availability of relevant footage. *Hongqi manjuan xifeng / Red Flag Sweeping the Western Region* (1950) records battles of The People's Liberation Army fighting against the Nationalists in the country's north-west from Yan'an in Shaanxi, Lanzhou, Yinchuan, Xining, to Urumqi. *Da xinan kaige / Victory in the Southwest* (1950) shows the Liberation Army fighting against the Nationalists in Guiyang, Chongqing, and Chengdu and Kunming. *Siye nanxia ji / Journey to the South by the Fourth Army* is a cinematic record of the Liberation Army's approach from the northeast to Shanhai Guan, Tianjin and Beijing, then on to the provinces Guandong and Guangxi. *Dazhan Hainan dao / Battles in Hainan Island* (1950) chronicles the liberation Hainan Island, while *Jiefang Xizang da jun xing / Marching to Liberate Tibet* (1951) and *Guangming zhaoyao zuo Xizang / Bright Sun Shining Over Tibet* (1952) celebrate the liberation of Tibet and the Army's welcome by the Tibetans. A somewhat different mode of representation characterises the 1959 documentary *Pingxi Xizang panluan / Calming Down the Tibetan Riots*, which offers a carefully selected view of the suppression of the Tibetan uprising by the Chinese armed forces. While in this film oppositional views are included, they are strictly identified as the voices of the enemy of the nation. Consequently, this inclusion does not amount to a breaking of the rule of the monological voice of the Party. None of these counter voices is permitted to take on the role of an equally valid position. Quite the opposite, they are denounced as the voices of aggressors and deprived of any possible legitimacy. As such, they merely reinforce the domin-ance of the film's overall dogmatic style. This should not be surprising, since the inclusion of Tibet as an Autonomous Region within China has been one of the most highly sensitive political issues to this day. Of the many docu-mentaries made about Tibet in China since that time, all have asserted rather than questioned the legitimacy of Chinese rule.

War documentaries made during the 1950 to 1953 Korean War, such as *Chaoxian xixian jie bao / Good News from Korea* and *Kang Mei yuan Chao / Fight America, Support Korea* (1951) above all else display the bravery of the Chinese soldiers and their victories won in the Korean battles; the films promote Chinese heroism, patriotism and nationalism. *Fandui xijun zhan / Against Chemical Warfare* (1952) records the event of a Chinese delegation visiting North Korea to investigate American attempts at launching a chem-ical war. *Gangtie yunshu xian / Steel Transport* (1954) shows the competency of the Chinese transportation workers, the drivers and road workers who ensured that weapons, medicine and food arrived in North Korea on time. On the Indian front, the documentary *Zhongyin bianjie wenti zhenxiang / The Truth of the Sino-India Border Dispute* (1963) presents images of the Chinese government trying in vain to achieve a peaceful resolution. When India attacks, the film records, China had no option but to retaliate. *Xin Shahuang fan Hua baoxin / Anti-China Violence by the New Royals of Russia* (1969) and *Zhenbao dao burong qinfan / No Permission to Invade Zhenbao Island* (1969) address the Sino-Russian border dispute on the River Amur, while *Fengqi huanji / Fight Back* (1979) documents the brief war with Vietnam in 1979. All these documentaries engage with international disputes and large-scale confrontations against which individual human fate appears irrelevant. Compassion for civilians does not appear to be addressed and where there is an interest in individual human suffering it is in terms of celebrating the heroism of Chinese soldiers and others in support of the war effort.

The Military's loyalty to the Party is the theme of *Xiang Mao zhuxi huibao / Report to Chairman Mao* (1964), with parades by the Beijing and Jinan Army in front of Mao Zedong, Liu Shaoqi, Zhu De, Zhou Enlai and Deng Xiaoping. In the film Mao looks relaxed, kind and loving while he is smiling and talking to the soldiers. *Weida de zhanshi / A Great Soldier* is a cinematic document in honour of the truck driver Lei Feng who died in an accident and was praised by Mao Zedong as a model for the nation to follow. The Army's participation in national construction and reconstruction has been a well-worn documentary topic not only in order to demonstrate that their assistance is indispensable, but also that they are a key stone in the social cohesion of China. This is why the Party promoted numerous documentaries representing the army as 'renmin de zidi bing' ('sons and brothers of the people'). In this spirit, *Yingxiong zhansheng beidahuang / Heroes Win the Barren Land in the Northeast* (1965), *Jungen zhange / The Army's Victory* (1965) and *Lüse de yuanye / Green Grassland* (1965) show soldiers along with hundred thousands of youth and minorities working hard to turn barren land into abundant agricultural fields in the northwest and northeast. *Yishan tianhai / Moving Mountains to Fill the Ocean* documents the labour of soldiers building tunnels and bridges for the railway from Yintai to Xiamen in Fujiang. *Zhansheng Nujiang tianxian / Overcoming the Nu River* (1954) and *Tongxiang Lhasa de xinfu daolu / The Road Brings Happiness to Lhasa* (1954) are monuments to the heroic deeds during road and bridge construction accomplished by the Liberation Army in remote areas of the country. In documentaries such as *Yingxiong zhan zhen zai / Heroes Overcoming an Earth Quake* and *Junmin tuanjie kang zhenzai /Soldiers and People Unite to Fight Disasters* and *Huo de kaoyan / Fire In Helongjiang Forest* (1986) a series of natural disasters is recorded in which the Army is summoned to come to the rescue.

Minorities

Presenting China as a unified nation and achieving equality amongst its constituency has been a long standing aim of the Communist government. This is why cinematic documentations of the Chinese minorities also occupy a special rung in the official ladder of priorities. *Zhongyang fangwen tuan zai xibei / Delegation of The Central Government in the Northwest* (1951) was scripted and shot to broadcast Government assistance to 17 Muslim minorities in the country's northwest. *Huanle de Xinjiang / Happy Xinjiang, Renmin de Nei Menggu / People's Inner Mongolia, Kaili Miaojia / Miao in Kaili* showcase government policies on minorities, emphasise the friendship between the Han and minorities and the improvement of social structures, such as the abolition of remnants of the serf system and the replacement of primitive agriculture by modern production methods. *Zhongguo minzu da tuanjie / The Unity of Chinese Nations* (1951) is a record of Mao's meeting with representatives of minorities at the first Anniversary of the People's Republic, and a display of minorities playing their part in the nation's celebration of the National Day.

Again, Tibet occupies a special position amongst the minorities. It is the only minority that constitutes a clear majority in its traditional territory and has had a particularly complicated relationship with China over at least a thousand years since the Tang dynasty. Portraying Tibet on film is sensitive for many reasons. There is an emphasis in the West on émigré Tibetans who support the Dalai Lama, a perspective that tends to exclude the unpalatable portrayal of pre-1959 Tibet with its considerable social brutality, wholesale illiteracy, and a serfdom that involved more than 90 per cent of the population. Chinese officials complain that the Communist redistribution of land to individual Tibetans and their families, the introduction of schools and access to higher education, a functioning health system and the imposition of a massive infrastructure are hardly mentioned in the West, except as doing damage to the country's religious tradition. At the same time, the Chinese government is wary of being reminded of the excesses of Red Guards in Tibet during the Cultural Revolution and is trying its utmost to present a picture that foregrounds progress in social justice and the economic welfare of the region. It is against this background that we need to view documentaries such as *Kangba de xinsheng / New Life of Tibetans* shot by Tibetan cinematographers about social progress in Tibet, and *Baiwan nongnu zhanqi lai / Stand up, Million of Serfs*, which presents happy Tibetans who were the beneficiaries of the Chinese land reform and reconstruction projects. The abolition of the serf system is further explored in *Jinri Xizang / Today's Tibet*. Other themes addressed in these documentaries are the friendship between the Tibetan people and the Chinese Liberation Army, as celebrated in *Shangao shuichang / Mountains High, Rivers Long* or the fortieth birthday of Tibet under Communist rule, as shown in *Zai Xizang de rizi / Days in*

Tibet (1992). The film introduces seven Tibetans who shared their birthdays with the liberation day of Tibet. By describing the course of their lives, the film shows the great changes that have taken place in Tibet over the last 40 years. *Women zouguo de rizi / Days We Have Experienced* (1991) shows images of Tibet taken by four Tibetan cinematographers, focusing on economic change and the improvement of the lifestyle of the Tibetans. Even as late as 1993, we find a similarly celebratory mood in *Congfang Xizang de lianxiang / Thoughts on Re-visiting Tibet* (1993), which tells the story of a Chinese cinematographer who revisits Tibet after 30 years.

There exists, however, another body of documentary films about the minorities, as mentioned earlier. These are ethnographic films produced in the 1950s on Mao Zedong's instructions to keep records of the primitive social structures and production methods of minority cultures. For about thirty years, these ethnographic records were made only by government controlled studios and held in special archives. Since the 1980s, however, minorities science research institutions, television stations and increasingly also independent documentary filmmakers have added their voices to minorities cinema. Today, there is a flourishing industry in cultural and ethnographic filmmaking across China, the scale and complexity of which has so far escaped critical attention. I will address this body of documentary production in Chapter 6.

Foreign affairs and foreign countries

The majority of films on foreign affairs are about Chinese leaders and delegations on formal visits to foreign countries and prominent foreign visitors. The visit by American President Richard Nixon, for example, spawned a documentary entitled *Nikesong fang Hua / Nixon Visiting China* (1973). Likewise there is a documentary film covering Deng Xiaoping's visit to the United Nations (1974). International meetings held in China, such as *Shijie funü dahui / The World Women's Conference* proved an attractive topic for cinematic documentation. Yet it was not just event based film that flourished under the foreign affairs category, more abstract themes, such as the principles underlying Chinese foreign policies, proved good propaganda topics for the studios, as for instance China's increasing distance from the Soviet Union and, in turn, its attempt to become the leader of the Third World in the 1960s and 1970s. Some of these themes have their roots in a Pacific Peace Congress in 1952 held in Beijing, with 364 delegates from 37 countries of the Pacific region. The subsequent documentary, *Heping wansui / Long Live Peace* (1952), offers a message of 'peace', while focusing on anti-American images: a Korean representative denouncing the US Government as an American representative hands him a bunch of flowers. A French representatives is shown hugging his Vietnamese counterparts; British representatives are filmed as they offer flowers to Malaysians in support of their country's independence; while India and Pakistani are recorded signing a joint declaration. Other, similar documentaries followed, as for example, *Yafei huiyi /Asia and African Conference* (1955), a cinematic record of the Bandung Conference at which Premier Zhou Enlai announced China's well-known Five Principles of Peaceful Coexistence.

Denunciation of the US and Chinese international leadership aspirations go hand in hand in the documentary *Yazhou fengbao / Storms in Asia* (1965), a compilation of documentary footage about Korea, Turkey and Japan in conflict with the USA. *Shijie renmin gongdi / The Enemy of the World* is made up of edited news mainly from America, shows the US as the main instigator of invasions in the world, with images of wars in Africa, Asia, Vietnam and South America. With a Chinese script and a number of per-spectives, the film shows how Third World countries have consistently demanded independence from the imperialist West in the late 1950s and 1960s, as for instance, Laos, Vietnam, Cuba, Iraq, Iran, Cambodia, Algeria, the Middle East and African nations. An uptake of Mao Zedong's 'Theory of the Three Worlds', this film demonstrates China's claim as leader of the Third World countries. China's success story of the completion of the Tanzanian railway project in record time is well documented in *Zhongguo yiliao dui zai Tanzanian / Chinese Doctors in Tanzania* (1975). These films continue in the familiar dogmatic mode, while introducing foreign geograph-ical locations and a historical overview of anti-imperialist campaigns in pursuit of independence as seen from a Chinese perspective.

In the 1960s and 1970s, documentary films about foreign countries focused almost exclusively on the Third World, in particular on nations in Eastern Europe, Southeast Asia, Africa and South America. With the new open door policy after 1980 and China's foreign policy foregrounding 'peace and development', more films about the West were commissioned. The shift from the political ideologies of the Cold War also meant that in the 1980s documentary filmmaking was able to take into its sights such economically advanced countries as Canada, Australia, West Germany, Japan, America and Italy, as well as new topics such as sightseeing, lifestyles, consumerism, tourism, culture and the arts.

Culture and art

Documentaries about culture and art emerged in mid-1950s, especially after Mao's call for the bloom of 'One Hundred Flowers', and while the Anti-Rightist Movement and the Great Leap Forward meant a setback for docu-mentary film art, large numbers of documentaries were produced after 1972. Documentaries about culture and art are typically educational, introducing history, geography and anthropology to the viewer. In the 1970s, quite a few films were made about anthropological discoveries, including such docu-mentaries as *Wenhua dagemin qijian de chutu wenwu / Artefacts Dug out During the Cultural Revolution* on the Xi'an terracotta warriors and *Manchen hanmu / Han Tomb Discovered in Man City* (1975). After the Cultural

Revolution, documentaries reflect the new approach to the construction of Chinese identity through culture, as is the case in *Kongzi guli / Confucius' Hometown* (1983). Films like *Zijin cheng / Forbidden City* (1985–87) and *Lao Beijing de xueshuo / From Old Beijing Residencies* (1984) bring to the viewer the architecture and art hidden away in the capital. Documentaries on Chinese pictorial art covering nearly all the schools and masters in Chinese history include *Zhongguo hua / Chinese Painting* (1987), *Zhongguo gongyi meishu / Chinese Art* (1988); folk culture is the focus of *Shandong minjian muban nianhua / Woodcuts from Shandong* (1978), as it is in *Nisu xinhua / New Soil Characters* (1979), *Wukang shuhua / Painting Exhibition from Five Amertus Painters* (1987), and *Congfang huxian / Revisiting Hu County* (1992), the latter displaying peasant paintings from Hu County. Likewise, there is a large number of films about Chinese music, including music activities inside and outside China, as well as films on Chinese operas and traditional Chinese cooking. On the whole, these documentaries suffer less than others from the dominance of the dogmatic formula. In spite of plenty of national pride and the occasional intrusive voice of praising achievements of the Party as guardian of Chinese culture, the tone in these works is less stridently political, more expository and explanatory, and offset by rich image chains based on good research. Needless to say, these films also have a political function; above all else the dissemination of the themes of Chinese identity and cultural nationalism.

As far as the documentation of religion is concerned, a series of documentaries is dedicated to the representation of different religious communities and the official policies that protect them. *Zhongguo Mushilin / Chinese Muslims* (1985) informs the viewer about the country's ten Muslim minorities who occupy a special place amongst China's 56 officially recognised minorities. *Zhongguo Jidujiao / Chinese Protestants* (1987) documents the existence of four million Protestants and ten Protestant colleges in China under the government's protective policies enshrined to ensure respect for different religious beliefs. This body of films also includes Catholicism as shown in *Zhongguo Tianzhu jiao / Chinese Catholics* (1988), Chinese Buddhism and Daoism, portrayed respectively in *Zhongguo fojiao / Chinese Buddhism* (1988) and *Zhongguo Daojiao / Chinese Daoism* (1988).

From 1979 onwards cinema travelogues added considerably to China's documentary film production. In this category we can view films such as *Huangshan guanqi / Spectacular Scenes in the Yellow Mountains* (1980), *Zhongzhou daguan / Scenery of Zhongzhou in Henan* (1982), *Gudu Chang'an / Ancient City of Chang'an* (1983), *Yuanlin miaoguan / Chinese Gardens* (1982), or *Jinxiu Zhonghua / Colourful China* (1983). After 1984, when China's tourist industry experienced a massive expansion, an impressive number of documentaries swelled the list about tourist sites, remote areas of natural beauty, and the minorities. Not unlike the culture and art films, the presentational style of documentaries here shifts from an emphasis on political messages towards a foregrounding of spectacular cinematography.

As a result, the effect of the dogmatic formula tends to be toned down in favour of scopophilic pleasures.

Sport

In the 1960s and 1970s the cinematic representation of sport had been limited to domestic sports activities such as mountain climbing and table tennis. *Yuanzheng shije gao feng / Climbing the Highest Mountain in the World* (1961), *Zaici dengshang Zhumulangma feng / Once More, Climbing Mount Everest* (1975) recorded Chinese sportsmen climbing Everest. In the early 1980s, Chinese men and women won major volleyball matches in Asia, and the Chinese teams' spectacular performance in international competitions were shown in documentaries. The Chinese women's volleyball team won several world championships, and as might be expected, the players were presented as national heroines. But where in the past such heroism was as a rule documented in political terms, now the emphasis was on their sporting skills. The following documentaries broadly fall into this category: *Pinbo – Zhongguo nüpai duo guan ji / Fighting – The Chinese Women's Volleyball Team* (1982), *Dierci jiaofeng / The Second Match – The Chinese Women Volleyball Team vs. the Japanese Women's Volleyball Team* (1980), *Lidui zhihou / After leaving the Team* (1985), *Shijie nüpai mingxing sai / The World Volleyball Match of the Women's Team* (1986), *Xin de boji-ji Zhongguo nüpai si lianguan / Four Times Winners of the World Female Volleyball Competition* (1986). In another major sports documentary, *Ling de tupo / Breaking Records from Zero* (1984) we witness the Chinese win 23 gold medals at the Summer Olympics in Los Angeles from a zero record in Olympic history. *Minzu tiyu zhi hua / Minority Sports* (1986) brings the Chinese minorities into the picture, while *Xinling suixiang qu zhi yi / Singing from the Heart* (1988) records the Chinese disabled athletes attending the Disabled Olympics in South Korea. In these documentaries the dogmatic formula is much diluted, leaving the impression of a strong sense of national pride and achievement.

Film style and presentational mode

I said earlier that there was a marked difference between semi-scripted documentaries, short news documentaries and compilation films. Let me start with the last category. The fact that compilation film is made up of existing footage has a profound impact on its style and presentational mode. Apart from the raw footage, what the film looks like in the end is the result of editing and editing alone. Historically, compilation film production in China peaked twice. Once in early 1960s when China faced serious economic difficulties in the wake of the Great Leap Forward and the subsequent break down of the Sino–Soviet relationship, making film production almost unaffordable. The second time, compilation film flourished immediately after the Cultural Revolution when the Nation started to review critically what had gone wrong.

Based on the 1936 footage of the Red Army in Yan'an Shaaxi shot by American journalists Edgar Snow and Harry Dunham, a documentary was made in 1963 entitled *Zhongguo gongnong hongjun shenghuo pianduan / Pictures of the Red Army*. Likewise, *Yan'an shenghuo sanji / A Few Clips of Yan'an Life* (1963) is based on footage taken by Hong Kong youths in 1938 and by Soviet Union cinematographers in 1939. These compilation films of the early 1960s are edited with the intent to reassure the nation that the Communist spirit of self-sufficiency was able to overcome the worst difficulties and that the Party was well placed to lead China through hard times. Based on old footage taken in Yan'an, the documentary *Nanniwan / Nanni Bay* shows Yan'an soldiers planting their own food in response to Mao's call for self-sufficient production. *Liangzhong mingyun de jiuzhan / Fighting against Two Destinies* (1961) addresses China's dilemma of facing two possible destinies after the Second World War, the Nationalist or the Communist route. The film leaves no doubt that in following the Communist leadership China chose well. *Renmin zhanzheng shengli wansui / Long Live of the People's War* documents the anti-Japanese war under Communist leadership. Typical of the compilation genre is *Guanghui de licheng / Glory History* which celebrates the fortieth birthday of the Communist Party and narrates its achievements. In a very similar vein, *Xinghuo liaoyuan / A Single Spark Can Start a Prairie Fire* looks back on 34 years of the People's Liberation Army under the guidance of the Communist Party and Mao Zedong. Other compilation films are used to expose the exploitation of workers. In this subject category we find films like *Yangong xuelei chou / The Salt Workers' Hatred of Exploitation, xuelei de kongshu / Tears of Bloody Stories, zuie de dizhu zhuangyuan / The Farm of Evil Landlords, Kuangshan xuelei / Tears and Blood of Miners*, or *Laoji jieji chou / Remembering Class Hatred*. In terms of style and presentational mode, little can be said, except that here the dogmatic formula exerts its full effect, resulting in a heavily monological presentation and single-minded ideological messages. Simply put, the mode of presentation in these compilation films uniformly serves the goal of reinforcing Communist belief.

After the Cultural Revolution, compilation film again became popular. In part this is so because Chinese society felt that it needed to review the past since 1949, especially the Cultural Revolution, to see what had gone wrong, and in part because such a review was an opportunity to publicly argue the necessity of the nation's support for economic reform. After the Party had declared the end of the Cultural Revolution and class struggle in late 1970s, the government was able to begin its compensation process of both financial recompense and political rehabilitation, admitting wrongs committed during the Anti-Rightist Movement and the Cultural Revolution. A large number of compilation films were produced to respond to this change in the Party's policies. Horrendous injustices had to be acknowledged and, where possible, redressed. Some three million cadres wrongly accused during the Cultural Revolution were permitted to return home from exile or jail. About 500,000 rightists and counter-revolutionaries were returned to society as Chinese citizens. In addition, the policy of giving an individual a class status which was dependent on their family background, which had been going on since 1950, was to be cancelled. This meant that about 20 million people would be given a new status as peasants or workers, in order to extinguish their previous classification as landlords, rich peasants or counter-revolutionaries, and all because their grandparents or parents were once so labelled by the authorities. The compilation film was the ideal vehicle for such a large-scale reassessment of policy because existing footage provided all the evidence which could be shaped by competent editing. Not surprisingly, the presentational mode of these documentaries neatly complies with the new political agenda.

Many of these compilation films were about individual Communist leaders. *Jing'ai de Zhou Enlai zongli yongchui buxiu / Forever our Beloved Premier Zhou Enlai* (1979), *Zhu De weiyuan zhang huo zai women de xinli / General Zhu Lives in our Hearts Forever* (1979), *Zhou zongli he women zai yiqi / Premier Zhou Lives with Us* (1979), *Liu Shaoqi tongzhi yongchui buxiu / Comrade Liu Shaoqi Forever* (1980), *Shaoqi tongzhi renmin huainian nin / People Remembering You, Comrade Shaoqi* (1980), *Hao zai lishi shi renmin xie de / Luckily, History Is Written by People* (1988) *Xianqu ze zhi ge / Song of the Pioneers* (1981) are all in full celebratory mode, with a one-directional narration and political message to support it. These compilation films, including *Guanghui yeji / Grand Contribution* (1982), highlighting the contribution to the Revolution made by five major generals, all emphasise that the success of the Revolution was not accomplished by one person, but was a social event in the service of which many people sacrificed their lives, a not so subtle critique of the sole leadership by Mao Zedong. However, to avoid any radical public anti-Mao feelings, this critique is qualified by the documentary *Mao Zedong* (1983) in which Mao's early contribution to China is acknowledged without covering up the many mistakes made towards the end of his leadership. In the 1990s further compilation films were made acknowledging the contributions of individuals to the Revolution, including women leaders and the wives of Communist officials, Deng Yingchao, Kang Deqing, He Xiangning, as well as scientists, writers and painters. *Yangmei jian chu xiao / Raise Your Eyebrows and Draw Your Sword* (1979) documents people at the memorial of Premier Zhou in Tiananmen Square in 1976 showing their anger at the Gang of Four and Mao Zedong. Compilation films were also made in the service of rewriting history. For example, *Jindai chunqiu / Modern Chinese History* (1984–89) presents the viewer with a new Chinese history in stark contrast to that written during the Cultural Revolution. This internal revision does not mean, however, that the presentational mode has changed equally drastically. The dogmatic formula is still dominant, though the usual doctrinal tone is somewhat less strident.

Another type of documentary is the government produced newsreel. Pre-scripted, it is similar to standard documentary film, except that its brevity imposes a marked style on the way images are put together. Narration cannot expand at leisure but is strictly ruled by topic sentences and sum-mary, while image sequences are pruned to the minimum required to convey information. Weekly or monthly newsreels of this kind were often screened before feature films. Newsreels include *Xin Zhongguo jianbao* / *Brief News of New China, Jiefang jun xinwen* / *News of the Liberation Army, Budui shenghuo jianbao* / *Brief News of the Army Life, Renmin shijie* / *People's World, Guoji xinwen* / *International News, Jinri Zhongguo* / *Today's China, Xin nongcun* / *New Countryside, Shaoxian dui* / *Young Pioneers*, and *Tiyu jianbao* / *Sports News*. As in most other countries, though this occurred somewhat later in China, these newsreels were gradually replaced by the popularity of televi-sion from the early 1980s.

Apart from compilation films and newsreel films, the bulk of Chinese documentaries were scripted or semi-scripted and driven by narration. Foot-age in this mode of presentation was to be shot after the film plan had been approved. The 1952 meeting on news and documentary films had supported this production method in which scripts and proposals were well advanced before shooting to avoid an unnecessary waste of celluloid and to guarantee that official planning was respected in terms of subject matter and presentational mode. The result was a script controlled by political dogma; it was narration driven with a leaning to reportage, a minimum of location sound and non-diegetic music added in the editing process. The only vari-ation of this presentational style was a relaxation of political ideology in documentaries where a more poetic or lyrical mode was called for in order to celebrate China's landscape, culture and art.

The poetic mode in documentary filmmaking could be called the 'the great escape' for the simple reason that it was the only presentational style that could be chosen by Chinese filmmakers who wished now and then to escape the constraints of the dogmatic formula. These filmmakers foreground the aesthetic side of the Leninised conception of film, paying attention to images in their own right and by matching them with Chinese poems, that is, expressing cinematic images according to the rules of Chinese poetry. Once more we need to recall that according to traditional Chinese aesth-etics, art and teaching had to be combined in such a way as to avoid the frivolous. During the Mao period that principle was modified by adopting the Soviet emphasis on ideology and political instruction, relegating the artistic side of production to a subordinate role. So a return to a more poetic tradition could be achieved only by compromising Lenin's doctrine in two significant ways: one, undermining the dogmatic formula by the introduc-tion of traditional literary and especially poetic language into the cinematic narration; and two, by reviving the tradition of pictorial art via cinematic images themselves. A *poetic mode* of documentary filmmaking was thus created that produced a number of intriguing deviations from the political norm. The most outstanding in this group of films is *Xinghua chunyu Jiangnan / Jiangnan in Spring* (1956) which pays special attention to the cinematic beauty of the south side of the Yangzi River in a lyrical style. The film is a collection of fragmented images of Jiangnan in spring, on a rainy day, with rain dropping into little ponds causing waves, flowers floating on the river downstream, the setting sun on tidy fields, the cozy white houses of peasants, fishing boats on the Yangzi River, a small tranquil bridge, boys on buffalos playing the flute, women sewing and picking tea leaves in the field, silk worms, and red flowers on a hill. In 1957 this documentary was heavily criticised for failing to follow the dogmatic formula, that is, for failing to praise the new socialist China and its leadership.

It took some 20 years before similarly deviant documentaries appeared on screen. *Zhu / Bamboo* (1977) is a documentary in the poetic mode celebrating the bamboo. A traditional symbol of strength, nobility and unsullied life, the bamboo is presented from different perspectives and situations, some are shown to be tall and straight, others as delicate, loving and charming, or strong, rough, and mysterious. The film also works with two traditional themes, 'banzhu yizhi qian di le' ('one branch of bamboo has a thousand tears'), a love poem written by Xiang Fei, and 'guzhu fan qing cheng lin' ('dry bamboo returns to the green forest'). The film emphasises *yijing* (the mood of a work of art) stimulating the viewer's imagination by using lighting, colour and camera movement to produce images of bamboo from all sorts of angles. It has close up images to show fresh and light greens, and the dark green of the bamboo trunks and mature leaves. Bamboo leaves shot against the background of flowing water makes them look greener, fresher and even transparent. We also see the bamboo forest in the setting sun, the leaves collecting the red light to produce a red bamboo forest. It is not unlikely that this film inspired Zhang Yimou in his magnificent portrayal of the bamboo forest in the fiction film *Shi mian mai fu / House of the Flying Daggers* (2004).

In spite of the relative success of such filmmaking, the *poetic mode* turned out to be a double failure. It failed to deliver the promise of escape from the ideological straightjacket; at the same time the *poetic mode* undermined the very notion of documentary film by shifting it towards fantasy and so fictionalisation. However, the poetic mode was successful to the extent that it introduced a conflict in the conception and practice of documentary filmmaking in the late 1950s, which contributed significantly to unease in the official studios and so helped to force the government to review its documentary film policy in 1961, as discussed above. As in many other areas of the political process in China, the dogmatic univocality of documentary film already contained the seeds of its own demise, seeds that were beginning to sprout as soon as the hard grip of power on Chinese society was forced by the very consequences of Mao's policies to give way to a more open approach to the economy and all that it depended upon. Yet it was only towards the end of the Cultural Revolution that the positive effects of such filmmaking began to become effect. And even then, we cannot say that the poetic mode constitutes a full liberation from the fetters of the dogmatic formula. It was only a minor, though significant, step in that direction. A more thoroughgoing liberation of documentary cinema had to wait until the new market economy came into full swing during the last few years.

The dogmatic formula

In the light of the film policy, film industry, and film text discussed in this chapter, I am now in a position to sum up what I mean by the 'dogmatic formula' in Chinese documentary filmmaking. I want to emphasise that the formula covers more than just the film text; indeed the entire documentary cinema during the Mao era was affected, from film policy through the production process to film viewing and film criticism. The features that define documentary cinema in China between the 1950s and 1980s can be summarised as follows.

- A film policy which focused on film serving politics, developed by leaders such as Lenin, Mao, Jiang Qing and other prominent politicians;
- A film theory that combines communist ideology and traditional Chinese aesthetics;
- A tightly circumscribed and detailed subject plan;
- A budgetary and quota system for film production articulating with the national economic plan;
- Fully controlled film studios;
- Production often interrupted by changes in policy;
- Control over and continual screening of production crew and other personnel;
- Anonymity of director, cinematographer and crew;
- Selection of a range of social realities appropriate to the current political line;
- Selection of footage appropriate to political message;
- Foregrounding of slogans and supporting image chains;
- Strict control over the editing process;
- Tightly controlled narration;
- Predominance of voice-of-God narration;
- Prominence of the colour red;
- Political selection of extra-diegetic music;
- Absence of cinematographic innovation;
- Fictionalisation (staging, heroisation, unacknowledged re-enactments);
- Screening (compulsory viewing and captive audiences, screening prohibitions);
- Tightly controlled film criticism (mostly written in response to political ideology or the political movement of the time);
- Documentary filmmakers were uncredited on films during the Cultural Revolution.

What makes this list a tight dogmatic formula is its exclusivity and the inextricable interaction of its components. No film quite escapes the authoritarian grip of the formula. In terms of the subtitle of this book, the dogmatic formula marks one extreme pole on the spectrum between monological and polyphonic documentary filmmaking. In the remainder of the book I will show how the dogmatic formula is beginning to lose its grip, giving way gradually to a more inclusive documentary cinema in today's China.

The period of transition

I want to conclude this chapter with a brief sketch of the beginning of the gradual transformation of documentary cinema. The crucial period here is the time between the end of the Cultural Revolution in 1977 and 1992 when Deng Xiaoping's agenda for establishing a market economy with Chinese characteristics had finally won through. Three factors characterise this transitional period. First, changes of the government media policies allowed a certain degree of pluralism, although the dogmatic style for a while remained dominant in documentary cinema. Second, the expansion of the television industry, especially the introduction of new technologies and the birth of a new subgenre of television documentary, *zhuanti pian*, which fostered the coexistence of remnants of dogmatic style and observational as well as interactive modes of presentation. Finally, the emergence of independent filmmakers and their products in the late 1980s, albeit of only a small number, also contributed significantly to the emergence of a new style of documentary filmmaking in China.

Having said this, we need to address the question why in spite of this political shift the dogmatic mode was able to continue its influence to a certain extent during the 1980s. First, although the range of documentary subject matters increased, the perspective from which they were presented remains virtually unchanged. Whilst in the 1980s documentaries were still characterised by the dominance of official policy, their counterparts of the 1990s reversed this relation. Now documentaries offer bottom-up perspectives on society as seen by individual filmmakers. Second, the 1980s were still dominated by a dogmatic version of Grierson's expository presentational mode with dramatic music for emotional emphasis and written narration preceding a selection of images to fit. Of the 109 documentaries about the Liberation Army, 95 per cent were shot after the narration was completed; only for 4.5 per cent of these films was the narration written during shooting, and only in 0.5 per cent of cases did the shooting come first (Leng and Ma 1998: 137). Third, as to production method, in the 1980s the government was still the major force and organiser. Top television stations typically chose a topic suitable to fostering government policy, such as 'the promotion of economic reform', praise of the 'market economy', the celebration of the beauty of the landscapes of the motherland, of teachers and scientists. A film crew was then selected, including prestigious scriptwriters and composers. Given the political changes, it was only a matter of time before this type of production was bound to decline. Above all, it proved to be incompatible with the new 'self-responsible producer system' subject to public ratings that emerged by necessity in the evolving market economy.

Media reform

Two years after Mao's death, Deng Xiaoping began to lead the nation away from ideological dogma to a pragmatics of economic development and social reconstruction. In December 1978, at the third plenary of the Eleventh Central Committee, Deng Xiaoping called the Party to 'emancipate the mind', to 'seek truth from facts' and to 'make practice the sole criterion of truth'. After intensive debate raging day and night between Mao's followers and Deng's supporters, this one-month long meeting ended with an agenda for making economic reconstruction the number one national priority. Its aim was to achieve 'four modernisations' by the end of the twentieth century in the areas of industry, agriculture, defence, and science and technology.

In the area of media and film, reform began from the resurrection of advertising and business operation. In 1978 the government gave the green light to allow eight newspapers, including the *People's Daily*, to operate as businesses, though remaining under the state's administrative control. On 14 January 1979 the editorial of the *Wenhui Daily* in Shanghai spoke of the 'restoration of the good name of advertising', (Ding 1979) and 14 days later on 28 January Shanghai TV broadcast an image of a herbal wine. This advertisement not only kick-started China's advertising industry, but also signaled a shift from the media's reliance on state funding to self-funding by way of advertising. Only six years later, in 1986, Shanghai Broadcasting of Television and Radio earned more from advertising than it received from the government, 19.58 million RMB compared to 16.6 million RMB (Lu and Xia 2001: 115).

In 1980 the Tenth National Broadcasting Conference identified the promotion of economic development as the central task of broadcasting. Above all, the Conference agreed, the media sector needed to learn to 'walk on its own' (*ziji zou lu*) (Zhao 2004: 350). In terms of industrial operation, 'walking on its own' encouraged the media to be self-sufficient, reducing its reliance on government funding by exploring business ventures. In terms of content, the slogan urged the media to produce a variety of programmes across all media in the place of tedious, dogmatic repetitions. It was argued at the Conference that media decentralisation was essential to accomplish these goals. Accordingly, what had to be actively encouraged was the increased involvement of local governments, gradually replacing media dependence on national and provincial governments. To accelerate the process of building a broad based communications network, especially with respect to reception in remote rural areas, the new Ministry of Radio and Television, established in 1983, proposed a policy enabling city and country areas to establish television stations. Previously this was a privilege restricted to the national and provincial levels. In 1986, China launched its first communication satellite, significantly boosting the transmission of broadcasting programmes. By 1988, the number of television stations increased eight times from 47 in 1982 to 442 in 1988. Since then, all national and provincial television communications have been transmitted via satellite. By 2003, reception areas had likewise expanded sharply, from 57 per cent to 88.3 per cent nationwide (Zhao 2004: 346, 386).

The rapid expansion of the media communication network in China over the last 20 years was accompanied also by a change of attitude towards the media industry. This showed itself first in the recognition of the commercial value of the industry and second by the introduction of specific media laws aimed at regulating the industry. In 1986 the CCTV started to pay serious attention to the media market opinion by conducting its first television ratings research. In the same year, the first series of regulations and laws were decreed on film censorship, advertising, the import and export of films and television programmes, as well as cable and satellite television control. From the mid-1980s, terms like *shouzhong* or *guanzhong* (audience, viewers) are gradually replacing *renmin* (people) and *qunzhong* (masses).

In spite of the *jingshen wuran* (spiritual pollution) campaign since 1983 against bourgeois ideologies and lifestyles, once a sense of pluralism had taken hold it could not be easily stopped. The types of news, broadcasting hours, the number of local news outlets, and news in minority languages all increased significantly, with a simultaneous reduction of the length of news broadcasts. The result has been that we now have more of 'today's news instead of 'recent' news (*jinlai*), or news of 'not so long ago' (*bu jiu*), while the manner of reporting news has shifted away from 'reading a political textbook' (Yu 2002: 6; Zhao 2004: 353–4). News analysis, current affairs, investigative news and identifiable television personalities began to fill the screens. In terms of drama, the new pluralism also included imported soaps from Hong Kong, Japan and the USA. In the documentaries, new and different voices began to emerge. Although the nationwide broadcasting of the 'infamous' documentary series *Heshang / River Elegy* was condemned by the conservatives for 'advocating bourgeois liberalism and promoting the idea of saving China through capitalism' (*People's Daily*, 19 July 1989), its voice was certainly heard. The documentary legitimated at one stroke the call for further and faster reform and profoundly inspired the student democracy movement of 1989 that was to be squashed in the Tiananmen massacre. Compared to the pre-economic reform era, media topics on lifestyle, leisure, culture, technology, and entertainment have all been radically expanded, though of course not without creating serious tensions between Maoist conservatives and the Deng reformers.

New technologies and the use of television

China established its first television station in 1958, and yet its development in the Mao era was slow. Access to television was limited to a circle of the political elite. In 1976, the year of Mao's death, China had increased the number of its television stations to 39 covering 36 per cent of the nation. It was only in the 1980s that we witness a more rapid development of the television industry. In 1978 Beijing TV, established in 1958, was elevated to a national station by renaming it Central China TV. Furthermore, the CCTV was equipped with new technology, the Electronic News Gathering camera invented in 1968 in the West. The portable camera with location sound recording capability launched Chinese documentary cinema into a new era. However, after three decades of the domination of documentary filmmaking by ideological dogmatism, a new technology on its own could not be expected to bring about any rapid change in the way documentaries were produced. Other factors need to be considered. In August 1979, the CCTV signed China's first television co-production with Japan's NHK for a documentary project about the Silk Road. After 21 months of shooting, the CCTV crew discovered that their conventional way of making documentaries, with the completion of the narration script preceding the shooting, staging of objectivities to be documented, concealed re-enactment, and post-production sound and music, were out of date. While the previous Chinese 15-episode series portrayal of the Silk Road had hardly raised any interest amongst the audience, the 13-episode Japanese version immediately sparked a flourishing fad of Silk Road tourism. This experience alerted the Chinese documentary filmmakers and scholars to the attraction of documenting perceptual actuality and a new style of filming, as well the need for clever marketing. The role the new portable cameras played in this shift in reconceiving documentary filmmaking cannot be overestimated.

The second co-production with the Japanese in 1982, a documentary on the Yangzi River, taught the CCTV documentary filmmakers to pay attention to the characteristics of television as a medium. When Japan failed to deliver the completed version of the project according to the contract, the CCTV was forced to change its plan from broadcasting a translation version to making its own version from the raw footage. With an investment of three million US dollars, the CCTV decided to make the most of the footage by editing it into a series instead of screening it as a standalone documentary film. Instead of the old style of simply dictating media product to a captive audience, the CCTV documentary adopted an interactive process with the audience for optimal communication. For the first time the CCTV designed a weekly programme with regular presenters for the 25 episodes. It also invited the audience to submit words for the theme music of the series. Within 13 days, the station received more than 4,000 words for the lyrics. In addition, the CCTV received more than ten thousand letters from viewers commenting on the programme. The success of the series seeded the interactive mode in Chinese television documentary (He 2005: 55, 60–4).

Following the popularity of the *The Yangzi River*, China continued to produce a number of documentary series throughout the 1980s, to the extent that documentary series became the main genre of documentary film on television. A term was created to identify this popular style of filmmaking as a new subgenre of documentary: *zhuanti pian* (films on a special topic). The genre was instrumental in the process of the gradual dismantling of the dogmatic mode. On the one hand, the *zhuanti pian* continues the tradition of the Grand National theme, and the collective production efforts under the supervision of the Party.[3] On the other hand, the main differences lie in the style of presentation. Unlike films in the dogmatic style, *zhuanti pian* introduces interactive and observational modes, such as the foregrounding of interviews, with location sound and diminished staged shooting, allowing alternative voices to be heard. A typical example is *Wang Changcheng / The Great Wall* in 1991. The grand theme of the national symbol, the Great Wall, is presented with several new characteristics: location sound instead of voice of God narration; recording through the series presenters and the impressions of cameramen experiencing the Great Wall, as well as a focus on the people who reside along the Great Wall instead of historical heroes. In a similar style, both *The Yangzi River* and *The Grand Canal* include the voices of ordinary people and make use of audience feedback to enhance communication with the film viewers. Televisually-driven documentary cinema had arrived.

The emergence of independent documentary filmmaking

Wu Wenguang's *Liulang Beijing / Bumming in Beijing* (1990) is widely recognised as a pioneering success in independent documentary filmmaking in China. Made on the eve of the 1989 democracy movement, the film attracted considerable attention outside China when it was screened at the Hong Kong Film Festival in 1990. Its good reception was partly due to the sensitive historical period when the film was made, and partly to the freshness of both subject and style. *Bumming in Beijing* is a portrayal of five artists, a writer, a photographer, a playwright and two painters. They are described as *mang liu*, 'blindly mobile' or 'self-exiled'. The film has six sections dedicated to their reasons for staying in Beijing, their life in Beijing and their dreams of the world outside China. The six sections are presented largely by way of interviews. The five artists are articulate, emotional and individualist, with their 'marginal' status as freelance artists being presented as a typical social phenomenon among young people during the late 1980s: depressed, in search of an ideal life, and resistant to the socialist mould.

Quite apart from its artistic merits, the film is a record of the emergence of a new form of cinema: independent documentary filmmaking. After he left Kunming television station, Wu Wenguang came to Beijing looking for a creative space he could not find in Kunming. In Beijing he had various project contracts with the CCTV, a time during which he was given the opportunity to view non-Chinese documentaries and learned to appreciate the variety of documentary styles in the West. At the same time, he had access to camera and recording facilities that allowed him to make *Bumming in Beijing*. The key characteristic that Wu Wenguang and the five freelance artists in his documentary shared with other independent filmmakers is that they chose a 'free' life without attachment to a state run workplace. Their status of being 'allowed' to be 'free' and survive 'depressed' was a direct consequence of the economic reforms that encouraged employees to try their luck in the market before a new social welfare system was put in place.

From the late 1980s onwards, with reformed television stations, more students graduating from film courses and the availability of digital videos, the number of independent documentary filmmakers increased at a steady rate. Some of the independent filmmakers share with Wu Wenguang the experience of retaining their professional contacts with television stations and working on contracted projects, while at the same time making their own films. Some bought their own digital videos and editing suite in pursuit of their documentary dreams, as for instance Yang Tianyi who made the well-known DV piece *Laotou / Old Men* (2000). In spite of such successes, there are a few major problems for independent filmmakers not faced to the same degree by their colleagues in the West: production costs and access to distribution and exhibition. Nevertheless, the emergence of independent documentary films in the late 1980s and early 1990s marks a sharp deviation from both the dogmatic documentary mode and televisual *zhuanti pian* in the period of transition of 1977 to 1993. Present day semi-independent and independent documentary filmmaking owes a great deal to those pioneering achievements.

Part II

4 Media reform, documentary programming and the new citizen

Introduction

The year of 1993 is a significant marker for Chinese documentary. In that year television replaces film to become the dominant medium for documentary film. In the same year the government also abolished its central control in film distribution. As a consequence, all film studios had to face a new market challenge by seeking their own distribution mechanisms. The Central News Documentary Film Studio formally ended its era of four decades of domination in documentary cinema. In 1993 the Studio was transferred to the CCTV, which was now responsible for most television documentaries. Also in the same year, the CCTV adopted a producer responsibility system, permitting programme producers to recruit their own crew, outsource projects to freelance filmmakers and manage their own budget. At though still constrained in many respects, what is new is that the system provided some space for independent documentary filmmakers and the screening of their work. The year is also marked by the emergence of 'television *pingmin hua*' (shift to present the ordinary). Images of a variety of ordinary people (*laobaixing*) as individuals now appear on television. This new trend was pioneered by two popular documentary television programmes in 1993, *Dongfang shikong / Oriental Horizon* screened on CCTV and *Jilu pian bianji shi / Editorial Room for Documentary Film* on Shanghai TV. *Oriental Horizon* contracted a number of independent documentary filmmakers for its production, while *Editorial Room for Documentary Film* is regarded as 'China's first documentary programme independently run by filmmakers themselves' (He 2005: 79). On another front, the China Television Documentary Academic Association is founded for the promotion of a documentary culture through its journal *Jilu shouce* (Documentary Handbook) and the hosting of an annual documentary award festival. Internationally, the independent film *1966: Wo de hongweibing shidai / Red Guards in 1966* (1993) by Wu Wenguang won the best film award at the Yamagata International Documentary Film Festival, ahead of six other Chinese documentary films competing at the festival.

As television has become the main medium for documentaries, my focus in this chapter and the following will be on documentary television programmes. The main difference between documentary film and documentary programme is that the former is typically shot on location, while in the latter studio shooting usually plays a significant role. Indeed, some documentary programmes are entirely filmed in a studio, for example talk shows. What makes documentary television programmes a sub-genre of documentary is the documentation of objectivities in their own right, quite apart from the range of presentational processes they may favour. Given this dependence of documentary programmes on studio technology, we must also address television as an institution and managerial frame. We need to look at the rationale that informs, and the mechanisms that are involved in, the production of documentary television programmes. This is why this chapter begins with programme reform, introducing the reader to the broader background of contemporary Chinese television. The chapter will then illustrate how the institution manages to meet the demands of both market and government by a narrowed focus on documentary programmes produced by the China Education Television (CETV). The CETV is China's only education television station with covering about 85 per cent of the entire nation. With China moving towards a market economy, the station has been facing a conflict between its educational mandate, on the one hand, and on the other, its new commercial task of self-funding by way of advertising. So one of the themes in our focus on documentaries produced by the CETV will be how China is negotiating its traditional *wen yi zai dao* in the market economy.

Media policy and television reform

Since Deng Xiaoping's Southern Journey and the Fourteenth Party Congress in 1992, the collective goal of the state has been to make China one of the strongest national economies in the world, and under the leadership of the CCP. For the media, this meant the establishment of self-sufficient enterprises able to compete with Hollywood and other Western media industries in the domestic market. This became an especially urgent task when China joined the WTO in 2001. So far, progress in this context has been impressive both with regard to speed and content. Compare, for example, the statistics of 1991 when government funded a total of 130 films, (Ni 1994: 165) with 2004 when only 30 out of 212 fiction films were produced by the state (Yi and Wang 2005: 332). Clearly, in terms of film production, what we are seeing is a transformation from a state monopoly to a heterogeneity of producers, including state, private industry and trans-national companies. Changes can also be noticed in the broadcasting area. In 1978 the nation had 106 radio stations and 38 television stations covering only 53 and 40 per cent of the country, respectively (Zhao 2004: 346). In 2004 China registered 282 radio stations and 314 television stations with a coverage of 92.74 and 93.65 per cent of the country, plus 2,119 newspapers, 9,074 magazines, 570 publishers and 320 sound and video publishers, and 668,900 internet websites including .CN, .COM, .NET, .ORG (Cui 2005: 31). Furthermore, private investment has begun to enter television since 2004: a Shanghai private media company bought 15 years management rights of the Inner-Mongolian satellite TV; a Beijing private media group signed a three year contract with CETV Channel One for exclusive broadcasting rights; and in 2005 Qinghai satellite TV started to be run in cooperation with Hong Kong Xing Kong satellite, owned by the American News Group (Lu 2005: 232). Not only could the Chinese television industry boast to have the largest television audience in the world with 1.15 billion viewers, its Internet population of 94 million in 2005 is also growing rapidly, according to the CNNIC (the China Internet Network Information Centre). Last, as to the variety of media genres and media technology China does not lag far behind the developed countries.

Three major factors contributed to this rapid media development: media reform towards commercialisation, the growth of the advertising industry, and the steadily expanding participation of consumers. As a result, we witness a marked increase in programme variety and hi-tech media products. With regard to media policy, especially television, while the 1980s focused on the expansion of communication networks, the 1990s saw media policy favouring market innovations promising greater professionalism and internalisation. In the wake of a 1985 governmental document, *Guanyu jianli di san chanye tongji de baogao*, which declared cultural production the Third enterprise, the State advocated a market-oriented reform in its 1992 'Report on Speeding up the Development of the Third Enterprise' (*Guanyu jiakuai disan chanye fazhan de guiding*). In 1998 the Ministry of Radio and Film was abolished, and the Film Bureau was transferred from the Ministry of Culture to the newly established SARFT (State Administration of Radio, Film and Television). The primary purpose of this reshuffle was to strengthen the competitiveness of the domestic media industry, especially in preparation of China's anticipated entry into the WTO. In response to the government's call for a bigger, stronger (*zuo qiang, zuo da*) and more competitive media industry in its No.17 document of 2001, media institutions have gradually merged into larger conglomerates on the national as well as provincial levels. Perhaps the most competitive group amongst these is the China Radio, Film and TV Group consisting of the CCTV, China Central Radio, China International Radio, China Motion Picture Group, China Radio and TV Networks, and China Radio and TV Internet.

From 2003 onwards the government began to urge system reform (*tizhi gaige*) in the cultural sector. In December 2003, the government issued several documents demanding institutional media reforms, through such official channels as the Ministry of Publicity (previously Ministry of Propaganda), the Ministry of Culture, the State Administration of Radio, Film and Television, the Central News Publisher on the Reforming of System of Cultural Institutions, and such documents as 'Two Policies Addressing the Reform of the System of Cultural Institutions: In Support of the Transformation of Cultural Institutions into Cultural Enterprises'. In 'Encouraging the

Development of Broadcasting Enterprises' issued by the State Administration of Radio, Film and Television, we read, 'channels which show a potential for profitable business such as sports, transportation, film and television, arts, music, lifestyle, finance, science and technology, should be allowed to become independent from the centre to establish individual production companies outside the system, as long as the state's resources and equipment are not regarded as saleable commodities, and the final broadcasting rights are controlled by and remain the property of the stations,' and we should also 'explore possibilities of operating television channels on business terms.' At the National Broadcasting Conference in 2004, the Vice Minister for Publicity and Head of the State Administration of Radio, Film and Television, Xu Guangcun, suggested that the media reform should 'create a new system: face the masses, face the market, using the mouthpiece function of the media to promote business, and using its business function to support its mouthpiece function, and separate those functions which could be operated in the market economy apart from the institution to allow them to develop their own business, according to market economic principles'. The SARFT states that the government would retain ownership and broadcasting rights of radio and television stations. Apart from news production, all other productions, including fiction and non-fiction films, talk shows, entertainment and sports programmes should be outsourced to production companies outside the broadcasting system. However television broadcasting was to remain responsible for the political and social content of the programmes they screen. The separation of production from broadcasting was to turn television stations into buyers of programmes, with advertising functioning as a quality control mechanism for the market. In early 2004, the President of the CCTV, Zhao Huayong, indicated that all CCTV channels would be commercialised except for the news channel. Ratings and advertising income were to determine the continuation or discontinuation of programmes (Lu 2005: 233). According to media scholar Wu Xinbin, in 2004 the CCTV made only one third of their screened programmes themselves, provincial stations made one out of six, and city stations one out of nine of their programmes (Wu 2004: 67). Considering that the private productions screened on these stations make up only half of the total output by private enterprises, we are witnessing here a major explosion of commercial industries. It also made sense that the significant portion of production that failed to be publicly screened reappeared in the VCD and DVD market for private purchase. I will address this market in some detail in Chapter 7.

As to the external market, China started to trade with international media corporations as early as 1979, even if only on a small scale, when the open-door policy came into effect. After 1992, the exploration of the global market became a priority. China is now hosting a number of international television and film festivals, media conferences and trade fairs in Beijing, Shanghai, Sichuan and Guangdong. International exchanges are beginning to exert their influence on media structure, content and style in China. After China joined the WTO, media institutions had to change from being 'policy directed' to being 'guided by law'; from being 'limited open' to 'fully open'; from 'individual opening' to 'a mutual opening amongst the WTO members' (Shen 2003: 11). In the long run, Shen predicts, 'globalisation and China's entry to the WTO will challenge current media policies and management' (Shen 2003: 11). Anticipating this development, the CCTV focused on the following areas in its 2001 reform document: (1) the separation of production and broadcasting, and increased production by independent companies; (2) the elimination of lowly rated programmes; (3) broadening income sources beyond government funding and advertising (Shen 2003: 22). Such attempts at bringing the Chinese media up to international speed, says Shen, can be predicted to yield the following changes. China's media will soon be characterised by the separation of ownership, censorship, and management; while the industrialisation of China's media will include two core goals: allowing all capital cities to enter the media industry; and reducing government interference (Shen 2003: 14,12).

As McCormick and Liu observe on the question of control, 'censorship in China is less visible for being integrated into media management'; yet, like Shen, they do not doubt either that 'the introduction of new technologies has transformed the Chinese public sphere in ways that make a more open and reasonable debate more likely' (McCormick and Liu 2003: 155,145). The move towards media professionalism is something China has recognised as a key element in its competitiveness in the global media market. This can be seen in the increase in new media laws regulating the industry throughout the 1990s, with the splitting of media laws according to specific areas: film, cable and satellite television management, film censorship, the import of films and television programmes, non-domestic involvement in film and television programme productions, screen materials archives, co-production of transnational television soaps, domestic television series, licensing, VCD and DVD productions, broadcasting management, copyright, advertising, and national media security. Another significant change concerns human resources. In 1993 the producer responsibility system granted producers the right to contract their own crews as well as accountability for their programme budget. In 2005, for the first time in China, Sichuan TV station publicly recruited four Deputy Presidents for the station. Such high profile staff appointments used to be the prerogative of government.

Media policy is only one of the main elements in the process of kickstarting the media industry on its way to a market economy, professionalism and globalisation. Yet these top–down policies would not have been successful without the immediate response by the advertising industry in China. Over a very short time span, the advertising industry proved to be instrumental in the change of the financial relationship between media and state. For example, in 1979 Shanghai Broadcasting received advertising income in the order of 600,000 *yuan*, with government funding at the level of 4.55 million *yuan*. When the system of 'self-responsibility' commenced in Shanghai in 1985 to 1986, which put programme producers in charge of ratings and budgets, advertising income increased to 19.58 million *yuan*, leaving government funding behind at 16.63 million (Lu and Xia 2001: 115). In 2004 the total income of radio, film and television in Shanghai had risen to 82.47 billion *yuan*, of which 41.45 billion came from advertising, and 8.86 billion from state funding (Sun, Huang, Hu 2005: 60). Another example is the income of a small television station servicing a population of 2.44 million in the north of China (Wu, Bingxin 2004: 45). In 1986 the government funded the TV station to the tune of 224,000 *yuan*. Now, the government contribution only covers salaries of tenured station staff, while advertising income has risen to over three million *yuan*. In an ironic reversal of the funding process, of the three million *yuan* earned, 2.5 million are returned to the government, the station being allowed to keep 50,000 *yuan* for operations, maintenance, production, and salaries for contractual filmmakers. Similarly, the government funding covers basic salaries for forty tenured staff at the Hunan Media Group. In comparison with the 1.9 billion *yuan* of advertising income, the significantly reduced funding by government is to be regarded as no more than a 'symbol of the identity of the Group as government property' (Shi 2001: 148). In actuality, of course, the fact that government is continuing its obligation of paying the salaries of the tenured station staff means that it also retains the right of ultimate control.

The former prominence of political messages and nationalist slogans has given way to the ubiquitous screen presence of advertising. Television programmes have become characterised by product branding for improved ratings so increasing investments by advertising agents. Advertising is now the lifeline of Chinese television; currently nearly all television stations have achieved self-sufficiency through advertising. Even a cursory glance at the television screens will drive home the forceful presence of product brand names, modern interior design, hyped-up herb medicine for the aged, medicines for the improvement of the IQ of the young, an overwhelming amount of cosmetics for women, potions for the enhancement of masculinity, all of which are portraying China as an avid consumer society. In spite of the possible charge of empty consumerism, this appears to be indeed what the majority of Chinese viewers like to see and the kind of China they approve of in their imagination (Wu, Bingxin 2004: 50). For the rapid growth of the advertising industry is guaranteed by the purchase power of the consumers of media products. Without this burgeoning consumption, the advertising industry would not be able to carry the media industry. But where, we may wish to ask, does this leave the traditional Chinese emphasis on educational ethics, its *wen yi zai dao*?

The case of the CETV

Station reform

The CETV provides a good example for an examination of the mechanics of a radically modernising Chinese television organisation. Here, we are able to gain insights into the interaction between television and its market, official policies and programme reform, programme production, distribution, the transformation of an industry from political mouthpiece towards semi-independent commercial enterprise, public reception, as well as the rise of the new style of participatory television audience. The CETV is one of four broadcasting institutions at the national level along with the CCTV (the Central China TV), the CNR (Chinese National Radio), and the CRI (China Radio International). However, the CETV has two identities. As a media enterprise, the CETV is responsible to SARFT, and as educational television, it is responsible to the Ministry of Education. With a reception area covering 85 per cent of the nation, the station potentially addresses all of China's 300 million students at the tertiary, secondary and primary levels, and provides training services to more than 40 per cent of the population in the rural areas. It feeds its programmes to 71 educational television stations at provincial and city level. In doing so, it provides courses in such disciplines as accounting, computing, English, Chinese, arts, maths, agriculture, primary and secondary school teaching, and political philosophy. Currently, the CETV has four channels: Channels 2 and 4 dedicated to professional education; Channel 1 for general national broadcasting; while Channel 3 provides a variety of programmes mainly for the greater Beijing region.

The CETV is a product of the post-Cultural Revolution era. In 1978 a response to Deng Xiaoping's call for an efficient strategy to raise the nation's educational standards after the Cultural Revolution, the Central Television University was established with 28 provincial Television Universities, to alleviate a serious shortfall of qualified personnel and places in tertiary education. As the demand for Television University education had increased rapidly by the mid-1980s, the Ministry of Education decided to found a centrally controlled television station in Beijing for education news and teaching programmes via satellite in 1986: the CETV. Inevitably, new and not entirely predictable citizenship qualities were to emerge from this government initiative, which suddenly legitimised the pursuit of new skills, new technologies, wealth creation, market orientation, employability, upward mobility, electronic and computing expertise, and a certain freedom in fostering personal goals.

There can be little doubt that the CETV has had a major educational and informational impact on Chinese society since 1986. It boasts millions of graduates at various levels, with millions of qualifications in accounting, agriculture, and a range of technical disciplines. The CETV has also contributed greatly to training primary and secondary teachers, and technicians, providing the peasantry with agricultural programmes, and students with general knowledge in science, history, arts, society, literature and moral education. As Professor Yin Hong at Qinghua University observes, education has once more received the recognition it deserves and the Television University has played an important role in getting the best results from a limited national budget. 'Using television to broadcast teaching programmes, broadcasting culture, civilisation, science and technology, lifestyle and values, allows society to share limited resources. Teaching via television has played an important role in democratically distributing knowledge and information' (Yin 2002: 52). The significance of the innovations at the CETV lies in the expansion of its narrow subject offerings to a broad transmission of general knowledge. As a consequence of this shift, not only does the traditional teacher now function as a conduit of knowledge, but also experts from various technical and professional fields, as well as members of the general public, are able to offer new perspectives on a wide range of topics. The democratising effects of such televised education programmes should not be underestimated. In principle at least, a broad spectrum of Chinese television viewers now had the means of improving their personal levels of knowledge and skills and if they chose to do so, experienced the chance of acquiring for themselves a new conception of what it meant to be a Chinese citizen in China's transition from the planned economy to a market economy.

Yet at the same time, the idealised notion of a better informed, more highly trained, and more broadly educated citizen fits well into the top–down reform agenda initiated by the government. What is missing in this picture is one of the major *raisons d'etre* of television in China today: the bottom–up force of public approval. Like most television stations in China, the CETV faces serious market competition and, perhaps, more severely so than most others. After all, the CETV was regarded as a specialist television station for broadcasting educational programmes, and not mandated to broadcast commercial viable programmes, such as popular dramas and soaps, certainly before 2003. Furthermore, the current emergence of new specialist channels, especially in science and technology, does not favour the CETV. At the same time, the trend to compact large conglomerates of stations into powerful regional media groups is further challenging the leading role of the CETV. In particular, education television providers at the provincial level are now in the process of forming their own local television groups, such as Sichuan Television, or Jiangsu Television (Yuan 2002: 7–9). In addition, foreign media groups are beginning to offer educational programmes in the wake of relaxed media regulations after China's entry into the WTO. The Minister of Education, Chen Zhili, has warned that as a result it will now be 'difficult to maintain national sovereignty in education; there is increasing competition in the educational market; an increasing imbalance in education; an increase of conflict in the employment structures; and new problems are emerging for the mobility of human resources and talents' (Chen 2002: 135). By 'imbalance' Chen is referring to the gap between privileged and underprivileged access to education, while her comment concerning conflictual 'employment structures' draws attention to discrepancies especially between rural and urban employment practices.

In this atmosphere of competing demands, the CETV faces a serious 'identity' problem, doubting its role and service as educator, its function and pedagogical methods, as well as how its traditional conception of education is to fit into the new market economy. As much as some would like to believe that the CETV 'should not sacrifice its role as educator to screen those vulgar programmes for increasing ratings,' (Chen 2002b: 73–4), this however fails to address the key issue of how to make the station commercially viable. As You argues, the problem lies in a muddled conception of the CETV in the market economy: (1) teaching via television and educational television are two different concepts; (2) students and the general public are different types of audience; (3) the demand for the CETV to transform one-way education into a multiple interactive system is challenging; (4) making media educational or education media-like for public consumption are two different aims; and finally (5) the reconciliation of income via ratings and securing high ratings for education is a long term task (You 2002: 31).

In spite of such difficulties, the President of the CETV, Dr Kang Ning, strongly believes that the station needs to reform. 'We have been overstressing our function of classroom teaching,' she explains, 'an outdated pedagogic style in a changing society, where the traditional relationship between campus, teachers and students is no longer relevant. As a result of keeping this concept, the reputation of the CETV is now marginal; in particular, it has a reputation of wasting resources.' (Kang 2004). The need for reform has been widely recognised in China well beyond the CETV. She believes that policy reforms should firstly address the fundamental changes of the CETV as to its 'position, identity, attitudes, and perspectives'. In order to improve its ratings, the reform should focus on reducing the role of the CETV as the centre and pay more attention to balancing top–down regulative directives with public ratings. 'Education News', declares President Kang, 'should be in close touch with the campus, students and teachers, as well as parents: knowledge should be defined by the audience'. The attitudes of the CETV are to change from 'educating' to 'learning', from 'training talents' to 'discovering and exploring human resources and abilities', and from supervisory 'teaching' to the 'three principles of closeness': close to life (less idealisation), close to reality (less ideology), and close to the people (more audience input). This has direct implications for the production of a new kind of citizen, one who is able to exert an influence on the media by voicing approval or disapproval on a broad range of issues, except basic Party doctrine. As a consequence of this change in pedagogical goals, a new type of citizen is likely to emerge whose personal involvement, problems, failures and difficulties, begin to be recognised publicly as legitimate concerns and matters of public debate.

In her reform proposal to the Ministry of Education, and the Ministry of Publicity in February 2004, President Kang encompassed a series of fundamental principles. (1) To create the biggest forum for 'learning via television in the world'. She thinks that the main attraction of 'the CETV lies in all areas of study and training for employability'. She views this as a pedagogic plan on a broad scale: 'our concept of what a student is has become all-embracing; it should include the whole of society, as long as there is a need for study'. This requires a shift of attitude from a narrow conception of education limited to school education towards a broadly conceptualised educational model relevant to society and embracing lifelong learning. (2) The bridging of school and lifelong education, of formal and informal education means that the CETV must include rural education, without losing sight of the cities, using the multiple products of television, media-print, radio broadcasting, VCD, DVD, and newspaper, free public television, pay channels, as well as channels that are co-operating with other stations. The CETV is to assist in making learning fashionable. (3) A gradual reform of the CETV infrastructure by separating news and propaganda tasks (the 'mouthpiece' function) of the CETV from the other programmes, which are to be relocated to the newly established 'China Education Media Group' operating under the principles of the market economy. (4) In accordance with this change, all employees are to be placed on a contract system within two years. At the same time, the CETV commits itself to the following goals: (a) developing a system likely to attract human talent; (b) installing digital channels and producing appropriate, reputable programmes; (c) exploring the market, since income does not only come from advertising, but also from pay television and long distance education; and (d) establishing a China Education Media Centre in co-operation with the Beijing Media University.

What is significant here is the sheer size of the envisaged audience, with the implication of citizenship training on a vast geographic scale, as well as a continuing process. Moreover, such training is to be expanded from the rural areas to include city audiences and to make learning a 'fashion' trend. A clearer separation of official pronouncements from infotainment and learning is envisaged and far-reaching goals, such as continuing technological innovation and cross media co-operation are embraced. If these proposals are indeed realised in practice, we can predict that they will not only enable the CETV to thrive in the new Chinese market, but will also have noticeable effects on the formation of its vast audience. So it is not surprising that in light of this two-pronged reform package, one prong addressing the demands of the CETV audiences, the other securing government input and protection, the President of the CETV expressed her confidence in the continuing success of the station, in spite of her worry about an increasingly competitive television market. Her reasons for this optimism are as complex as is the situation of the CETV itself, positioned as it is half in the market and half in the direct sphere of government interest. Since the Ministry of Education continued to regard educational news as a priority, the CETV will remain a high priority. After all, the government itself is promoting the idea of reform in the media and the idea of *wenhua chanye* (cultural enterprise). So the CETV will be secure 'as long as the government retains the ultimate control'. Moreover, the government explicitly supports the role of the CETV in the creation of a 'learning' society by providing 10 million educators catering for 300 million students. In addition, China's entry into the WTO in 2001 has accelerated the already serious crisis of unemployment, and the government expects the CETV to play a significant role in re-skilling the labour force nationwide. There is the project of a comprehensive long distance education under the auspices of the CETV for the rural sector, primary and secondary education and the training of more than 20 million cadres, as well as teaching the displaced peasantry that is streaming into the urban environment. On the technical side, it is likely that the CETV will be able to introduce digital media in education in addition to the creation of advanced internet networking and broadband programmeming for primary and secondary education. Last, and certainly not least, it is a considerable advantage for the CETV to remain located in Beijing, that is, close to the centre of policy making.

CETV post-reform programming

In the wake of the 2003 government pronouncements on education, the programmes of the CETV now include such formats and topics as classroom teaching, seminars, games, narrative educational programmes (learning through storytelling), computing, reporting, panel discussions, mathematics, English, philosophy, Chinese language and literature, nursing, mechanics, engineering, electrical and electronic training, health consultation, insurance, and teacher training among others. In short, the range of educational programmes offered by the CETV covers almost the entire spectrum in the Chinese education system. Of the four channels of the CETV, channels 2 and 4 teach courses offered by the Central Broadcasting and Television University and the Central Agricultural Broadcasting Television School, as well as educational news, training programmes, programmes on cultural morality, the arts and technology. They are discipline and subject oriented, teaching people how to gain specific qualifications. In contrast, channels 1 and 3 are general educational channels, focusing on all sorts of educational programmes, but more generally, airing such topics as daily lifeskills, consulting, information about and interpretations of contemporary society and lifestyle, and a range of documentary programmes.

In late 2003 the CETV conducted policies and programming reforms aimed at improving its ratings in an increasingly competitive Chinese media market. In the process, education in the CETV appears to be gradually moving from an authoritarian style of political indoctrination to the provision of technical training on a broad scale and an acknowledgment of the principles of consumption. An essential part of this transformation is a significant awareness of audience, and hence, an increase of audience participation in media programmes. In the hunt for an increase in its ratings, the CETV has invited private media companies to be part of its scene since 2004. In February that year the CETV signed a contract with a Beijing commercial media company for its Channel 1 to be run by the company including production, programming, marketing, and advertising. All the CETV reserved were its rights in general policy decision making and broadcasting (Lu 2005: 232).

From this rough picture of objectives one can see that Channel 1, and to a lesser extent Channel 3, are especially well suited to respond to public demand and changing audience expectations. The 2004 reforms mainly concern Channel 1, with a new emphasis on 'global perspectives', the development of 'human resources', and the provision of a 'forum for study and debate' (Kang 2003a). In this scenario, the CETV functions as a mediating forum in which Party policy and media audience enter into a dynamic relationship of negotiation. As a result, CETV programmeming is responding at the same time to the pressure of top–down guidelines and to the market forces of a rapidly changing horizon of expectations amongst a new citizenry in the making. Such demands cannot be reconciled evenly across all programmeming, and so it should not come as a surprise that the programmes of CETV Channel 1 can be shown to fall into two types: government directives and general as well as specialised information. In terms of presentation styles, participatory strategies play a major role in half of these programmes.

Government directives are concentrated in *Guoshi xinwen Educational News*, *Xibu jiaoyu West Education* and *Live Broadcasting* which is a news conference held by the Ministry of Education. These programmes continue the tradition of official information distribution, with an emphasis on political education, reassuring the population of responsible leadership with regard to educational standards and the achievements of Chinese education in comparison with developments abroad. Here applies what C. C. Lee has characterised as 'nationalistic packaging' which without doubt 'contributes to market success' (Lee 2003: 25). *West Education* (types 1 and 3) is a programme responding to a government directive to 'explore the West' in talk show format, involving the audience to comment on proposals for education about the West. In this programme, official policy and audience participation enter into a novel relationship, reflecting as it does the dual pressure of government guidance and media market forces. Viewed as a coherent set of offerings, these programmes generate a sense of security, stability, and an image of a government in control and dedicated to looking after the interests of its well protected citizenry.

The majority of the CETV programmes can be described as constituting a broad based service, providing information on international and national current affairs. Focusing on current affairs in culture and the economy, *Guancha Observation* and *Guoshi zhishi Reporting* offer analytical commentaries by panel discussion and debate following a short documentary in reporting style. *Fuxiang cai zhu xue bang / Scholarship* informs viewers about the availability of government assistance to students in financial need. *Qingchun jia nian hua / Youth Party, Yangguang huoba / Sunshine and Shaji banhui / Super Classroom*, which target youth audiences, report on campus activities, various sports, IQ games, and music bands. *Trendy Vehicles* and *Kuche didai / Car Knowledge* provide viewers with the latest information on cars and lifestyles. Programmes like *Anquan didai / Safety, Jiaotong zongheng / Traffic*, and *Zheng juan da xuetang Stock Market* convey insights into contemporary living conditions in China's mega-cities. *Baoxian zhongguo / Insurance in China* discusses such issues as the statistics of 300 million teachers and students needing to be concerned about insurance. In doing so, the programme provides the much needed service of advising viewers how to deal sensibly with insurance. *Zhongguo zhichang / Consumer Survey* pays attention to consumer rights and advice on how to avoid mindless consumption. *Zhongguo zhichang / Chinese Human Resource* is dedicated to practical news on employment for college graduates and job hunting, taking into account the economic situation in China and the human resource needs of enterprises. The programme makes forecasts on the human resources market in various professions, providing the latest analyses of national human resources, as well as information about professional training and certificates. *Guoshi dao hang / Direction on Tertiary Education* specialises on information about tertiary institutions, news on courses provision and various disciplines. *Baishou qijia / From the Bottom* tells stories about successful business enterprises and the secrets of their success. *Fanyue rili / Looking at Calendars* and *Wenming Zhonghua xing / Journey of Chinese Civilization* looks at China's past and introduces the audience to historical heritage sites. Lastly, the programme *Guoshi jiangtang / Academic Seminar* invites scholars and other experts to talk about strategies for strengthening the nation in fields varying from the humanities to science, engineering, and education.

Turning to the presentational modes prevalent in the CETV programmes, various participatory styles have emerged and are strengthening. Explicitly participatory programmes make full use of debate, journalistic investigation, independent expert advice and audience feedback, both in the studio and via remote response. *Observation, Reporting, Information, Consumer Survey, Chinese Human Resources*, for example, are programmes that typically focus on a documentary report followed by debate and panel discussion. In these programmes, there emerges the goal of training a new kind of citizen, one that is reassured that the government is maintaining responsible control of the nation's education system, one that recognises that self-advancement is a legitimate goal and that self-discipline and self-reliance are good qualities to achieve success in the new market economy, as well as one who is encouraged to actively participate in national debate on a broad range of topics, including criticism of government corruption and incompetency. Given the specific structure of these programmes, it is misleading to write the contemporary Chinese media off as mere mouthpieces of government dogma. While this was an appropriate characterisation of the media in the Mao period, Chinese television today is undergoing a gradual but nevertheless fundamental change towards accommodating the demands of modern media audiences and the media market. Certainly, in at least some areas of the CETV the claim that the media are no more than 'conduits, interpreters and enforcers of legal and policy pronouncements' is misleading (Lee 2000: 23). For the kind of description that emerges from the details of CETV programmeming applies in principle to many other media enterprises in China today. And if this is so, the kind of new citizen that is likely to evolve as a result of the style of information offered in CETV programmes may be assumed to become a generalised actor in a modestly defined Chinese 'public media sphere'.

How precisely do CETV programmes encourage the formation of citizens inclined to see themselves as participants in public debate rather than recipients of official doctrine? The following documentary programmes are introduced to demonstrate in more detail the kind of media discourse conducive to this new form of citizen education. In the remainder of the chapter, I will select a few examples to illustrate the kind of educational programmemes offered by the CETV. What I want to emphasise here is my claim that authoritarian education via television is gradually being replaced by a multi-perspective approach and the beginnings of training in critical thinking.

Programme analysis

EPD zai xingdong EPD in Action (Environment, Population and Development in Action) is a programme encouraging primary and secondary students to become aware of the problems of the environment, population, and technological development. Each episode addresses one particular topic, such as 'Can we still get water from the well in the future?' alerting the children to the preciousness of a resource which we tend to take for granted, or 'The world heritage site – Zhoukoudian', which introduces the students to questions of anthropology and archaeology, or 'Looking for the dangers in the environment', raising awareness of both natural diasters and those caused by humans. The format typical of this documentary show is first to invite six children, who are then given a topic to research on site. Their actions are recorded and later, in the studio, the host asks them about their findings, their experiences, what they have learned, and discovered, while at the same time the film is being screened, recording their on-site research. The programme typically ends with the TV host guiding a debate amongst the students and the studio audience, who are usually of the same age group and from the same school.

In the show 'Can we still get water from the well in the future?', for example, the children are taken to a village near Beijing, where they experience the hardship of carrying water for miles, tasting dirty water, learning to dig a well, collecting data from the field, and other chores. In the studio, they are all eager to tell their stories, their feelings, the fun they had, and details about the site, their friends, and what they have discovered. They use body language, imitating the action of carrying water and walking in the hills. Their conversations are guided by the TV host, while the entire process of knowledge acquisition and discovery is a lively interaction between host, guests and studio audience. The participatory strategy here makes for engaging entertainment, especially because of the imaginative naivety of the children, their mimicry, facial expressiveness, comments and questions adding a comic element to the programme's didactic intent.

In the second topic, 'The world heritage site – Zhoukoudian', secondary school children visit the site where the famous Beijing Man or Beijing *ren* (200,000 to 700,000 years old, according to the programme!) was found. The audience is introduced to the familiar story of 1929 when a Chinese archaeologist discovered human remains. In the studio, the children participate in a discussion on the origin of the human species. They are asked how they imagined Beijing Man lived thousands of years ago. Opinions are freely expressed, and although they have all been trained to be polite and wait while others are talking, the viewers witness the children interrupting others, eager to express themselves, passionate about the subject. When being asked about their thoughts on the discovery that humans are originally from Africa, some students express their doubts. They argue that it is impossible for humans to have travelled on foot halfway around the globe to China; some are happy with having the evidence of Beijing Man in Zhoukoudian, while others say they don't particularly care, arguing that it might indeed be possible for those people to have moved from Africa to China while hunting and playing. The debates and discussions are humorous, intelligent, and relaxed, not so much competitive as focused on discovery and knowledge. At the end of the show, an academic is invited to answer the children's questions. Again, the children's participation is crucial, distancing this format from earlier, more authoritarian modes of presentation.

Perhaps one could say that *EPD in Action* not only demonstrates the attractiveness of a television-led evolution of 'learning by participation', but also introduces Chinese society to the public negotiation of different views and perspectives. The third topic 'Looking for dangers in our environment' encourages a group of 13-year-old children to search for potential dangers in an ordinary street. They discover that people washing their cars in the street face potential dangers, especially if they are in a rush or in case the water on the street turns to ice, on which old people could slip. The children discover a bridge without fences, a well without a lid, a broken street lamp, a burning cigarette, and a fly on the electric pole. The students then meet to discuss and define the term 'danger', and debate how we should prevent, or act upon danger, or which cause more damage to our life: natural disasters or human accidents. Later in the studio, a father talks about how he would sacrifice his life to help his children out of a dangerous environment. His talk touches his daughter to shed tears in the studio. Apart from the occasional show of such emotions, the programme typically emphasises rational debate. Using a participatory format, the episode highlights the children's eagerness to explore their practical world and learn useful lifeskills and in so doing succeeds both as a teaching mode and as entertainment.

Jintian wo zai jia / Today I am at Home was initiated during the SARS period when many children were not able to leave their homes. The episodes of the programme use interactive methods, inviting children to email a television host about their views, their studies, and their concerns. Here the host takes on the role of a virtual babysitter whom the students can call and talk to. The programme employs a variety of games. For instance, in the 'yes or no' game the children call two hosts live to ask them questions about general common knowledge. Each of the two hosts links with one child over the phone, creating a competition between two teams. Another version presents the hosts taking children outside to play. The whole process is recorded without editing, employing long take filming. In yet another format the producer invites children to organise a reporting club, or a television host competition. Children are invited to submit their applications to the station, the only rule being an age limit. After only a few hours of training, each little reporter, on different campuses, uses a camera to report whatever they think is worth reporting. The children also establish a reading club. They present their views, reviews, comments on books and their bookshelves. There is also a talent show, with an open invitation to all children to participate, as long as the talents displayed are not harmful to health and their talents have not otherwise already been formally recognised. In agreement with the aim of the programme, the show's emphasis is not only on 'participation' but also on inviting 'as many children as possible to become themselves the host of the programme.'

In *Today I am at Home* audience participation is maximised. Without it the programme would not exist. Both education and entertainment mingle to produce an effective television performance. Its interactive character depends on the dynamic relationship and negotiatory practice amongst the hosts, the CETV studio personnel, and the children, outside the formal channels of school, teachers or parents. The children learn from their own actions, discoveries, research, and above all, debate. In addition, what is being learnt is knowledge relevant to society, rarely formally taught at school. This is particularly useful in a society in transit to an increasingly competitive market economy in which skills of analysis, negotiation, the assertion of needs and wants, self-reliance and initiative are in high demand. The optimisation of participatory activities aimed for by the CETV producers certainly announces an entirely new style of social interaction, one which encourages the emergence of a new kind of citizen and one which could be viewed as a necessary prerequisite of an evolving public media sphere.

In documentary films, we can likewise observe a turn from authoritative, if not authoritarian, styles of presentation towards a more multi-voiced kind of cinema. We can illustrate this trend by comparing two documentary films made by the CETV, *Xiao yuan bao wei zhan / Fight Against SARS on Campus* (2003) and the series *My Sun* (2005 and 2006). The former very much presents a monological view of the government broadcasting its achievement in dealing with the SARS epidemic. The documentary is presented in expository style with dominant narration, assisted by music for emotional effect. The film uses techniques of zoom shots, close-up and fast editing to create a sense of dramatic effects, with hospitals, patients, ambulances, and security soldiers. The film begins with a series of snap shots of Beijing to illustrate its intertitles informing us that its economic growth rate is 9.9 per cent, the fastest growing economy since 1997, but suddenly interrupted by the SARS epidemic. The rest of the film shows how the Chinese leadership, President Hu Jingtao, Premier Wen Jiabao, President of the National Congress Jia Qinglin, Minister of Education Zhou Ji and Chen Zhili, and a number of Deputy Premiers visited universities, showing their care for and solidarity with the people of Beijing. Against the background narration of concerned parent letters commending the leaders, the images show officials shaking hands with the masses, visiting a university dormitory, eating and singing with students, and talking over the phone to students unable to attend school. A number of interviews combine to convey one and the same message: how universities have achieved to protect students on campus. The documentary also shows students coping with the National Tertiary Entrance Examination, and how all primary and high school students were able to access education via television when the schools were closed for two weeks. Apart from the splendid handling of the SARS epidemic by government, the death of a number of dedicated doctors and nurses in the process, and the survival of the students, the documentary shows us nothing about the government's embarrassing bungle of denying the epidemic to the World Health Organisation. There is no mention of errors made, of conflicts or complaints; there is no debate and no lessons to be learnt from mistakes. We miss at least a modest dose of self-criticism and the question whether SARS would have caused the damage it did to Beijing from April to July, had China had not concealed the information that the epidemic started in Guangzhou in late 2002. Nor is there any mention of the crucial role of the World Health Organisation in fighting the disease worldwide.

In contrast, the documentary series *Wode taiyang / My Sun*, produced in 2005 and 2006 also by the CETV displays a more sophisticated presentational process. Part of a group of documentaries in grand style with a focus on contemporary society, the series consists of four episodes screened during the May Labour Celebrations and the October National Celebrations in 2005 and 2006. The first series, screened in May of 2005, presents a day in the lives of 64 individuals across 52 different occupations. The second series was screened in October 2005, turning from the representation of individuals to groups, their lives, feelings, and social relations. The groups include an airport security team, a Party unit at Dazhai Village, a university research team, social workers in a residential district, a blind football team, and female anti-drug personnel. The 2006 series has as its theme 'creation' in response to the government's call for the education of a self-reliant, creative society. Traditional occupations are gradually disappearing in the market economy, but new skills and new kinds of professionals are still in short supply. First broadcast in May 2006, the film introduces 70 individuals working in the new professions. We see how enterprising and diligent people from all walks of life invent market niches for their special skills. The latest series in the programme will be screened in October 2006. It is about 70 managers in small and medium-sized businesses, including graduates, foreigners working in China, peasants, laid-off workers, and retired soldiers. The four episodes are the collective result of co-operation amongst film directors from the CETV, the Television Documentary Academic Association, and China Media University. *My Sun* is advanced in its use of a new 'fast management style' in the sense that it pursues participatory strategies by collecting ideas from the public via the internet as part of the pre-production process, by employing a large number of film directors, including freelance filmmakers, and large crews working together at high speed, with their filmed subjects selected from anywhere in China. In terms of content, the series provides a broad spectrum of snapshots of individuals and professionals actively engaged and contributing to the thriving market economy. In this way *My Sun* provides documentary evidence of the human resources and creativity behind the anonymity of China's burgeoning market.

My Sun attempts to portray a broad and up-to-date picture of ordinary people in contemporary Chinese society by pointing its cameras at middle and lower middle social groups, individuals as well as collectives. The film's documentary, presentational mode combines an expository mode with observational style and an emphasis on interviews. Its participatory character is achieved by involving a large number of people, whose competing voices make up a significant portion of the documentary. In addition, interactive strategies are harnessing audience responses for promotion of the film and as an integrated cinematic technique. Each filmed subject is given a time limit of ten minutes, with the result of each occupation being restricted to its postmodern surface. As the title *My Sun* indicates, the documentary deliberately depicts energetic people with a positive attitude and consistency in seeking success. In this respect, the series reveals its government driven, didactic agenda under the commercial pressure of ratings. As a consequence, we witness the emergence of a specific documentary mode, one that fulfils the pedagogic task of demonstrating to a mass audience how self-employment and success in the market can be accomplished by being creative, hardworking, optimistic and positive. At the same time, the presentational style of the series acknowledges the demands of the media market by a significant reduction in top–down narration, the foregrounding of observational camerawork and interviews, and the active role of an increasingly participatory audience. The resulting mix of pedagogy and entertainment has become the hallmark of CETV productions.

What we should also note here is that the state is actively promoting a new citizen: technically qualified and self-oriented, though of course not critically democratic so far. Yet as the media, especially media such as the CETV, are forced to survive in an increasingly publicly challenged market, they cannot but also produce a kind of citizen who is not only a commercial survivor but also one who will gradually make more broadly critical demands. This seems likely to be the case also for another reason, which as early as 1991 James Lull termed the 'electronic amplification of contradiction' conducive to the generation of 'alternative, competing visions of China's collective future and the personal dreams of millions of Chinese citizens' (Lull 1991: 209). In this context it is instructive to note that in spite of the CETV's inevitable closeness to the government, it has not only introduced a certain degree of liberation in the presentational style of its own pro- grammes, but has also acted as a conduit for the nationwide screening of documentaries by independent filmmakers. Instrumental in this respect is the initiative at the CETV of a special programme dedicated to amateur DV documentaries.

In spite of such innovations, the CETV forum cannot yet be called a public media sphere in the sense in which it applies to advanced democratic states, for what is lacking still is the legitimate expression of oppositional opinion of a genuinely political kind. And yet, while at the level of content there is still a fundamental top–down constraint, at the level of training polyphonic, dialogic behaviour, citizenship education appears highly suc- cessful. What kind of contribution, then, is the CETV making towards the production of a new kind of Chinese citizen able to operate effectively in such an environment? It would be insufficient to approach the question from the narrow angle of programme content and programming style. To arrive at a reasonably realistic answer we need to consider a number of pathways enabling us to address the way the CETV mediates government directives, programme reform and programme policy, commercial pressures, programme content and mode of presentation, public feedback and audi- ence participation. In turn, each of these entails a different way of con- structing television audiences and citizens, from Foucauldian 'docile bodies' and bodies as 'effects' of power to critical participants in public debate (Foucault 1988: 78; 1980: 98). As to content, what is being emphasised now is a modern, internationally-oriented lifestyle (fashion, new technologies, consumption, modest wealth) and the know-how likely to make such a style affordable (marketable skills, ways of increasing employability, fostering talent in a broad range of fields, acquisition of information and knowledge). As far as the programmes' presentational style is concerned, the stress is on encouraging debating competence, the expression and negotiation of differ- ing views, the interaction between individuals and groups, the recognition of different perspectives and their significance, as well as criticism of public institutions, of local and provincial officialdom, within the boundaries of shared but tacit constraints. Given this reshaping of the conception of the Chinese citizen on the mass scale of CETV audiences, we may well ask whether we can speak of the birth of a genuine 'public media sphere' beyond the bourgeois sense in which Jürgen Habermas introduced the term in his paper of 1964 and elaborated in *The Structural Transformation of the Public Sphere* (Habermas 1974; 1989).

To be sure, the presence of large numbers of citizens in media events does not in itself constitute an advance in democratisation. The organised assembly of large members of the public can equally well serve authoritarian purposes. Nor does the occasional expression of views contrary to official policy constitute a tendency towards democratisation. For genuine media democratisation, what is required is the evolution of public opinion out of private opinion by way of rational debate open to the general public and free from domination. This is the route Habermas' argument on the bourgeois public sphere takes from its beginnings in Kant (Thompson 1995: 260). With reference to the specifics of CETV programming, we can speak of an advance in democratisation by increased media participation where at least some of the following conditions are fulfilled:

- when the participants take part as a matter of their own choice;
- when the media event organisers encourage the participants to express their own views rather than any preconceived position or message;
- when the organisers stimulate the exchange of opposing opinions amongst participants,
- when the media event is designed to foster the negotiation of heterogenous positions held by the participants; and/or
- when the organisers themselves offer views that modify or qualify official policy;
- when the media event is designed to tolerate the expression of views critical of government.

If media participation is defined in this way and if democratisation is characterised by the increasing pressure of publicly expressed views held by people with ideologically heterogeneous positions, then the kind of citizenship education conducted by the CETV suggests the gradual emergence of a style of social interaction congenial to the formation of a genuine public media sphere. The jury is certainly still out on such claims. According to C. C. Lee, 'the very concept of a "public sphere" may be dubious in China' (Lee 2000: 23), and for Lowell Dittmer the media remain 'coopted by the state and heavily regulated' (Dittmer 1994: 92). On the other hand, for writers such as McCormick and Liu 'it is at least possible that globalisation offers audiences enough new resources as to significantly tip the balance toward a more open and reasonable public sphere' (McCormick and Liu 2003: 156). And while it is too early to speak of 'consumer sovereignty' in the domain of the media, (Donald and Kean 2002: 9) there is ample evidence that the 'Chinese media are increasingly dependent on revenues generated from advertising' as well as on public ratings (McCormick and Liu 2003: 150). As a result, the public voice can be predicted to play an increasingly powerful role in the way the media will be able to negotiate their position between government directives and the demands of the market. I suggest that the CETV is a persuasive case in point.

As we have seen, since late 2003 the CETV introduced policies and programming reforms aimed at improving its ratings in an increasingly competitive Chinese media market. To achieve this goal, the station's education mandate had to be gradually transformed from an authoritarian style of political indoctrination to the provision of technical training on a broad scale and an acknowledgment of the principles of consumption. An essential part of this transformation proved to be a significant increase in audience participation in the CETV programmes. Although China's media in general, and the CETV in particular, are still far from being inclined to integrate the public in a comprehensive political sense, the kind of education now conducted by the CETV suggests at the very least the likelihood of a new viewing and debating consciousness on a mass scale. What is required then, I suggest, is a conceptual narrowing of the much used phrase introduced by Jürgen Habermas in the 1960s to restrict its semantic scope to a 'public media sphere', since in China a general public sphere is not a realistic option (Habermas 1974;1989). If there is any chance for the emergence of a public forum of debate at all, it seems to me to have to grow out of the increasingly participatory programming that we witness in television stations across China today. In the broad sense of the term, then, Chin-Chuan Lee's observation is probably right that 'the very concept of a "public sphere" may be dubious in China, where the primarily top–down media are conduits, interpreters, and enforcers of legal and policy pronouncements' (Lee 2000: 23). Likewise, John B. Thompson had earlier critiqued attempts at generalising Habermas's notion of the 'bourgeois public sphere' to apply to other social constellations (Thompson 1995: 73). So the modification of 'public media sphere' may be a more promising avenue to discuss the expression of public opinion on a mass scale in China today. Surely, when millions of viewers are able to have an input into television programming nationwide, a new participatory consciousness is emerging even if the topics debated so far exclude politically sensitive issues. Perhaps, we could say that what we are witnessing in present day China is a *televisual rehearsal of democracy by means other than the obviously political*. With the proviso I have suggested, one should be able to accept McCormick and Liu's defence of a loose application of the Habermasian term in an analysis of contemporary China, because of the politically communicative emphasis which we now associate with the 'public sphere' (McCormick and Liu 2003: 139). This choice finds support also in Nick Stevenson's argument that Habermas's notion 'remains germane' for media analysis not because 'it provides a model that could be realised or copied' but because 'it perhaps delivers the principles within which public cultures might best operate' (Stevenson 2003: 48). In this generous sense, then, the notion of a public media sphere seems to me useful for a description of television programme providers and participatory consumers in today's China.

Taking a broader perspective, why should what can be observed at the level of televisual media not also apply to the market driven social transformation of China as a whole? While Mark Seldon saw 'a democratizing political process' as a precondition for 'successful economic reform', the research presented in this chapter suggests that the relation is probably the converse. Today, few would doubt China's staggering economic success, while indeed 'many of the social and political controls remain intact' (Seldon 1993: 229). Yet in spite of many such constraints, this chapter has documented a quite radical transformation of media audiences from passive recipients to active participants. What Seldon failed to see is the 'critical issue' of the 'changing configuration of institutions', the less 'centralised, less politicised, and more commercially oriented institutional frameworks', as well as the transformation of the 'public sphere' as a consequence of 'the introduction of new technologies' which 'makes a more open and reasonable debate more likely' (McCormick and Liu 2003: 145). At the same time, the participatory style observed in the programmes of the CETV and now characteristic of most media offerings in China, is unlikely to be reversible. On the contrary, the chapter concludes, what is much more likely to evolve is a televisually trained citizen who will strive to extend the privileges of participation to a more fully political representation.

5   Documenting the law

Introduction

This chapter explores the themes of this book by considering how television documentaries, particularly on the law, are being used as a vehicle of citizenship education in China, and how they are often made more effective by using audience participation. If we accept the idea that 'education for citizenship is not an optional extra, but an integral part of the concept' of citizenship (Heater 1990: 319) then citizenship pedagogy via the electronic media is of paramount importance to our understanding of citizenship in China today.

While citizen training appeared broadly conceived in the programmes provided by the CETV, we find highly specialised forms of public education in programmes screened on other television stations. At the centre of the current citizenship pedagogy is the most popular of the television law programmes, a documentary produced by the CCTV: *Legal Report* (*Jinri shuofa*). The documentary series has proved to be one of the most effective government driven instruments in shifting public awareness from traditional thinking in terms of morality towards recognition of the increasing importance of legal processes everywhere in Chinese daily life. The chapter addresses this phenomenon in four steps: Interpretive Framework; *Legal Report*; Case Studies; and Narrative Structure.

Citizenship, morality and law

In 1994 Zhang Yimou presented to the public a social realist comedy which two years later inadvertently spawned a television documentary programme, *Legal Report*. With more than a thousand episodes, this documentary programme was to become a central feature of government sponsored citizenship education. *Qiuju da guansi / The Story of Qiuju* (1994) portrays a pregnant woman who takes her *cunzhang* (village chief) to court. In a minor dispute, Qiuju's husband insults the *cunzhang* by telling him that his family line will be terminated. Outraged, the village chief kicks the husband in the genitals, injuring him seriously. Qiuju asks for a *shuofa* (an official statement explaining his reason for the assault), which however is refused. Much of the film shows the pregnant Qiuju travelling from her village to courts in the district, town and city, in search for justice. Finally, justice appears to be done when the *cunzhang* is taken away by the police. Qiuju is confused by the result. The film ends with a medium shot of Qiuju, puzzled: she did not want her *cunzhang* to be arrested. All she wanted was a *shuofa*.

A number of specific themes and motifs help to explain why Zhang Yimou's film became the pilot for a television documentary series at the centre of current citizenship education. There is the traditional motif of an initial injustice requiring the righting of a wrong, the theme that a request for justice remains unsuccessful until someone in a position of authority takes an interest in the plaintiff's case and its 'differend' (Lyotard 1988), the motif of *taoge shuofa* (begging for an official explanation), and the all important tension between expectations of traditional morality and the law. In *Legal Report* these themes are integrated into a highly successful narrative formula which has been able to keep millions glued to the television screen since 2 January 1999.

The interaction of a new legal awareness and traditional moral thinking is at the heart of a number of television documentaries other than *Legal Report*, which are likewise designed to train ordinary Chinese to learn how to reconcile their traditional values with an increasingly complex legal perspective. Before we are in a position to appreciate this relationship in some depth we need an interpretive framework within which both citizenship television documentaries and their focus on the relationship between law and morality make sense. At the same time, we should rid ourselves of such clichéd contrasts as 'Western citizen standards are individualistic and adversarial whereas those of Asia are communitarian and consensus-seeking' (Davidson 1999: 222). I take first the negative approach of listing the types of citizenship concepts that form much of the content of recent discussions of citizenship in the Anglosphere and Europe, but appear inappropriate for the Chinese situation, at least at present. I will then turn to a number of Chinese sources in order to provide a background relevant to the phenomenon of the television documentary, in particular its subgenre, the TV law programme and my example, *Legal Report*.

'There is no more dynamic social figure in modern history than The Citizen', observes Rolf Dahrendorf (1994: 292). Perhaps the most radical use of this figure is the concept of the 'global citizen' or 'world citizen' in the sense that people are primarily 'citizens of the world' (Dower and Williams 2002: 1). That such a notion is an inappropriate horizon for our understanding of Chinese citizenship at present should be obvious from the observation that 'being a global citizen is not merely a matter of accepting a global ethical framework, it is belonging to and participating in a wider community which finds expression in a variety of institutions within global civil society' (Dower and Williams 2002: 40). In this perspective, citizenship 'ceases to be synonymous with nationality' (Delanty 2000: 127). Neither such 'decoupling of citizenship and nationality' (131) nor the picture of a 'fluid world' in which 'the ironic citizen needs to learn how to move on, how to adjust and to adopt to a world of cultural contingencies' (Turner 2000: 30), nor the kind of 'normative cosmopolitanism' that is emerging in the European Union (Follesdal 2002: 71) can be said to apply to present day China. Nor can I find any contemporary theorisation in China of such notions as the 'polyethnic rights' of 'multicultural citizenship' (Shafir 1998: 171;167) 'regional citizenship' (Falk 2002: 23f.), 'supra-societal rights' (Turner 1994: 473) let alone 'differentiated citizenship' and the 'special rights' of underprivileged group. (Young 1998: 288).

A telling handicap in Western perspectives on citizenship and citizenship education if applied to Chinese social phenomena and the law is the assumption that ethics, especially in their utopian global form, should be premised on the way in which morality has emerged out of religious traditions. While it may be true that 'there will be no new world order without a global ethic' (Küng 2002: 134), such an ethic is not of necessity tied to any form of religion. The tenacious emphasis on morality in China today is the result of a 2,500 year tradition of non-theistic and secular moral practice as well as its continuous theorisation. Perhaps we should also remember in response to Küng that almost all the democratic rights that citizens in advanced democracies are enjoying today have been achieved since the European Enlightenment against rather than with the assistance of any religious group. A more appropriate interpretive path suggests that China is gradually warming to the notion of modern citizenship, as long as its leadership is confident that it can restrain and channel the dual forces of democracy and capitalism. With capitalism on a leash, early ideas of European citizenship appear relevant, especially those that emphasise responsibilities rather than rights, from the Treaty of Westphalia (1648), through the writings of Pufendorf, Mendelsohn and Kant, to the *'devoirs'* of the French Revolution in 1789. If, as Kenneth Minogue notes, the trajectory of citizenship curves from 'compliance' towards 'participation' (Minogue 1995: 16;13), China could be said to be gradually approaching the latter, having achieved in its recent history at least some of the requirements stipulated by Thomas Marshall in 1950, such as old-age pensions, unemployment benefits, public health insurance, legal aid, a minimum wage, and a modicum of other entitlements.

From a Chinese perspective, one could approve of Dahrendorf's view of citizenship as 'the institutional counterpart of rationality, not merely an idea but a reality, the crystallization of rationality into a social role' as long as such a reality does not 'cross a line beyond which it defeats its own purpose', a threat that he terms the 'suicidal strain' of citizenship (Dahrendorf 1994: 307). Perhaps the transformation of the workers of European modernity into postmodern consumers signals to the Chinese authorities the crossing of that suicidal line. What is more realistic for contemporary China is the transformation of a society grounded in public morality under state control into a community under more specific legal constraints, what Dahrendorf calls a '*Rechtsgemeinschaft*', a community based on the principles of law (Dahrendorf 1994: 292). Certainly, as public announcements, as well as a massive wave of media pedagogy, suggest, Chinese authorities have taken seriously the task of educating their citizens towards a better grasp of the role that the law is increasingly playing in their everyday lives. For in the past, as Li and Wu observe, 'the dignity of the law has been a foreign notion for most Chinese' (Li and Wu 1999: 165). What has been familiar to all Chinese instead has been the long-standing tradition of common, that is, Confucian morality. In the absence of a history of acquaintance with a complex and detailed body of laws, the new citizenship training programme appears as timely as it is necessary if China is to optimise its position in a rapidly globalising world.

Today China has its own practices and interpretations of citizenship, a social phenomenon in which morality plays a fundamental role. The term 'morality' here refers loosely to what remains active of traditional Confucianism: the particular way of understanding the nation-state, government, the relationship between rulers and subjects, the rank relations within the larger social order, and the familial hierarchy. The signifier 'nation-state', in Chinese, is constructed as two characters *guo* (country, kingdom) and *jia* (family): *guojia*, the family as nation-state, or the nation-state as an extended family. This notion of seeing the state as an extended family is illustrated by Li and Wu's observation of the relationship between state and the citizens on the issue of right and duties. 'For most Chinese, the rights of citizens are given by the government, and a citizen is part of the state: citizens perform their duties and, in return, government gives them their rights' (Li and Wu 1999: 165). The relationship between state and citizens in China mirrors the family relationship in that children are an integral part of the family; the parents give children certain restricted rights, while in return the children do as they are told. This perspective is reflected also in the Chinese popular saying, *Guojia younan, pifu youze* (when a country is in difficulty, every ordinary citizen has responsibilities). The emphasis on the state as an extended family, foregrounding duties rather than rights, is invoked by the leading intellectual in the late Qing Dynasty, Liang Qichao, when he admonishes the *guomin*, the people, to increase their efforts to strengthen China in the face of Western imperialism. He felt that it was a 'lack of a sense of obligation – to pay taxes and serve in the military, for example – rather than the lack of rights, [that] constituted the root cause of China's problems' (Goldman and Perry 2002: 6). So it makes sense that even in the twenty-first century, Chinese patriotism and nationalism are still built on the idea of an extended family. For instance, in the discourse of Chinese nationalism, Taiwan, Hong Kong and Macau Chinese are referred to as *Taiwan tongbao, Gang'Ao tongbao*, that is, as full brothers and sisters of the mainland Chinese, while the Chinese minorities are regarded as cousins and nephews of the Han.

The Chinese view of nation-state as an extended family transfers the singular relationship between the state and the citizen into a complicated dual relationship between citizen and the state, and citizens and rulers, where the rulers are perceived as parents responsible for running the family. That this perspective should have survived through the Mao era is perhaps as surprising as it is significant for an outsider trying to understand China. In Western terminology, citizenship focuses on the relationship between state and the citizen, on rights and duties through ideas of 'justice' and 'equality'. In China, citizenship is complicated by the relationship between state, rulers and individual. Since the state is viewed as an extended family, the rulers of the state and the rulers of the family become interchangeable: it is not the state that looks after the citizen, but rather the rulers of the state who perform the duty of looking after their 'children'.

In Chen Yuanbin's novel *Wanjia shusong* (1991), on which Zhang Yimou's *The Story of Qiuju* is based, Qiuju complains,

> *Cunzhang* (the village chief) is in charge of the whole village, just like being in charge of a big family. The person who is charge is, of course, allowed to hit and scold his subjects. But he should not kick my husband's *yaoming de difang* (his place of life). I asked him [the chief]; he didn't even have a *shuofa* (reason).

When the Chief is taken away by the police, Qiuju does not understand that *cunzhang*'s behaviour of hitting a villager is a breach of law. What she understands is that the Chief has a right to punish the villagers (his children), but not by assaulting that particular part of the body. Since Qiuju does not yet know the gender of her unborn baby, her husband's reproductive organs are crucial to the continuation of the family line. Seeing the ruler as the senior (parent) of the family connotes a sense of gratitude for the contribution he has made to the welfare of his subjects, a firmly established theme of Confucianism. This makes it difficult to see citizens' rights as a product of a contract between individual and state on an equal basis. And it is likewise difficult to see how an ordinary citizen (son/daughter) should participate in decision making in the affairs of the state (family) on an equal basis with the ruler (parents).

As a consequence of this metaphoric and yet real extension of the family relationship to that between rulers and citizens, people in China tend to 'accept' situations where the relation between state and citizen is overruled by decisions made by the rulers of the day. For instance, in the CCP's categories, people (*renmin*), nationals (*guomin*), citizens (*gongmin*), the *renmin* enjoyed the rights to elect or to be elected, have freedom of thought, speech, and the press, while *guomin*, which includes *diren* (the CCP's political enemies within China), were required to perform their duties but could not necessarily enjoy all the political rights and liberties of the *renmin* (Li and Wu 1999: 158). Between 1954 and the late 1970s, Mao's 'two kinds of contradiction', contradictions between the people and the enemy and contradictions amongst the people themselves, tended to overrule the legal notion of 'citizen'. The former could be mended by education, the latter required harsher intervention, including extermination. To complicate matters, as the meaning of *renmin* changed according to Party needs, so did their rights and duties. For example, what is deemed 'urban' and 'rural' became more important than the concept of 'citizen' (*gongmin*). These different guises of citizenship have been created, recreated and practised by the CCP since the early 1950s.

This authoritarian and pastoral practice of citizenship only worked as long as Confucianism played a more significant role than the rule of law. Throughout twentieth-century China, rulers and intellectual élites developed a series of moral criteria to guide citizen behaviour. In the 1910s, the national government and the intellectuals called for citizens to perform their duties to make China strong. In the 1930s, the Jiang Jieshi government called for the return of Confucian morality in the *xin shenghuo* (New Life) movement proclaiming that every *guomin* (national) had a duty to participate in nation-building. In the 1950s, the Communist government developed the *wuai* (five loves: love the nation, the people, work, science, and socialism), the standard measurement for a *hao gongmin* (good citizen). In the 1960s and 1970s, following to the letter the Party's fast changing instructions was the sole measure of the good standing of a citizen. Lei Feng, the heroic Communist soldier killed in a road accident, was hailed by the government as an exemplary good citizen because of his unselfish behaviour and collective spirit.

As China entered the period of economic reform, the idea of 'governing the country according to law' became the new revolutionary idea. The government gradually realised that a market economy cannot function without a highly complex legal system. In 1979, one year after his return to power, Deng Xiaoping stated that China 'needs to develop a high degree of democratic and comprehensive system of laws'. He urged the government that the People's democracy must be systematic and legal: '*youfa keyi, youfa biyi, zhifa biyan, waifa bijiu*' ('We must have laws that we can rely on, we must carry out the laws we established, we must abide strictly by our laws, and we will investigate to the end if our laws are breached.'). In September 1979, the CCP developed the new concept of *shehuizhuyi fazhi* (socialist legal system). In April 1980 at the National Congress, the government launched the idea *yifa zhiguo* (governing the country by law). In November 1985 the Central Committee of the CCP and the State Council declared the *yifa zhiguo* a binding principle, and passed several five-year plans for mass eduction on law. In 1996 at the Fifteenth Party Congress '*yifa zhiguo*' and 'the establishment of a law governed country' became the nation's fundamental credos for running China's domestic affairs. In 1999, basic strategies for governing the country by laws were written into the constitution (*xiuzhen an*).

However, given China's traditional reliance on public morality, it is not surprising that as the nation has been gradually changing into a society governed more and more by laws, government and conservative intellectuals have expressed concerns regarding the demise of traditional Chinese morality. Questions are being raised, such as: What is the role of morality in citizenship education? Is it sufficient to govern the country by law? What if citizens are more aware of their rights than the morality that guides their duties? (You 2002: 27). There is a fear that, while awareness of laws is rapidly increasing, moral education is lagging behind. Even to those who see no contradiction between law and morality, the former is regarded as inferior. Wei, for one, argues that law is the lowest form of morality (Wei, Yongzheng 2001: 199–121), whereby law is regarded as punishment enforced by the state; law is about rights and duties, about restrictions imposed on both self and others. Most importantly, in Wei's perspective, the law cannot act as a ground for all social relations. In contrast, he argues, morality is to be viewed as the highest status of human beings; it is about beliefs and cultural values; about sacrifice and the performance of duties; and it can modify all existing social relations, and predict possible social relations for the future. Thus, for Wei, morality ought to be recognised as the supreme law. A somewhat different view is offered by You who argues that law is a nation's legal spirit, a state's value system and basis for judgement, whereas morality involves differences between class, institutions, race and ethnic groups (You 2002: 21–24). Law, he says, requires a formal process to be carried out within the institution, whilst morality relies on self-evaluation within social constraints. All social relationships covered by laws are also covered by morality, but not all social relations covered by morality can be covered by laws. Morality is a treasure of Chinese traditional ideology. Morality is the basis, law is a method. Law belongs to political construction and has a political spirit; morality is about ideological construction, reflecting the spirit of civilisation (*People's Daily, Editorial*, 1 February 2001). Like many other Chinese, You insists on the necessity of a return to moral education, for 'if there is only the law, then there is no spiritual civilisation' (You 2002: 27).

The government has now embraced the idea that moral education is not only necessary in the long run, but is also an immediate and urgent task in balancing citizenship education. They recognise that the nation is facing a morality crisis caused by 'the contradiction between a fast developed economy and a moral system that is lagging badly behind' (Jiang 2001: 241). As Hao writes,

> We had a socialist morality but that was the morality of the planned economy which was relative simple and direct (in organisational format, employment methods, distribution of wealth). Now we are in the market economy, and our system is empty.
>
> (Hao, Tiechuang 2002: 15)

The document, *Gongmin daode jianshe shisi gangyao* (*Outline for Carrying Out Citizenship Moral Construction*), issued by the Central Committee of the CCP on 20 September 2001, warns that the current moral degradation will seriously 'disturb the economy and social order' if the following social phenomena cannot be stopped.

> In some social areas and aspects, moral degradation is on the rise. Boundaries between right and wrong, kindness and evil, beauty and ugliness, are being violated. Materialism, hedonism, and individualism are on the rise. At times we forget what is right at the sight of profit, and seek private gain at public expense. Loss of credibility and cheating are harming our society. Corruption and the use of power to gain private benefits are serious issues.

Calls for the restoration of *minde* (morality for the masses, the ordinary citizens, or people) and *guande* (morality for the officials) are getting louder (Jiang 2001: 247–9). In January 2001, the General Party Secretary Jiang Zemin declared that 'in the process of developing a socialist market economy, we must persist in strengthening the socialist legal system, in order to govern the country by law. At the same time, we must also persist in constructing and strengthening socialist morality, in order to govern the country by morality' (Meeting of Media Ministers).

What precisely is this morality the CCP has been calling for? How does the morality they have in mind differ from the Confucian ideal, especially in its perception of the relationship between state and individual? Does the kind of morality the CCP wants in any way assist in the transformation of the perspective of rulers and society as an extended family to a legal contract relationship between state and individual? The CCP acknowledges that the notion of 'governing the country by morality' has been inherited from a cultural tradition that has informed the management of ideology and the state apparatus (Gao and Liu 2002: 3). The Party also acknowledges that the differences between distinct kinds of morality stem largely from the differing ideological positions that produce them. Hence the current CCP wants to produce a 'system of socialist morality' that best suits their idea of a 'socialist market economy' (*People's Editorial*, 1 February 2001 and *Xinhua Daily*, 13 February 2001). This moral blue print contains as its core message: serving the people; the principle of collectivism; the five loves (of the nation, the people, work, science and socialism) and three domains in which morality is to be primarily employed, the social, the professional and the family. These guidelines are echoed in the *Zhongguo gongmin daode shouce* (*Chinese Citizenship Morality Handbook*) which highlights knowledge of morality; learning about the law; social behaviour; the idea that law is subordinate to morality; and *wuai* or the 'five loves' as the legal duty and moral responsibility of every Chinese citizen.

Though differing in content with time, the principle of citizenship education has always been at the centre of the government's agenda under the guidance of the CCP since 1949. The main difference between the Mao and post-Mao period lies in the content rather than in the pedagogic method. What remains similar is mass education through targeted campaigns. In the post-Mao period, the content of political ideology has been significantly reduced. In its place, awareness of the law now occupies centre stage in citizenship education. This is to ensure China's smooth transition from its planned economy to that of the market. In the planned economy, social and familial problems were usually resolved through government mediation with the help of Party committees in the workplaces and neighbourhood, with an emphasis on the spirit of collectivism, harmony, and various moral codes. In the market economy, the government encourages society to use laws as solutions to their problems. Where competence in legal matters is proving a necessity is in the arena of international trading relations, a fact that has had significant reverberations in the domestic market. However, this shift towards a collective legal consciousness is not just a matter of a new way of solving problems but a new way of thinking, including evaluating the individual's position in relation to family, society and state. In other words, retraining docile, ideologically constituted bodies into competent users of legal processes amounts to more than just another government campaign. It amounts to a significant social transformation, perhaps even a special kind of revolution.

Although Jiang's slogan 'governing the country by law' significantly accelerated public thinking in terms of a contractual relationship with authority, Jiang did not want to let go of the notion of morality, though what he wished to retain was a 'socialist morality' suitable to the new 'market economy'. While in Mao's period morality was subsumed under 'political ideology', the CCP under Jiang's leadership revived a modified notion of morality compatible with the demands of the market. In 1990, the Jiang Zemin Government insisted that moral education was to remain part of citizenship education. In 1996 the government specified that a modern citizen should have these qualities (*suzhi*): ideologically correct morality (*shixiang daode*); knowledge of science and culture (*kexue wenhua*); and awareness of the law (*minzhu fazhi guan*). In 2001, Jiang proclaimed that while 'governing the country by law is important', it is equally important to 'govern the country by morality'.

Throughout Chinese history, governments have defined, and redefined, 'morality' to accommodate what they felt was required for the specific circumstances of their rule. In their studies for the methodology of governing the country by morality, Gao and Liu (2002: 4–5) write:

> [Jiang's] 'morality' in 'governing the country by morality' refers to a socialist and communist' morality. The ancient morality is the morality of slave society and feudalism. Morality under socialism and communism emphasises unity between individualism and collectivism, between the interests of the nation and those of whole human beings, between collectivism and self-interest.

The tension between collective obligation and the interests of individual citizens remains a pervasive theme in all things Chinese. It does therefore not come as a surprise that the television law programmes that play such a prominent role in citizenship education should reflect this tension in the way their episodes are constructed. In *Legal Report* the relationship between social obligation and the rights of the individual are negotiated in a complex structural dialogue between morality and the law.

Legal report and legal consciousness

Documentary films and television programmes featuring legal processes and their application occupy a central place in the evolution of the genre in China. In no other country has the law received as much televisual attention as it has in China since the start of its socialist market economy. What are the reasons for this sudden popularity of law on the Chinese television screens? Several answers appear plausible. First, as I have argued in the previous section, it had become obvious to the burgeoning business sector and the government that traditional Chinese legal processes were glaringly inadequate for their rapidly developing interaction with advanced Western countries in terms of technology and commerce. The largely punitively conceived and rough grain traditional law of China proved incompatible with the intricate legal networks that make national and international trade efficient and reliable amongst advanced capitalist societies. So it is perhaps not so surprising that the creation and implementation of a compatible legal system has been one of the most urgent tasks faced by the Chinese legislature since the early 1980s.

Second, if such a transformation was to be successful at all, Chinese society at large had to be retrained in terms of legal thinking. A society reliant for over two millennia on Confucian morality, which included as an essential feature competence in the art of the social negotiation of conflict rather than litigation, could not simply be told by the CCP and the government that they now had to live by a completely different set of rules and way of thinking. Nor had the communist reign from 1949 to the end of the Cultural Revolution in 1977 effected any fundamental changes in this respect. A mass education programmes was therefore required to introduce legal thinking in addition to, and sometimes even in competition with, traditional notions of morality. Such a programmes was first instigated by the government through one of its main official channels, the CCTV, and subsequently taken up as a commercial hit by many other television stations.

Third, and this is a theme at the heart of this book, programmes addressing legal matters cannot hold the attention of a mass audience unless they reflect in some detail the social realities within which the law functions. It became obvious to producers that to achieve commercial success all they had to do was to let the various components of actual legal conflicts and the ways in which they could be reported 'speak' for themselves. In this sense, the typical law programmes is a natural candidate for a participatory, documentary style. After all, the reporting of legal cases typically involves victims of a crime, perpetrators, investigative journalists, the police, court officials, and lawyers. The combination of an initial top–down encouragement of television programmes and the generic conditions of televised legal reporting resulted in an unprecedented upsurge in the popularity of the discourse of law in the form of television shows.

Fourth, a further factor for the popularity of television law programmes gradually emerged as television stations began to expand the commercial measurement of ratings by introducing other feedback mechanisms into their programming. Audience responses were increasingly built into the programmes themselves and the public began to appreciate being able to air their own legal grievances or simply welcomed the opportunity of expressing their views on a particular episode. In this respect, law programmes have spearheaded developments in documentary filmmaking and television documentaries in general. Indeed, many of the presentational techniques in the current digital video contributions by individual directors and amateur filmmakers in the style of 'let the people speak' were pioneered in televisual law programmes.

Lastly, not only did the feedback strategies of the new television law programmes permit ordinary people across the country to have their voices heard, such voices also contained a critical element. Televisual audience feedback proved conducive to critical intervention in cases of public and particularly lower level governmental fraud and corruption. As such, the law programmes began to function as an effective social safety valve for letting off steam, that is, the airing of a degree of public dissent within tacitly accepted parameters. This served the double purpose of relieving some of the social tensions that were accumulating in the post-Mao era, and had exploded in the student democracy protest of 4 June 1989, and at the same time allowing the government to continue its reform programmes in strictly specified areas and at a slow pace. But how did it all begin? In the following sections I draw selectively on observations made by Hu Shifeng and Yi Li in their 2003 book *Dianshi Fazhi jiemu tezhi, chuangzuo yu kaifa* (*The Television Law Programme*) in addition to my own data.

In July 1980, the CCTV launched *Guancha yu sikao / Observation and Thinking*, a programmes with in-depth commentary on current affairs, politics, morality, education, and law. This initiative very much reflected Deng Xiaoping's words that social practice should be the 'only criterion for truth'. Law, among other facets of social reality, had become an object of televisual scrutiny. Between November 1980 and January 1981 the CCTV presented court proceedings of the trial of the 'Gang of Four', thus introducing a modicum of transparency into the court system and at the same time making legal process a topic in its own right. This was followed in November 1985 by a new government policy making television law education programmes mandatory (Hu and Yin 2003: 1–3).

On 22 May of the same year Shanghai TV had already started the first officially recognised, full law programmes, appropriately named *Falü yu diode / Law and Morality*, with viewers being invited to participate as co-editors, acting contributions, and with short plays on legal problems. Legal experts were asked to contribute to the programmes their explanations and interpretations of the emerging legal system. Four months later, in September 1985, Nanjing TV broadcast *Fazhi yuandi / The Garden of Law* the episodes of which addressed the intricacies and subtleties of the new legal process. In December of that year the CCTV started its own law programmes *Guiju yu fangyuan / Law and Harmony*, a weekly programmes with 20-minute episodes. As its title indicates, Chinese culture is highly sensitive to the conciliation of legal principles and the ideal of harmony in the face of the complexities of social reality. Four years later the CCTV changed the title of the programmes to *Shehui jingwei / Social Latitudes and Longitudes*, now including a police hotline, reporting, commentary, a letter box for the audience, a focus on 'hot issues', and detailed analyses of individual cases (Hu and Yin 2003: 8).

From 1985 to 1994, more than 50 television stations across China, as far as Urumqi in Xinjiang, introduced programmes on law, most of which proved highly popular. These programmes often focused on local cases and issues in relation to new, nationally binding laws. 1994 also saw the first awards for outstanding programmes on legal topics being handed out by the 'Television Law *Programmes* Committee', established by the Ministry of Broadcasting and Television. In the same year Nanjing TV offered a new programmes entitled *Fazhi chuanzhen / Court Alive (Fax)*, a weekly documentary on actual legal proceedings in the court room, making good on an earlier promise of rendering the court system more transparent for the public. By 1997 more than 70 television stations had established a share in the new market niche and a year later 150 television stations were vying for audience approval. They did so with resounding success, having become the main TV genre in China, its ratings even defeating those of soap drama.[1] By 2001 the number of television stations broadcasting law *programmes* had risen to over 200 (Hu and Yin 2003: 9–22). Confident that the law education programmes, including its televisual format, was being successful, President Jiang Zemin announced at the Fifteenth Party Congress in 1997 that it was appropriate to 'use the legal system to govern the country', the first step perhaps on the way towards a state founded primarily on legal processes rather than on CCP directives. It is against this historical background that we need to read the significance of the launch by the CCTV on January 1999 of the most successful of these television programmes, *Jinri shuofa / Legal Report*. Here, the principles of the legal process are carefully combined with didactic purpose, made attractive by participatory strategies both within each episode and by keeping in close touch with the audience by way of a number of feedback strategies.

Ironically, media events often turn out to be more real in terms of their effects than ordinary events, such as crimes or road accidents, and *Legal Report* is certainly no exception. *Legal Report* is a half hour daily programme on CCTV, from 12:30 to 1pm, following the lunchtime news at 12:00 noon. The programmes aims to introduce concepts of law and the mechanisms of the legal process to the public through documented case narratives. This is why the programmes is commonly referred to as *Zhongguo ren de falü wucan* (The Chinese People's Legal Lunch). The programmes typically consists of two sections. The first section is a documentary report on a case lasting between 15 to 20 minutes. The second section is a discussion about the case between the host(s) of the programmes and guest experts, usually an academic from a jurisprudence faculty of a university or some other legal specialists. Since 2 January 1999, *Legal Report* has produced more than a thousand episodes. The production team includes some 50 documentary specialists – producers, journalists, cameramen, sound recorders and editors, in front and behind the camera. The programmes is broadcast nationwide to China's 900 million plus television audience, maintaining top ten ratings from day one, initially capturing 1.78 to 5.24 per cent of the population and with a growth rate for a while of 2 million viewers per day. On the average, the station receives more than 1,000 letters every day. There is a professional team ready to respond to audience queries via a 24-hour telephone answering service dedicated to receiving audience feedback. A sizeable number of Chinese citizens involved in actual law suits approach *Legal Report* team for professional advice. A website and an email service add to the didactically interactive character of *Legal Report*, guaranteeing a high degree of public involvement, including the wider audience of the Chinese diaspora world wide.

The English titles '*Legal Report*' or 'Law Today' do not quite capture the significance of the cultural and political connotations of the original Chinese *Jinri shuofa*. '*Jinri*' means 'today', while *shuofa* can be understood as 'statement' or 'the way you reason a matter'. As pointed out before, '*Shuofa*' is borrowed from Zhang Yimou's much loved film, *The Story of Qiuju* in which the protagonist, Qiuju, makes a superhuman effort in requesting the law courts to provide an official *shuofa* (statement, reason) why the *cunzhang* (the village chief) should be permitted to kick her husband's reproductive organs without having to offer an official reason. *Jinri shuofa* targets millions of Chinese television viewers like Qiuju, who have little or no knowledge of the legal system and its laws. The chief editor, Yin Li explains the purpose of the programmes as follows:

Over the 20 years since the economic reform, the creation of laws has accelerated to such an extent that 300 new laws have been established. 'Governing the country by laws' has been written into our constitution, Qiuju's '*taoge shuofa*' (begging for an 'official' statement or reason) has entered the homes of thousands of families over night. However, how many people in 1.2 billion have received education on the legal process? How much do they know about laws? How much do they use laws as principles to protect themselves and, at the same time, as principles to regulate their own behaviour?

(Yin 2001: vol. 3)

Placed in this context, the title *Jinri shuofa* could be understood also as 'today's reason(ing) from authority'. Implicitly the title indicates that we are dealing here with an official explanation of individual cases involving a legal dispute. The title could also be seen to refer to a programme with a certain temporal limitation: legal reasoning for today rather than reasoning applicable to the past and the future.

As hinted at above, there are specific reasons why millions of Chinese, very much like Qiuju, lack knowledge of the law. First, in Chinese traditional society, law is mainly associated with punishment. The law is there above all 'to protect rulers' and regards 'citizens as subjects to be controlled'. In this sense the 'law does not protect citizens' property rights, nor does it recognise the individual right of freedom' (Li and Wu 1999: 167). Civil law was only gradually developed out of the government's emphasis on criminal law (Li and Wu 1999: 167). Second, in the Mao period from the 1950s to the late 1970s, the concept of law was undermined to the point of an absence of the law, since *zhengce*, or policies, more or less replaced the legal process. The leading criterion of a good citizen in the Mao era was to be a member of the proletariat (workers, peasants, or soldiers) who actively participated in political movements by following the Party's instructions. As citizenship is a relationship between an individual and the state, and since the Chinese constitution enshrines the CCP as the only governing Party of the nation, a good citizen during the Cultural Revolution was measured by a citizen's distance from or closeness to Party rule. Only from the 1980s when the Party introduced the principle of *yifa zhiguo* (governing the country by law), began legal consciousness to be promoted on the Party's agenda for nationwide education. For most of the twentieth century, China had been governed by a mixture of traditional morality (Confucian values, *liangxin* 'conscience') and CCP policies. To a certain degree, and in spite of all its innovative features, *Legal Report* still reflects this mixture.

The central aim of *Legal Report* is to develop China's law culture by assisting the masses in developing a legal consciousness – to use laws to regulate social behaviour, and to establish mass confidence in China's new and expanding legal system. After all, the motto for the programmes is *zongzai pufa* (making laws accessible), *jiandu zhifa* (inspecting how laws are being carried out); and *chujin lifa* (encouraging laws to be established) (Yin 2001: 3). This directive covers matters dealing with civil laws, such as marriage, extra-marital affairs, family, inheritance, adoption, children's rights, property rights, and other civic matters; traffic laws; security; administration, law scrutiny, business laws: contracts, product quality, business fraud, insurance, advertising, enterprises, consumer rights; labour laws; intellectual property rights, natural resources, land management, elections, and organisational laws. At the same time, the traditional idea of morality is never far from the central intent of the programmes. For example, on 30 May 2002, *Legal Report* organised a quiz show dedicated to the theme of 'Knowledge of Citizenship Morality' screened nationwide.

As my sample analyses will show, *Legal Report* programmes support the ideological apparatus of the government, while at the same time catering for the needs of a vast and growing market. In addition to the reasons given at the outset of the chapter for the popularity of all the new television law programmes, the appeal of *Legal Report* also lies in its structured format combining storytelling with expert discussion, and partly, of course, also in its spectacular pandering to voyeurism. Given the programmes' aim of creating and nurturing a new legal consciousness in society in the style of fast-food consumption, *Legal Report*'s formulaic programmes structure is well suited to providing introductory lessons in law within a half hour time slot at lunch time to a mass audience with some high school education. The majority of cases televised over the last six years (1999–2006) can be distributed broadly over three categories: (1) introduction of the audience to laws and the legal process; (2) examination of the efficiency of the way laws are being applied; and (3) situations in which the law has been deficient or absent. No matter, however, to which category we may wish to allocate individual episodes, they are all variations on the deep theme of the intricate relationship between legal process and moral behaviour. With this proviso, the chapter now turns to an interpretive description of five selected *Legal Report* episodes covering three cases.

Case studies

(1) *Hainan / Ocean Accident* is about an investigation into the compensation awarded the families of 14 victims of an accident at sea. The 14 victims, all fishermen, drowned as a result of a collision between their trawler and a large commercial fishing vessel. The accident occurred on 6 April 1997. Although the courts granted the families of the victims full compensation, the money was never received. *Ocean Accident* consists of two episodes, *Hainan* (I) and *Hainan* (II), exploring the details of the fraud. The first episode opens with three images setting the scene and the theme of the investigation:

- Image 1: a rural, middle-aged woman, the wife of one of the victims, tearfully describes the moment when her family receives the news of her husband's death. 'My child is in tears, wailing "How can I live without my father? I want my father"'. Below the image the caption reads: 'Perished in the ocean, the fishermen will never return'.

- Image 2: an old man, the father of one of the victims, speaking in anger: 'My name is false, all of these names are false'. The caption reads: 'Inventing false names; who is responsible for the theft of 1.26 million *yuan* in compensation?'
- Image 3: a middle-aged woman in her court uniform, admits: 'The court too has been cheated'. The caption repeats the title of the episode.

Legal Report usually opens its episodes with attention-grabbing images announcing the investigation of a crime and the search for social justice. *Ocean Accident* is a story of fraud which certainly could not have occurred without the involvement of officials in local government and legal institutions. Soon after the accident, the Ningjing Fishing Company, who had employed the fishermen, paid 15,000 *yuan* to each family for their loss. At the same time, the company asked the bereaved families to sign an agreement that they would make no further claims should the ship involved in the accident not be found. However, within less than a year the ship was identified by the Company. Without informing the victim families, the Ningjing Fishing Company initiated legal action. The Company first sought documentation from the Rongcheng Court to the effect that Rongcheng City testified that the victims had families and therefore a compensation claim should be pursued on behalf of those families. The Ningjing Fishing Company then employed a lawyer to represent the victims' families in the Qingdao Ocean Affairs Court to seek two separate compensation claims, one for the Company's loss of its boat, the other for the victims' families. The Qingdao Ocean Affairs Court resolved that a total of 2.2 million *yuan* be paid by the convicted party, 1.4 million to the 14 plaintiffs, and 800,000 to the Ningjing Fishing Company.

However, the Ningjing Fishing Company, the lawyer and the guilty party decided to settle out of court, reducing the compensation claim from 2.2 million to 1.26 million. As the Ningjing Fishing Company was a state-owned company of the Town of Ningjing, the Deputy Mayor instructed the lawyer to transfer 1.06 million to the Ningjing Government minus legal fees and other deductions. The Government then drew 200,000 *Yuan* from the account, paying for road construction, and transferred the rest to the Lingye Fishing Company, which happened to be a branch office of the Ningjing Fishing Company. The fraud unfolded unimpeded, mainly because the plaintiffs had been excluded from the legal proceedings. As Professor Zhao Ling, guest law expert in the episode, points out, the fraud could have been stopped if the Rongcheng Court had followed the rule that a court of law could issue death certificates only after checking the identities of the victims' family members, the family registrations, and the marriage certificates. The fraud could also have been prevented had the lawyer met with the families whom he was supposed to represent in court. The Rongcheng Court inspectors, while admitting their error, insisted that they themselves had become victims of fraud. Likewise, the lawyer conceded that he should have met with the plaintiffs to discuss their case. The question that is implicitly posed then is whether this massive fraud was the result of no more than a few deplorable acts of unprofessional behaviour or whether large-scale corruption was to be blamed.

In the *Ocean Accident* episodes, broadcast over two lunch times, we are given several perspectives. One is provided by the reporter of *Legal Report*, Sun Hui, who is also the narrator and the investigator of the crime. The second perspective is that of the host of *Legal Report*, while the third is the analysis offered by the guest of the show, a legal expert. Further minor perspectives are added by various persons speaking during interviews. Sun Hui represents the plaintiffs. She interviews the families, the deputy court judge and inspector, the lawyers, the Party Secretary of the Ningjing Town Government, and unsuccessfully pursues the Director of the Ningjing Fishing Company for an interview. She appears non-aggressive, modest and yet determined. Her investigation is presented from the victims' families' position and their claim for compensation. Her investigation proceeds from the families to the Qingdao Ocean Affairs Court, the Rongcheng Court, the lawyer, the Ningjing Government, and finally the Ningjing Fishing Company.

As part of the documentation of the case, Sun Hui also uses the strategy of the hidden camera to record encounters between the victims' families and the lawyer, the Party Secretary and herself. Her sympathetic attitude towards the defrauded families is shown in her relationship with the family members, the corrupt and unresponsive governmental officers and lawyers, and the critical images taken of government buildings. We see her sitting closely with the families in the rural family yard. We also see her casting herself in opposition to government officials, the Rongcheng Court inspector, the Qingdao Deputy Judge, and the lawyer. She employs her hidden camera to capture the Party Secretary's unsophisticated manner and lies. In between, the sequence cuts to a shot of Mao's words 'Serve the People' which is painted in large characters on the government building. The montage leads the viewers to critically judge the function of government against Mao's motto for the CCP. Almost all the images of the governmental buildings, the courts and the offices are composed from low angles to highlight their authoritative, if not oppressive and threatening, status. The two *Hainan* episodes end with symbolic images of the reporter, Sun Hui, in relation to the plaintiffs and the government: the peasants in tears seeing Sun off at the village gate, grateful for her efforts to present their case; and Sun climbing up the steps leading to the Qingdao Ocean Affair Court with her concluding remarks, 'hopefully the relevant institution will be able to make an early and speedy decision.'

While Sun investigates the crime on behalf of the victims, the programmes host anchors the themes and conclusions by commenting and asking questions from the perspectives of ordinary citizens. The host does not ask questions such as 'Should the Rongchen Court be sued for failing to check the identities of the families?', 'Should the court be punished for breaches of the laws?' or 'Should the Ningjing Government be sued since without their support, the Party Secretary and the Deputy Mayor, the Ningjing Fishing Company and the lawyer could not have been successful in committing the crime?' Instead, she points out that the old man, the woman, and the children are all too trusting, though she admires their faith in the legal system and justice. Rather than challenging the authorities and asking what kind of punishment they should face, the host directs the viewers to sympathise with the victims. Two messages appear to be suggested by the host and the guest speaker: first, that one can sue lawyers for failing in their duties; and second, that the misfortunes of the families portrayed are the result of the inability of the relevant authorities to guarantee justice.

The questions that are posed by the host address the reasons why such frauds can occur in the legal process, why it is possible for a lawyer to represent his clients without informing his clients about his presence, and alter a decision made by the courts on behalf of the victims, and what the defrauded families can do in pursuing their claims for compensation. These questions are understood by the audience not only as revealing the legitimate legal concerns of the public but also as rightly provoking general moral outrage. 'What kind of persons could be so cruel', she asks, 'to cheat the old, the women, and the children?' As frequently in *Legal Report*, the reference to morality serves as a method to guide the audience's attention to the question of what has gone wrong in the application of the law.

The guest of the programme, a legal expert, offers a third perspective, though his answers are constrained by the host's questions and comments. In *Ocean Accident*, Professor Zhao Ling identifies the Rongcheng Court and the lawyer as responsible for the crime since they have failed in their professional duties. He also points out that the Ningjing Government has failed in its responsibility to distribute the legally allocated money to the families, and that the lawyer should be sued for failing to perform his professional duty of transferring the money to the victims. Zhao further informs the viewers that a lawyer has no right to alter a court decision without being re-appointed by his clients. Accordingly, the 1.26 million *yuan* should, in his legal opinion, belong to the victims' families *in toto*. As to a solution to the problem, Zhao offers two choices: one is to reopen the case, the other is to redistribute the compensation funds to the families. In addition to this legal advice, Professor Zhao's concluding remarks emphasises the moral issues involved in the case:

'Whatever the options, I think, as a public institution the Ningjing Government should show their sincerity in their support of the suffering families and so conclude this matter in peace.

(2) *Jiayao de laili / The Origin of Fake Medicine* is likewise presented over two episodes. While the first episode informs the viewers about the law on

consumer rights, the second develops from an investigation of the source of fake medicine to the exploration of government corruption. Both episodes aim to solve a puzzle: where is the fake medicine from? As usual the reporter is the investigator as well as the narrator. While the episodes praise the government's achievement in market control, they expose at the same time corruption and unprofessional conduct, as well as inefficient supervision of the market by certain government officials.

The first episode introduces viewers to consumer rights, while also addressing the question of morality in the medical profession. The opening contains:

- Image 1: The victim, 47-year-old factory worker Jing Gang asking, 'The medicine comes from my *danwei* (the state government workplace where I work), how can that be fake?' with the caption reading: 'After having taken false medicine, Jing *shifu* (master) *paian erqi* (slams his fist on the table and rises angrily to his feet)'.
- Image 2: The distributor of the medicine, claiming innocence, concedes: 'Yes, we distributed the fake medicine. This is a fact, and we have pointed out that the mistake was made by the original supplier'. The caption reads: 'Insisting that he has been implicated unjustly, the distributor tells his story in detail'.
- Image 3: The accused, the state clinic manager, saying 'He (Jing Gang) did not give any evidence'. The caption repeats the title of the episode; 'The Origin of Fake Medicine'.

The episode introduces legal knowledge that most people in China are unfamiliar with. It presents the viewers with two types of law that consumers are able to invoke in the case of justifiable claims for compensation. After a serious cancer operation, Jing Gang is advised to take medicine provided by the state factory clinic. A year later Jing becomes seriously ill. Assuming that his cancer had returned, he terminates his employment, awaiting his inevitable fate. His wife, however, is somewhat more sceptical. Because Jing often vomits after taking his medicine, she asks him to consider the possibility of a connection between his sickness and the prescribed drugs. Jing takes her advice and writes a letter to the pharmaceutical factory to inquire into the reason for his sickness. To his surprise the factory informs him that the medicine he has been taking is not the product of the factory. Worse, the medicine he has inquired about turns out not to exist officially at all. In disbelief, Jing takes the medicine to the Bureau of Medicine Inspection, where the result is confirmed. In anger, Jing takes the state clinic and medicine distributor to court for damages suffered. The court decides that the clinic should return Jing's medical fees, and furthermore, that Jing is entitled to receive a 10,000 *yuan* compensation for mental stress from the clinic and the distributor.

In the dispute between Jing and the accused, a moral question is raised by Jing's lawyer. Both the clinic and distributor have argued that there is no compelling evidence proving that Jing's sickness was caused by the medicine he took. The distributor claims that 'like animals, humans get sick without taking medicines'. In defending themselves against the payment of compensation for mental stress, they argue that their relationship with Jing was no more than a contract between a seller and a buyer. Hence, they say, compensation for mental stress does not apply. In reply, Jing's lawyer has this to say:

> You prescribed the medicine, and my client took it in good faith. Your medicine is fake, and now my client is getting sick from taking it. How can you say that you have done nothing wrong? Strictly speaking, this is not a question of law; it is a question of *liangxin* (conscience or morality).

Professor Ni, legal expert and guest in this episode, addresses the concept of contracts between seller and buyer; the notion of violation of customer rights; laws governing compensation for mental stress; and the regulations for the control of the pharmaceutical market. He explains that the court's decision was rightly based on the consequences caused by the clinic and the distributor. In spite of the fact that they themselves have been defrauded – trusting products issued by government agencies – they are guilty of failing their professional duty of checking the products they sell. By selling fake medicine they have violated Jing's rights as a consumer, leading to the termination of his employment and his considerable anxiety.

The second episode exposes unprofessional conduct and corruption in local government, as well as the tension between the central government's determination to control a poorly regulated pharmaceutical market, and the resistance by local officials to the uncovering of the scandal. The investigator of the episodes, the reporter, leaves Baoji for the capital city of Shanxi province, seeking the answer to the question of 'how fraudulent medicine is able to infiltrate government controlled channels of distribution.' However fruitless the search for an answer to the question proves to be, it reveals more than the viewers were led to expect. We learn that, as the manager of the head distribution in Xi'an admits, they did not as a matter of course check pharmaceutical products supplied by providers before releasing them onto the market. The reporter then travels to Puning in Guangdong province, South China, with Xi'an's receipt signed by the provider Xu Chuangshen, at *Canrong* Company. It turns out that Puning had already been listed as one of the centres in China known for producing fake medicines. From September to March, the local government had dealt with 90 such cases, with 16 people receiving jail sentences between 6 and 10 years. The local official praises this achievement by saying that 30,000 *yuan* awards for informers have not been claimed since March that year, and the reporter concludes the introduction by remarking that 'the methods to eradicate the crime employed by the government of Puning leaders are forceful; and their strict ruling is putting us at ease'.

The next scene introduces the theme of corrupt local officials. The manager of Canrong Company is summoned to be interviewed by two officials from the local Bureau of Medicine Inspection, of which the uncut footage presents the following dialogue.

The reporter in the background: Can I trouble you to speak Mandarin?

The officer to the manager of Canrong in Chaozhou dialect: You speak Chaozhou dialect with ease. Let him (the bookkeeper, the other official) write whatever he wants to write. Let's meddle things around, and the trouble will pass. Just say there is no such person called Xu Chuangshen. The person is a fiction. Say you have never produced such medicine.

The Bookkeeper: But how are we going to explain the receipt?

Officer: Have you used this invoice before? Which date? November 2000? Just say that the stamp has nothing to do with your company. You haven't used this stamp since 1996.

As a northern Chinese, the reporter does not understand the local Chaozhou dialect. The scene makes sense to him only after he returns to Beijing, when someone familiar with the dialect exposes the fraud. The documentary ends with a promise made by the Director of the Bureau of Medicine Inspection in Puning that the local government has established a special committee to investigate the case. The reporter comments that 'his promise makes us believe that the case will be cleared up and that the people involved in the production and distribution of fake medicine will not escape punishment'.

In discussing how it is possible for fake medicine to enter the market, the guest for the episode, Professor Qu, points out that cover-ups by local government have made the system dysfunctional. He explains further that the central government has various kinds of punitive control for such crimes, ranging from heavy fines to the death penalty. By way of conclusion, the host lists government achievements for the previous year, including the handling of about 50,000 cases, worth 40 million *yuan*; the arrest of around 1,000 people; the suing of 197 companies for producing fake medicine; and the termination of 14,219 distribution contracts. So much, the viewer may be tempted to say, for traditional morality in China. The episode ends by pointing out that the media has played its role in guiding public opinion and, by doing so, stabilising society.

(3) The episode *Wang Honger de bugui zhi lu* / *Wang Honger's Road of No Return*) tells the story of a murder committed by a desperate woman. The documentary conveys three messages: rape needs to be reported; bigamy is a crime; and a woman should ask for custody of her children and a fair share

of finances and property in the case of divorce. These three messages are delivered through a portrayal of a rural woman who has killed her ex-husband. As usual, the episode starts with three images presenting the major parties involved in the case.

- Image 1: A policeman describing the murder as 'very cruel' against the caption 'With a single wave of her hand, her ex-husband passed away'.
- Image 2: Wang, in hand-cuffs, weeping, says 'I have suffered too much', with the caption reading 'Whispering her secret with a sigh of regret'.
- Image 3: Wang's daughter's memory of happier days with her parents. The opening lures the viewer into Wang's secret motivation for the murder, the caption reading 'She has suffered; she has also been loved; why choose murder?'

Wang's story is presented in a realist manner by a non-sympathetic male voice, the reporter. Images are the collections of Wang and her husband's residences in their rural home town in Anhui and Shanghai, with cuts in between the interviews of Wang, her children, her husband's second wife and policemen. The less than 15 minute documentary begins with Wang's confession in the police station on June 13 2002. Eighteen years ago, Wang recalls, she was a raped by the man who later became her husband. After she discovered that she was pregnant as a result of the rape, Wang married the rapist. Though they lived in rural hardship, Wang conceded that the first 15 years of marriage were reasonably happy because of her husband's devotion to their three children. In 1996 the husband left the village for Shanghai. Two years later Wang is told that her husband is living in a de facto relationship with a younger woman. In disbelief, Wang travels to Shanghai, only to return to her village realising that her husband has started divorce proceedings, claiming custody of their three children and all of their finance. Wang accepts his demands for the sake of her children. She starts a new life in China's northwest. Two years later, the husband calls her, asking her to abandon her job and new family in order to return to him. He offers her the chance of remarriage. However, Wang soon discovers that the husband has no intention to divorce his younger wife. With memories of having been raped, forced into marriage and divorce, and betrayed once more, Wang is unable to suppress any longer her tortured feelings and assaults her ex-husband with a hammer until he is dead.

The discussion of Wang's case focuses on female crimes in China, and their relation to gender difference. No doubt, Wang's tolerance reflects the traditional moral rules for women, the 'three forms of submission and four virtues'. From the point of view of traditional morality she has done everything to serve her husband's needs! Wang's case is an example of the negative consequences that adherence to traditional moral codes can have on women. Interestingly, neither the host nor the guest speaker mentions the role that traditional patriarchal culture plays in such cases. Instead, their explanations remain within the confines of the debate of the 'natural' characteristics of the female sex. This may also indicate that the state is reworking elements of an existing 'moral' public culture about men and women into its current citizenship education, without cognizance of the global debate on gender.

According to Professor Li, the guest speaker of the episode, the weakness of women, in tolerating violence and repressing their needs inevitably leads to social catastrophe. Leaving aside the question whether this is a characteristic unique to the female sex, the result of biological factors, or shaped by the cultural environment, Li argues that Wang's murder is caused by years of tolerance and repression of her husband's crimes of rape and bigamy, and the loss of her children. In her transformation from 'an obedient, dutiful and kind woman' to a murderer, Wang is said not to be uncommon among female criminals. A list of women's crimes is provided on the screen to demonstrate the relationship between women, crime and personal relationships.

- The two most common crimes perpetrated by women are murder and financial fraud.
- 60% of women who commit crimes are married;
- 60% of violence and murders are caused by unhappy marriages and love relationships;
- Victims are usually close associates, including husband, lover, and children.

In Li's analysis, the suggestion that women should use the law to protect themselves is based on the traditional assumption in patriarchal culture that women are naturally weak. Wang is shown to be a victim of traditional morality. To avoid the tragedy, Li suggests that Wang should have sought legal protection at least three times in her life: after she was raped; after she discovered the fact that her husband was living in a bigamous relationship; and during her divorce. What is new is that 'legal consciousness' is now encouraged to enter the private domain, such as the domestic relationship between husband and wife. Yet 'thinking about laws' is still articulated from the perspective of traditional moral assumptions about gender. Concluding the episode, the host concludes,

> We all have misfortunes in life. Women have more misfortunes than men. In addition, women's ability for bearing misfortunes is inferior to that of men. When facing misfortunes, we should remember that every choice we make leads to options that will change our fate. So the best way to protect oneself is to use laws.

Narrative structure

Two narrative patterns are dominant in these documentaries. The major pattern portrays how and why a perpetrator has committed a crime. The minor narrative pattern is often used for the investigation of a dispute. In both structures, some incidence of injustice usually opens the story. We witness actual events, actual people, in specific temporal frames and specified spatial co-ordinates. The story *Wang Honger's Road of no Return* is a typical example of the first narrative type. The reporter gives the date and the place where Wang Honger, in the company of her daughter, tells the police that she has just killed her ex-husband. The story then explores the reasons why Wang has committed murder against the background of her being por-trayed as a 'kind', 'submissive wife and dutiful mother' and her ex-husband as 'hardworking' and 'always willing to help others'. A similar story (5 December 2001) deals with a woman who has killed her second husband in order to protect her first disabled spouse. Again, the reporter investigates the motivation that has led a 'kind and dutiful wife' to commit murder. In each case, the reporter's narrative is based on data available in police and court documents and recorded during interviews.

The other, less frequent structure, the one concerned mainly with some kind of legal controversy, typically shows how an investigator presents a disputed case and interviews the various parties involved, including third parties and witnesses who present their views. The law is usually portrayed as providing a solution to the dispute. *Ocean Accident* and *The Origin of Fake Medicine* are two examples in this narrative pattern. Another repres-entative episode in this mode is the case of a resident who sues her district security for failing to protect her home against robbery (10 April 1999). After the court decides that her evidence is insufficient a jurisprudence expert explains the court verdict. In another case, a child is the victim of alleged medical malpractice in the Yidou Central Hospital in Qingzhou (24, 25 April 1999). During a small operation the boy is given an anaesthetic overdose resulting in brain damage. The parents complain to the local police. After an investigation a comprehensive, written report is submitted to the court. When the Bureau of Health is informed about the case they object to the intervention of the police, arguing that they should have been approached first. A dispute arises about which legal procedure is applicable for such medical accidents, criminal law or ordinary regulations. Yet another case in this mode deals with an eight year-old girl who is seriously injured by a motorbike in a National Park, in Shenzhen (10 May 1999). When the parents sue the National Park authorities for damages a dispute arises as to where the complaint should be lodged. The park authorities argue that such a case is not covered by park regulations but falls under general civil or road accident law and therefore is a matter for the police who should apprehend the motorcycle rider. In the end the court decides that all three parties are responsible to some degree, the parents because they have neglected their duty of care, the park authorities because the accident occurred within the park precinct, and the motorcycle driver because he failed to drive with caution.

In all episodes, the investigator's narration is the dominant voice within the 15–20 minute time frame. The interviews are selected for the reporters to demonstrate different sides of the argument; the interviews are highly focused, direct, with no additional, alternative or multiple explanations. The reporters have very clear aims, the messages they present are straightforward and the style of the investigation is kept simple. There is no room in these narratives for psychological development or other forms of narrative evolution. A glance at the basic facets of documentary narrative structure will support these summary observations.

Documentary style

- Tight image sequence of 15–20 minutes;
- News report style of documentary: narration by the reporter dominates; images and interviews are selected and cut to fit the narration;
- No location sound except during interviews;
- Although the narration tends to be fast (a complicated case explained within 15 minutes), it appears 'objective' and 'calm' in the style of news presentation; most of the reporters are invisible; they tend to be situated as sympathetic to the victims and seem to know who the perpetrator is from the beginning, quite apart from the process of investigation;
- Real events (location and time are actual); the parties involved do exist;
- Opening questions – what happened? Followed by an investigation of motivation and who is responsible for the crime;
- Cause and effect relations: every cause is shown to lead inevitably to an effect(s); the impression of documented event and an investigation contradicts the fact that all the events, as well as their investigations, have been completed before shooting the film;
- Cases are sometimes unfinished either because the courts have not yet given a verdict or because the perpetrators have disappeared;
- The majority of cases happen in the rural areas; or in small or medium cities; 99.9 per cent of cases involve lower middle class families; few celebrities appear in the stories;
- Corruption cases mainly refer to the lower cadres, such as village chiefs, township Party secretaries, low-ranking clerks in legal institutions, and lower rank of policemen;
- Cases of civil law are the rule: family issues (children and parents; marriage, extra-martial affairs, divorce, adoption, children or senior parents rights); business (fake products; contracts); disputes (between relatives, the neighbourhood etc); accidents (traffic accidents, work related accidents);
- Violence and sex are barred; most cases are unusual, some have comic effects, most are attention grabbing: vistas of private backyards, portraits of uneducated peasants, rural leaders, exploration of corruption, family gossips, the display of emotions, such as anger or despair.

Typical events, acts, and agents

1. Haozhuang xiangshui yu Village in Taiyuan has rat problems apparently caused by the pillows used by the villagers (3 December 2001). The reporter interviews the workers in the pillow factory, who it turns out never use the pillows themselves because they stuff them with biodegradable rubbish. Using a hidden camera, the reporter interviews distributors and retailers at the market and more than ten shops to find out if they are aware of the fraud. The reporter then hands the case over to Consumer Affairs, which bans the pillow production and fines the factory owner.

2. A man receives a letter from his father who had died 11 years ago (1 November 2001). Making matters worse, his bad relationship with his late father had been caused by this missing letter. The son sues the Post Office. In the interview the son argues that the Post Office must be at fault if it took the letter 22 years to arrive. The Post Office manager defends himself by pointing out that the postal staff of 22 years ago had all retired and some had died, so how could he be held responsible. The son insists on a *shuofa*, an official reason for the delay of the letter. The court rules that since it is impossible to be accurate about long past events, the complaint is rejected. The discussion supports the court's verdict. What is noteworthy in this case, I think, is that the Post Office manager defends himself and his office as a group of persons rather than an institution. His emphasis on persons rather than structures appears symptomatic of a society that is only now beginning to think in legal rather than primarily in moral terms.

3. On World AIDS Day, 1 December 2001, a programmes is screened portraying Wenlou village in Henan (population 800) where two-thirds of the population are HIV-positive. The cause of the disease is traced to the villagers' habit of selling blood to untrained blood bank personnel. The documentary first shows the details of the blood trade, then switches to a national report on the 600,000 AIDS patients in China. Two blood merchants admit that they were not aware that they were breaching any law; all they wanted was 'to earn some money'. The two are charged and are shown to be awaiting a court verdict.

4. Zhou Litai, a philanthropist lawyer in Shenzhen, has offered shelter and legal representation to a group of about 100 disabled workers who are waiting to receive compensation (2 December 2001). When asked about his clients Zhou claims that 'only 60 out of 500 have gained compensation'. The interviewed plaintiffs offer a similar picture: they are typically out of work; in their early twenties; with family responsibilities; waiting for a court decision. The concluding discussion addresses existing labour laws and the correct procedure for compensation claims. Here traditional morality can be said to have been violated by the employers, but it lacks the specificity required for decisions on appropriate

compensation, a case where the new legal procedures are indispensable for a just outcome.

5. A two and half-year-old child dies after falling from a balcony when the nanny goes to take the rubbish away (16 December 2001). A number of interviews flesh out the background to the accident: the child's parents say that they had not asked the nanny to do any work except looking after the baby; the nanny, a 50-year-old woman from the country is crying helplessly, unable to speak; the court rules that she has to pay RMB 60,000 compensation; her husband says to the interviewer, 'her fault is that she has been trying to do too much'. The discussion informs the audience that Shenzhen has just passed China's first nanny regulations, including rights and duties of nannies. This is another case, where specific laws are beginning to regulate social relations in a way unachievable by any vague moral consensus.

6. A man takes a five star international hotel to court (4 February 2001). Having done some shopping the man enters the hotel garden for a rest, where two security guards ask him to leave, explaining that the garden is reserved for hotel guests. They also point to a sign written in Chinese supporting their demand. The man then sues the hotel for offending Chinese national pride. In support of his complaint he says that since the sign is written only in Chinese rather than in Chinese and English, as is the custom at international hotels, it reminds him of a Chinese sign put up by the French in a park in Shanghai in 1850 that read 'No Dogs and Chinese'. The reporter informs that the man's case is supported by a large number of ordinary citizens. The court however disagrees, ruling that Chinese signs are not exclusively meant for the Chinese. While the discussion that follows airs feelings of national dignity, the legal expert suggests that it would be wise to restrict questions of national pride to incidents of greater import. Perhaps a point being made here by the law specialist is also that personal moral outrage becomes an immoral use of the court system if it is out of proportion in comparison with the suffered offence. This implies that a new sense of morality has to be taught together with the law education.

7. In Gongyi, Henan province, an old man drives without a licence and kills a person on the road (7 December 2001). His son goes to the police to confess to having caused the accident. He is sent to jail, while the daughter-in-law, deprived of a husband, fights with the father. Later, the daughter-in-law tells the truth to the police. The father asks whether he can go to jail so that his son could be released. However, now his son is charged with concealing a crime. When the villagers are interviewed they refer to the proverb *Fu zai zi huan* (A father's debts are paid by the son). In their view, the son behaved responsibly, and he should not be punished for his filial piety. The discussion addresses the question why a proverb encapsulating high moral standards should be declared invalid by the new legal processes of a market economy, a tension between

morality and law that will inform the legal transformation of China for some time to come.

8. A 87-year-old sick lady, a widow of 58 years, takes her 63-year-old son to court for failing to look after her (6 February 2001). The son explains that he has an agreement with his elder brother who is to care for their mother in exchange for inheriting their mother's property after her death. The court rules in favour of the old woman, arguing that the agreement between the two brothers is illegal. The discussion emphasises that nobody has a right to ignore the duty to look after parents. Whether there is any legal basis for the judgment is unclear. It would seem that in this case the court is guided by a sense of traditional morality rather than any specific law.

9. A man leaves a will according to which his superannuation and half of the property are to be given to his de facto spouse (with whom he has a four-year-old daughter, whom he has treated well, though he has never acknowledged her publicly) (26 November 2001). His legal wife discovers the will after his death and challenges the will. The de facto spouse takes the wife to court, but only attends the court at the beginning of the case where she faces pressure from a hostile public. The popular opinion is that the court should protect the wife even if the marriage had not been satisfactory and in spite of the fact that the husband had requested a divorce, which however was rejected. Some community members are outraged that a mistress should be able to sue a legal wife. They are concerned that if the de facto spouse were to be successful in her claim this would amount to society supporting the legitimacy of having a mistress. After the hearing a clear majority of people attending the case applaud the court's decision that the man's will is illegal. In the discussion, existing marriage laws are explained and the notion of a de facto relationship rejected as inappropriate for Chinese society. Only time will tell whether the law will be modified in the future to provide more differentiated guidance for judges in such cases. As matters stand, traditional morality here clearly has the upper hand.

10. A dispute has arisen between an 87-year-old woman who loves a tree she planted many years ago and from which she earns a living by selling its fruit. However, her brother's son claims that the tree belongs to him as it is in his garden (7 February 2001). According to forest law, the tree belongs to the woman, but according to the land law, the tree belongs to her nephew. The court decides that the tree belongs to the old women, but the profit from selling its fruit must be shared between the two families. The host of the episode reports that the old lady had died two months after the court decision, perhaps because she could not bear the thought of strife between the two families and concludes by saying: 'I believe laws can solve certain problems, but shouldn't we be more tolerant, more giving and loving when we face disputes between friends and relatives?'

At the end of many of the episodes of *Legal Report* the discussion addresses the fact that awareness of the law has certainly increased and that it is useful to know how to use laws to solve specific problems. At the same time, the discussion acknowledges that traditional thinking, which tries to avoid such problems in the first place, still has a role to play in Chinese society. And this is why, the host usually argues, we should continue to support people who defend some moral values, no matter whether they win or lose in court. Other episodes address such matters as China's entry into the WTO and the effect of this event on Chinese laws; copyright laws and pirate control; extra-marital affairs; a girl suing her parents for not providing tuition fees; a tourist taking a travel bureau to court for false advertising; a woman filing a complaint against the wine industry for failing to point out that alcohol consumption may lead to death; and hundreds of episodes in a similar vein and on a broad spectrum of social events.

Thematic and audience response

All episodes of *Legal Report* are constructed, as we have seen, as variations on the theme of the tension between traditional morality and the new legal process. Depending on the topic of each individual case, the different structural components of the episode are weighted towards the one or the other. As a result, *Legal Report* as a whole presents a picture of morality being tempered by laws and the law as modified by moral expectations. It is this common theme that sharply distinguishes *Legal Report*, as well as the entire Chinese citizenship education campaign, from the citizenship debate in Europe and the Anglosphere with its current emphasis on citizenship beyond national boundaries. Another important message we take from the Chinese law programmes is that television audience feedback is not merely an incidental, additional attraction to keep the ratings up, but an integral feature that affects the didactic effectiveness of each episode, as well as the task of legal consciousness raising of the series as a whole. By involving the viewers on a massive scale via email, telephone and letters, the editors are able to plough public response back into the evolving series, resuming topics, referring back to earlier discussions, and keeping the debate topical and alive as if in a vastly extended college lecture theatre.

Narrative formula

If we distil from the empirical story materials the core pattern we arrive at a succinct narrative type. From a narratological perspective, the myriad variants of *Legal Report* share a common structure that can be summarised into a formula with ten main ingredients, as follows: (1) an initial situation of injustice or suffering (a crime, a dispute, an accident, a moral infringement); (2) a confrontation between one or more perpetrators of a crime and its victim(s) or between opponents in a dispute; (3) an investigating reporter;

(4) interviews; (5) a court verdict (given or pending); (6) an expert providing specialised legal knowledge; (7) a discussion of the case and its legal and moral implications; (8) a tension between traditional moral expectations and the legal process; (9) audience response; and (10) an overarching ideological, didactic component: citizenship education in matters legal.

In the fleshed out individual episodes these core ingredients all play their part in the forging of a new kind of citizenship through media pedagogy. What is new in these exemplars and their emphasis on morality is the legal argument introduced by professional experts and a certain degree of democratisation via investigative journalism and audience feedback. In this way, *Legal Report* can be said to make a significant contribution to the creation of a shared cultural citizenship through the medium of television. In its one thousand plus episodes to date *Legal Report* reflects an anxiety deeply embedded in the social pathology of Chinese society today. On the one hand, there is the realisation by government, the intelligentsia, and the leadership in technology and commerce that the development of a complex network of laws and legal processes is a *sine qua non* if China wishes to compete successfully in the global economy. On the other hand, China fears that the shift towards a legally managed rather than authority controlled social system could seriously damage its time-honoured, pragmatically proven, and all-pervasive, ideational system of traditional morality. As my analyses, as well as the overview discussion of a number of episodes shows, the dialogic tension between law and morality is not only present as a motif in every single episode of *Legal Report*, it informs its every structural feature from the reporter's data collection to audience feedback. The staggering popularity of *Legal Report* can now also be traced to a highly formulaic narrative structure able to meet a number of viewer expectations at the same time: informative topicality, practical applicability, legal and moral pedagogy, and narrative entertainment. In this, the programmes revive, in a televisual mode, the traditional Chinese demand on art to *wen yi zai dao* ('art must convey a moral message').

In conclusion, what are the effects of this kind of citizenship education? Or, to speculate about government expectations in sponsoring such *programme*s, what is the political purpose behind *Legal Report?* Perhaps the following summary propositions will provide at least a tentative answer to both questions. Internally, that is, nationally, the consistent thematics and didactic direction of *Legal Report* appear to achieve a new social awareness that combines increasing knowledge of legal processes with traditional moral values, perhaps resulting in a renewed social cohesion. Externally, that is, internationally, it is no accident that *Legal Report* should emphasise something that is essential to the functioning of late capitalist democracies: an intricate web of laws and a complex hierarchy of juridical institutions that regulates it. Instead of aiming for Western global citizenship aspirations, however, China appears to have embraced the more realistic goal of achieving compatibility in cultural, political, technological and economic domains.

In this, the kind of law education offered by *Legal Report* plays a crucial and effective role. While it is true to say that the notion of the 'dignity of the law' is foreign to China, it is equally true that the dignity of morality remains a mainstay of Chinese thought. The documentaries on law, it would seem, very much support this observation.

6   Documenting the minorities

Introduction

Documentaries on Chinese minorities are a good illustration of my theme that Chinese documentary films are evolving from a dogmatic mode towards a multi-voice or polyphonic style. Members of the minorities themselves are beginning to contribute, mostly to the latter style, as participating subjects and as directors of films. Throughout this evolutionary trajectory from 1949 to the present, documentary films on minorities are produced in accordance with the political and economic conditions of the time. In the planned economy, such documentaries are designed to illustrate and promote the CCP's policies on minorities. Minority groups are shown supporting the Party leadership; actively contributing their share to the heroic socialist construction programme, to political movements and economic reforms; and enjoying and appreciating a better life in the new China. In the planned economy, themes and stories are framed within CCP policies, while the presentational mode is dominated by the monological voice of a narrator whose utterances are neither contradicted nor even qualified. There are no interviews and the entire film typically offers a top–down perspective of minorities as objects of authoritative as well as authoritarian depiction. More recently, government directed and sponsored minority representations have changed to the degree that they now contain interviews with local people expressing how they are coping with the demands of the market economy, that is, the tourist industry. Typically, these films portray minorities as flourishing in the new socialist market, which allows them to maintain and display their traditional cultures as a tourist commodity, with an emphasis on their harmonious coexistence with the Han majority and on the theme of the unity of China. Such films are produced mainly by the CCTV under the term *zhonghua minzu da jiating*, understood as the big family of the nation made up of different Chinese ethnic groups. Here, *minzu* should be understood as including such notions as 'people, ethnos, nationality, nation and ethnic group' (Luo 2005: 1).

At the same time we now witness the rise of documentary films representing minorities from a non-government perspective. Examples include documentaries portraying the market economy as a threat to the traditional lifestyle of minorities and highlighting the differences between urban and rural China. Examples of this type of semi-independent filmmaking are the documentaries of Zhou Yuejun and many others. A further step towards the freeing of government constraints in the documentation of minorities are films produced from within university research centres funded by external sources. An example of this kind of development are the films led by Yunnan University with funding from the University of Goettingen, Germany, and by Professor Guo Jing at the Social Science Academy founded by the US Ford Foundation. What is remarkable about these films is that members of the minorities themselves are starting to participate as filmmakers.

Historical and political context

Documentaries about minorities play a significant role in Chinese screen culture. Internationally they present the case for China's identity as a unitary country with ethnic plurality. Domestically they demonstrate each ethnic group's special political and cultural location in relation to the People's Republic as a whole. From the perspective of film culture, these documentaries enrich the cinematic variety and richness of the nation, and from the view point of the economy they enhance the Chinese national industry by providing products that appeal to wider markets. China now has 56 officially recognised ethnicities distilled from the 400 self-claimed nationalities of the early 1950s. Fifty-three out of the 56 ethnic groups live in the provinces mostly along the national boundaries, and mostly in the western region of China. Apart from Han, the remaining 55 minorities share about 64 per cent of the national territory, yet they make up less than ten per cent of the nation's total population. Because of their geographic locations they play an important role in the stability and the defence of the nation and, in addition, in the overall picture of the Chinese economy. Although people from the minorities are increasingly moving into the urban areas, the majority remain in their rural and remote regions, typically in plateaus, high mountains, grasslands, the desert and other dry stretches of land in Xinjiang, Gansu, Ningxia, Qinghai, Tibet, Inner Mongolia, or in the tropical forest regions of the table hills of Yunnan, Guangxi, and Sichuan, as well as in the deep forests in the northeast. Their main productivity lies in agriculture and animal husbandry, as well as in the craft industry and small trading.

Interactions between the Han and the minorities have a long history. In many ways, China's imperial history is a tale of Han territorial expansion as a result of battles and wars with the minorities. Although the Han were for a while ruled by the Mongols, the Manchu and other minorities, the Han have continued to see themselves as the Centre under the heaven, distinguishing themselves as *zhuxia* from surrounding ethnic groups, the *siyi* foreigners at four frontiers, *yi, man, rong, di,* that is, the east, south, west and north. This kind of description can be found in the earliest ethnographic records of China. To cite from the *Liji: wangzhi*, an ancient Chinese book written about 2000 years ago during the Han dynasty,

> People in the east, known as *Yi*... grow long hair hanging down over their necks, they have tattoos, and some of them eat their food without cooking. People in the south, known as *man*, tattoo their foreheads and cross their feet when sleeping, and some of them also consume their food without cooking. People in the west, known as *Rong*, grow long hair hanging down over their necks and wear pelt, and some of them do not have grain for food. People in the north, known as *Di*, wear feathers and live in caves, and some of them do not grow grain as food.
>
> (Hao 2005: 3)

In addition, the Han also distinguished the minorities according to whether they had been Hanised, and whether they were dealing with the Han, absorbing Han philosophy and technologies as a result of war or the tribute system. Indeed, it was the political and cultural standards of the tribute system, the *tusi* system, and the *jimi* policy, developed and modified in various dynasties, that proved the most effective ways of expanding the Han territory, consolidating Han authority, as well as settling conflicts and problems at the frontiers (Luo 2005).

In contrast, the CCP and its government adopted a different approach to the minority question. Following Marxist theory, the CCP interpreted differences in ethnicity and religion between the Han and the minorities primarily as differences in social class. The Party acknowledged that the minorities had throughout history been exploited and oppressed by the ruling class of the Han. However, they were quick to point out that the Han by no means had a monopoly on exploitation. The elites of the minorities, such as feudal autocracy, religious leaders, and landowners were likewise identified as social oppressors. In addition, the presence of Western imperialists since 1840 had further strengthened the authority of the ruling class. This is why the CCP strongly encouraged the minorities to participate in the Communist Revolution in order to overthrow the governing bodies of the Han, the rulers of minorities, as well as the imperialists and to build a new nation under a proletarian dictatorship. The Party's strategy of using class differences to replace differences in ethnicity, ethnic culture and religions gained the support of the minorities in the Long March during the 1930s. It is in this context that we should view the 1940s establishment of the Communists in the liberated areas in the South, Northwest and the North. Notwithstanding various kinds of political and cultural opposition by the minorities, the CCP gained sufficient support from the minorities themselves to allocate them a place in the new political order of the People's Republic with the establishment of participatory autonomous districts, counties and regions after 1949.

Acknowledging ethnic and religious differences between the Han and the minorities by establishing autonomous administrative regions however in no way hindered the Party's political and economic vision. Placed under the National People's Congress and the Central Government, the autonomous regions were, and remain to this day, subject to the central political and economic plans. Since 1949, the minorities have participated in the national political movements and economic programmes in land reform, the Great Leap Forward of the 1950s, the Cultural Revolution in the 1960s and 1970s, the economic reforms of the 1980s, as well as the emergence of a socialist market economy since the 1990s. These movements and reforms, plus the establishment of a centralised national education system, the promotion of Mandarin as unifying national language, and the domestic mass migration programmes from Han areas to the autonomous regions during the 1950s and 1970s accelerated the breakdown of ethnic differences and the political integration of the nation (Ren and Zhou 2003: 170–75, 253–58).[1] Nevertheless, since 1949 the central government has implemented various programmes to preserve the ethnic cultures of the minorities, including their languages and religions. Yet again, no matter how much ethnic autonomy is granted the minorities, their new status is designed fundamentally to contribute to the consolidation of the image of China as a unitary country with ethnic plurality.

The economic reforms of the 1980s and subsequent market economy signalled a new relationship between the Han and the minorities. While in the planned economy the central government can be credited with trying to achieve a balance between the well-developed regions in the east and the less developed west, where the majority of the minorities live, market competition has significantly widened the economic gap between east and west China. The fast developing east is increasingly demanding natural resources from the west at low prices. Lack of sound infrastructure, poor production conditions, dependence on soil and weather, and with agriculture as their main source of income, the west is unable to compete with the rapidly industrialising and urbanising east. Furthermore, voluntary migrants flown from the east to the west in search of economic opportunities are intensifying the problems between the Han and some of the minorities. International pressure on China's human rights performance is adding to the existing historical tensions especially between the government and some of the minorities. In particular, a continuing conflict exists between the Chinese government and the Tibetans supporting the Dalai Lama, as well as the Islamic minorities in Xinjiang, who are demanding independence as a new nation under the name of East Turkistan.

To ameliorate some of these problems, especially the clamouring for independence by Muslim groups and the widening economic gap between the east and west China, the central government has committed itself to a series of investments, including infrastructure, education, technology and agricultural development programmes in the western regions. Such radical, top–down interventions however come at a price. They affect the balance between economic development and environment protection. Some of the forest logging is destroying the very livelihood of minorities who raise deer and still hunt for survival. There is a serious conflict between traditional and religious values and modernity; certain traditions are reluctant to embrace the market economy, while religion sometimes sees itself in competition with state education. Lastly, there is a clash between the new consumer culture and minority traditions based on communal rites. This is conspicuously the case where minorities continue to rely on ritual performance instead of medical technology and the pharmaceutical industry.

Ethnographic film: the tyranny of difference

At the heart of documenting the Chinese minorities we find not only issues endemic to Chinese culture and society but also certain theoretical questions pertaining to ethnographic filmmaking as a special form of documentary cinema. The documentaries about Chinese minorities to be discussed later in this chapter, to differing degrees all participate in this genre. So before I embark on a discussion of the details of cinematic representations of minorities in China, I feel it is appropriate to draw attention to at least some of the general theoretical problems faced by the ethnographic filmmaker. I do so partly to provide a general, though minimal, theoretical background and partly to make it easier for the reader to be able to better appreciate the specific conditions under which Chinese filmmakers are working and how these conditions affect their products.

Perhaps the most striking feature about ethnic filmmaking is that it thrives on the sharpening, celebration and often exaggeration of cultural difference. This applies equally to popular films depicting other cultures as it does to the scientifically oriented ethnographic film. Without exception, I suggest, this observation likewise applies to the cinematic representation of Chinese minorities, whether in documentaries produced by official government agencies, by semi-independent filmmakers or by independent individuals. At the same time, it is also important to point out that there is no generally agreed set of principles governing such filmic representations either in the West or in China. Instead, we find in the literature a broad spectrum of opinions ranging from a strictly scientific code for ethnographic productions to the much looser constraints typical of documentaries in the mode of cultural representations.

I want to illustrate this situation with the help of a few examples. According to Peter Fuchs, scientific ethnographic film should be rigorously governed by a number of principles: 'unity of place, time, group, and action, together with strict obedience to the chronology of action in the final version of the film. Artificial manipulation in either shooting or cutting is not permitted. A scientific film rules out the use of staged scenes.' (Fuchs 1988: 222). The position advocated by Fuchs could be called purist, a stipulated ideal that is hardly ever aimed at and in practice never achieved. Certainly, the vast majority of ethnographic films fail to measure up to his strictures. Nor can such rules be laid down for a broad range of popular ethnographic depictions. Nonetheless, citing the conception of ethnographic film held by Fuchs here is not altogether spurious; after all, a substantial number of ethnographic films are produced from within university research departments that are sometimes funded by universities from abroad. I will later refer to the case of film production by the Academy of the Social Sciences in Kunming, Yunnan, as a case in point.

As Karl Heider describes the documentary subgenre in his book *Ethnographic Film*, 'film is the tool and ethnography the goal' (Heider 1990: 4ff). But Heider also makes a much broader claim. For Heider, 'all films are "ethnographic": they are about people.' (5) He refers to this as 'naïve ethnography'. (5) However, he goes on to say, 'the most important attribute of ethnographic film is the degree to which it is informed by ethnographic understanding' and based on 'interpretive holism'. (5–6) Consequently, 'ethnographic film can only be as good as the understanding which precedes the filmmaking.' (10) Heider also suggests that 'no ethnographic film has suffered from focussing too much on an individual and many are flawed by not doing so.' (22) Given the prominence of ethnographic film on television, however, Heider's demand that 'ethnographic film must be supplemented by written material' (127) is unlikely to be fulfilled in the vast majority of screenings. Nevertheless, like most theorists today, Heider is fully aware of the impossibility of accurate ethnographic documentation. 'It is inconceivable', he concedes 'that an ethnographic film could be made in such a way that it did not distort or alter or select its images of reality in a myriad of ways.' (49) As the film director of *Nanook of the North*, Robert Flaherty, once remarked, 'sometimes you have to lie. One often has to distort a thing to catch its true spirit.' (Calder-Marshall 1963). This leaves open the question of whether or not any filmmaker can be trusted in representing precisely whatever the 'true spirit' of an ethnic group might be. So it should not be surprising that in Flaherty's case the critical literature abounds with observations of the inevitability of distortion of ethnic realities by documentary representation. Nor, as will be shown, do the Chinese films about minorities escape this kind of critique.

For Marcus Banks it is important that 'ethnographic films should reveal whole persons, whole objects, whole actions.' (Banks 1992: 119ff). He regards 'any film which represents non-western people doing non-western things' as 'inherently ethnographic.' (120) At the same time he draws our intention to the event of filming itself as a significant part of ethnographic filmmaking. Every filmic event includes 'the fact that a crew has arrived somewhere and has selected some aspects of someone else's life to enshrine on film. . . . Event is thus a category which is precipitated by intention.' (120) And so 'one of the most important things happening in any ethnographic film is the fact that the film is being made at all.' (120) These observations are supported by

John Collier who notes that 'the personality of the filmmaker can still be detected in most documents; the schooled rapport and low-profile "invisibility" of the camera-person does not guard against observational selectivity, and this continues to have a major distorting effect on ethnographic film.' (Collier 1988: 74–5). For Collier 'reflexivity is a fisherman dislodging a stone into a quiet pool teeming with fish that dart into the shadows.' (75). Likewise, the arrival of any Chinese film crew in a remote village in Yunnan, Xinjiang or Manchu will of necessity disturb the web of symbolic interaction that sustains the minority community on a daily basis.

A more sharply critical perspective on documenting the Other is offered by Kathleen Kuehnast. She asks 'who has the power to represent whom and what are the effects of these represented images in shaping our attitudes and our memories about other groups?' (Kuehnast 1992: 183ff). Such a question is indeed warranted if we accept that ethnographic films, like all visual representations, are bound to 'perpetuate dominant ideologies and operate as economic currency' and that ethnographic filmmaking is part of a 'visual imperialism' (183–4). By this Kuehnast means 'the colonisation of the world mind through the use of selective imagery that acts as a representation of a dominant ideology.' (184). Visual imperialism in ethnographic film, then, produces 'insiduous effects' (186). Some of these effects, Bill Nichols has argued, move ethnographic film close to pornography (1991), a thesis vigorously rejected, for example, by Peter Loizos (1993: 206–7). In China, the perspective offered by Kuehnast requires a number of adjustments. First, the question of who has the power of representation has now begun to be answered by a plurality of filmmaking, from official governmental documentation to the most idiosyncratic documentaries using independent, cheap digital video production, as well as minorities filming themselves. Given this heterogeneity in the production of ethnic documentaries, the homogenous ideological critique offered by Kuehnast requires refinement. Second, while there is no doubt that official ethnic representations indeed attempt the perpetuation of China's dominant ideology, this very ideology is both different from the one Kuehnast is pointing to and by no means uncontested. Indeed, we can observe at this very moment something like an explosion of alternative filmmaking with competing ideological commitments. A heterogeneous polyphony of documentary voices is emerging from the dogmatic slumber to which filmmaking had been condemned in the Mao era.

All these general issues and many more specific ones prove themselves relevant to the researcher of the topic before us. There should be no doubt that the complexities of the present, dynamic economic and social conditions of the emerging new China place specific constraints on our brief theoretical excursion. In important ways, documentary ethnographic filmmaking in China reflects the starkly differing styles of the planned economy and its market driven successor. In the next two sections, I will address some of these differences and the kinds of film production that have emerged as a result.

Images of minorities in the planned economy

Screen images of minorities echo political, economic and social conditions of the time. In a broad sense, the unity of the nation is the determining theme for minority representations. Images of the minorities are shown as part of the national news, emphasising the political location of the minorities as part of the nation. Like most news and documentaries at the time, as discussed in Chapter 3, these images are harnessed to promote the achievements of the CCP with regard to their policies towards the minorities. This is why the majority of documentaries focus on how the minorities willingly and actively participate in the nation-building programmes; how they have progressed from backward, feudalist societies to become equal partners in the new China; and how the minorities on their own accord oppose separatist ambitions. Apart from political doctrine, images of minorities are presented as entertaining and as tourist objects, with their living conditions in a natural environment, and their colourful culture demonstrated by ethnic songs, dances, costumes and rituals.

In this chapter I want to focus on the ethnicity side of documentaries for these reasons. When minorities were mentioned in Chapter 3, I stressed their dogmatic mode of presentation. Here, I want to draw the reader's attention to a conflict between, on the one hand, representing minorities as a form of 'scientific' anthropological study, and on the other, as a way of supporting Communist political ideology and its theme of the unification of the nation under CCP leadership. To be sure, the news documentaries of the time do not reflect market demands, nor are they designed to mirror the actual realities of the minorities at the time. Yet gradually, questions began to nag the official conception of the documentary film genre as a result of the rising tension between documentaries made for public consumption and documentaries produced as archive materials for selected policy makers and researchers. Five years after the first economic plan of 1956, Mao Zedong issued instructions to the effect that traditional social structures and lifestyles of minorities needed to be documented as historical evidence for policy makers. This double task of political information and scientific, ethnographic knowledge contained the seeds of generic innovation. The policy was handed to the *Minzu* (Ethnicities) Committee of the People's National Congress, which in turn requested the assistance of some of the nation's leading anthropologists and filmmakers. Since these films were not designed for public viewing, the *Minzu* Committee appeared to feel free to relax the customary dogmatic frame and instead instructed the studios that documentaries had to be 'truthful'. This is ambiguous, if not ironic, in the sense that 'truth' had already been redefined in ideological terms. As to the selection of subject matter and theme, priority was now given to the documentation of ethnic traditional social structure, lifestyle, customs and cultures, especially those already in the process of changing and disappearing. Now the recording had to be 'truthful' as far as actual persons, locations and events were concerned. Re-enactments, so popular in the dogmatic mode, were discouraged. Fictions, subjective views and other products of the imagination were now prohibited. Now cinematic styles were being called for which were simple, natural, without artifice, and conducive to 'truthful' and 'scientific' documentation (Fang 2003: 256; Zhang et al. 2000: 196–7).

Here, it would seem, we have a case where contradictions within a highly controlled political schema lead to changes in documentary film production at a time when outside influences such as film criticism, let alone theorisation, virtually did not exist, with the exception of Soviet film theory. There simply was no critical discourse to contest the orthodoxy of the dogmatic presentational mode. However, as a result of the double standard for governmental in-house productions and productions for the public, the generic tensions between the two modes had to be aired sooner or later. So it may not be too surprising that in 1961, after seven films about the minorities of the Li, the Wa, the Ewenki, the Kucong, the Dulong, the Yi and the Tibetans had been made, the *Minzu* Committee and the Ministry of Culture felt it necessary to call a meeting for a reassessment, with filmmakers and anthropologists from the Beijing Social Science Academy, the Minorities Linguistics Research Centre, the Central Minorities Academy, and the Yunnan Minorities Research Centre. Their debates centred on the following five questions (Fang 2003: 456–63):

- Should film be loyal to historical actuality or to the political perspective that the film enunciates?
- Should film portray the contrast of a minority's social structure and lifestyle before and after the Communist liberation?
- Should documentary film be permitted to incorporate re-enactments when they serve the overall content?
- Should a documentary film cover all aspects of a minority, its social structure, systems of tribe or clan, religion, art, culture, relations and forces of production force, as well as its economic institutions?
- Should such cinematic, scientific studies of the minorities emphasise Chinese educational values or should they demonstrate the artistic aesthetic values of minorities?

The five questions all address a core topic of the documentary genre, the troublesome notion of 'truth'. In the context of the orthodox *dogmatic mode*, this amounts to asking to what extent political ideologies, scientific description and aesthetic values should be allowed to interact. From the perception of the Chinese government, answers to these five questions ultimately rested on how one defines the function and purpose of documentary film. For instance, should images of the Dalai Lama and Bancan Lama be included as important political leaders in representations of Tibetan politics and religion? Should films attempt to document the differences the minorities have experienced between before and after the liberation? Are re-enactments reconcilable with scientific intent and political purpose? And if so, to what extent should they be permitted? (Fang 2003: 456) Such questions also address the issue of intended audience and the purposes the films are meant to serve. The achievement of a close portrayal of historical reality must have been a priority for both policy makers and research purposes, even if policy makers intended to keep such information for themselves and if it was only a select group of privileged scholars that made up the film audience. Significantly, apart from the debate about re-enactments neither generic questions nor ethical concerns appear to have mattered much at this historic meeting. One question of film ethics was raised, though, but only to be resolved in the paternalistic fashion typical of documentaries suitable for the public. The question was whether documentaries should represent things a minority would not like to have recorded and shown. The answer given was that of a parent speaking about small children: 'they [the minorities] may resist now, but they will welcome and appreciate our work in the future' (Fang 2003: 463).

The issue of what can and what cannot be made available for public viewing is consistently illustrated by documentary cinema during the Mao period: the firm belief that cinema as a public space in which specific educational and ideological values are to be instilled in the film viewer, while policy makers and their academic elite could be safely trusted with documented facts. Dogma, then, reveals itself as the transformation of ethnographic documentary records into filmic vehicles of ideological storytelling in which scientific investigation is replaced by the 'voice' of an unerring and indisputable rendering of exotic cultures. Such are the vast majority of publicly screened minority documentaries during that period.

The methods used in the 1950s for producing ethnographic films were not much different from those employed in other documentaries (Zhang et al. 2000: 236–46). They fell within a standard process of writing outlines and shot-by-shot descriptions, followed by shooting, developing, editing and the adding of sound. The written outlines were based on the field research of anthropologists and other academics. The filmmakers would then work with the anthropologists to turn outlines into shot by shot descriptions before selecting representative villages for filming with the assistance of local ethnic cadres and village leaders. In spite of the scientific emphasis, the actual style of filmmaking also involved such things as paying for people to act, and for directing and organising if not pre-staging events for shooting. This can only partly be blamed on a lack of understanding of the concept of documentary or ethnographical films – the term did not appear in China before the end of the 1960s. Such non-documentary intrusions have to do more with the difficulties of transporting camera equipment into the remote areas, persuading local people to overcome their traditional reticence to participate, and a notorious shortage of film stock. However, as Yang Haiguang recalls, (Zhang 2000 et al.: 246–51; He Yuan 2003) some footage, such as that for the film *Wa zu / The Wa Nationality*, was shot strictly by following the filmed subjects according to the film outline, meticulously recording their ways of production, lifestyle, and religious activities. In filming the Kuchong ethnic community, organised shooting is involved but both location and people are actual. Re-enactment was part of the making of *The Dulong Nationality*, where images were needed of Tibetan aristocrats beating Dulong people who were unable to pay them. Re-enactment also occurred when there was difficulty transporting heavy equipment to remote areas. In such cases, the narration is usually written after filming. Here, narration plays an anchor role in that it is always strictly constrained by political principles and typically read several times by various political organisations and their leaders.

After 17 years of filming minorities, Li Yimin summaries three distinct ideological strategies by which images of minorities are presented as part of a cohesive national picture of China (Y. Li 1997: 177–8). In each of these strategies the recurring themes are the liberation from Japanese occupation, and the harmonious relationship with the Han and socialist nation-building programmes. The strategies Li observes are (1) Reconstruction of social structure: ethnicity and religious differences are replaced by *class* identification by foregrounding Marxist class theory. Class theory is also used to analyse the legends of an ethnic group, as well as religious practices, witchcraft and sorcery. (2) Ethnic consciousness is to be replaced by a *national Chinese consciousness*. This is the goal in a number of films presenting the patriotism of ethnic communities under the leadership of the Chinese Communist Party in anti-Japanese battles. (3) The dichotomy between advanced and backward societies is used to replace traditional beliefs by a new trust in *national progress*. Han socialist atheism is contrasted with the feudal, religious superstitions of the minorities.

Given the Marxist agenda of filmmaking during this era, every single documentary reflects in some way the ideological and theoretical commitments to that agenda. For example, in *Xizang Nonglu zhidu / The Serf System in Tibet* of 1960, Li identifies eleven steps by which the social structure is gradually revealed to build up to the inevitable climax of class struggle in the end. The narrative structure meticulously reflects this revolutionary principle: (1) introduction of the natural environment; (2) display of the feudal government, the theocratic class, and the aristocracy, constituting the three groups that make up the ruling elite; (3) representations of the serf class ; (4) production methods and agricultural products; (5) crafts; (6) exploitation of serfs (*nongnu*) by their masters; (7) details of how the three ruling classes exploit serfs; (8) religious belief and temple architecture, as well as the theocratic hierarchy; (9) the lifestyle of the ruling class; (10) hardship and suffering of the serfs, as well as cruel punishments meted out by the legal system; and (11) resistance by the serfs, their struggle and victory (Y. Li 1997: 172–85).

The Serf System in Tibet (1960) is by no means exceptional in terms of the transparency of its ideological superstructure. Marxist class theory and the contrast between the pre-Communist and post-1949 China are the dominant themes pre-structuring the way in which minority societies are portrayed in the films before 1961. Films such as *Wazu / The Kawa* (1957), *Liangshan yizu / The Yi Nationality in Liangshan* (1958), *Lizu / The Li Nationality* (1958), *Ge'er guna heban de Ewenkezu / The Ewenki Nationality near the Ge'er guna River* (1959), *Kucong ren / The Kucong Nationality* (1960), *Jinpo zu / The Jingpo Nationality* (1960), *Dulong zu / The Dulong Nationality* (1960), *Xinjiang xiaheleke xiang nongnu zhi / The Serf System in Xiaheleke County Xinjiang* (1960), or *Xishuangban na Daizu nongnu shehui / The Serf Society of the Dai Nationality in Xishuangbanna* (1962) all reflect this agenda. The dominant themes are a feudal social and political structure, religious rituals, weddings and funerals. While the specifics of the documentaries vary somewhat according to region, tribe, and ethnicity, we typically view tribal alliances, the transition from late-primitive society to a serf society, as in the Kawa and Yi nationalities; traces of primitive social structures in the Li and Jingpo nationalities; or feudal serf systems in Tibetan and Uygur nationalities. The films also capture economic production methods, such as the slash-and-burn agriculture in the Kawa community, the training of deer by the Ewenki; the ritual of the bull sacrifice, the cutting off the bulls' tails, and headhunting among the Kawa; as well as exchange rituals between tribes, religious rites, marriage ceremonies and a variety of other social customs. Seasonal migration, for example, is shown to be at the centre of the life of certain ethnic communities, as in the case of ethnographic documentaries about the Kucong and Oroqen people, depicted in *Kucong ren / The Kucong Nationality* (1960) and *Elun cun zu / The Oroqen Nationality* (1963).

The thematic preoccupation with the periods before and after 1949 gradually diminished. In this respect, 1961 once more proved a turning point in that the focus then was increasingly on typical lifestyles or particular features of the social customs of ethnic communities.[2] For instance, the documentary *The Oroqen Nationality* (1963) highlights the traditional hunting life of the Oroqen, their arranged marriages, weddings and funeral practices, dress, ornaments and handicrafts, and their shamanistic religious performances in tune with the four seasons. The film presents the social system of the Oroqen in its evolution from a hunter and gatherer society to that of an agricultural community, from the equal distribution system of a classless society to its transformation into a class society. Amongst the ethnographic documentaries of the Mao era, *Oroqen Nationality* is regarded by Chinese filmmakers themselves as one of the most successful. Perhaps the reason for this judgment is the fact that the film contains few political messages, focusing as it does on displaying the traditional way of life of the Oroqen. The film starts with a winter image, a master shot of a forest with tents. Then there are a number of long and medium shots of the Oroqen as they are getting ready for the day, walking out of their tents in the snow, and preparing for the hunt. They are shown as they draw a picture on a tree and perform a pre-hunt ritual. There are no intertitles, the viewer's knowledge is provided by the narration. People are shown eating in a communal manner. The food is distributed fairly and equally and as it appears also in sufficient quantity. Hunting scenes are depicted by way of a collection of images of huntsmen posing for the camera, teams on horseback passing by, and shooting poses. Spring scenes follow, with people singing, though we do not hear their songs or music. There is a focus on women and children with contented, smiling faces, and images of children picking flowers. We are told that flowers are regarded by the tribe as a protection against illness until death. The film viewer also notices that the cameras tend to focus on the personalities of a few selected characters. We see images of the Oroqen building their store houses, highlighting communal collaboration and use. We gather information of gender relations from the division of labour between women and men. Women feed the children, and children are playing and eating on horseback, while adults are busy making shelters for themselves. We are introduced to the inside of the tents, with the male narrator elaborating on each section of the tent and furniture. We are informed that the females sit separate from the men. In the summer and autumn seasons, we see close-ups of women and children in the fields. One of the Oroqen songs can be heard, but is not translated. We see images of the Oroqen shooting birds, and picking up food for their own consumption as well as for trading. There are also images of the Oroqen crafting wood, and making chopsticks, tools, toys and musical instruments. We witness images of the Oroqen giving a mock performance, dressed up in bear furs. The making of fur clothes is another ethnic detail captured for the viewer. The film then provides some in-depth insights into marriage customs. A male matchmaker is shown in the home of a bride-to-be, discussing a marriage proposal, negotiating with the woman's parents. From the narration we understand that women are typically engaged at 15 and all marriages are arranged by the parents. After a few drinks shared between the matchmaker and the parents, the proposal is finalised, and the wedding is ready to begin. The bride and the groom are filmed using one and the same pair of chopsticks to eat a bowl of porridge. The lengths of these shots are such that the editing is in accord with the narration. As a result, our knowledge about the Oroqen is not so much delivered by the images, but by the narration. There is not a single image sequence at long distance or long take to allow the audiences to gain knowledge via the action itself. Within the time frame of about 90 minutes we are informed about the four seasons of the life of the Oroqen. Even in what has been called the most successful ethnographic documentary of the period, then, the viewers are not permitted to judge for themselves from the dynamic image chain. Nor would the prominence of staged performances be a sound basis for such judgment. Rather, we are univocally instructed, a method that not only curtails any interrogative reading but radically reduces interpretive agency altogether.

After the Cultural Revolution, ethnographical filmmaking continues very much in the same manner. While the Cultural Revolution profoundly altered many of China's institutions, as far as ethnographic filmmaking is concerned, no fundamental reorientation is visible either in cinematic theorisation or in documentary practice. Rather, the Cultural Revolution appears as no more than a slowing down of cinematic production, a temporary hiatus, after which the principles laid down in 1961 resurface and production resumes. The period between 1976 and 1980 is characterised by five ethnographic documentaries focusing mainly on the Deng and the Miao nationalities. *Dengren / The Deng Nationality* (1976–77) shows the means and forces of production amongst the Deng people, their family organisation, trading habits, and music. Roughly the same pattern can be identified in *Miao zu / The Miao Nationality* (1978–1980). A much sharper focus on ethnic details characterise such films as *Qingshui jiang liuyu Miao zu de hunyin / Miao Marriage in the Qingshui River Delta* (1978–80), *Miao zu de gongyi meishu / Crafts of the Miao* (1978–80), *Shidong Miao zu de longchuan jie / Boat Festival of the Miao in Shidong* (1978–80), and *Miao zu de wudao / Miao Dances* (1978–1980), where attention is paid to the minutiae of specific customs.

In terms of cinematic style and presentational mode, ethnographic portrayals of minorities in news and news documentaries very much adhere to the standard features of the *dogmatic formula*. Ideologically structured narration is the dominant, common cinematic practice of the time. Images are carefully connected through the largely monological narration and sometimes qualify the narrative monologue. The film viewer is directed by the narration, as is our knowledge so gained. Owing to technological constraints, little location sound and few interviews are shown. Some background music is in fact puzzling, as for example when images of primitive living appear against the background of popular Western music. Documentary convention is also often violated by the practice of posing before the cameras, a feature that reminds us that, traditionally, performance in Chinese feature films tends to be regarded as theatrical. The ethnographic filmmaker of the period apparently does not view such posing as an unwarranted rupture of the documentary brief.

Representations of minorities in the market economy

Since the 1980s ethnographic documentaries portraying minorities have undergone some significant changes. This somewhat simplifies the historical transition period from 1980 to 1993, which I have addressed separately in Chapter 3. Suffice it to emphasise here that as a consequence of the shift towards the new market economy, the media industry entered an entirely different terrain. It was plunged from the dubious security of government control into the unexplored waters of commercial competition. This meant that instead of having to adhere to a fairly simple, even if censorious, set of regulations, the screen industry had to reorient itself towards such notions as popularity, variety, innovation, and ratings. Not that government control diminished overnight. Indeed, a whole range of official guidelines and prohibitions are in place to this day. But such guidelines are now premised not only on greatly reduced government funding but on the demand that studios and television stations respond proactively to market forces and audience expectations. Now the government encourages minority representations that foster economic development in the remote regions and assist in the development of a tourist industry on a broad scale. Even the well-trodden theme of promoting the unity of the nation with ethnic pluralism is now being restructured to emphasise minority problems with which the Han majority is able to identify. The disappearance of tradition, poverty, unemployment, the education of children, success in the market economy, the mastery of Mandarin, dressing, media consumption, access to news-papers, radio, and television, a shared political and economic history since 1949, new diets, the consumption of similar products, and changes in social structures are all topics that are now available to make the document-aries of minority cultures appear very different not only from pre-liberation portrayals but also from the dogmatic formula representations of the Mao era.

What is different now for the producers of minority film is that because the official guidelines are much looser than they were in the planned market, large areas of decision making are left to those in charge of programming and filmmaking. Popular appeal, diversity, competition and technological innovation, as well as the demands and opportunities of tourism now to a large extent dictate the kinds of films to be made as well as their presentational techniques and style. Above all, the economic transformations since the 1980s have resulted in a sharp increase in the diversity of minority represen-tations. The dogmatic, monological formula film is being replaced by a range of films based on a very different kind of thinking. All kinds of new ways of reasoning now affect their production. Under the influence of inter-national models, diverse political, economic, cultural, and practical options, as well as novel equipment are beginning to interact, producing an entirely new palette of cinematic representations. At the same time, the singularity of government instituted studios and television stations is being replaced by a plethora of official, semi-independent and independent production sites, including the recent expansion of film production into the digital video market. Both filmmaking itself and cinematic consumption are in a state of rapid expansion.

If this suggests a change in the Chinese cinema scene from authoritarian control to democratic diversity, this is of course not quite the case. After all, media ownership by and large remains in the hands of the government. And, as a result, government steered documentary film production likewise continues to display the marks of top–down, politically motivated filmmaking. What is new is that in addition to official media programming, reforms within the industry, the emergence of semi-independent filmmaking and private video and sound production companies significantly broaden the spectrum of images that can be offered to the public about the minorities.

One could argue that it is precisely because the non-government owned media industry needs to produce alternative images to be able to compete with government controlled television programmes, non-government production tends to foreground alternative minority representations. In turn, an entire new market can be shown to have emerged ready to respond to alternative cinematic products.

In spite of the explosion of opportunities for all kinds of filmmaking in China in recent years, it appears that the representation of minorities, ethnographic or otherwise, remains uneven. While there is an abundance of films about the Tibetans, Naxi, or Dai, and many others, in comparison there are few films available representing the communities of the Hui. This is the result partly of the resistance of Muslim culture to representation in principle and to what many Muslim people regard as an unwarranted, secular intrusion into their religious communities and partly a result of the reluctance of Chinese authorities to interfere with matters to be regulated by the Hui leadership. Certainly, filmmaking about Muslim minorities in China is a delicate matter. I raise it here because it may appear odd that one of the largest minority groups in China, the Hui, as well as other Muslim communities in various regions of the country, hardly figure at all in documentary filmmaking.

As to the remaining minority cultures, three thematic modes appear to dominate government sponsored cinematic documentations. The first continues a favourite subject matter of the Mao era, namely the promotion of a unitary China with plural cultures. This theme underlies many documentaries, of which the cinematically spectacular *Budala gong / The Potala Palace* (2004) as a recent example. Other films, such as *Xizang wushi nian / Fifty Years in Tibet* (2001) and *The British Invasion of Tibet* (2000) favour the same topic while showing how the minorities have faced problems not unlike those faced by the Han Chinese themselves. In this way, such films tend to conceal actual ethnic concerns. The second theme is tourism, which the government wishes to promote by a series of documentaries characterised by colourful representations of minority cultures, foregrounding customs, such as dancing and singing, weddings and other community events, costumes, art and crafts, as well as a sense of hospitality extended to visitors. The former dogmatic voice of monological narration is replaced here by the promotional voice of advertising, showing minorities as flourishing and picturesque communities open to the nation and the world. Ethnicity is now above all a marketable commodity spiced for consumption. The third theme of documentaries produced under the auspices of the government is mass education about the social structure and ethnic characteristics of minorities. This mode is *informative*, with a nod towards anthropology. Representative examples of such films are Hou Yaojun's *Shandong li de cunzhuang / Village in the Cave*, Liang Shaobo's *Sanjiecao / Sanjiecao, Shenluo Ai! Women de Shenluo / The Deer Story* (1997). One could argue that the information provided is nevertheless steered by a set of political principles, even if these principles are now far less in the foreground and very much toned down in the interest of capturing as broad a viewing market as possible. After all, neither education nor information have escaped the new agenda of the market economy. In particular, audience appeal and visual pleasure as an increasingly popular consumer product are now officially held to be praise-worthy properties of documentary cinema. In the following I offer the reader a series of summary analyses of government sponsored documentaries about minorities which, I think, well illustrate these introductory remarks.

Fifty Years in Tibet is a four episode television series celebrating 50 years of Chinese rule in Tibet. The four episodes in turn show the country during its 'peaceful' liberation, 'democratic' reform, as an autonomous region, and promising a bright future. The first episode concentrates on the historical period from 1950 to 1951, from Mao Zedong's launch of the 'liberation of Tibet' to the signing of the Seventeenth Peaceful Agreement with Tibet. The viewer here encounters two levels of liberation, one that deals with the conflict between the People's Liberation Army and Tibetans; the other, the higher level conflict between the Tibetan government, the religious leadership, and the Chinese central government. On the first level, we are shown the Liberation Army, the soldiers of the Tibetan resistance and the local peasants. The footage consists of images of the Liberation Army entering Tibet in a harsh environment, the crossing of mountains and rivers in winter. The climax is the battle of Changdu on 12 October 1950 between the Chinese Army and the Tibetan soldiers, followed by images of the Chinese releasing Tibetan prisoners, as well as of Tibetan peasants and village authorities welcoming the Chinese army. At the political level, the film addresses the negotiations between the Chinese government and the Tibetan delegation, and the signing of the Seventeenth Peaceful Agreement. The narration draws the viewer's attention to two thorny issues in the Agree-ment, the question of how long the Liberation Army should stay in Tibet, and the status of the Chinese backed religious leader, the Panchan Lama. The episode ends with a medium shot of the Chinese flag against the roof of the Potala Palace.

The second episode shows the historical period from the liberation in 1951 to the establishment of Tibet as an autonomous region in 1959. It shows the transformation of the serf society and the 1959 riots that led to the departure of the Dalai Lama and his entourage of about 100,000 land-owners, theocratic leaders and monks. The episode opens with an analysis of the Tibetan serfdom system combining Tibetan Buddhism and secular rule in a unique form of theocracy. The traditional Tibetan society is por-trayed as consisting of serfs, the serf owners of local governments, religious leaders and aristocrats. The viewer learns that in traditional Tibet five per cent of the population owned all the available land. The film also shows museum evidence and photos of some of the brutal customary punishments still practiced in the middle of the twentieth century, with people being skinned alive, having their hands cut off, their eyes gouged out, and death sentences being imposed for stealing. The viewer is made witness to the efforts of the CCP to encourage the unity of the country, with power sharing between the Dalai Lama and Panchan Lama, to the effect that both religious leaders were to occupy positions of high rank in the overall Chinese political structure. The Tibetan aristocrats are recorded as denying their support for the Liberation Army in Tibet, a situation that is shown to have led to the Army becoming self-sufficient in developing modern agriculture in Tibet. The Army is depicted as instrumental in improving local conditions by offering help to the serfs in health, education, accommodation and employment. In 1956 two opposing positions emerge on political and economic reform in Tibet. One group, represented by the Chinese backed Panchan Lama, is shown to be in support of the reforms, while the other, led by the Dalai Lama, resists the changes. The narration then turns to the support by the USA of the establishment of the Tibetan Independence Army and, in March 1959, the founding of the Tibetan People's Congress. We also learn that the Congress encouraged people to join the military movement to protect Tibetan religion, and assisted the Dalai Lama in his escape from the country, and of the military attack on the Chinese Army in Tibet. Eighteen days after the uprising, the episode shows, the Beijing government abolished the Tibetan government, and within the same year announced the establishment of Tibet as an autonomous region within China. This, the film tells the viewer, brings Tibet in line with the other Autonomous Regions of Inner Mongolia (1947), Xinjiang (1955), and Guangxi and Ningxia (1958). The episode ends with footage of celebrating serfs in tears, happy to receive their certificates as landowners, and united with families no longer separated as a result of belonging to different serf owners.

The third episode documents the progress of Tibet as an autonomous region. It starts with the election of its new government. We learn that 80 per cent of the government representatives are former serfs, and by 2001, 79.9 per cent of the cadres are shown to be Tibetans. The film emphasises education, health, scientific development in agriculture and animal husbandry, infrastructure in transportation, electronic communication, energy development, the protection and renovation of the religious architecture, the renewed development of Tibetan Buddhism, Tibetan language and literature, the founding of research institutions, and assistance of the local craft industry and Tibetan medicine. The final episode 'The Road towards a Bright Future' focuses on the construction of Tibet, with the customary contrast between before and after the 'peaceful' liberation. The documentary makes a special point of how every development is now bringing benefits to the Tibetan people. Footage of the road construction from 1951 to 1954 shows the completion of two roads to Tibet, one from Sichuan, the other from Qingchuan. We also witness the 2000 opening ceremony of the railway project, completed in October 2005 and now open to tourists. We see the first bookshop in Tibet, the establishment of light and heavy industry, electronic development, telecommunications, and hospitals. In addition, the documentary offers statistics on the growing population, usable land, and ongoing projects funded by the Chinese government.

The presentational process of *Fifty Years of Tibet* is in typical governmental style, with narration, interviews and old footage. The narration tends to emphasise a form of poetic and heroic language, relying heavily on metaphor, and ideological, symbolic usage of mountains and rivers to stand for political ideas, instead of information and data to indicate time and place. The music corresponds neatly to the narration, whether we see something happy, heroic, sad, or horrific. The interviews function in the main as witness and evidence supporting the theme and arguments of the film. The persons interviewed appear to have been carefully selected. There are two types of interviewees, Han Chinese who participated in the construction of Tibet in the 1950s period. They tell of the hardship, the poverty of Tibet, and the restrictions following the government's policies with regard to respecting local and religious customs. The second type of interviewees are Tibetans, including beneficiaries of the new policies, the new Tibetan local governmental authorities, policy makers, the professional classes, scholars, historians, doctors, agricultural scientists, technicians, teachers, singers, and monks. The majority of these people came from the serf class and received their education in Beijing. The film also contains a certain per centage of footage shot in the 1950s to 1970s by the Chinese News Documentary Film Studio in Beijing. The contemporary Tibetan images portray mainly the different landscapes, clean and tidy interiors of Tibetan houses, and modern buildings. The presentational style here is characterised by the absence of oppositional voices. There is no mention of the Cultural Revolution or its impact on Tibet. Nor do we learn of the independence movement outside Tibet or of the reactions to it by Tibetans inside the country. The entire series is very much a sanitised version of events in the manner in which Chinese government wishes the nation to see and remember them. Such are the remnants of the dogmatic style that have survived in Chinese cinematic documentation into the era of the market economy.

If it is fair to say that in such documentaries as *Fifty Years of Tibet* and *The Potala Palace* we can recognise remnants of dogmatic filmmaking as the main agenda for presenting minorities, in the period of the new market economy the major alternative trend could be described as propaganda for tourism. *Zhongguo Mingzhai / Famous Villages of China* (2004) is a television series shown on the CCTV's half hour programme: *Zhongguo minzu / Chinese Ethnicities*. The series contains 63 episodes, each depicting the lifestyle of one minority village. The 63 villages of the Bai, Dai, Dong, Li, Jing, Miao, Qiang, Shui, Tujia, Va, Yi, Yao, Zang, Zhuang, Hani, and Naxi are scattered across four provinces in the Southwest, in Yunnan, Guangxi, Sichuan and Tibet.

The episodes show three main aspects of village life, basic economics and means of production, cultural features such as rituals and festivals, the environment, the natural surroundings of mountains, and the man-made environment of village architecture. The episodes usually start with a series of glossy and colourful images of green mountains, blue skies, misty valleys, clean rivers, ancient forests, a white beach, golden terraced fields, with fascinating village architecture favouring wood, natural stone, bamboo or straw, shot against the backdrop of picturesque nature, reminiscent of the *locus amoenus* of European antiquity. Amongst such scenic images, we are typically presented with close-ups of individual villagers, or wide shots of minority groups, in colourful garb and unique national costumes. Slice images of a village dog and a group of buffalo are added to make up a picture of a peaceful world where nature and culture are in harmony, away from violence, pollution, and poverty. Minority rituals and celebrations occupy centre stage in the series. There is an abundance of elaborate ritual ceremonies, as for example birth rites in *Qianhu Miao zai / Miao Village with a Thousand Households*, a wedding in *Duanqun Miao fengqing / Miao Skirt*, an initiation ceremony in *Zhonglu Zang jia / Tibetan Households*, a beauty contest in *Meiren Xiang, Meiren Xiang / Village of Beauties*, and a funeral in *Gebo Yi xiang / Yi Village*. The documentation of folk festivals draws our attention to alternative forms of civilisation in minority villages to contrast with the efficiency based lifestyles of our modern world. All episodes display rich and colourful costumes adorned with animal fur, leather, beans, and silver embellishments amongst the Zang, Miao, Li, Bai, Zhuang, and Dai.

Instead of the primitive agricultural production methods and animal husbandry so prominent in ethnographic film, these episodes foreground the contemporary village lifestyles of the minorities by focus on arts, crafts and tourist hospitality. Each minority is shown to excel in one craft or another. There is a variety of bamboo baskets to be seen in a Naxi village in the episode *Aini meimei / Aini Sisters*, silver craft in *Diaoke shiguang / Carving Time*, wooden Tibetan suture and Tibetan paper in *Junke chuan han / Everlasting Wood Craft*, Tibetan scent in *Tunba cun chuanqi / Legend in Tunba Village*, musical instruments in *Boge Yi xiang / Yi Village*, and sewing with horse hair in *Bangao shui zai / Shui Village*. Motels and restaurants managed by village families are a main theme in *Beauties in Zang Village, Miao Village of a Thousand Households, Ruili Daijia / Dai Family, Shitou zai / Village of Rock, Taoping Qiang zai jishi / Qiang Village at Taoping*. Folk songs and dancing for tourists are at the centre of such documentaries as *Awa renmin cang xinge / New Songs of the Va, Daboqi xiao banding / Miao Stool Dance at Daboqi, Miao Skirt* and *Duchang zai xun men / Tujia Village*.

Almost all episodes contain interviews of local people. Some interviewees express ideas and values easily identified by the Han Chinese, as for instance, young people who do not conceal their desire for a better and more interesting life in *Li Village at Hainan Island.* Some speak of the aesthetic value of historical architecture, indigenous languages and crafts in *Rock City in Baoshan, Zang Village at Ganbao*, and *Wangwei Island*, and of the new entrepreneurial spirit that rules the market economy in *Qiang Village at Taoping, The Beauty Valley in Zang, Shui Village, Dai Village at Ruili,*

Rockie Village, and in *Miao Village of a Thousand Households*. *Zang Village at Wongda* portrays a middle-aged man who intends to start a hot house to grow vegetables. In the interview, his mother supports the idea but does not allow him to borrow money. In the end, he seeks support from his young brother, a monk at a temple, and things turn around. In contrast with ethnographic films, these documentaries avoid the theme of the tribal and communal character or spirit, except for the surface presentation of costumes, village architecture and local production geared to attracting tourists. Although these surfaces differ from village to village, we would not be able to abstract from them the more profound differences that distinguish the traditional cultures of Tibetans, the Li, Miao, Bai, Yao, Shui, Tu, Va, and others.

The people interviewed fall into four different groups. First, there are the young people who speak of their experiences in the city and rural areas, and what they would like to do in future. *The Va Village, Aini Sister, Yi Village at Gebuo, Ni Nü / Zang Village, Li Village at Hainan Island* all select a number of young people who have been to cities for employment and returned disappointed. However, all the young women are presented as ambitious and yearning for a better life than that of their mothers at the village, if only they could change their rural situation. In contrast, a young man of the Naxi minority, Li, praises the contented lifestyle at the village. It is perhaps not an accident that far fewer young men are being interviewed in these documentaries than women. This may reflect the fact that so many more of the young men seek employment in the cities or that the men are less expressive than their counterparts or perhaps even that the women are more determined to change their situation at home.

The second type of interviewees is made up of persons committed to the protection of local culture. In *Rock City in Baoshan* a man in his forties is shown to collect historical materials in order to be able to apply for world heritage status for his village, which is over a thousand years old. In *Ganbao Zang zai / Zang Village at Ganbao*, a doctor uses his own money and the support of an American friend to renovate the 2,500 year old village architecture. A 60-year-old man tells of his life long passion of collecting opera songs from amongst his nationality, *Jing zu*, and studies, researches, and teaches the Jing language which is now in decline.

The third group consists of senior citizens and village heads who are interviewed for their knowledge about the origins and history of their villages, as in *Miao Village at Babei*, and *Beimei yingxiang / Impressions about Beimei*. In *Zang Village* and *Zang Village at Wongda*, the elders and village head introduce local customs and family life. For instance, an old man remarks that respecting seniority at home and reading are the two essential features of his family life. He proudly tells the viewers that in their remote village all young people pass their Tertiary Entrance Examination. In the documentary *Bai Village in Dengruo*, an 82-year-old man is chuffed to be able to let us know that all his grandchildren are at university, and that education is a well-established tradition not only in his own family but in the entire village.

Fourth, we are presented with villagers who tell of their skills in arts and craft production. Some say that they are thriving in the new market economy, as for instance in *Silver Carving at Bai Village*, and *Tibetan Wood Carving of Sutran*. The exception is a musical instrument maker in *Manjiang Yao Zai / Yao Village* who is having difficulty selling his products as more and more people enjoy popular music. On the other hand, sewing minorities' costumes have become one of the major sources of income for women supporting their families, as interviewees tell us, for instance, in *Shui Village*. Lastly, the majority of the interviewees share an engagement in the tourist industry. They typically manage their family motels or restaurants, organise local dancing and singing teams, welcome visitors to local museums, and act as tourist guides. Good-looking, well-spoken and confident in their national colourful costumes, young women are presented as enthusiastic about their tourism jobs in such documentaries as *Tibetan Beauty Valley*, *Stool Dancing at Miao Village*, *Skirt at Miao Village*, *Tujian Village*, *Shui Village at Bangao*, *Dai Village* and *Qiang Village at Taoping*. Middle-aged men cheerfully display their national culture to the outside world in the *Va Village*, *Miao Village of a Thousand Households*, and *Rock Village*. All minorities are shown to be hospitable to the Han tourists, offering rice wine and introducing them to their way of life.

What the programme fails to address is the widespread poverty amongst the minorities. Most images are external, directed at an unpolluted nature to avoid the primitive living conditions of the villagers. We hardly see more than the odd interior of a house at a wedding celebration, with glasses and bowls on the floor. No questions are asked about the precarious balance between local culture, tourism, and the environment. Negative aspects of the market economy are played down, as for example the increase of the gap between rich and poor. What is being promoted in these documentaries is above all the tourism potential of minority cultures and their proactive participation in the new market. It is easy to see that these documentaries are produced according to a recognizable formula, which can be summed up roughly in the following ten points: (1) an opening series of montage images of a village against the background of nature, with a few poetic sentences anchoring the place somewhere between tradition and modernity; (2) a series of montage overview shots alternating between landscape, architecture, and medium or close-up shots of a minority group or individuals in their traditional costumes against a natural background; (3) one or two major personalities are introduced as representing typical life in a village; usually they engage with local tourism, local crafts, or they are village leaders or seniors, whose activities function as threads connecting the display; (4) occasionally there are images of interaction between minorities and Han tourists; (5) amongst 63 episodes, there are only two episodes containing long observational scenes; the majority of shots consists of montage and interviews; (6) cheerful minority music easily identifiable by averagely educated Han Chinese; (7) except for *Qingkou zai shan ji / A Few Things about Qingkou Village*, all episodes are narrated by male narrators, urban and positioned outside the documented reality, idealising, romanticising, and praising the content of village life in poetic terms; (8) there is an absence of social, demographic analysis and comparative perspectives; (9) the exceptional, single female narration in the series is presented from a young, local woman's perspective, but even here the voice appears to function as a stand in for a filmmaker's voice, the reading of an external script which she is presenting to the viewer; and (10) the ubiquitous theme in all episodes of the promotion of tourism.

A documentary film well worth seeing for its spectacular landscape and colourful Buddhist Tibetan culture is *Potala Palace* (2004) produced by the CCTV. The Potala Palace is the focus and background of the documentary against which the filmmaker presents a Tibetan monk's life, as well as the historical and political relationship between the Tibetans and the Han Chinese. The film is narrated in Tibetan by an 80-year-old monk, Byams-pa-skal-bzang, who has lived inside the Palace for almost all his life. *Potala Palace* is divided into an introduction and five sections, Red Hill, White Palace, Red Palace, Birth and Death, and Earthly Life. The documentary opens with a couple of shots showing the old monk climbing the stairs of the Potala Palace from one side of the palace to the other. These images are filmed from low angles and long distance to heighten the grandeur of the Potala Palace against the sky, emphasising the insignificance of human beings. Colours of white, red and blue against the background of echoing Tibetan long horns present a bright, inviting, but also sacred, grand, mysterious and foreign land. At the very beginning of the film, the narrator, Byams-pa-skal-bzang, speaking in his calm, content and rhythmic language, introduces us to his childhood desire to see the Palace, his first reaction in seeing the palace, and his feelings as he is looking back at his 60 years of life inside the Palace. The narrator's authority and legitimacy as narrative voice of the film is strengthened by the close-up images of his weather-worn, wrinkled face and the medium shots of him assisting a young monk to dress in his shawl on the roof balcony of the Palace.

With Chinese and English subtitles preceding each of the five sections, each part relates a different story, from the construction history of the Palace, the functions of halls and rooms inside the Palace, the old man's life, and the longstanding relations between the Tibetans and the Han. The first section, Red Hill, illustrates the early history of the Palace in the seventh century. We are told that the founder of the Tubo Kingdom, the first King of Tibet, Srong-btsan-sgam-po, chose the red hill as the site for the Potala Palace. At the Palace, he marries the Han Chinese princess Wen Cheng after her three year journey from Chang'an to Lhasa in 641 AD. Although the King also had a Nepalese princess as his wife, the old man points out that the Tibetan people were very fond of the Han Princess, referring to her as an incarnation of the white Tara Goddess. On screen, we see the intertitles of an official record.

> In 641 AD Princess Wen Cheng set out on a three year long trek to Tibet. She brought with her classical works on astrology and calculation, books on prescriptions and technology as well as for such crafts as papermaking, carving and brewing (*the rest is shown in Chinese but not translated into English*). These have contributed greatly to the Tang and Tubo economy and culture.

The intertitles further testify to the fact that in 710 AD the thirty-fourth Btsan-po, Khn-srong-Ido-btsan married the Tang Princess Jin Cheng. While the old man is telling the story of how the Han and the Tibetan alliance was established as a result of these two marriages, images of The Uncle–Nephew Alliance Pledge Tablet are displayed on screen. We learn that while the ninth century saw the collapse of the Tubo Kingdom, the red hill has forever remained in the heart of the Tibetans.

This early Tibetan history is told with a mixture of the legendary content of a traditional oral song, wall pictures in the palace, the earliest written records to be found in Tibetan, and a narrative spoken by an official Tibetan historian. The cinematic illustrations are richly coloured images supported by location sound and added music. We hear traditional singing, scholarly analysis and the old man's narration. We see the oral history teller in her blue, white and fur costume singing against the background of the vast landscape facing the snow covered mountains, green grass and sandy ash at the bottom; we see the yellow and red of the wall pictures, and the golden glow of the written records inside the palace. The government sponsored style comes to the fore when we note that the oral history presented by the rhapsode, the scholarly analysis, and the old man's story all produce *one and the same* version of history. As the Tibetan historian states: 'Her [the princess Wen Cheng's] arrival created a solid foundation for relations between the Han and Tibetans, particularly for the later unification of the country.' Thus the documentary legitimates the present status of Tibet as part of China.

While the first section, Red Hill, establishes the uncle and nephew relationship through royal marriages, the following two sections of the White Palace and Red Palace advance the Tibetan historical relation with China first from a feminine point of view and folk knowledge and then a masculine, official and military legitimation of the current political status of Tibet. Two kinds of Tibetan history between the seventeenth and early twentieth centuries are presented in parallel. One is offered via intertitles summing up the significant dates of Tibet's relationship with China and Britain. The other is presented through the personal memories and folk knowledge of the perspective of the protagonist, the monk Byams-pa-skal-bzang. His narrative authority is framed in three ways, by his long life inside the Palace, the construction history of the Palace, and by his intimate knowledge of the functions and history of the main halls, religious statues, gifts, wall paintings, as well as the sarcophagi of past Dalai Lamas.

The old monk tells how he was born into a poor family 200 kilometres from the Palace. At twelve, his brother took him to Lhasa for work. He was sent to the Palace to commence his training as a Buddhist monk in the following year. He does not remember life in the Palace as impressive, though he presents his story without anger or complaint. His description is rich in detail, such as the chanting of sutras, meetings, and service to the senior Lama, strict restrictions (no celebration of the New Year), no reluctance in getting up in the morning, and punishments (being beaten for falling asleep during meetings and chanting), and back pain caused by long hours of sitting. The narrator considers himself lucky as he has only been beaten three times, and successfully passed all his sutra tests on his way to becoming a senior monk. However, a long take of the old monk slowly getting up, pouring himself a cup of milk, drinking and eating alone, and a medium shot of him sitting in a tiny room, a solitary figure looking outside through a miniscule window, suggest quite another side of the story. Longing for a warm, loving home and freedom outside the Palace, he and one of his peers once escaped the Palace in their teens. Hoping to be able to sell their sutras to pay for their journey, they are caught and returned to the Palace. The monk recalls that he saw in his dreams, 'a beautiful young woman brushing past me; I even sought pleasure with her'. This memory is presented with pictures of topless Tibetan women bathing in a lake against the background of a female voice singing a traditional song. This reminds the viewer of the narrator's dream at the beginning of the film, with the first King of Tibet, the handsome and brave Srong-btsan-sgam-po, flying across the valleys on his horse. The viewer of the documentary cannot but wonder at a central contrast in the documentary. On the one hand, there is the image of the weather-worn monk and his romantic fantasy of masculinity and femininity in his youth, together with the luxurious decorations of the living quarters of the Dalai Lama and, on the other, the monk's remark 'all we do is chanting sutras'. Awareness of this contrast is certainly part of the overall 'voice' of the film, urging us to contemplate the question whether this kind of religion has not perhaps wasted this human life, as well as countless others. It is no mere coincidence that this kind of reading very much reflects the official Communist position on religion and its class analysis of society.

The merging of personal, authentic knowledge of Tibet and official Chinese historiography is most evident in the editing of the documentary. The old monk's story of Tibet is intertwined with an official Chinese presentation of the history of the Palace construction. The narrator combines a rare performance of a fire ritual held at both ceremonies of the Palace construction by the fifth Dalai Lama in the thirteenth century and the Palace renovation by the Chinese in 1989. He explains a wall painting portraying the fifth Dalai Lama visiting Beijing in 1645 with 3,000 men and gifts to pay homage to the Emperor in exchange for his official confirmation of the title of local ruler of Tibet. The Emperor Shunzhi is recorded as having granted him 'a cordial reception and bestowed upon him a gold seal and a gold album written in Manchurian, Han, Mongolian and Tibetan, irrefutably confirming his political and religious power over Tibet'. At the same time, intertitles inform us of the historical, political connections between the Han and Tibetans:

- In the thirteenth century, the Yuan Emperor appointed a Central Government Official in charge of Tibet, marking its official incorporation into China.
- In 1642, the fifth Dalai Lama and the fourth Panchan Lama established the Local Regime. Lhasa once again became the political centre of Tibet.
- In 1696 Emperor Kangxi learned that the fifth Dalai Lama was long deceased. Sang-rgyas was severely censured over this.
- In 1751 Emperor Qianlong issued the thirteenth article ordinance for *the Efficient Governing of Tibet*, establishing the Dalai Lama as the political and religious leader of Tibet, and instigated a system to dispatch officials to Tibet.
- In the year 1791 the Emperor Qianlong sent Fu Kang'an and 17,000 men to Tibet to drive out the Gurkha invaders and established a system of drawing lots from a golden urn to confirm the reincarnation of souls in children.
- In 1888 Tibetan troops defeated British invaders in Longtu.
- In 1903 British troops again invaded Tibet. The British encountered fierce resistance from the Gantse Battery. Their supplies and ammunition exhausted, the Tibetans jumped off the cliffs rather than surrender. [In Chinese it is added that] There also were Qing soldiers amongst them.
- In 1904 British troops occupied Lhasa and resided in the Potala Palace. The Tibetan government representative refused to sign the Lhasa Convention.

The film viewer cannot but notice that the narrator hardly comments on the Tibetan relations with Nepal and India. Likewise, there is very little information on the monk's life after 1950. We learn that he went to Beijing to accompany both the Dalai Lama and Panchan Lama in 1950 and that he worked for the Buddhist Association of Tibet, away from the Palace during the Cultural Revolution. All we are told about this period is that 'things happen in the most unexpected ways. Incredibly, the Potala Palace survived China's Cultural Revolution'. Naturally, Buddhism looms large in this documentary. There are the themes of reincarnation and monastic performances filled with rhythmic and mysterious chanting. We see colourful illustrations of life and death and monks writing on sand and swiping away their ephemeral works of art, and we are moved by the monk's solemn monologue:

> My mother brought me into the world after ten months of pregnancy. But she will end up lying naked on the celestial burial platform. A man grows up only to bend low again. His teeth fall out. His hair and beard turn as white as snow. He yearns only for the delights of the past. His cloudy eyes survey the crowding relatives, his shaky hands clutching at their clothes. The air is filled with the breath of Death. A weak and shivering body, he has one final valiant struggle with Death. He breathes his last breath and leaves all behind him. His soul departs his body on its lonely journey. His body is bound with ropes. His old friends fare well him, tears in their eyes. So he leaves his bed for the celestial burial platform. Either his body is taken to the mountain top, a sharp knife slicing through his limbs, his innards scattered over the ground for the vultures and wild beasts to tear apart. Or else his body is thrown into the river, his blood dissolving into the yellow waters while fish and other animals nibble and gnaw at this flesh and bones. Or his body might be thrown into raging flames, his flesh and bones turning to ashes, while earthly men inhale the rising smoke. Or else his body is buried deep in the ground where flesh and blood turn putrid sucked out by worms like bees gathering nectar. You alone are the Saviour. Show us how to escape the cycle of birth and death. I live a good life now, with genuine personal freedom. We are truly our own masters now. You could say this is a brief or a statement. That is about all I can say about my life.

The monk's powerful monologue on death, the cinematographic spectacle, the Palace and landscape, the music and the Tibetan language, and the mysterious religious life lift this documentary well above the official government fare of tourist propaganda. The film viewer cannot but admire the stylish camera work with its wide, medium and close-up shots, and mostly high and low angles, the colour contrasts of white, red, and blue, the snow capped mountains, vast grasslands, and beautiful lakes, the exotic interiors of the temple, the golden sarcophagi, richly decorated halls, religious performances, costumes, and music with Tibetan instruments, and songs in Tibetan. The editing achieves a rhythmic lure, while the dominant, personalised narration differs from the earlier Chinese voice-of the Party style. The monk's individuality contrasts effectively with the formal and official intertitles that provide the historical framework. We find ourselves asking whether the film is primarily the old man's story. His narration no doubt suggests a performative documentary mode with shots of his posing for the camera on the balcony of the Palace, presented in long take. Certainly, the film presents Tibet from a Tibetan's point of view, even if this view is interspersed with an official Chinese historical perspective. This is accomplished without the presence of a single Han personality in the entire documentary. Nevertheless, remnants of dogma shine through the Buddhist imagery. After all, the interlinked discourses of Chinese national unity and the plurality of its cultures, as well as the attractive presentation of Tibet as a place well worth visiting leave no doubt in the viewer as to the film's origin in the Beijing Film Studio.

Semi-independent portrayals of minorities

A very different type of documentary about a minority is *Zuihou de muxi sh zu: guancha mosuo* / *The Last Matrilineal Society: Observing the Mosuo* presenting as it does a strikingly unfamiliar world to the Han Chinese. At the beginning of the film, the narrator informs the viewer that 50,000 tourists have visited the Mosuo society, not because the Mosuo reside by one of the most beautiful and unpolluted lakes in China, the Gulu Lake located 2,685m above sea level, but because of the Mosuo's intriguing social structure, the matrilineal family and the so-called roving match. With a population of 40,000, the Mosuo live a mountain area in southwest Yunnan. About 67 per cent of their families are matrilineal and 70 per cent of the Mosuo practice 'roving matches'.

The film is made from a sociological and anthropological perspective. Neither the government nor any state agency is granted any role on the screen, and there are no political sections featuring village heads or committees. Neither minority education, health, cadres nor police is thematised. The only modern insignia we see on the screen are a television satellite dish, young men's motorbikes, and a few pubs for tourists. At a Mosuo family breakfast a child is filmed reciting a Mandarin text. The filmmaker asks the child what she knows about Beijing. The young girl answers that Beijing has animals, like at her home, ducks and chickens, cows and horses. The interviewer asks the adults whether they knew who the current leaders of China are. No one knows the answer until a family member, a monk, having returned home for breakfast, proudly offers two names, adding that he had seen them on television. While the film does promote local tourism to a minor extent, and there are some shots of the picturesque landscapes, local dancing and singing, the main focus is elsewhere. At the centre of the film is the social structure of the minority, the matrilineal family and the 'roving matches'.

The subtitle *Observing the Mosuo* is not entirely appropriate for what we see, for observation is only part of the documentary. A more distinguishing feature is the interactive format of the film, with its emphasis on personal exchanges with and amongst the Mosuo society. The documentary not only shows us the filmmakers as they follow the unfolding events, but also how they interview the subjects and their participation in a ritual ceremony. There are four sections in the film, the Grandmother Hall (*Zhumu wu*), the Sutra Hall (*Jing Tang*), the Flower Hall (*Hua lou*) and Farewell to the Soul of the Dead (*Song hun*). The Sutra Hall and the Flower Hall sections each are further subdivided into two parts. Apart from the Funeral, the other three sections present a typical Mosuo courtyard. Similar to Beijing's *sihe yuan*, there is a four sided courtyard, with different functions for each of the four side rooms. The Grandmother Hall and the Sutra Hall are dedicated to family and religious activities. The Flower Hall is reserved for women to meet their men at night, while the Grass Building (*Cao lou*) houses the domestic animals. For the Mosuo, the definition of the 'family' is highly inclusive, comprising all persons covering several generations in the hall, pigs, cows, and horses in the stables, and chickens, ducks and geese in the courtyard.

Observing the Mosuo introduces three families. The first two sections, Grandmother Hall and Sutra Hall, tell of the life of the 20-year-old receptionist Bingma and her Mosuo family, spanning four generations. Bingma has a 96-year-old great-grandmother, Ahshi, a grandmother, Ahri, and her partner Ahpu who has finally moved in after many years of enjoying their 'roving match'. Bingma's mother, Ahmi is the head of the family. She organises and largely looks after all the domestic work of feeding 15 people and dozens of horses, cows, pigs, chickens, ducks and geese. Ahmi has five brothers and one young sister, all of whom live in 'roving matches'. The younger sister assists her in domestic work during day time and meets her roving men at night. The five brothers contribute financially to the family, but at night they likewise meet their roving matches and their children. Bingma has four siblings. The section on Bingma's family depicts the daily life of the matrilineal family, where women are the main supporters of the family, and men offer occasional assistance. The filmmakers follow the grandmother, the mother and her younger sister, and Bingma's teenage sister, recording their domestic chores of cutting wood, transporting grass, planting vegetables, sewing, cooking for the animals and family members, and generally looking after the old, the young, the men, and the animals in the house. The presentational process avoids long takes, favouring cuts and parallel editing. The documentary highlights changes in the matrilineal family by interviewing Bingma, the eldest daughter who, according to tradition, is expected to return to the family to gradually take over her mother's role. When asked how she sees her own future, Bingma begs the film crew not to raise the question. Later she appears on camera to express her desire for a monogamous marriage. She also admits that she perceives her mother's heavy duties as an injustice in the division of labour in the matrilineal family. Should she be forced to stay in the matrilineal family as *kama*, Bingma tells us that she will instruct the male members of her family, especially her uncles and brothers, to support themselves by sharing more of the family chores.

The documentary also acquaints the viewer with the men of Bingma's family, the grandmother's partner, Ahpu, and the third uncle, a local monk who features in the second part of The Sutra Hall. We follow the events leading to the renovating of the Sutra Hall in Bingma's house. We watch Ahpu looking for a suitable sutra wall painter, and witness his six-hour walk to a Yi village in a mountain valley to buy a couple of sheep to be roasted at the completion ceremony which is to crown the renovation of the Hall. That this is not an ordinary event in a Mosuo family's life becomes clear when we see a shot of a wooden label above the gate: Bingma's family has been chosen as a documentary research site amongst the Mosuo minority. From this the viewer can assume that in exchange for the filming, the family is receiving welcome remuneration, which allows them to renovate their run down premises. But this realisation in turn suggests the reality of the stark poverty in which many members of the minorities live. There is no bath, the 13-year-old girl has never been to school, the hygienic conditions of the house are of a very low standard, and Bingma's mother is seriously over-worked; there is Ahpu's memory of his roving matches in the past, which, according to the custom, are not to be mentioned in the woman's house in which the man wishes to settle. There is also the contradiction between the roving matches as a custom and the indignity of women not even to be able to discuss the matter in their own homes. The documentary indicates that at least some of the traditions of the Mosuo are likely to be challenged in the not so far future and that it is the women who are taking the lead in this social transformation.

The Flower Building consists of two parts focusing mainly on two men. One is a young male, in his twenties, Li, the owner of the local pub. The other, a middle aged man, Geke, a father of three, works as a rower and enjoys a stable roving match. Having experienced life as a waiter and worker in a northern Chinese metropolitan city, Li decides to return to his roving match in spite of his admiration for a Han Chinese woman. Geke, by contrast, has settled in his tradition. After a day's work, he rows for three hours to his woman and three children, who live on the other side of the lake, and returns to his mother and sister early in the morning. Throughout this section, we see that men, young and middle aged, are full of praise for the tradition of the 'roving match' and the freedom it affords the men, but we do not hear the women's position on the matter. The film ends with a recording of a traditional, highly complex funeral ritual in a Mosuo family.

The sociological approach to this documentary series is reflected not only in the style of the narration, explaining the action, but also in the mode of presentation of the events, and the interaction with the filmed subjects. Interaction between film crew and cinematic subjects is a vital characteristic of these films. We see the filmmakers following the grandmother's partner to the Yi village on a six-hour trip, recording his trading negotiations; we see the mother's third brother inviting the filmmaker to participate in a ritual ceremony when a helping hand is needed. There are images of the filmmaker attempting to blow a Mosuo horn, we see him appear on screen during an interview, and we hear his voice off camera. This interactive mode is mixed with an observational style whenever the filmmaker is waiting for things to happen, as for instance in the funeral section. All in all, the series stands for a new and exciting way of making documentary films about minorities in China. Perhaps the most remarkable observation we should make is to say that the films highlight a broad variety of speaking positions, some of which are clearly oppositional and so suggest a polyphonic hetero-geneity of voices which, together, reflect a dynamic social picture without government interference.

The documentary celebration we see in CCTV productions about the beginnings of the tourist industry amongst the minorities, in for instance its well-made television documentary series *Zhongguo Minzai*, contrasts with some of the films made by Yunnan independent filmmakers, who take a more critical view of the impact of the market economy on their cultures. Rong Li's DV *Wenhua xiu / Culture Show* (2003) critically records some of the changes of the Sani village that have taken place as a consequence of tourism. Many villagers have opened hotels and restaurants, while aban-doning their farming activities. They now advertise themselves to outsiders. With the assistance of scholars, many villages in a similar situation have recreated, as well as created, public performances to display their 'culture'. And so, under the pressure of outside influences, local people are gradually changing their views of 'themselves' and 'others'. Advertising, a new 'mater-ial' culture, and cultural performance as commodity combine to produce a profoundly transformed village 'self' and self-understanding. In his docu-mentary, the filmmaker Rong Li is trying to find out whether the villagers are really happy about the transformation of a peaceful tranquillity of their agricultural existence into a life disturbed by hundreds of tourist 'intruders'. Almost all the local people she interviews comment on the positive eco-nomic benefits of tourism, while complaining about some of the bad habits of the tourists. At the end of the film, when the question is repeated, the camera captures a local assistant reminding the organiser in local dialect not to tell. After all, the filmmaker is not only an outsider but also appears counter productive to tourism. A remainder of actual cultural difference between the village and the outside world shows itself in a certain degree of distrust by the local minority vis-á-vis the Han tourists.

Zhou Yuejun's award winning documentary *Wugu / Misty Village* (2005) explores some of these issues in greater depth. The film documents a story of a television crew filming a minority renowned for its singing and dancing. The filmmakers are seeking help from local people who would like to appear on television. A young man in his late teens offers help. However, after the man takes the crew to the village, he demands more money for procuring a buffalo and local costumes to film. Annoyed with the young man's haggling, the filmmaker sacks him, although the shooting is incom-plete. A little local boy offers his help without asking for payment. By the end of the shoot, the director invites the boy for lunch in a restaurant. He accepts, but shares some of his food with his group of friends. The filmmaker rewards him with a generous tip. On the way back, Zhou Yuejun sees the young man working in the field. He asks him how much he is charging for his work. He replies 'I don't ask for payment from my people', a reply suggesting that the government portrayal of the harmonious unity of Chinese nationalities is not quite the full picture.

Zhou Yuejun's *The Lake of Romance* (2006) documents social changes in the Mosuo community. The film presents parallel footage of the growing scepticism towards the tradition of the 'roving match' and, at the same time, the beginnings of tourism at Lake Gulu where the Mosuos have lived for hundreds of years. The film starts with a long take of Mosuo people, mostly women washing and chatting near the lake. An old man amongst them begins to tell the women about his memories of his 'roving matches'. He cheerfully recalls his amorous adventures as a young man, while the women are teasing him in good humour. As the film progresses, we see women of three generations talking about the tradition of the roving match with a female filmmaker. Now we hear of their dissatisfaction with the outmoded custom, the women condemning their hardship and suffering as a result of male irresponsibility towards their offspring. As to the theme of Han intrusion into the world of minorities, Zhou Yuejun shows a long take of himself following a four-year-old boy. We see the boy herding his cows. The boy carries a bag with the word Marlborough, indicating that global commerce has now reached the remotest areas in China. The boy is uncomfortable being filmed and asks the filmmaker to stop shooting: 'Don't shoot, don't shoot'. Zhou ignores him and continues filming. The boy picks up a stone, threatening 'If you don't listen to me, I will hit you'. He throws a stone at Zhou, but to no avail. After a while, the boy gives up and continues with his task. This perhaps symbolises the hopelessness of resistance by the minorities in the face of tourist development, modernisation, and Han domination. As to tourism, we learn of the way a Mosuo family runs a motel catering for Han tourists. The motel is managed by two of the family's three sisters. One of them is practising a roving match, the second has married a Chinese man, while the youngest, the central personality of the film, refuses any proposals, but instead concentrates on her business. The father who was not happy about one of his daughters' marriage to a Han, says he is now reconciled to the fact after he has trained the son-in-law to be a good Mosuo man. We witness the Mosuo's daily routines, the young women chatting with Han visitors, waiting outside the family motel to attract tourists, and the management of their tourist facilities. The youngest daughter is not at all shy about expressing her thoughts: she is no hurry to settle down; she will continue for a while enjoying the attention of admirers; her favourite Chinese popular songs, her admiration for the Japanese; her colourful traditional costume; and her ambition to sleep on her grandmother's bed, the most powerful symbol of status in her family. On the one hand, then, we see a generation of young Mosuo women who are competent, ambitious and in control of their own destinies; on the other hand, we see the Mosuo culture in the process of disappearing, or at least being fundamentally altered by the impact of tourism.

The irresistible pressure exerted by Han culture on the minorities is also the theme of *Shenluo Ai! Women de Shenluo / The Deer Story* (1997), which is about the destiny of three generations of women of the Ewenki nation (*Ewenke*) at the mountainous boundaries of Inner Mongolia and Manchu in north-east China. The Ewenki tribe is traditionally a nomadic society entirely bound up with the migration of the deer. The deer is the focal point of the people, providing shelter, food, trade, and materials for art work. In turn, the tribe care for the herd, raising young animals and accepting the lead deer as a divine creature. We are told that the central personality of the documentary, Liu Ba, has graduated from the Visual Arts Department at the Minorities College in Beijing. After she has received her degree she has worked as editor for an arts magazine in Inner Mongolia for seven years, after which she returns to her tribe in the forest in 1992. However, neither her grandmother, the Shaman of the tribe, nor her mother accept her any longer as a full member of their society, regarding her now as a city person. Trapped between the image of an educated woman from the city and her desire to remain an Ewenki in love with the forest, Liu Ba is profoundly unhappy. When the family deer dies and development encroaches on the forest, her life together with that of the Ewenki appears doomed. Liu Ba leaves home in 1993 and gets lost in the forest, but is found and saved by a Han Chinese man. She marries him and gives birth to a daughter. After the film has been completed, Liu Ba, unable to reconcile her two forms of existence, commits suicide. The decline of the Ewenki culture appears tragic, because it is both a terrible loss and inevitable.

Throughout the 1990s, hundreds of documentaries about minorities are produced, many of them presenting voices that deviate markedly from those of the official channels. Independent filmmaker Duan Jinchuan, for example, shot his *Baguo nanjie shiliu hao / No.16 Barkhor South Street* (1997) when he was commissioned by Beijing Television to make a documentary film about Tibet. *No.16 Barkhor South Street*, which won an award at the Prix-Cinema du Reel International Documentary Film Festival in Paris, depicts a neighbourhood Committee on Barkhor Street in Lhasa, the bottom level unit of the CCP, responsible for the implementation of government policies. The film captures the daily routines of the committee dealing with issues involving both secular and religious perspectives. *Gongbu de xinfu shenghuo / Gongbu's Happy Life* (1999) documents a Tibetan peasant who leads a simple and somewhat monotonous life, singing and gambling with his friends, in spite of his worry about his loan and his elder son. *Jiayuan / Home* (2001) records the government enforced relocation of the Yao minority. After centuries of living in a remote mountain range, the Yao minority has been told that they are to be evacuated to a more accessible area to reduce their poverty and isolation. Ji Dan's *Laoren men / Elders* (1999) documents the religious activities of a group of old Tibetan men in the village of Latsu. Although their engagement with the religious life is motivated by their consciousness about old age and death, the film shows that their religious preoccupation with death actually infuses them with a passion for life. Hong Kong sociologist Zhou Huashan has made *Sange mosuo nuzi de gushi* / *A Documentary about Three Mosuo Women* (2001) using interviews to present three generations of a Mosuo family, their relationships and daily life. He shows that in spite of modernisation, their attitudes to life and human affection has changed very little. Although the three women have little in common as to their fate, they share the priority of the happiness of their families as the priority, suggesting that Mosuo matriarchy and the harmonious relationship it produces between men and women could be continued. Xu Han's *Meili de heici* / *The Beauty of Black* (2003) focuses on two girls of the Daisai minority, a branch of the Dai ethnic group on the Ailao mountains and the Gasai River. The Daisai women stand out for their tradition of dying their teeth black. The film shows some of the changes occurring in this minority by letting the girls air their problems in the face of a declining tradition. *Wo yao shenghuo* / *Mr. Cool* (2003) looks at the conflicts of the young people of a minority trapped between tradition and modernity. The film captures the feelings of young people towards city youths as well as the influence of the media. *Nanlin cun de geshen* / *Song of Nanlin* (2004) documents a community singing event in a Hani village. Traditional songs sung by elders confront popular Han songs sung by the children of the minority. *Nongcun funu Yulan de wenhua shenghuo* / *A Country Woman's Cultural Life* (2004) looks at Yulan, a Naxi country woman's life, at how she prepares herself to be able to go to an open air screening of a film organised by a political team in charge of culture, science and technology. *Xiao Shengmin* / *Small Lives* (2003) is a documentary made by a young Tibetan woman who captures images of a group of Tibetan people trying to save some frogs trapped in a hole dug for an electric pole. No great cinematic achievement, one might say, but nevertheless a documentary account of a scene of some symbolic import: a demonstration of the Buddhist respect for life in its most humble forms and in the face of encroaching technology.

The recent trend of 'letting the people speak' is well demonstrated in a series of documentaries produced by a group of filmmakers in Yunnan, especially around Yunnan University and the Academy of the Social Sciences in Kunming. Some of these films address the culture of the Tibetan minorities in the mountains of Yunnan. The documentary *Bingchuan* / *Glacier* (2002) produced and edited by Guo Jing and co-directed by the Tibetan poet Zhaxi Nima portrays the people of Mingyong Village in the Deqin County of Yunnan. It is the result of a 'Participatory Video Education Project' funded by the Ford Foundation, aimed at reviving and teaching village traditions to students. Part of the project was to provide Tibetan villagers with video cameras to record and speak of their own cultural traditions. Filmed by Zhaxi Nima, a Tibetan resident of the village and a poet, the documentary presents the multiple perspectives of villagers, mountaineers, journalists, tourists, and a visiting CCTV film crew interviewing the rural population. The title of the film points to its central concern, the tourist and mountaineering activities that have arisen around the Minyong Glacier on Mount Kawakarpo. Contrary to the typical Government sponsored representations of minorities, the amateur style of filming of *Glacier* and, above all else, its polyphonic assemblage of voices and positions, amounts to a highly effective, realistic picture of the clash of traditional cultural values and the demands of the new market.

Mount Kawakarpo also features in the documentary *Cizhong shendan jie / Christmas Eve in Cizhong* (2002), *Wo keai de jiaxiang / My Lovely Home* (2002), produced by the BAMA Mountain Culture Research Institute, again with Guo Jing as co-director. A sacred mountain well before the introduction of Buddhism to the region, Kawakarpo achieved notoriety when in 1991 seventeen mountaineers from China and Japan lost their lives in an attempt to reach the summit. To this day, the film informs us, the peak has never been reached. As a result of a Tibetan mass demonstration on the mountain in 2003, the government has now introduced legislation protecting the mountain and its environment from tourist encroachments unacceptable to local Tibetan beliefs. Renqin Duaoji, a Tibetan villager and scholar, together with Stephan Kranz and Guo Jing, use DV cameras to record their own and other people's impressions of the mountain and its place in Tibetan culture. The documentary is remarkable especially because of the foregrounded 'image voice' of a Tibetan local and the indigenous perspective this provides for the viewer.

A similarly participatory style characterises a number of other films about minorities produced by Guo Jing, his group of film scholars and their associates in the mountains of Yunnan. Here, as is the case in a wide range of DV films being now produced throughout China, the formerly leading voice of the official studios and through them those of the government and the Party appear to be disseminated across a broad band of local and indigenous voices constituting a polyphonic heterogeneity that promises a certain degree of democratisation in filmmaking and the media. In this process, I suggest, documentary film is playing a substantial and leading role in the sense that it is introducing into Chinese culture a critical discourse hitherto absent in the tradition.

7 The many voices of Chinese documentary

Introduction

Early in the book I gave a definition of polyphony as the simultaneous interaction of many, and especially, of competing voices. In this last chapter I look at documentary film and television programmes of the recent past, as a collective, heterogeneous polyphony of voices. An important new player on the scene that we need to consider here are documentaries produced in the DV format. Since 2000, DV documentaries have made up an increasingly powerful portion of the overall production in the documentary mode. DV production includes a variety of amateur filmmakers from tertiary students and artists, to the unemployed, hairdressers, entrepreneurs, in short anyone seriously interested in shooting films in the new technology. Currently most television stations have a programme dedicated to DV films. From the late 1990s, there have been specialised DV programmes screened by Phoenix, the CCTV, the CETV and provincial stations. A further outlet for DV films is the internet, now also used by mobile phone filmmakers. In addition, there are various weekend exhibitions, many of them organised by non-government organisations associated with companies selling cameras. Some such gatherings are organised by university students, and some are sponsored by print media groups, by newspapers and popular magazines. Here are a few examples. In September 2001, Beijing *Shijian She* and *Southern Weekend* organised the first non-government DV exhibition at the Beijing Film Academy; in August 2003, the biggest independent DV exhibition so far took place in Zhujiang, billed as 'Independence Day: Screen Exhibition'; and in 2004 the 'Contemporary Chinese Independent Screen Exhibition' was held in Chongqing. In 2005, the 'Multicultural Visual Festival' in Yunnan welcomed many independent DV documentaries to its second gathering. I was able to view a number of these films, to be discussed below, at the festival archives. DV production, I suggest, is a film practice that is not only of statistical significance, but one that is already beginning to cause a shift in the very conception of documentary cinema itself. Nor should we assume that this trend is the result only of a critical groundswell of creative expression amongst the growing number of DV filmmakers. Once more I emphasise that the major television stations, such as the CCTV and CETV, have played a role in the emergence of mass DV documentary production.

In this concluding chapter, I single out individual documentaries as exemplary in the use of a multi-voiced presentational mode. Before I do so, I want to give a brief elaboration of the notion of *voice*. The most well-known definition of voice in documentary cinema is that proposed by Bill Nichols who describes voice as 'a text's social point of view' (Nichols 2005: 18). We could call this the socio-political statement that a film is making as a whole. This is a useful definition, one which to which I resort at times myself in this book. However, if we were to restrict our definition to this summary version, we would be in danger of always homogenising and collapsing the many voices that constitute the potential of the documentary mode into a singular perspective. There are other options, useful for close analysis of a documentary, when it is precisely the nuanced interplay of voices that is of interpretive significance. This is why I want to suggest a more differentiated sense in which the terms 'voice' and 'voices' can be employed in the analysis of cinematic documentation and its televisual variants. By 'voice' I mean in the first instance that someone is entitled to speak and so is able to make use of a variety of 'enunciative modalities' (Foucault 1986: 50–5). In this sense of the term, individual speakers can be recognised as persons able to present opinions, observations, judgments, explanations, to clarify their social position, their political leanings, their cultural alliance, their gender views, their agreements and disagreements. Such a voice can be minor or major, intentionally foregrounded or merely sketched as an incidental participant. In addition, and in a more subtle sense, a voice can also just be a visual presence, such as a displayed yet unheard voice in ethnographic film or in war footage. It is in this sense that Guo Jing has argued for the 'voice of image-making'. New technologies such as DV and computers, he says, enable 'ordinary people' to fulfil their wish of making their own visual images and so empower them to express themselves as individuals beyond their verbal capacities. The 'voice' of the image, for Guo Jing, is a liberation from authoritarian description and gives freedom of self-representation (Guo Jing 2005: 68–9).

I would also like to suggest that the polyphony of voices can be argued to emanate from documentary subject matter and representational mode. My justification for such an expanded use of the term voice is this. Both are accessible to the viewer and hearer as discursive domains, visual and verbal. As such, any restriction of subject matter that can be dealt with in documentaries is a restriction of discourse at large and so a stifling of the free exchange of social voices, as we have seen in the discussion of the dogmatic mode. Likewise, the limiting of the representational potential, that is, the presentational possibilities of documentary cinema, amounts to a censorship of the exchange between filmmaker and the public. Where a single voice dominates we can speak of personal voice, a dominant, authoritative, and an authoritarian voice, the most restrictive of which is the dogmatic voice of ideological cinema, as we saw in Chapter 3. The opposite is the cinema of many voices, or polyphonic documentary. This is particularly so when such a polyphonic structure is made up of opposing voices and so constitutes what I call a polyphonic heterogeneity. This multi-voice structure can be employed in a single film or television programme where different voices compete with one another. More typically, polyphony is spread across a cinema culture as a whole. In this last chapter, I argue that Chinese documentary cinema today, supported by a range of television programmes, and significantly expanded by the emergence of DV documentaries, constitutes the emergence of such a polyphony in *individual speech positions, including those of filmmakers themesleves, subject areas,* and *representational modes.* I suggest further that in this extended and specified sense of voice the polyphonic cinema of today's China amounts to a rehearsal of democracy by means other than the conspicuously political. What we are witnessing today, the chapter demonstrates, is massive evidence for the increasing exchange of competing positions in documentary cinema and television programmes. And since television is now the main site at which these films and programmes reach their audiences, I suggest, this situation indicates the tentative beginnings of a televisual public sphere and the evolution of a genuinely critical discourse.

Polyphony in contempoary documentary film texts

Compared to the reforms of the financial structures of media institutions and their role in the media market, reform in the media content area has been much more cautious. Although the variety of media programmes and genres in China is now not only huge but also diverse, sensitive political topics nevertheless remain a public taboo. And in spite of the appearance of a certain degree of diversity in the reporting of news, what is to be broadcast remains an object of political scrutiny under the watchful eye of the Party. The most conspicuous change in media content is that 'ordinary people' (*putong ren*), that is, those who are not in a position of power, such as policy making or financial influence, now fill the television screen, which in the past was reserved mainly for the political leadership, or Communist heroic characters. With this shift also goes a less 'authoritarian' and more informal representational style. The participation of ordinary people in television programmes is especially prominent in talk shows, debating programmes, phone-ins, SMS exchanges and email feedback facilities. The evening news, especially in provincial areas, is now typically focused on difficulties and problems in the social services sector, such as hospitals, housing, education, traffic regulation, natural disaster measures, environmental programmes and inflation.

To make the most of this new, relative freedom in the choice of subject matter, the CCTV established a number of popular programmes on current affairs *Dongfang shikong / Oriental Horizon* in 1993, *Jiaodian fangtan / Focal*

Point in 1994, and *Xinwen diaocha / News Probe* in 1996, to provide more objective, systematic and authoritative information about events of public interest. Investigative reports on the corruption and incompetence of lower level government officials, false products and fraudulent marketing are frequently exposed with the support of the government. *Focal Point* has also become a popular place for seeking justice. During several visits to the CCTV between 1998 and 2005, not once did I fail to notice people outside the CCTV gate with slogans such as '*Focal Point* for Justice'. A number of taxi drivers told me that what corrupt officers feared the most was to be interviewed by *Focal Point*. It is widely believed, as de Burge has pointed out in his book, that President Jiang Zemin and Premier Zhu Rongji instructed their ministers to initiate investigations after watching *Focal Point* (de Burgh 2003: 42).

When in 1998 Premier Zhu Rongji described the CCTV as *qunzhong houshe* ('media as the voice of the masses'), he signalled a sharp deviation from the Party's principle of the 'media as the mouthpiece of the Party'. To increase ratings across the country, the then Minister of Propaganda Li Changchun in 2002 furthermore announced the principle of *san tiejin* (three proximities) for media representations, proximity to reality (focusing on social issues), proximity to the public (more programmes and information relevant to the population at large), and proximity to daily life (with topics concerning everyday life instead of grand political ideologies). This principle has been perceived by media scholars as a significant revision of the long-standing Chinese Communist doctrine that the media is no more than the monological propaganda organ of Party and government (Zhang 2003: 34–8). From the perspective of our argument here, an important aspect of this policy shift is the fact that the relaxation of the rules of what can now be legitimately represented on screen, immediately resulted in an increase in the voices and speaking positions that can be heard and seen in television documentaries.

This nascent documentary polyphony shows itself first of all in the increasing spread of the variety of subjects available on screen today. Compared to the tightly controlled topic range and its dogmatic representational style in the Mao era, this development strikes us now as a major transformation of the visual media. This impression is strengthened further when we consider that even during the transitional period between the early 1980s and 1990s documentary film topics were still focused on a very restricted palette of such grand themes as Chinese culture, the Yellow River, or the Great Wall. In contrast, we are now witnessing an explosion of documentary themes of which only a handful can be put to an interpretive test in this chapter.

It is not easy to generalise this new diversity of subject matter in Chinese documentaries, not least because we are now not only dealing with productions by government sponsored television stations, but also by semi-independent and independent filmmakers, DV amateurs, as well as community and transnational producers. Not surprisingly, then, both documentary subject themes and presentational techniques now constitute a broad and varied collection. While some of the dominant subjects of the dogmatic periods still appear on the screen now and then, such as nationally significant events, socialist economic construction, history, geography, minority, culture, and sports, their representational style now usually involves more perspectives than the earlier single-voiced and idealised, wishful world of the CCP. No doubt, the majority of documentaries on historical topics continue to be produced by the government, but at the same time more and more alternative visions of the past are now being screened.

DV historiography

One of the main sources of this new body of films are DVs by independent filmmakers. A good example is Ban Zhongyi's 130-minute DV *Gaishanxi he tade jiemei / Gai Shanxi and her Sisters* (2004) which broaches the subject of Chinese 'comfort women' during the Japanese occupation. We learn that during that period some 350,000 Chinese women were raped by the invading enemy forces. The documentary traces the tragic life of a peasant woman from Shanxi province, Gai Shanxi, a member of the Chinese resistance, who is taken by the Japanese to one of their strongholds as a sex slave. She twice rescues girls from her village by offering herself to the Japanese. The brutal rapes cause permanent damage to her body. After the war, her bravery is rewarded by contempt from her own husband and the villagers. Physically scarred and psychologically devastated, Gai Shanxi commits suicide. One of the main differences between this documentary and officially produced films on similar topics lies in the critical stance the director takes not only towards the Japanese invaders but also towards Chinese society, which is presented as heartless and cruel. Another difference lies in the way the evidence is assembled in terms of the image chains of the film. The narration is subdued and largely replaced by interviews with the older people of Gai Shanxi's village, some surviving Japanese soldiers, and other Chinese 'comfort women'.

Another DV documentary in the same subject area is the *Yaoyuan de jia / Home Far Away* (2000). It tells the story of a young Korean girl who is kidnapped by Japanese soldiers on her way to the market with her father. She is raped by the Japanese and taken to Manchu as a 'comfort woman' of the Imperial army. Later the unit that keeps her captive moves to Shandong where she continues to be raped daily in spite of her pleading and constant crying. An old Chinese man in the service of the Japanese army takes pity on her and frees her. As he is shot dead by the Japanese guards for his intervention, the girl manages to escape. She is taken in by a village in Shandong where after a while she marries a Chinese man. During her many years of marriage she never loses her yearning to return to her Korean village. When she lies sick in hospital, a young man, a social worker, listens to her story, comforts her and offers to become her substitute son. When she leaves hospital she and her husband welcome the young man in their home, where he looks after the old couple, providing money and food, and visiting them whenever he can. In gratitude to his new parents, the young man tells a local newspaper his mother's personal tragedy. The story is published and incidentally read by a young Korean woman who is studying Chinese at Nanjing University. She includes the story in her Masters thesis and visits the old woman as part of her research. The two Korean women sit many hours together looking in the direction of Korea and lamenting the old woman's fate and shame, as that of thousands of other Korean and Chinese 'comfort women'. Together they visit the grave of the old Chinese man who had sacrificed his life to give the captive Korean girl a chance to escape. The young Korean woman then offers to take the old lady on a visit to her old home. On their arrival in the old woman's village she finds her birthplace intact and is welcomed by her brothers. She is led to her father's grave where she prays and cries. She also meets other Korean former 'comfort women' with whom she shares memories of the war before returning to China.

The film is observational, with some brief narration as background information. The camera follows the woman over a period of time, starting from when she meets the Korean student. Interviews with a number of key persons are prominent. The viewer learns most of the story from the perspective of the old woman herself, the remaining information between provided through the voices of the old lady's husband, her son, her brothers, villagers, and Korean 'comfort women' survivors. The narration is kept to a descriptive minimum, the bulk of the information being garnered by the film viewer from the speaking positions of the persons telling their stories.

One of the subject matters avoided in official documentary accounts is the violent and often deadly struggle that sometimes took place amongst opposing factions of the Red Guards during the Cultural Revolution. This is an area of documentary where independent filmmaking is now making a significant difference. In a 23-minute DV, *Qingchun yuanmu / Cemetery of Youth* (2004), the young filmmaker Zhang Ke takes as his cinematic focus a cemetery in Chongqing that few people like to mention. As the gravestones tell us, 103 youths lie buried here, the victims of ideological squabbles within the Communist ranks. Similar skirmishes raged at various flashpoints across the country at the time. In 1968 some 300 young people were killed. It has been said that Chairman Mao enjoyed watching the raw footage of this internecine slaughter, testimony perhaps to the insanity that characterised the final stages of his rule (Fang 2003: 276). Zhang Ke's documentary is reopening old wounds by his visual indictment of irresponsible policies that encouraged the brigades of the Red Guards to fight amongst themselves, to decide which faction represented the true revolutionary thought of Mao Zedong. The DV looks back at the Cultural Revolution in dismay as a disastrous phase of Chinese politics with its fanatical hordes of youths, blinded by ideological hatred, destroying their own country and themselves.

Zhang Ke spent six months in the graveyard, interviewing visitors to the site. He made compelling visual documents of the parents and families of the dead in order to uncover a past that no one wants to talk about. The film makes ironic use of Mao's words addressed to the Chinese youth: 'The world belongs to you. You are like the sun at 8 and 9 o'clock in the morning.' This quotation is juxtaposed with the harrowing descriptions by the mothers, the sisters and fathers of the slain youth. We learn how the young Red Guards were killed, and how their families survived after their deaths. Some of the visitors decline to be interviewed. Also included in the documentary are image sequences of children who are asked who they thought was buried in the cemetery. The children give various answers, such as 'Those who died for the revolution', 'What kind of revolution?', 'Anti-Japanese', or 'Fighting against the Guomindang'. The wilful forgetting inscribed in these answers only heightens the sense of tragedy the documentary is able to convey. At the same time, Zhang Ke's use of a heterogeneity of voices not only sharpens his realist message but also testifies to the presence of a new cinematic consciousness in China today. Unlike the sanitised versions of recent history offered by the CCTV, CETV and other stations close to the government, Zhang's and other filmmakers' voices are announcing the emergence of a new generation of independent Chinese filmmakers ready to usher in a period of genuine critical discourse.

Rural topics

It should not be surprising that the majority of documentaries about the countryside are made from the perspective of city dwellers. After all, television stations with the technology and personnel for producing documentary films are typically located in urban rather than in rural environments. Moreover, the new user-friendly digital video cameras have so far largely been taken up by urban populations. But even this limited perspective has already produced a variety of rural documentary vistas.

From the perspective of the city, the rural is sometimes presented as an ideal place, comparable to the *locus amoenus* of the European literary tradition. Leng Shan's DV *Women de dong* / *Winter at 3000 Meters* (2001) produced by Sichuan TV documents a village of the Qiang minority living at an altitude of over 3,000 metres in the southwest of China. At the centre of the film is a nine year-old school girl, Cong Huan, her village, her family and friends during a holiday season. The film starts with a few images of the magnificent view of a village – a collection of wooden houses on top of a mountain covered in thick white snow under the deep blue sky. There is no road to the village, and a normal shopping trip to the nearest town will take five days, season and weather permitting. There is neither electricity nor television. In spite of, or perhaps because of, this backward remoteness, the social relations in the village appear pure and simple. Cong Huan is shown to be growing up in a loving family. A clip of a family dinner shows the caring and happiness that pervades the household: her parents paying attention to the senior members and the young of the family; the mother teaching her children singing and dancing after dinner. Cong Huan's father takes her to the village's elders so she can learn the local Qiang language and study the family line, while her mother teaches Cong Huan the art of Qiang sewing. The social relations in the village appear harmonious, somewhat like the relations within one large family. Indeed, as it turns out, in the entire village of a hundred households, each one is related to the rest, as an elder proudly declares. The villagers work together, the women cook, wash and sew. The men are filmed as they cut wood, and the children are engaged in communal games while their parents are busy. We see no argument or disputes, and the images of the innocent chatting of the children, their playing and laughter altogether produces the impression in the viewer of an ideal society in an environmentally intact, beautiful and socially peaceful world, of which city dwellers can only dream. It would seem that the strong yearning for idealisation, so prominent in traditional Chinese culture, has survived even in the new DV era of documentary film.

Feng Lei's 20-minute DV *Xueluo yili / Falling Snow in Yili* (2001) follows a similar line of filming. The focus is on an eight year-old Kazak girl and her family in a remote family station with sheep and cows during a fine winter's day. Unlike *Winter at 3000 Metres*, in *Falling Snow in Yili* music plays a prominent role at the beginning and end, signifying the music saturated culture of the Kazak. The film shows a single day in the girl's life from the time she wakes up to the time she goes to bed. Although there is strict discipline in the household, her life appears blissfully content, with happy moments of playing with her lamb, accompanying her elder brother to collect snow for water, assisting her mother milking the cow, doing her homework, listening to the radio and singing with the family after a meal. When the family say prayers at the dinner table the girl is instructed in the gestures and words of the ritual. Shyly she complies, but finds the ceremony funny. The parents do not reprimand her. As evening settles on the house, a long take of falling snow against a black sky completes the daily cycle of Kazak life. The poetic portrayals of the snow landscape, long takes of a group of sheep passing by, leaving a lamb to catch up, followed by the warm inside of the house, with the little girl's singing and her family's praise once more present the nostalgic view of a rural existence where nature and human relations are in harmony.

The popular theme of melancholy yearning for the simplicity and peacefulness of rural existence is likewise at the centre of Zhang Dali's DV *Hanya / Crow in Winter* (2004). Once more we are presented with an urban perspective, informed by the hustle and bustle of commercial life, where young and old alike chase after employment opportunities and where speed covers up people's spiritual emptiness. The filmmaker portrays his hometown, somewhere along the railway between Beijing and Kowloon, which has turned into an urban wilderness devoid of the spiritual depth that only close human relations embedded in a continuum of traditional culture are able to afford. The villages too, we are told, are affected by rapid urbanisation, leaving the women, children and the elderly to wait for the men to return from the cities to celebrate the Spring Festival.

The countryside is also the place where traditional culture is 'discovered'. Zhu Jili's DV *Chunjie yinxiang / Spring Festival* (2002) documents the traditional way in which a typical household celebrates the Spring Festival in Nan'an, Fujian Province. Hundreds of such DV documentaries are now adding a new perspective to the standard presentations of village customs screened by the CCTV and other official television stations. Liang Bibo's *Hunshi / Marriage* (1999), for example, documents the intricacies of arranged marriage from its early negotiations to its culmination in a wedding in a mountainous country area. Unlike the more relaxed procedures of marriage in the city, country life is shown in this film as carrying on the traditional procedures involving matchmakers and the cautious dealings between the two families. The film follows two couples. The first are two young lovers who ask a 54-year-old matchmaker to discuss their marriage plans with both their parents. The second case depicts a woman who would like to be married to a young man in order for her to be able to continue to look after her sick father. The film documents the matchmaker's negotiations with the four families in the hope of reaching a solution acceptable to all parties. The process extends roughly over a full year. At its successful conclusion we witness a typical country wedding, with the bride and her family in tears, a well prepared feast, and the bride's dowry consisting, among other things, of poultry and big bags of food. Using interviews and a mainly observational presentational mode of documentation, the filmmaker seems to be saying, 'Here life is still in its natural order; a pity we seem to be unable to retain such traditions in modern urban existence'.

Another kind of urban perspective on rural life is the presentation of the exotic. *Kuohun / Crying the Bride* (2004) records the details of a traditional wedding ceremony according to a Han custom, a way of life that has now died out in the cities and has almost vanished even from most rural areas. In this old style of marriage, ten days before the wedding, the bride's relatives begin to cry day and night to express their gratitude to the bride for her kindness, to bid her farewell and wish her good luck in her future life. The more intensive the crying, according to this custom, the better a future the bride will enjoy. True to its purpose of highlighting what strikes us as a strange if not exotic practice, the filmmaker has done his best to emphasise cultural difference. In Chapter 6, I called this phenomenon of documentary filmmaking 'the tyranny of difference'. This observation also applies to Hao Yuejun's *Shandong li de cunzhuang / The Village in a Cave* (1996) a documentary about a village of some 280 people who have lived under the same cave roof as one single family in a remote area in southwest China for eight generations. With virtually no modern conveniences or material goods, the community functions by relying closely on all its members. Such intimate interaction amongst a large group of people surprises the viewer by its social success. Almost all activities are targeted to ensure the survival of the community, which makes for a simple life, which appears to be warm, rewarding, peaceful and meaningful. However, when an opportunity arises for access to electricity by the proposed construction of power lines, the village harmony is disrupted. The documentary shows the community's spontaneous reactions and what appear to us 'primitive' ways of negotiation in trying to cope with the promise, and at the same time the threat, of rudimentary modernisation.

Sometimes, the rural is often presented as mysterious, as for instance in Mao Chenyu's DV *Ximao jiawu chan jiashen yinyang jie* / *Between Life and Death*. The film records a Nuo ritual dance ceremony by which the Nuo people celebrate and sacrifice to the god Nuo. We are told by the filmmaker that he is able to shoot such a documentary only because he enjoys special access to the Nuos and their ceremonies. Having grown up in a family still practicing shamanic culture, the filmmaker has a grandfather who is regarded as a local god, while his father, a shaman, has inherited his grandfather's skills. Having received a modern, urban education, the filmmaker is intrigued to explore and reveal to the public his own tribal culture and heritage. A visually fascinating study of ancient folk practices in a family of shamans, the documentary offers rare insights into a mysterious, culturally and ritually rich rural area, peopled with hundreds of local gods and ghosts. Nothing could be further from the modern transparency of practical urban existence and its commercial culture.

A number of documentaries take as their task a critique of the poverty of certain rural areas, demanding that the basic needs of rural populations should be more seriously addressed by the government. In Chen Xueli's *Buzhai chanjiao* / *No More Bound Feet* (2003) the viewer is once more treated to a rural wedding. The film shows a Yunnan family hosting a village feast in honour of their daughter, the bride. We witness the father and mother speaking to their daughter before the wedding, the mother offering the bride valuable instructions for her future life as a wife. There is abundant food for the merry wedding guests and a group of grandmothers commenting on how much better off today's brides are in comparison with the circumstances of their weddings, including the custom of bound feet. Yet, the camera does not miss the opportunity of driving home to the viewer the poor conditions of the village. There are muddy roads, the houses are dark inside, with only basic furniture, and the village as a whole gives a run-down appearance. As the rain sets in, walking and driving becomes hazardous and dirt dominates the picture.

There are many such films highlighting the backward conditions of rural living, with some addressing poverty with a focus on remote country schools. One such documentary is *Long Qi* / *Long Qi* in the late 1990s which has as its theme the shocking conditions of a village school. The film displays the school surviving on broken desks and chairs, the desperate efforts made by the school teacher to get by with what is available, and his innocently cheerful pupils. In a similar style, Wei Xing's *Xuesheng cun / A Student Village* (2002) documents the difficulties in providing basic education for children in remote country areas. In order to guarantee all children elementary training in numeracy and literacy, the village committees decide to build a primary school. The film shows the efforts involved in achieving such a goal in a mountainous area, where building itself is extremely difficult. Images of school children carrying water are mixed with footage of well-meaning but incompetent builders and villagers. The degree of impoverishment of the villagers is also highlighted by a sequence showing two students who, in order to be able to buy a pocket dictionary, are digging up herbs and selling them after a day's walk to the nearest town. The filmmaker's message is clear: with proper interest in the rural population shown by federal and local governments, these conditions surely can be improved on.

Rural poverty is likewise the topic of Peng Hui's light-hearted documentary *Beilou dianying yuan / Cinema on the Back* (1999) which addresses the length to which some peasants have to go to provide some modest form of entertainment to villagers. We see an image chain of two peasants carrying a projector and rolls of film on their backs, walking from village to village across valleys and hills to show films. On a more sombre note, *Zai yiqi de shiguang / Wellspring* (2002) shows the difficulties faced by a rural couple in trying to find a doctor for their brain damaged 15-year-old son. In the end, they are left alone, feeding their son water and fruit juice for two months to safe his life. Another such tragic story is told by Jiao Bo's DV *Yaba de zhenyue / Last Spring Festival* (2002) which documents the final 25 days in the life of a peasant, Jiao Yuqing. We find out that Jiao is disabled with a hearing problem and has never married, but has looked after his blind old father and brought up the four children of his divorced brother. Due to financial difficulties, his younger brother could not afford to take him to hospital. Jiao dies 25 days after the Spring Festival and, 15 days later, is followed to the grave by his old blind father. The film leaves no doubt in the viewer's mind that with minimal financial assistance, Jiao's life could have been saved. Where, the DV appears to ask, in Communist China is the social welfare system for the poor?

Watching these documentaries, one cannot escape the suspicion that the materials for such stories are infinite and what we see is a tiny selection taken from a vast and heart-rending social scene. Some of these documentaries combine tragedy with a sense of the pathetic, as does Hu Zhong's DV *Moo / Moo* (2004). It shows the hard life of an old blind man and his wife, both over 70, who manage to survive on their own. Notwithstanding his blindness, the old man has been able to raise cows for a living. He follows their 'moos' which guide him to feed them, he shovels dung and takes them to pasture up the mountainside. Sometimes he falls off the bridge leading to his house. However, eventually his cows had to be sold, as the village decided to open a tourist industry. Again, what we are shown testifies to the endurance of the peasants against all odds. But at the same time, the documentary functions as a visual indictment of a political leadership unwilling or unable to provide sufficient support for the poor, in areas such as education, health, and especially for the disabled and senior citizens.

In addition to the urban perspectives from which many of the documentaries on rural conditions are filmed, there are also filmmakers whose position must be constructed as speaking from within the rural communities which they represent visually. Such a perspective characterises a documentary which addresses the specific difficulty that arises for families in rural areas as a result of the government's rigid land policy and the changing relation between allocated land and the increasing number of family members. In Zhou Yuejun's documentary *Ah Lu Xiongdi /Ah Lu's Brothers* (2004) the topic is persuasively handled by tracing the fortunes of several members of Ah Lu's family. The film demonstrates the impossibility of peasants of supporting themselves under the existing law. Within a 20-year period, Ah Lu's family has increased from six people, the parents and four sons, to four married families with children plus their ageing parents, and yet, the existing land policy does not allow them to acquire more land to feed themselves. To escape further threatening impoverishment, Ah Lu and his wife decide to accept the lure of employment in a dubious coal mine in far away north China. When they arrive there, the working conditions and pay are much worse than they had feared. Nevertheless, Ah Lu accepts work in the mine, while his wife cooks for the workers. For a while they both knuckle down under the most appalling conditions. In the end, however, they decide that working for the mine is humanly unacceptable, give up on the pay they are owed and prefer the risk of fleeing illegally to continuing their contracts. When they arrive in the capital of their home province, Kunming in Yunnan, finding work once again is proving an impossible task. Experiencing serious discrimination because of their peasant background, Ah Lu and his wife are getting more and more desperate, without any real chance of securing a life-sustaining occupation. The documentary ends ironically with Ah Lu and his wife sitting speechless in the capital's People's Park, unable to partake of the relative prosperity surrounding them, nor able to return to their village.

Yet another cinematic vista of rural life addresses the relation between village people and their local government officials. One such documentary is Dai Yi's DVD *Cun guan / Village Cadre*, cinematic testimony to the near impossible tasks facing village officials in an impoverished mountain site. Through interviews and follow-up filming over four years, village cadres are able to express their difficulties and their feelings about their thankless jobs. Likewise focusing on the interaction of officialdom and people in the countryside is *Haixuan / Election*, or 'Election at Sea', a translation that retains the original's allusion to the difficulties and risks involved in the election process. The documentary tells the process of a village election in Liaoning Province as part of the series *Newsprobe*, an investigative television programme broadcast by the CCTV. The documentary consists of images of a remote mud brick village, meetings, polling procedures, and a number of interviews conducted by a CCTV journalist.

The opening images show village people in conversation, talking about the coming election of a new village head. An official news speaker of the CCTV channel introduces the topic: an election in a remote village in Liaoning Province, beginning on 27 March 1998. A pan shot of Daguan village shows a cluster of modest houses in the early morning sun, with a red flag raised on a pole and red boxes in front of the polling station. We see red posters on the walls announcing a large number of candidates. The incumbent village head, Liu Xiaobo, is asked how he sees his chances of being re-elected. He concedes that it won't be as easy as last time when he was the sole candidate, appointed by the Party. 'I have done well, I am not corrupt, I have been honest, and simple. My shortcoming is that I have not been very forceful'. Nonetheless, he feels he has a good chance of success. At a village meeting there is loud verbal exchange, villagers shouting and interrupting one another. The leader of the Election Committee jokes, 'Don't vote for a dead person, as they did in a village nearby'. Someone interjects that they should vote for a real candidate, and not for the government, a remark rewarded with loud applause, perhaps more in acknowledgment of the speaker's courage than as an expression of the majority view. In a series of interviews the candidates tell the reporter why they are standing and what they wish to achieve if elected. One of them says that he is a Party member and will do whatever the Party wants. Another candidate feels that although he comes from a small village, his supporters think that he is well suited to the job and will vote for him. The narration informs us that the election consists of a two-tier process, with nominations and the selection of a shortlist of candidates, followed by the election of the village head and his five member executive committee. Polling takes place on 29 March 1998. When the votes are counted on a blackboard, a surprise candidate emerges, called Wang Chen. Of the 1,168 votes, 204 go to Liu Xiaobo, 187 to Wang Chen, with the remainder deciding the composition of the executive committee. The reporter quizzes the two leading candidates as to their election speeches. Liu Xiaobo has prepared his speech; he doesn't like the way his opponent goes around talking to individual people and making promises. After all, what counts, he says, is 'ability'. Wang Chen has no written speech: 'I just say what I think'. Nor is he interested in the kind of suit he will wear. When the villagers are interviewed, support appears evenly divided between the two front runners. A shot of the assembled electorate, neatly organised in front of a podium, introduces the election speeches. When Wang Chen steps up to the lectern the crowd laughs. He begins by saying that he is nervous and that it may look ridiculous that an old man of 49 years wants to be village head. He speaks freely, listing his election promises: transparent accounts; no big banquet; no use of public funds to feed himself; instead, road repairs; and saving money to drain the fields. He is generously applauded by the electorate before Liu Xiaobo reads his short speech. He will do his best for the community, he says, and will resign if the people are unhappy with him. He too is applauded. In question time both candidates are challenged as to how they are going to achieve their promises. Wang Chen's response is that he will grant no privileges to officials, while the incumbent candidate promises to continue with his honest style and try to be more forceful to achieve his goals. When the polling count is finalized, the result is 591 votes in favuor of a smiling Liu Xiaobo and a surprisingly close 536 votes for the challenger. The concluding shot once again shows the village under the red flag, while a radio broadcast announces the election result and date: 2 April 1998. The documentary, as all the CCTV productions, is neatly framed, with slick editing, producing the effect of a more rigorous order of the event than would be conveyed by the footage on its own.

This CCTV version of documenting an election process is nicely complemented by a semi-dependent filmmaker, Zhao Gang, who records the chaotic events of a village election in Dongpo. His documentary *Dongri / The Sun in Winter* (2002) testifies both to the growing participation of ordinary people in the political process that determines the fortunes of their village and the sobering realisation that electoral participation is no guarantee for the protection of their existence. In this documentary we follow the activities of a member of the village electoral committee, a socially committed woman who is single and looks after her children. She is filmed talking to villagers and candidates, emphasising the importance of elections for the continuing existence of the village and their livelihoods in the face of a major threat by developers who are demanding land for urban expansion. The camera records the electoral process with the nominations of candidates on 7 November 1998, speeches and a public debate. An independent candidate, Zhou Wei, is standing against the established village leaders, offering a new, commercially oriented political platform. He speaks in front of a fairly large crowd in the street with the promise of a better future. The main spokesperson in support of elections, the single woman, is not convinced by his promises and recommends an older candidate as the village's best chance. Three candidates are recommended for nomination as a result. This is followed by a chaotic meeting of village representatives chaired by the local Party Secretary. There is a dispute as to the legality of the process and it becomes obvious to the viewer that what is missing is a clear and shared understanding of the proper electoral procedures. The nomination process is then declared invalid by the officials. On 24 November 1998 the camera shows a group of villagers consulting a fortune telling book to guide them in their political decisions. When the election finally takes place, there are four polling booths. Very much like the preceding debates, the polling is chaotic. Nevertheless, when the votes are counted, the independent candidate, Zhou Wei, has won by a landslide margin. However, the villagers' hope for proper political representation in their fight for survival is soon dashed when they realise that the government and developers are pressing on with their expansion plan. In a public display of dissent, the villagers protest against what they regard as inadequate compensation for their houses and land, and the government representative is howled down unable to complete his announcements. The camera affords us a view of an official meeting at a provincial level where it appears that Zhou Wei's impact on the decision-making process is negligible. We also witness the Dongpo spring festival of January 1999, when the village is celebrating their communal life for the last time. Now Zhou Wei receives death threats from villagers who are enraged that their elected candidate is ineffectual in the negotiations with government and developers. In 2000 the camera records the assault and beating of Zhou Wei in his office by members of the furious mob and in 2001 we witness the beginning of the demolition of the village. Thus ends both an attempt at a quasi-democratic election process and the existence of an entire village. What is important in this DV, it seems to me, is that the overall 'voice' of the documentary in Bill Nichols' sense is not so much construed by the director. his narration and the camera, but more indirectly by the multiple aspects of the chaotic electoral process and the heterogeneous, individual voices of the voters, nominees, candidates, local Party leaders, government representatives, and villagers at large. That the recorded outcome of the election is what it was is an indictment of a system that cynically uses the promise of democratic reform at the level of village politics to cover up the rampant development strategies of the new market economy.

The urban environment

The tension that I have observed between documentaries produced by television stations close to government on the one hand and those produced by semi-independent and independent filmmakers on the other reappears in the cinematic representation of urban themes. Whereas the former highlight successful reforms and rapid growth by way of modernisation, Westernisation, and globalisation, the latter tend to explore the social consequences of the new technologies and market economy. For instance, a documentary series *Gaige kafang 20 nian / Twenty years of Opening and Reform* (1999) presents stunning views of Chinese capital cities shot from a helicopter. We are treated to the aesthetics of the layout of new cities, vast construction sites and freeway clover leaves like works of art, a sky show spiced with interviews in praise of progress. Not all Chinese documentaries are however that celebratory. There is a large and growing number of more probing visual accounts by semi-independent and independent filmmakers screening their work on television and at international film festivals, addressing the downside of capitalist expansionism.

A recurrent documentary theme about Chinese cities is the observation that modernised urban life is beneficial neither for the elderly nor for children. In *Laonian hunyin zixun suo jianwen / Senior Citizen Dating Service* (1990), the chief agent, Ms Zhao, tells us that loneliness and their children's failure to meet the demands of their filial duties are the two major reasons driving *laoren* (the elderly) to register their interest in a second marriage. Another emphasis in the film is a critical shortage of housing for the poor. The person at the centre of the documentary, Ms Lu, has brought up her two sons and a daughter alone after her husband died when she was 40. A few years ago, she gave her house to her youngest son so that he could marry to continue the family line. In order to find a place to live herself, Lu comes to the Senior Citizen Dating agency in search of a partner. The theme of housing shortage for senior citizens is explored in some depth also in *Dexing Fang / Dexing Lang*. Wang Fengzhen lives in a room of 14.4 square metres with her daughter's family of four. At the age of 75, she goes out every night and returns after ten in order to grant her daughter's family a bit more privacy. In another family, rain or shine, and even in temperatures below zero, an old lady of 75, Wang Mingyuan, has slept on a balcony for eight years to leave the 12.3 square metre room to her son's family of three. In Yang Lina's independent DV *Lao Ren / Old Men*, it is not the shortage of living space that is an issue but rather loneliness and isolation. Acclaimed at the Tokyo Documentary Film Festival, the film captures the daily routines of a group of male retirees in Beijing. Every day they gather to sit in a shady place in summer or a sunny place in winter along the street. They chat aimlessly about trivial matters, and about the unfair treatment at the hands of their children. No assistance, the film shows, is available for those who live alone and those who take care of their aged spouses. The image of a group of old men in their black Zhongshan jackets sitting against the white wall under the chilly blue sky poignantly reflects the coldness of an urban society.

The theme of the city as a place where children have no childhood is likewise a favourite amongst documentary filmmakers. Unlike the rural children who are facing difficulties gaining basic education, city children experience the opposite problem. Ambitious parents are pushing them ruthlessly to achieve academic success. In an award winning documentary in 1994, *Gangqing meng / Piano Dream* documents a mother who gives up her job and leaves her husband on his own in order to accompany her teenage son to Beijing in preparation for the entrance examination he must sit if he wishes to enrol in the Central Music Academy. The boy has already been under enormous pressure during a childhood filled with piano practice which denies him the pleasure of playing football or joining a sightseeing outing. Similarly in *Kaoshi / Exams*, four girls aged between 7 and 12 are under pressure to gain entry to the Central Music Academy. To achieve this, all four have had to sacrifice their childhood to piano practice. What we see is the fulfilment of parental dreams, the youngsters' dislike of endless practice, their fatigue, their worries about not being able to pass, and their tears after receiving their disappointing examination results. Another award winning documentary in 2003, *Youer yuan / Kindergarten* depicts children aged between three and five in a Shanghai kindergarten. Without narration and music, except intertitles providing background information, the film consists of long sequences of children eating, sleeping, playing, learning, singing, displaying their skills, talking, fighting and watching television, presented predominantly in the observational documentary mode. A contrast emerges between the interviews which show the children's innocent body language and individual thoughts and shots of the system by which the kindergarten transforms individuality into stereotypical behaviour to suit collective activities. A large number of images show children crying, or fighting, with teachers trying to maintain control. The film ends with a sequence of a little boy standing near the winder searching for his parents' shadow. He has been waiting for four hours to be picked up.

This kind of social critique is made even more poignant in documentaries addressing the theme of the city as a place of broken families. In the 30-minute DV *Yuanyuan / Yuanyuan* (2005) by Yu Shaobin, the 20-year-old Beijinger Yuanyuan portrays herself as having grown up in a single-parent family. When her parents were divorced, her father took off to South America, only to return to Shenzhen in the early 1990s, while her mother headed for Xinjiang where she opened a fertilizer factory. Since then, Yuanyuan has been shuffled between various family members, her father in Shenzhen, her mother in Urumqi and her stepfather's mother, whom she calls 'grandmother', in Beijing. We meet Yuanyuan as she decides to leave her stepfather in Beijing to join her filmmaking father in Shenzhen. However, things do not turn out so rosy for Yuanyuan there. Her father is rather bohemian, with a girlfriend only four years older than herself. Yuangyuan can't stand living with them and often imagines that she is suffering from a mental illness. On her twentieth birthday, as she wishes her friends to get married soon, she realises that deep down inside her she wishes them quite the opposite. When her grandmother dies she loses her only source of emotional support. The documentary closes with a shot showing her alone, once more boarding a train.

In some documentaries, the city is also the place where babies are dumped. Zeng Yiqun and Zhao Xinjing's DV *Qiying yu tanmianhua jiang / A Daughter for the Cotton Mat Maker* (2000) presents a migrant family who produce cotton mats as the source of their livelihood in the city. They find an abandoned infant whom they take in as their own child. In a similar vein, Jiang Yue's *Xinfu shenghuo / Happy Life* documents two middle-aged men who are security officers at Zhengzhou railway station, and their disillusionment with home and work. One sequence of the film shows an abandoned baby that has been found at the station and taken to the office. While the security officers look at the infant and chat about it, an old man enters and asks whether he can have the baby. He has no children himself, but makes a modest living selling fruit as a street peddler. Without checking his identity or reporting the matter to the police, the old man is permitted to leave with the baby. He promises to bring his identity the next day. All the old man is asked is to leave his address. The viewer is led to wonder whether the society is able to distinguish between a baby and a puppy.

The city is also represented as a contradictory place for which country people yearn and yet where migrants are discriminated against. *Houjie / Houjie Township* (2002) made by Zhou Hao and Ji Ianghong documents the filthy living conditions and hardship of country migrants who have settled near Guangzhou. The film presents images of the fighting in the district, the migrants' fears and their concerns about unstable jobs. Many of the manufacturing industries had been financed by investors from Hong Kong and Taiwan and are now shown to be collapsing due to the economic downturn after September 11, 2001. *Jietou tanfan / Street Peddler* (2003) by Zhao Weidong is a DV of 24 minutes depicting the daily struggles the street peddlers have to endure with city inspectors. City officials regard street peddlers as a nuisance and a blemish on the urban, social environment. The sudden appearance of the inspectors is a constant threat to the business of street peddlers. The camera follows a couple of country migrants, documenting their efforts to survive in a city, the hardship and nerve-wracking conditions under which they work. Officialdom is portrayed as inhuman and the city as a precarious place for earning a living. Much in the same critical spirit, *Chuang / Lost in the City*, a DV by Jin Xueli and Zhang Hai, has as its focus the childhood of rural migrant children growing up around rubbish bins while they are waiting for their parents to return from their odd jobs, such as shining people's shoes in the street. Old Lao Wang in Zhang Hongfeng's DV *Beiyin / In the Background* (2003) is unable to return to his rural home for the Spring Festival because he feels he has to earn a bit of extra money for his elder son's wedding and to keep the younger ones at school. During the Spring Festival when most of Beijing citizens keep warm at home and celebrate, Lao Wang rides his bicycle carting coal through back alleys during the cold winter nights. Zhu Lingfei's DV *Zai lushang / Migrant* looks at how the city attitudes to workers from the countryside impact on migrants. The film shows two types of rural migrants: one, who prefers urban life to returning to the country in spite of poor living and working conditions; the other, a clerk in a five star hotel with better working conditions, is not happy with his social status and is working hard to be accepted as a 'real' urban citizen. Yan Lin's DV *Zai Kunming / In Kunming* (2004) has as its theme the massive number of country migrants who are entering the city in search for jobs. Looking at the not so pretty underbelly of China's rapid economic growth and urban expansion, the film captures the hopes and hardship of the migrants. So determined are many to make their choice of city life a success that they confess that 'even if we died in the process, we must keep on struggling'. The statement is taken from an interview with a group of peasants who want to work in the illegal mines, fully aware of the real risk of being buried alive. Given the deplorable safety records especially of the private enterprise mining industry, the documentary's claims do not appear to be exaggerated.

In many documentaries, the city is painted as unstable and insecure. Han Lei's *Doudong de 20 fengzhong / Trembling for Twenty Minutes* captures the mobility of city life, with desperate scenes of human activity day and night across Beijing, Kaifeng, and Guangzhou. Wang Yiqun in *Buanding de shenghuo / An Unstable Life* (2003) portrays the lifestyle of a go-go dancer, Jiujiu, and her precarious existence. Lonely, anxious and fearful, Jiujiu finds it hard to survive in the prosperous city. The theme of 'trembling' is also explored in depth in Li Yifan and Yan Yu's DV *Yanmei / Before the Flood* (2005), but from a somewhat different perspective. In order to build the world's largest hydroelectric dam, the area surrounding the Three Gorges will be turned into a vast reservoir. The independent filmmakers record in detail the process of the first trial flooding as waters submerge a city. I will discuss this film in some detail below.

Another urban theme is the city as a place where creativity is oppressed. In 1990 the pioneering independent filmmaker Wu Wenguang documented five freelance artists living in Beijing but without Beijing residence identity in *Liulang Beijing / Bumming in Beijing*. Interviewed by the filmmaker, the five artists, a writer, a photographer, two painters and a playwright, express their dissatisfaction with the jobs allocated to them by the state, and explain that they have left their home towns to come to Beijing in pursuit of their artistic goals. However, their lives in Beijing turn out to be most depressing. Without stable income and proper work identity, their social status as *mang liu* (drifters) is low. It is perhaps not surprising that the image of city life that emerges from the interviews is not exactly flattering. Their nostalgia for traditional architecture and contempt for high-rise progress contrasts with the standard celebration of the modernisation of Beijing and other megacities. In much the same mould, Tang Danhong's *Yeying bushi weiyi de gehou / Nightingale, not the Only Voice* (2000) follows the lives of three artists, a painter, a performer, and a poet in Chengdu, and their feelings of oppression in the market economy. *Piao / Floating* (2005) documents a guitar player, Yang, who dreams of becoming a pop star. Drifting from Henan, Yang plays his guitar for a living in the streets of Guangzhou. Constantly threatened by security guards and city inspectors, as well as competitors in the street, his love life is a mess, his life is anything but enviable. On turning 30, Yang is caught by the city authorities and sent home.

The city is also often filmed as a place for gays, where men are confused, and where marriage and divorce have lost all meaning. *Wo shu she / The Snake Boy* (2001) a DV by Chen Miao and Li Xiao, tells the story of a Shanghai homosexual jazz singer. The documentary follows the snake boy to his hometown, tracing his family and the cultural environment that influenced his artistic career and gender preference. By means of interviews with his teachers at the Shanghai Music Academy, and his friends in Shanghai, the film shows the disappointment of the singer and his mother when his gay identity proves a major hurdle to his career. The theme of the emptiness of the life of men in the city is the focus of Hu Xinyu's DV *Nanren / Men* (2004) which documents three unemployed bachelors living together in a flat. Their life seems gloomy and dull, their only hope being female company, and waiting for calls from women. Similarly depressing is Wang Fang's DV *Jiehun / Marriage* (2004) a documentary about the second wedding of two divorcees. The film questions the apparent lack of depth in urban, human relationships and the ease with which human bonds are established and dissolved. Zuo Yixiao's *Shisang / Losing* (2004) records the process of his own divorce from his wife. The 33-minute film does not give us any clue why the couple divorce. We witness them one day before they go to the Shanghai marriage registry, where they received their marriage certificates, and the day they launch their divorce proceedings. At the beginning of the film there is a series of photos of the happily married couple and proud parents. On the way to the registry office, they pass the place where they first met and we learn of the start of their love affair. At the office, they film each other in a calm, friendly and rational manner. After their submission of the divorce forms, they take photos of each other, and leave in different directions. The film focuses on the process of divorce, not on any of its reasons, indicating contemporary attitudes towards marriage and divorce, in contrast to those of previous generations.

The theme of the shallowness of urban life is also at the centre of Huang Wenhai's *Xuanhua de chentu / Floating Dust* (2003) presenting lower middle class existence in a small city, where money is everything. The documentary focuses on a mahjong parlour and its regular customers. Beyond that, the film also provides a general impression of gambling as part of city life. The mahjong parlor is run by an unemployed disabled man and his wife. Their regular customers are all under 30, either out of work or not happy with their work. Xiao Qiu is the unemployed leader of a small gang. His girlfriend, Azi, runs a massage shop after having been made redundant at her factory at the age of 26. A gambling couple, Niu Zhenyu and Wang Rong have lived together for three years. She is pregnant, but wants neither baby nor marriage. Another customer is Xiao Cheng, a regular 21-year-old gambling addict. The film explores the obsession of city folks with 'getting rich quick'. A broad spread of people is canvassed by the camera: public servants, university graduates, and small businessmen, all spending their time in the mahjong parlour, buying lottery tickets, and asking fortune tellers about their chances. When it is announced that the winning number is hidden in an American children's show, *Teletubbies*, the entire city is watching the programme, hoping to win. A more serene perspective of the city characterises the DV *Kong / Empty* (2004). Although only 13 minutes long, the film nicely documents a monk's life in a temple, demonstrating how religious changes have been affected by the market economy, and telling the viewer that even 'a monk cannot escape the great Wheel of Life'.

Typical images of cosmopolitan life are icons of modernisation, economic growth, commerce, globalisation and speed. In many independent documentaries, the glimpses offered testify to a tradition in tatters. In a 15-minute DV entitled *I bumped into an Old Man in Wangfujing on March 16 2004*, the filmmaker literally bumps into an old man on the doorstep of a church in Wangfujing on 16 March 2004. The film briefly, but astutely, explores what is no more than an ordinary experience. Zhu Yingwen's DV *Qingguanlu shi hao / No.10 Qinghuan Road* (2004) homes in on a small tobacco shop in an ordinary alley in Shanghai. Although Shanghai has changed dramatically, the small shop still maintains its traditional way of management since its foundation some 60 years ago. The film is exceptional in the sense that it portrays the harmonious life of the shopkeeper and his friendship with his customers and neighbours. In contrast, a DV made by Xiao Peng, *Guirong xiyuan / Guirong Theatre* (2003), presents the transformation of the entertainment industry in the city from the period of the planned economy to the bustle of today's commercial market. As theatre troupes are now forced to survive in a world of cut-throat competition, the Guirong Theatre has been changed into a teahouse with opera performances. We see images of spectators who come to drink tea, and throw money onto the stage to see and hear their favourite piece. In turn, the performers try their best to satisfy the wishes of customers and gratefully acknowledge their patrons. Luo Lei's DV *Xiaoqu / Small Neighbourhood* (2004) uses simple scenes and montage to contrast the neighbourhood relationships of blue-collar workers in Jilin before and after the economic reforms. Dong Jun's DV *Wuyan meidian / Blind Coal Store* (2004) is an image sequence of a snowy night in an urban coal shop, drawing to our attention the hardship and monotony of one family: a father and his three children. For Zhang Hongfeng, the maker of *Beiyin / In the Background* (2003), Beijing is well characterised by the bent back of old Lao Wang, straining to ride his bicycle in a narrow alley, carrying coal in a fitful, snowy and cold winter's night. A more extended cinematic exploration of the hardship of city life is attempted in the 99-minute DV *Manchang shenghuo li d mukamu / Songs from Our Melody of Life* (2004) by Shao Lei and Yang Sheng who filmed intermittently between 2001 and 2004 to portray the daily drudgery of an Uighur family in Shanghai.

To cover comprehensively the variety of subjects and cinematic treatments of urban life in China today is well beyond the scope of this study. A representative selection of documentaries will have to do. What comes across when viewing them is that the topics and their perspectives generally focus on contemporary, ordinary, trivial, local and individual events and people that can be viewed in any Chinese urban environment. This above all distances the current wave of documentaries, especially in the DV mould, from the grand national themes so prominent up to the transition period after the end of the Cultural Revolution. With these provisos in mind, the following films can be viewed as a series of vignettes, together making up a more comprehensive mosaic of Chinese urban life.

Maibao ren / Qin, the Newspaperman (2000) documents a day in the life of a newspaper seller and folk song performer, Qin Baohu. Wu Wei's DV *Biye qianxian / Before Graduation* (2004) records a group of university students in their senior year. Cheng Long's DV *Binren / Icemen* (2004) looks at the simple, but happy life of an ice collector's life amongst the charming snow art works of Harbin. *Baitai / White Tower* (2003) focuses on lives of people with hearing problems. *Zhiye kuqi zhe / Professional Mourner* (2003) traces the movements of a professional mourner for some six months in order to explore her attitude to life. The filmmaker wants to know whether or not the professional mourner is still able to be compassionate and has any 'real' feelings towards death. *Chengme zhi lu / Silent Journey* (2003) documents a group of friends who set out on a journey, having made a bet to remain silent for 72 hours. In the DV *The Man Who Repairs Bicycles* (2003) we are privy to the struggle of a man from the countryside trying to survive in the city by opening a bicycle repair stand in the street. The camera follows 30-year-old Bai, called *gege* by the filmmaker, as he goes about his repair work, borrows money to be able to pay the 100 *yuan* monthly lease of his work space, and resists attempts at getting evicted. The day-by-day image account drives home to the viewer how difficult it can be for a simple, industrious, poor, and honest man to make even a modest living in the urban environment.

In a somewhat different style, the DV *Yemeng / Nightdreams*, experiments with an attempt at projecting the stream of consciousness of a young man while he is running along the streets of the city. The camera catches his face and panting chest, his forceful forward movements giving the impression of a desperate personal struggle. His heavy-breathing, pavement pounding progress is interrupted by intermittent shots of his fantasies of dancing girls in nightclubs and a series of other stereotypical images of urban desire. An ambitious film for its technological resources, *Nightdreams* introduces a sense of experiment into the Chinese DV scene not too frequently encountered. Two other significant aspects of this documentary are noteworthy: one is its turn to the representation of subjectivity, which contrasts with the usually communal spirit of Chinese cinema and signals a shift from social to psychological reality; the other, causally related to the first, is the film's foregrounding of the problem of cinematic mediation itself. These features seem to me to signal the opening of a new space for cinematic exploration at the margins of documentary filmmaking. A more conventional cinematic method informs the DV *Beijing Station* featuring staff at an underground station in the Chinese capital. Because the film relies heavily on interviews, the usual sense of hustle and bustle of rushing crowds trying to catch their trains is replaced by an almost unreal calm. In this island of relative tranquility, the filmmaker interviews three women staff members. The first woman tells us that she hates her husband but loves her job, the only really good thing in her life. She thanks the Party for her warm and satisfying employment, as well as the 1,000 *yuan* monthly payment she is receiving for doing what she enjoys. For the second woman, ticket collecting is far from what she really wants to do. So she escapes into a fantasy world of words and music, quoting from her favourite literature to impose a more aesthetically pleasing order on the chaos around her. The third woman, a former soldier, is a gentle and contented person who does her job with charm and good cheer.

When we are able to compare two versions of cinematic documentation of the same social event, we become aware of the degree of difference between their voices. Such a comparison is provided by the CCTV's documentary series *Beiying / On the Other Side of the Dam*, a record of the social impact of the Three Gorges Project on the people of Fengjie and the independent DV *Yanmei / Before the Flood* (2006), likewise documenting Fengjie and the responses of its population to the government's evacuation and compensation programme. The CCTV's documentary foregrounds the process of local government officials trying to instruct the population as to how to proceed with their evacuation to an alternative place of settlement and apply for compensation. We see officials talking to people, collecting information and gauging the collective feelings of the confused and disillusioned crowd. As the images tell us, the authorities are experiencing difficulties in persuading people to accept their fate, the place they have been allocated and the amount of compensation they are to be granted. The perspective here is a top–down look at local government, with an emphasis on official decrees issued in Beijing and their local administrative application. Although publicly expressed complaints and expression of dissent are included in this version of the events, the CCTV camera is directed mainly at those who appear happy with the lots they have drawn and accept their relocation and the government's compensation offer. All in all, the CCTV's evacuation process in Fengjie appears as a reasonably controlled operation. The presentational mode is characterised by narration, interviews, and an observational style, lending the documentary an air of objectivity.

In contrast to the top–down account of the CCTV, the independent documentary *Yanmei / Before the Flood* affords us a view from the bottom section of the population of Fengjie. We witness the difficulties faced by a retired soldier who has opened a 'coolie' hostel and finds it hard to gain appropriate compensation for his investment. Disappointed, he does not know what to do next. We are shown the office of a Christian church where the remaining members of the congregation discuss how to cope with the government's refusal to compensate them for their loss. In true Christian spirit, some suggest submitting false invoices and payment slips to get at least something in return for their efforts! The film also records the patience and frustration of the local cadres who are trying to impose some semblance of order on a chaotic social scene. In the town hall people are shown drawing lots for relocation and compensation, some accepting their offers, others tearing up their lots and shouting abuse at the government officials. Like the CCTV version, *Before the Flood* relies on interviews and observation. The DV captures well the overflowing emotions of a confused and dissatisfied public and the horrendous human cost involved in imposing the most massive engineering project ever to be attempted anywhere in the world and imposed on millions of residents in the Three Gorges region.

Competing voices also characterise the CCTV production *Yige ren he yizuo chengshi / One City and One Person*, a series that brings together a number of well-known contemporary writers sketching their impressions of Chinese cities. The writers contributing to the series include Liu Xinwu, Ah Cheng, Zhang Xianliang, Li Kuanding and Sun Ganlu. As a result of the scripts being produced by different authors, the series achieves a collection of perspectives somewhat different from those usually presented by government or commercial advertising. For example, Liu Xinwu, an old Beijinger, as he calls himself, does not even mention Tiananmen square, symbol of Beijing and the nation. Instead, he focuses on the traditional places, the old courtyards, the *hutong*, the area around Longfu Shi, the main Tibetan Buddhist temple in Beijing, and other places destroyed during the Cultural Revolution. He is also critical of contemporary urban design, accusing developers of destroying valuable traditional buildings only to replace them by hundreds of fake 'antiques'. Zhang Xianliang talks mainly about his hometown Yinchuang from his place of exile in the countryside nearby. A picture of Shanghai markedly different from the usual accounts emerges from the script by Sun Ganlu. Instead of seeing Shanghai as a pinnacle of economic achievement, Sun Ganlu paints a picture of a ramshackle place of 'letter boxes' and 'colonial architecture'. What emerges from this series of documentaries is a more artistic response to China's urban transformation and a critique of any naïve acceptance of cities succumbing too readily to economic expansion. What is documented here is of course the writers' individual voices and perspectives rather than the cities themselves.

An equally critical but less personal perspective of city life is presented by Du Haibin in *Tielu Yanxian / Along the Railway* (2000), a DV about a marginal social group, a motley gang of boys and young men living where the railway tracks cut into the city. What makes this documentary particularly fascinating is the fact that the filmmaker originally intended to shoot footage for a fiction film, but found what his camera discovered so intriguing that he decided to stay with the documentary mode of presentation. The film opens with a long take of an approaching passenger train passing the camera. We see the tracks, grey skies and the rear view of buildings of the city of Baoji. At the bottom of the railway embankment a group of shabbily dressed young men and boys is huddling around a fire amidst heaps of waste paper and rubbish. The camera follows a 20-year-old man, the apparent leader of the group. There are antisocial remarks and obscenities directed at the authorities. 'Fuck the police . . . I lost my ID card and they put me in the detention centre'. The man is from Sichuan. 'We sleep any-where on the ground'. The boys cook noodles, add some salt and lamb fat recycled from a rubbish bin. The youngest of the boys is nine years old; he comes from Xi'an. The oldest man is 30. They come from all over China. The camera focuses on a youth with a toy submachine gun against the tracks. Except when they warm themselves at the fire, or sleep in a wind sheltered niche along the embankment, the boys are constantly on the move, collecting rubbish and looking for discarded food, and cigarettes. Some pick up bottles to sell at the recycling plant for a few *yuan*. The film mixes images of the boys with conversational style interviews, letting them speak their minds. 'Who is Jiang Zemin? . . . The guards are dogs . . . I left my home to see more things . . . three years now'. Another boy wants to repay the money he owes his boss and then never leave home again. One boy gives a detailed account of his brutal father who beat his three wives until they left him. 'I was left with the baby . . . he sold my mother to Anhui . . . beat me . . . so I left'. The camera focuses on the boy in a very long take as the train passes closely behind him. 'When I got to Fuyang, I looked for a job . . . watched videos. A waiter served me some seeds and then charged ten *yuan*. When I couldn't pay he beat me. I got on the train'. A guard threw him out at Baoji. A long shot of the rail track is accompanied by television soap music: 'Mummy is the best in one's life. Children with a mother are like flowers . . .'. The members of the group have names such as 'Inner Mongolia', 'Fengxiang', and 'Yunnan'. A 16-year-old boy tells how his family went broke because his mother is addicted to opium. His father has been crippled in a mining accident. He would like to go home 'to open a shop'. Now he is saving money and tries to keep healthy and fit: 'I always exercise'. He has an odd job cleaning the local gym. Twenty-year-old 'Fengxiang' distances himself from those who 'walk in the night', that is, those who sleep during the day and steal when it is dark. He reminisces about his childhood, when he was running errands for a policeman. The camera briefly catches a sympathetic woman providing left over food and assuring them that the meat is fine. 'Inner Mongolia' is the only one who is committed to his life as a vagabond along the tracks. His parents are well off; he has a wife and a child, but left because of gambling debts. His parents have paid them off. He wants to stay here; he loves gambling and the freedom of the tracks.

After about six months the filmmaker returns to Baoji to resume his documentary. Some of the boys have left. Some now object to his filming on the grounds that their current existence is embarrassing. They ask him not to show the film in their province. The filmmaker promises, knowing full well that he will not be able to keep his word. One of the groups reminds him that their right to refuse being filmed is enshrined in law 151 and 152, which should be respected. 'Please don't film. I am not going to give a grand theory, but humans have human rights, rights to freedom, property rights, a right to their self-image, right?' One of the young men is philosophical about the law. 'What is the law? . . . a set of regulations protecting the rich . . . law is injustice . . .'. A 30-year-old, called 'King of Evil', collects stray children and takes them back to their parents. One of the missing boys has been picked up by a policeman who invited him to become a member of his family, an adopted son, and now found him a job in a restaurant. Otherwise the police and the guards do not get a good press from the railway kids. 'They beat us and steal our money'. Interviewed by the filmmaker, a nearby resident finds nothing good to say about the boys

'They are a nuisance . . . they steal . . .'. A railway guard concurs: 'These people are lazy; bad for our environment; no contribution to society; no respect for traffic regulations . . . they are too mobile; when we beat them the train passengers object and give them money. My boss said, "Kick them hard when nobody is watching"'. The group gradually dissipates, some returning to their home towns. The DV ends with the image of 'Yunnan' who does not want to go home. 'I can't go home. I am waiting for a friend who has been jailed for two years for stealing three *yuan* and seven cents'. 'Yunnan' wants to be here when his friend is released. The documentary offers us a glimpse of voices from the social bottom of the city. Its strength, it seems to me, lies in its strictly observational style and the total absence of any interfering, narratorial guidance. 'Look at these kids', the film seems to say.

One of the most disturbing documentaries to come out of China in recent years is the three-part film *Tiexi qu / District West of the Railways*. Directed by Wang Bing between 1999 and 2001, the documentary displays the plight of Chinese workers and their families in Shenyang, an industrial town in north-east China. Each of the three parts opens with a written introduction placing the film in its historical context. Established in 1934, the Tiexi District of Shenyang is one of the oldest and largest industrial estates in China. After the end of the Second World War, some 157 industrial projects had been financed here by the Soviet Union, with industrial equipment dismantled in East Germany and transported to China. In its heyday Tiexi District was able to sustain around one million people. In the early 1990s, however, when state enterprises began to be less and less viable, the entire area began to decline. By the end of 1999 one factory after another other closed down. At the centre of Tiexi District is a 20km long railway track linking its factories with the wider network of the country's industrial and commercial railway system. With ample use of carefully framed shots and often long takes, much of the film focuses on the tracks as the dying lifeline of industry and the population that sustained it. The remainder of the image chain depicts the rundown factories, work under the most hazardous conditions imaginable, the workers at rest playing cards and Chinese chess, families living in slum conditions and, above all, the verbal exchanges amongst workers and their families. Running through the three parts of *West of the Railways*, 'Rust', 'Remnants', and 'Rails', are conversations about the looming closure of factories, payment of outstanding wages, compensation, schemes for earning a bit of money, and ways of securing a better future.

The first part of *West of the Railways*, 'Rust 1' opens with a long take of a snow covered rail track viewed from a moving locomotive. From the starting sequence of images the viewer is presented with a cold, dirty, ramshackle industrial environment spelling hopelessness. This is achieved purely visually, without narration or voice-over to guide our interpretation, a technique consistently used throughout this documentary. We see workers in their rest area eating, having showers and haircuts, joking and quarrelling. There is dirt wherever the camera directs our attention. Again employing long takes, we witness how workers are trying to keep warm, and struggling to keep the factory going in spite of the fact that they have not been paid wages for a while and are desperately waiting for official instructions as to the fate of the factory and the future of the workers. The camera then introduces the viewer to what is supposed to be the central purpose of the factory, smelting lead. The working conditions look atrocious, lead poisoning being the most obvious hazard, with shockingly outmoded production methods well below third world standards, the productivity is minimal. More or less the same picture emerges from shots of two other factories in the district, a cable factory and a sheet metal factory. With most of the workers already laid off, no pay and serious doubts about compensation, the remaining factory staff express their frustration, anger, anxiety, and loss of trust in the factory as well as political leadership. At a dinner, women are presented in good cheer, hoping for better times. As the evening progresses, the conversations are becoming more strident. There is talk of demanding compensation, the privatisation of the factory and a share in the profits. This contrasts sharply with a woman singing a Karaoke song of 'spring, prosperity and a new grand era!'

'Rust 2' offers a similarly depressing scenario. Again opening with a long take of the rails, the documentary shows a copper foundry in the last stages of its existence. Rumours as to shutdown are rife amongst the workers. They can't believe it, having hoped against hope that management and government would ultimately do the right thing by them. An extended blue filter shot of the interior of the copper foundry on 9 June 2000, very much repeats the impression the viewer was given in 'Rust 1': an unsafe, run down, ramshackle workplace. Working under the most horrendous conditions, without wages and little hope for improvement, some workers are shown trying their hand at fishing in nearby dirt pond. Other desperate measures include trying to steel cable to sell at the wrecker's yard. Others dream of a better future. In one of the lyrical moments of the film, a worker plays a revolutionary song on a saxophone 'The Tibetan serf has become a master . . . Thank you Mao Zedong'.

Part 2 'Remnants' turns to the social conditions of the Shenyang working families at home where signs of demolition and decay are everywhere. Against this background, the camera moves amongst teenage youths whose personal problems intermingle with the dissolution of social life on a large scale. When the authorities announce the demolition of their homes to give way to urban development, some residents offer resistance without hope, while others give up and leave disillusioned. In the absence of narration, the social upheaval is entirely conveyed by slow moving image chains, painfully driving home a tragedy on a large scale. The viewer is particularly struck by the fact that it is those amongst the Chinese working class population that most trusted in the government, the CCP, and the factory management to reward their loyalty with proper wages and compensation who stay the longest and hence suffer the most. Part 3 'Rails' resumes the industrial theme by focusing on the demise of the railway itself, the lifeline of the factory district. The documentary ends on a minimally hopeful note by portraying a worker, Du Xiyun, and his son Du Yang who briefly return to their old factory after a year's absence in good health and apparently better off financially. There is hope after all, but elsewhere, these images suggest to Du Xiyun's old mates, as they do to the film viewer.

What Wang Bing's radical documentary style appears to be saying is that words could not describe what needs to be seen to be believed. His long takes, supported only by location sound, offer us a brute social reality uncontaminated by the director's verbal interference. Here, Guo Jing's idea of the 'voice of image-making' introduced at the beginning of this chapter, comes into its own, though not in the rural settings Guo has in mind. Certainly, Wang Bing's is a powerful and unique way of 'speaking' with the camera about the dissolution of SOE industrial plants in the era of economic reform and the transition from planned to market oriented management. Introductory texts and intertitles are restricted to the openings of the three thematic parts, while editing appears to be kept to a stark minimum. What we have before us on the screen is an almost unbearably slow unfolding of visual torture, made even more inquisitional for the viewer by the location sound of industrial noise and the voices of the workers. It is at the level of diegetic voices that the film speaks to us beyond its image chain of hopelessness. At this level, my earlier definition of individual voices and speaking positions becomes relevant. The cumulative effect of the utterances of the workers and their families amounts to a heterogeneous polyphony of voices that together cannot but form in the viewer's mind a critical discourse. In Nichols' sense of 'voice', or the overall socio-political statement a film makes, one could say that Wang Bing has captured such a critical, summary voice without recourse to editorial synthesis. Rather, or so it seems, the synthesis is already well prepared for by the cinematic unfolding of social phenomena.

To the traveller who visits Shenyang today a very different picture offers itself. The bulldozers have done their work and new buildings have been erected wherever we may wish to look. Economic progress is now writ large in Shenyang only a few years after the decay documented by Wang Bing and everywhere we notice the slogan 'One year – a new image; three years – great changes; five years – momentous development'. This however in no way invalidates the historical record put before us by Wang Bing.

Could we say, then, that documentary film, in the hands of directors such as Wang Bing, Zhao Gang and other likeminded filmmakers, is announcing a new critical discourse so rarely seen in the Chinese tradition? I suggest that we can. Looking back over the assemblage of documentaries discussed in this last chapter, it would seem that in terms of the range of subject matter, the presentational process, and the speaking positions encountered we cannot but notice the emergence of what I have called a polyphonic heterogeneity. The themes broached in the various documentary modes in the recent past include the failure of the planned economy and the tragic consequences of economic reforms, the human cost of vast engineering projects and the social engineering of massive relocation programmes, the chaotic conditions that characterise some of the elections at village level, backward conditions in remote areas, impoverished country schools, urban hardship and the difficulties faced by growing rural families under restrictive land release policies. The speaking positions we have encountered range from official voices describing controlled progress, to a critical reworking of history, personal and cultural perspectives, and scepticism and even cynicism towards electoral reform. In spite of the growing number of critical voices we should avoid, however, any narrowly ideological reading of this widening documentary forum as a struggle between individual critical creativity and authority. While this struggle is certainly part of the overall picture, it does not quite tell the right story. What is actually happening is both a challenge to the existing boundaries of public debate and co-operation between several parties, such as official channels, television as an industry, and semi-independent as well as independent filmmakers. To effect a difference that makes a difference, it is the latter two who need their work to be screened by television stations to mass audiences and so have their voices heard. The result is a burgeoning, multi-voiced public media sphere in the making.

Conclusion
Documentaries as critical discourse

How does the picture I have drawn of Chinese documentaries fit into the broader discussion of Chinese media and democracy? A persuasive approach to the topic can be found in *Media, Market, and Democracy in China* by Zhao Yuezhi (Zhao 1998). She is adamant that 'the question is not whether China should or can be democratised but which definition of democracy will prevail in the process' (Zhao 1998: 190). With respect to communication this should mean that democratisation cannot simply be seen in terms of increasing individual freedom or the protection of journalists but must also include such notions as equality and a 'sense of community' (Zhao 1998: 191). Zhao cogently locates television at the centre of the 'reconstruction of the media system' which has already achieved a modicum of diversity and is able to exert a huge influence on the nation. One could add that it is the growing number of semi-dependent and independent documentary filmmakers that have significantly contributed to that diversity. While she concedes that talk of democracy may sound idealistic at this stage, she also points to the important fact that 'a democratised media system does not have to start from scratch in China' (Zhao 1998: 193). This very much supports my arguments in Chapters 4 to 7. A space has opened up between political ideology and commercial interest, a space that is being negotiated by the media in a special way. As a result of the government having handed over to media institutions the task of self-funding, a certain degree of power has accrued to the media. The bigger the revenue, the larger the power, and the stronger the relative independence from government. One of the effects of this development has been, as we saw, the desire of television stations, from the CCTV down to local television institutions, to be seen as media professionals rather than propaganda instruments. However, as I have also been at pains to emphasise, we cannot therefore expect democratisation changes to occur as a groundswell generated by television and its audiences. As Zhao rightly cautions, 'there can be no single agent of change'. Without the support of reformers inside the CCP, the democratic forces in society at large, including journalists, television programme producers and filmmakers, will make little headway.

In any case, as Hugo de Burgh has pointed out in *The Chinese Journalist: Mediating Information in the World's Most Populous Country*, not all dissent by journalists and others are based on democratic principles. One of de Burgh's central arguments is that a large number of Chinese, certainly amongst the intelligentsia, and certainly the neoconservatives, are highly sceptical of democracy as a promising form of rule in China. Moreover, the Chinese that do celebrate democracy as an ideal for China are largely the émigrés. In China itself, says de Burgh, many 'share a scepticism about the appropriateness of democracy for China' (de Burgh 2003: 182–3). As to journalists, they 'may be championing rights', he writes, 'but this does not necessarily mean that they are imbued with a democratic spirit'. True, many of the expressions of discontent are 'no longer muzzled by a system of comprehensive repression' and 'it is permissible now to protest about local issues of corruption, maladministration, poverty or environmental plight'. At the same time more and more people are beginning to use the media to publicly present their interests. But even the 'emergence of a discourse of rights does not necessarily mean that the Chinese are adopting Anglophone notions of democracy' (de Burgh 2003: 180–1). Indeed, in the end the Chinese may very well find an advanced Continental European style of democratic discourse more to their liking. Although de Burgh shares Zhao's caution, and in spite of all the authoritarian remnants of the Mao era, he notes two kinds of evidence for change at least in the area of journalism. Now, there are 'contrasting views, fuelling the emergence of a public opinion; there is revelation; there is investigation'. At the same time, the 'language with which the journalists describe their functions' has changed: the vocabulary of 'public scrutiny' has replaced the 'throat and tongue of the Party' phrase and the term 'audience' is now being used instead of 'masses'. This, de Burgh feels, is a sign that journalists now are prepared to 'contribute to society's development in a fundamentally different way from their predecessors' (de Burgh 2003: 191).

Journalists are of course only one, and probably not even a leading, factor in the transformation of the media scene in China. As Michael Keane has argued, persuasively I think, television formatting has to be regarded as a major driver in the process. Part of formatting is the production of new kinds of audiences, something I have tried to demonstrate in detail in Chapters 4 and 5. Another factor is what Keane sums up under the term 'isomorphism', the way China is absorbing global trends. His distinction between 'coercive, mimetic, and normative' isomorphism reflects television practice under official pressure, under the guidance of leading stations, and in response to industrial best practice, respectively (Keane 2005: 89, 92). This three step description does not quite match the phases that I have argued characterise today's documentary films and television programmes in China – from remnants of the dogmatic mode to participatory strategies and critically observational styles, amounting to a polyphonic heterogeneity.

The discrepancy seems to be the result of a difference in analytical perspective. Where Keane looks broadly at television programming, including soap drama, reality television, and a variety of other entertainment formats, my narrower focus on the content and style of documentaries of necessity foregrounds the emergence of a critical dimension not visible from the industrial perspective.

As the analysis of a substantial number of Chinese documentaries has demonstrated, a polyphonic heterogeneity of voices is now emerging in China which, combined with a more relaxed attitude by the Party on appropriate subject areas, suggests the evolution of a new kind of critical discourse. Consider in this respect also the now flourishing Chinese talk shows on television, a documentary genre in its own right, in which the audience is invited to participate in the debate between programme host, experts, victims of crime, and people with specific achievements or experiences. Some audiences are divided into opposing sides for debate, in other cases, members of the audience are provided with signs with which they can signal approval or disapproval, enabling the host to select speakers from amongst the crowd. The signs also indicate when members of the audience change their minds as a result of the ongoing exchanges. Even when the debates are trivial, which often they are not, what we are observing here is a *rehearsal of democratic debate by means other than the obviously political*. As we have seen, some of the new DV documentaries, and certainly those that are screened on major television channels, are offering the viewing public a different view of society from that which is typically provided by the stations closely associated with government, such as the CCTV or the CETV. Marginal social groups, disastrous social and working conditions, or unpalatable historical topics are being aired in this new wave of documentary filmmaking. Nor is it the case, as we have seen, that the official channels themselves only present the staple fare of government propaganda. Indeed, some of the crucial innovations in Chinese television, such as audience participation and multi-voiced presentations, have their origins in the CCTV. The idea of democratisation from the top is not something that Western observers of China are likely to applaud. One could say that top–down and *demos* are contradictory and so the term 'democratisation' is misleading in this context. Nevertheless, there is ample evidence that many of the 'democratic' features of current documentary filmmaking have their origins in government controlled media institutions. For example, the government initiated separation of production and screen has been largely responsible, in conjunction with new technologies, for the rise of independent documentaries. Viewed in a larger context, this kind of government driven change is perhaps one of the reasons why Zhao Yuezhi insists that the reformers inside the CCP will be crucial to any future democratic movement in China.

Taking a bird's eye perspective of the chapters of the book and their contribution to the overall argument advanced, what kind of summary view offers itself to be abstracted? We have noted that from the historical beginnings of Chinese documentary in the 1920s to the present the question of 'truth' has been an issue in a way it has not been in the theorisation of the genre in the West. We also noted a drastic transformation in the role of the audience and the position of the filmmaker during the various phases of the evolution of documentary cinema in China. Let me try to characterise each of the major phases of this process in relation to these issues. In the twenty years before the Communist revolution, traditional Confucian morality exerted a powerful influence on the conception of the documentary genre (Chapter 2). The truth to be captured by documentary film was determined above all by social morality and a didactic narrativity to suit that purpose. This meant that represented objectivities as entities in themselves could not legitimately claim to be the primary goal of documentary cinema. Nor was the audience in a position to demand a deviation from this coherent cultural frame. After 1949 the definition of documentary truth changed radically under the pressure of Soviet film theory and Mao's adaptation of *wen yi zai dao* ('art must convey a moral message') to his Marxist goal, revolutionary art (Chapter 3). Again the represented objectivities of the social world were denied primacy. Truth now was identical with government policy, resulting in what I have called the 'dogmatic formula' of documentary film. Social reality was idealised to reflect the truth of policy and individuals were dissolved into heroic or enemy stereotypes. At the same time, viewers were truly a 'captive audience', one that was herded to film consumption sites and shown only what had been released for the 'masses'. All this underwent yet another radical transformation during the transition period from 1978 to 1993, when Deng Xiaoping's pragmatism gradually took root in China. Documentary film was then to address the actual facts of social reality. The cat, for example, was no longer to be viewed as holding a position in an elaborate moral scheme, nor as an expression of ideology, but in terms of its social function: no matter what its colour, a cat was supposed above all to catch mice. Now truth is what is in front of us in society and therefore identical with the social objectivities to be documented (see the end of Chapter 3). When this shift in thinking gradually spread through China and in particular through the ranks of filmmakers and television producers, something happened that had not been noticed, let alone theorised, before. A distinction opened up between the social fact to be documented and the manner of its representation. In other words, pragmatism ushered in a problem that had remained covered up in the two previous phases of documentary cinema: the problem of mediation. One could also say that the seemingly simple ontic of social reality suddenly revealed its logically necessary companion, the epistemic side of representation. The solution accepted by all, at least for a while, was the notion of 'truthful' or 'sincere' cinematic documentation. This eliminated, or so it seemed, the bothersome intrusion of the ideological or subjective distortion of social facts. Documentary filmmaking in the early stages of Chinese pragmatism was secured by truthful mediation, and film audiences across China were able to enjoy their liberation from dogmatic cinema without having to embrace rampant Western cinematic experimentation. But once the question of mediation had been raised at all, it was only a matter of time before filmmakers began to explore its potential (Chapters 4 to 7). As we saw, this was not only the result of a change of a philosophical and political kind, but also in part the consequence of the new film technologies of cordless camera, location sound, and later DV. The transformations that occurred, however, did not go as far as a general embracing by filmmakers of free experimentation with multi-perspectival filmmaking that would throw documentary truth to the wind. To this day, Chinese documentary has not adopted the principle 'the more, the merrier'; rather what we see in practice is the realisation of a principle of 'the more, the more truthful'. In other words, documentary film has extended and so questioned the idea of individual, 'truthful' representation by the introduction of multi-perspectival alternatives. If documentary truthfulness has proved to be an impossible ideal, its multi-voiced or polyphonic alternatives at least have the benefit of offering the viewer a range of alternative vistas. When audiences are invited to contribute to the polyphonic principle, the result is audience participation, a phenomenon that has been enthusiastically welcomed across China. When the combined innovations of internal text polyphony and audience participation constitute not just a numerical increase but also a spread of oppositional voices, we have what I have called polyphonic heterogeneity, a precondition of democratic discourse. For apart from avoiding a well understood and tacitly respected set of political topics, such as the status of Tibet, free elections, one Party governance, or the future of Taiwan; current television documentaries and in particular the rapidly evolving and highly popular debating programmes are demonstrating all the methods and techniques characteristic of similar forums in Western democracies. In fact, such programmes give the appearance of a deliberate practice of public debate in advance of any possible political application at a later date.

I said early in the book that documentary cinema and television programmes are a privileged arena for displaying a society's self-interpretation. In this respect Chinese documentaries demonstrate a historical trajectory from political idealisation to individualised representations of social realities, a shift from representing the heroic and grand to the particular and even pathetic, from a monologically homogenised society to one that is polyphonically disseminated. In terms of documentary styles, this process has shown itself as a transformation from documentaries made according to what I termed a 'dogmatic formula' to observational, interactive and participatory modes of presentation. What is still different in this picture if compared with the evolution of documentary genres in Europe and the Anglosphere is that we have found hardly any evidence of self-reflexive documentary styles in China to date. The leading edge appears to be a documentary mode of social critique, with self-critical styles perhaps waiting in the wings.

In the transformation of documentaries from dogma to polyphony the following factors, I argued, have played a substantial role: policy change at the level of government; institutional change at the level of television stations; new media technologies; steeply rising advertising revenues; ratings; increasing audience involvement in programming; a desire amongst filmmakers and media institutions to compete globally; and an emerging visual aesthetics approaching Western styles. In terms of the definition of Chinese documentary film and television programme, 'from dogma to polyphony' means a quite radical shift from representation based on an ideological conception of 'truth' to representation based on the 'truth' of perceptual actuality, an ideal stipulated at the beginning of the book. For China, perceptual actuality means above all the 'truth' of social reality. And once actual social reality is embraced as the legitimate basis for documentaries, the demand to 'let the people speak' inevitably leads not only to polyphony as a quantitative leap, but to polyphonic heterogeneity. One significant feature of this new multi-voiced picture of opposing speaking positions of directors, subjects and participating audiences has been shown to be the emergence of a significant, critical dimension of documentary filmmaking. While it is too early, I think, to describe this complex exchange of public opinion as a Habermasian public media sphere, I suggest that the rapidly expanding participation of television audiences in documentary programmes across Chinese society, including sectors of the peasantry, appears to be preparing the ground for the possibility of such a public media sphere in the making. Certainly, the style and methods of public debate on television in China today and the growing number of documentary films probing social issues make it difficult to deny that such a development is indeed likely to occur.

Notes

Chapter 2

1 Landscape documentaries include *Xihu fengjing* / *West Lake Scenery* (1919), *Lushan fengjing* / *Lu Mountain Sceneries* (1919), *Zhejiang chao* / *Zhejiang Waves* (1919), *Putuo fengjing* / *Putuo Sceneries* (1920), *Beijing mingsheng* / *Famous Places in Beijing* (1920), *Changjiang mingsheng* / *Famous Places along the Yangzi River* (1920), *Shanghai fengjing* / *Shanghai Sceneries* (1921), *Nanjing mingsheng* / *Famous Places in Nanjing* (1921), *Jinan mingsheng* / *Famous Places in Jinan* (1921), *Taishan mingsheng* / *Famous Places in Tai Mountain* (1921), *Qufu mingsheng* / *Famous Places in Qufu* (1921).
2 Others include *Shangwu yinshu guan fanggong* / *Workers leaving Commercial Press* (1917), *Shangwu yinshu guan yinshuan shuo quanjing* / *A View of the Commercial Press* (1918), *Sheng Xinsun da chu sang* / *Sheng Xinsun's Funeral* (1917), *Meiguo hongshizi hui Shanghai da youxin* / *American Red Cross Marching in Shanghai* (1918).
3 *Handa zhuo ze* / *Honest Man catching a thief*, *Daixu zhushou* / *Silly son-in-law celebrating father-in-law's Birthday*, *Sihao du* / *Gambling to death*, *De toucai* / *Winning a Lotto*, *Lidashao* / *Li Dashao*, and about ten more films in J. Cheng (1967: 36, volume 1).
4 *Aixi fen* / *Ancient Tome in Nantong* (1921), *Suzhou fengjing* / *Suzhou Sceneries* (1925), *Fuzhou fengjing* / *Fuzhou Sceneries* (1925), *Xihu fengjing* / *West Lake Sceneries* (1925), *Aihui jiuhuashan fengjing* / *Sceneries of Jiuhua Mountain in Anhui* (1925), *Luoyang fengjing* / *Luoyang Sceneries* (1924), *Chaozhou bajing* / *Eight Sites in Chaozhou* (1926).
5 Political events, *Wusanshi hu shao* / *May 30 Tragedy in Shanghai* (1925), *Shanghai wu sanshi shimin dahui* / *Shanghai May 30 Citizen Conference* (1925), *Shanghai guangfu ji* / *Shanghai Recovery* (1927), *Jinan canan* / *Jinan Tragedy* (1928), *Zhang Zhuolin can an* / *Tragedy of General Zhang Zuolin* (1928); *Shijie funu jie* / *International Women's Festival* (1924), *Guomin waijiao youxing dahui* / *Citizens March* (1923), *Jiangsu tongzi jun lianhe hui* / *Jiangsu Boy Scouts Association* (1922), *Fudan daxue yiyong jun jianyue dianli* / *Fudan University Volunteers Military Inspection* (1931), *Minnan shizhen jiaoyu* / *Fujian Government Education* (1927).
6 *Aiguo dongya liangxiao yundong hui* / *Sports Carnival of the Two Schools of Aiguo and Dongya* (1922), *Wanguo shangtui hui chao* / *Gymnastics of a Thousand Business Associations* (1922), *Guangdong quan sheng yundong hui* / *Sports Carnival of Guangdong Province* (1925), *Shanghai yuandong saima chang kaimu* / *Opening Ceremony of the Shanghai Racecourse* (1925), *Wanguo Zhonghua dui* / *Chinese Teams* (1926), *Shanghai liangjiang nuzi tiyu shifan xuexiao yundong hui* / *Sports Carnival of the Shanghai Liangjiang Female Teaching College* (1926), *Yuandong yundong hui* / *Far East Sports Carnival* (1928), *Diba jie yuandong yundong hui*

Zhongguo yuxuan hui / *The Eighth Far East Sports Carnival – China Preliminary* (1927).

7 *Zhou Fujiu da chusang* / *Zhou Fujiu Funeral* (1921), *Xu Guoliang chubin* / *Xu Guoliang Funeral* (1922), *Zhang Jizhi xiansheng de fengcai* / *Mr Zhang Jizhi* (1921), *Sun Chuanfang* / *Sun Chuanfang* (1925), *Xu Shuzheng chu sang* / *Xu Shuzheng Funeral* (1926), *Wu Peifu* / *Wu Peifu* (1924), *Feng Yuxiang* / *Feng Yuxiang* (1924).

8 *Nanjing de jingzheng* / *Nanjing Police* (1921).

9 *Shanghai jiuhuo hui* / *Shanghai Fire brigade Association* (1926).

10 *Beifa wanchen ji* / *Northern Launch* (1927) by Da Zhonghua (Great China), *Sun Zhongshan* / *Dr Sun Yat-sen* (1925) by Baihe Company, *Sun Zhongshan linmu dianji ji* / *Foundation Stone for Dr Sun Yat-sen's Memorial* (1926) by Changcheng (Great Wall), *Beifa da zhanshi* / *History of Northern Launch* (1927) by Minshen, *Gemingjun beifa ji* / *Record of North Launch by the Revolutionary Army* (1927) by Xinqi, *Gemingjun zhanshi* / *History of Revolutionary Army* (1927) by Sanmin Company.

11 This was caused by some Chinese protesting against American portrayals of the Chinese in the 1920s and some film companies were established in reaction to certain American films. For instance, a well-known film company, Changcheng (Great Wall), was established by a group of Chinese American students. Some documentaries were made by Chinese studying overseas, such as America, *the Great Wall* (1921). The reason for their entering the filmmaking business was that they felt the Chinese image was being insulted by Americans, and other foreigners. So they began to make their own 'legitimate' documentary films. Also, many drama films were made by using documentary footage, or using documentary films as a background (Du 1986: 60, vol. 1).

12 *Zhongguo jinji yuan fu riben di liu jie yuandong yundong hui* / *Chinese sports men attending the sixth Far East Sports Carnival in Japan* (1923).

13 *Sun Zhongsan xiansheng wei dian jun ganbu xuexiao juxin kaimu li* / *Dr Sun Yat-sen's Attending Opening Ceremony Yunnan Military Cadres School* (1924), *Sun Zhongsan xiansheng beishang* / *Dr Sun Yat-sen Goes to North* (1924), *Sun dayuan shuai chu xun Guangdong dongbei jiang ji* / *General Sun's Inspection of the North River in Guangdong* (1924, 1925: the date is disputed by Yu, Muyun (HK) and Cheng, Jihua (mainland)). In Fang Fang (2003) pp.44–45, Li Minwei followed Dr Sun Yat-sen in 1921, and produced *Sun Zhongshan jiu ren dazhongtong* / *Ceremony for Dr Sun Yat-sen Swearing in as the Chinese President*. But in Yu Muyun (1985), the film was made by Franch Baidai company, see p.48.

14 *Sun Zhongsan xiansheng chubin ji zhuidao zhi dianli* / *Dr Sun Yat-sen Funeral* (1925).

15 *Sun Zhongsan xiansheng lingmu dianji ji* / *Dr Sun Yat-sen Memorial Foundation* (1926).

16 Films made by Li Minwei, *Sun Yat-sen jiuren da zhongtong* / *Ceremony of Dr Sun Yat-Sen swearing in as President of China* (1921), *Zhongguo guomindang quanguo daibiao dahui* / *The Chinese Guomindang Congress* (1925), *Sun Zhongshan wei tianjun ganbu xuexiao juxin kaimu li* / *The Opening Ceremony of Yunnan Army Carder School by Sun Yat-sen* (1925), *Sun Zhongshan bei shang* / *Sun Yat-sen goes to the North*, *Sun dayuanchuai jianyun Guangdong quan sheng jinwei jun wuzhong jincha ji shangtuan* / *President Sun's Inspection of Military, Police and the Business Community of Guangdong Province* (1925), *Sun dayuanshuai chuxun Guangdong beijiang ji'* / *President Sun's Inspection on Guangdong North Rive* (1925), *Miao Zhongkai xiansheng wei Guangdong bin gongchang qingnian gongren xuexiao kaimu* / *The Opening Ceremony of the Youth School in Guangdong Military Factory by Mr Miao Zhongkai* (1925), *Sun Zhongshan xianshen chubin ji zuidao zhi dianli* / *Dr Sun Yat-sen's Funeral* (1925), *Sun Shongshan xiansheng linmu dianji ji* /

Foundation Ceremony of the Dr Sun Yat-sen Memorial (1926), *Hunghua gang / Hunghua Gang* (1926). Based on his footage of Dr Sun Yat-sen and the Party's activities, Li Minwei also made two compilation films, *Guomin geming jun hailukong da zhan ji* (*Battles of the Navy, Land and Air Forces of the Guomindang*) (1927) and *Xunye qianqu* (*Great Achievement Forever*) and *Jianguo shi de yiye* (*One Page on the Establishment of the Nation*) (1941).

17 Here is a list of documentaries on the Japanese attack on Shanghai in 1932. The war lasted about a month, and was mainly between the Japanese and Nineteenth Route Guomindang Army, a military confrontation which was quickly transformed into cinematic images for news documentaries: *Shanghai zhi zhan / Shanghai Battle* (1932), *Kangri xuezhan / Anti-Japanese Bloody War* (1932), *Shijiu lu jun xuezhan kang ri- Shanghai zhandi xiezhen / Real Images of the Bloody War of anti-Japanese by the No.19 Route Army* (1932), *Shijiu lu jun guangrong shi / Glorious Record of No.19 Route* (1932), *Shijiu lu jun kangri zhanshi / History of No.19 Route Army against Japanese* (1932), *Bao rihuo lu ji / Records of Violent Japanese Damage Shanghai* (1932), *Songlu kangri jiangshi zhuidao hui / Memorial for the Soldiers died in the Shanghai Anti-Japanese War* (1932), *Songlu xie / Blood along the Songhu River* (1932), *Shanghai kangzhan xuezhan shi / Record of Shanghai Anti-Japanese Bloody War* (1932), *Shanghai kangdi xue zhanshi / Record of Shanghai Anti-enemy History* (1932), *Zhongguo tiexue jun zhan shi / History of China's Remarkably Brave Army* (1932), *Shanghai haojie ji / Shanghai Tragedy* (1932). There are also news documentaries about anti-Japanese military activities in Manchuria, Inner Monglia and Manduran such as *Dongbei yiyong jun kangri zhan shi / History of Anti-Japanese Battles by Northeast Volunteer Army* (1932), *Dongbei yiyong jun kangri xuezhan shi / History of Anti-Japanese Bloody Battles by Northeast Volunteer Army* (1932), *Dongbei yiyong jun kangri ji / Record of Anti-Japanese Battles by Northeast Volunteer Army* (1932), *Rehe xuezhan shi / Bloody Battles in Rehe* (1934), *Rehe xuele shi / Bloody and tear Battles in Rehe* (1934), *Changchen xuezhan shi / History of Bloody War near the Great Wall* (1934), *Yuguan da xue zhan / Bloody War at Yuguan* (1934), *Suimeng qianxian / Frontier between Shanxi Province and InterMongolia* (1934), *Suiyuan qianxian xinwen / News from the Frontier between InterMongolia and Shanxi province* (1934), *Huabei shi women de / North China is Ours* (1939).

18 *Zhongwai zhuqun bisai / Sino and foreign Football Matches* (1931), *Quanguo yundong dahui / National Sports Carnival* (1933), *Shisan yingli changtu jinsai / 13 miles of long distance Competition* (1932), *Huiying malaixiya xueshou / Welcome sportsmen from Malaysia* (1935), *Diliu je quanguo yundong hui / The Sixth National Sports Carnival* (1935) (the title is disputed by Yu, Muyun (HK) and Cheng, Jihua (mainland) but we should rely on Cheng's work).

19 *Yang Hucheng yue bin / General Yang Hucheng Inspecting his armg* (1934), *Huanying Zhou, Hu chu guo / Farewell Zhou and Hu Visiting overseas* (1935), *Huanying Zhou, Hu fanguo / Weclome Zhou and Hu returning Home* (1935), *Ruan Lingyu shisi xinwen / News of the Death of Ruan Lingyu* (1935), *Lu Xun xiansheng shisi / Death of Mr Lu Xun* (1936) and *Lu Xun xiansheng shisi xinwen / News of the death of Mr Lu Xun* (1936).

20 Naou's article: 'Yingpian yishu lu' (Film Art), was published in *Zhongguo wusheng dianying* (*Chinese Silent Films*), pg. 493, originally published in *Dianying zhoubao / Film Weekly*, from 1 July to 8 October, 1932, Issues 2, 3, 6, 7, 8, 9, 10, 15.

21 Here is a list of well-known scenery documentaries. *Haining chao / Haining wave* (1931), *Beiping mingsheng / Famous places in Beijing* (1932), *Taishan / Tai Mountain* (1934), *Qufeng / Qufeng* (1934), *Xibei fengjing / Sceneries of the Northwest* (1934), *Xin Guangzhou / New Canton* (1934), *Xiongba Yazhou zhi da duohui – Shanghai / Shanghai* and *Manyou jianwen lu / Record of Journey* (1935).

22 Most anti-Japanese documentaries were produced in Hong Kong, after Shanghai film industry was destroyed and many filmmakers moved there. In China, Xibei (Northwest) Film company was established in 1935 in Taiyuan, Shanxi province produced a documentary *Huabei shi women de* / *The North is ours* (1940), which recorded how the Communists, the Eight Route fighting against the Japanese. It was the only documentary made under the Guomindang which showing the Communists fighting against the Japanese. (Fang 2003: 77).

23 *Baowei women de tudi* / *Defend for our Land, Rexue Zhonghua* / *Hotblooded Chinese, Babai zhuangshi* / *800 Brave Soldiers* all produced in 1938.

24 By trying to persuade commercial filmmakers to make 'progressive' films and by inserting Communist messages in commercial films.

Chapter 3

1 *Yongyuan nianqing* / *Young Forever* (1956), *Fengxue Pemier* / *Stormy at Pemier* (1956), *Xinghua chunyu Jiangnan* / *Jiangnan in Spring* (1956), *Guke de fannao* / *Worries from Customers* (1956), *Gongdi shang de langfei* / *Waste in the Workplace* (1956), *Huaer bu shi* / *Flashy and without substance* (1956).

2 Because of his essay, 'Dianying de luogu (Gongs and Drums of Film) published in the *Wenyi Daily* in 1956, Zhong Dianfei, the well-known film critic and scriptwriter was accused as a rightist and jailed for 20 years. This is just one example of how film criticism could become an ideological battlefield in China.

3 The documentary series *Huashuo Changjiang* / *The Yangzi River* (1983), *Yanhai mingzhu* / *The 14 Coastal Ports* (1984), *Huangjin zhi lu* / *The Golden Road* (1985), *Huashuo Yunhe* / *The Grand Canal* (1986), *Tangfan gudao* / *The Silk Road* (1987), *Huanghe* / *The Yellow River* (1988), *Heshang* / *River Elegy* (1988) and *Wang Changcheng* / *The Great Wall* (1991) are all well-known examples of documentary series in this period on the grand national themes of national and cultural geography, cultural philosophy, cultural history and political economy.

Chapter 5

1 There is a long list of TV law programs: Shanghai Station: *Anjian jiaoju* / *Case Focus*; Guizhou: *Jinfang jishi* / *Police Recording*; Guangxi: *Faxi renjiang* / *Law is among the humans*; Hubei Economy Station *Wuhan 110* / *Wuhan 110*; Taiyuan Station: *Zhi'an guangjiao* / *Security Corner*; Shaanxi station: *Shehui dang'an* / *Society File*; Yunnan: *Jintan 20 feng* / *Police 20 minute Forum*; Chengdu: *Jinshi lu* / *Police Records*; Shenzhen: *Fazhi congheng* / *Law horizon*; Ji'nan station: *Xiaodong rexian* / *Xiaodong's hotline*; Ganshu station: *Fangyuan tiandi* / *Law Space*; Dalian station: *Fazhi tiandi* / *Law*; Shandong station: *Jinjiang zhi guang* / *Gold Sward light*; Inner Mongolia: *Ren yu fa* / *Humans and Law*; Xinjiang Station: *Gongmin yu fa* / *Citizens and Law*; Congqin Station: *Bayu jinshi* / *Bayu Police News*; Jilin station: *Falu zai xindong* / *Law in Action*; Shangdong: *Daode yu fazhi* / *Morality and Law*; Guangdong: *Shehui conghen* / *Society horizon*; Shanghai: *Falü yu daode* / *Law and Morality*; Congqing: *Pai'an shuo fa* / *Talking about Law*.

Changsha has a law channel broadcasting 15 hours daily. Shangdong's *honghuanglu de huhuan* / *Calling from Red, Amber and Green*, specialises on traffic law. Jilin: *Jinji yu fa* / *Economy and Law*, Nanjing: tax *shuishou shijian* / *Tax cases*, Guangdong: protection of women *nüxing shikong* / *Women sky*. (Hu and Yin 2003: 18) Beijing station's *Fazhi jingxin shi* / *Law in Action now* and Hunan's *Lingdian zhuizhong* / *Seeking from Zero* are the two programs show police solving cases. They tend to be more dramatic, realistic, with exciting locations and are very popular. (Hu and Yin 2003: 23).

Chapter 6

1 According to the first national survey in 1953, the minorities made up 5.89% of the total population. 100% in Tibet, 93.06% in Xinjiang, 50.95% in Qinghai, 37%.51 in Guangxi, 31.59% in Yunnan, 23.69% in Guizhou, 15.53% in Inner Mongolia, 11.75% in Ganshu, 10.67% in Jinling, 7.89% in Helongjiang, 8.07% in Liaoning, 3.11% in Sichuan. In 1960, 140,000 Han were sent to Yunnan. Between 1954–61, 866,000 Han were transferred to Xinjiang from Shandong, Henan, Hebei, Suzhou, Shanghai. Between 1958–63, the government planned to transfer 570,000 Han Chinese from Hebei, Henan, Ganshu, Hubei, Hunan, Anhui, Jiangsu, Zhejiang, Shandong, Guangdong, and Sichuan to Inner Mongolia, Qinghai, Ganshu, Xinjiang, Ningxia, and Hainan. By 1978, about 16.23 million of Red Guards (Han Chinese) have been transferred to the remote areas, including 277,600 to Xinjiang, 492,000 to Ningxia, 232,500 to Yunnan, 245,200 to Gansu, 193,800 to Inner Mongolia, and 43,600 to Qinghai. See Ren and Zhou, *Zhonghua renmin gonghe guo minzu guanxi shi yanjiu* (*Minzu Relations in the People's Republic of China*), pp.17–5 and 254–55.

2 Here are a few more examples. *Dayaoshan Yaozu / The Yao Nationality in the Dayao Mountains* (1963) has as its main theme its social structure of a form of feudalism with traces of a primitive form of democracy, the 'system of Yao elders' (*Yao lao zhi*) or 'system of elders' (*shipai zhi*). The documentary also shows the tribe's origins, its history of migration, as well as the forces of production characteristic of the Yao community. *Hezhezu de yulie shenhuo / The Fish Lifestyle of the Hezhe Nationality* (1964) thematises the fishing economy in the Songhua, Hungtong, and Yusongli Rivers in Manchuria. It also briefly introduces the hunting practices, politics and culture of the Hezhe. *Yongning Naxi zu de ahzhu hunyan / Ahzhu Mating of the Naxi Nationality in Yongning* (1965) is a documentary about the characteristics of the matriarchy of the Naxi, the practice of matrilocality and the matrilineal organization of society under the feudal lordship system. We witness the Naxi practice of an *ahzhu* style marriage according to which a man visits a woman at night and returns to his own family during day time. The children produced in such love encounters are brought up by the mother. Men and women are shown to be free to choose and leave their partners. The 1966 documentary *The Culture and Art of the Naxi Nationality in Lijiang / Lijiang naxizu de wenhua yishu* shifts the attention to Naxi architecture, sculpture, crafts, music and dancing, as well as the Naxi *dongba* characters and sutras.

Bibliography

Aitken, Ian (1990) *Film and Reform: John Grierson and the Documentary Film Movement*. London: Routledge.
—— (ed.) (1998) *The Documentary Film Movement: An Anthology*. Edinburgh: Edinburgh University Press.
Bakhtin, Mikail (1973) *Problems of Dostoevsky's Poetics*, trans. R.W. Rotsel. Ann Arbor: Ardis Publications.
Banks, Marcus (1992) 'Which Films are the Ethnographic Films?' in P. Crawford and D. Turton (eds) *Film as Ethnography*. Manchester: Manchester University Press: 116–29.
Barnouw, Erik (1983) *Documentary: A History of the Non-Fiction Film*. Oxford: Oxford University Press.
Barsam, Richard (1988) *The Vision of Robert Flaherty: The Artist as Myth and Filmmaker*. Bloomington: Indiana University Press.
—— (1992) *Non-Fiction Film: A Critical History*, Indiana, IN: Indiana University Press.
Beattie, Keith (2004) *Documentary Screens: Nonfiction Film and Television*. New York: Palgrave Macmillan.
Burgh, Hugo de (2003) *The Chinese Journalist: Mediating Information in the World's Most Populous Country*. London: RoutledgeCurzon.
Calder-Marshall, Arthur (1963) *The Innocent Eye: the Life of Robert Flaherty*. London: W.H. Allen.
CCTV Jiangshu (Story) Programme (ed.) (2004) *Jiangshu: 2003 shoujie Zhongguo jizhe fengyun bang* (Reporting: A List of Leading Chinese Journalists 2003). Beijing: China Encyclopedia Publisher.
CCTV Jilupian Programme (ed.) (2003) *Yingxiang Zhongguo* (China in Documentaries). Guangzhou: Nanfang Daily Publisher.
Chan, Joseph M. (1993) 'Commercialization without Independence: Trends and Tensions in Media Development in China' in J. Cheng and M. Brosseau (eds.) *China Review 1993*. Hong Kong: Chinese University Press: 1–21.
Chang, Wo Ho (1989) *Mass Media in China*. Iowa: Iowa State University Press.
Chen, Fuqing (1994) *Dianshi xinwen* (*Television News*). Beijing: China Broadcasting Press.
Chen, Hanyuan (2001) 'Zhongguo dianshi jilu pian de lishi yu xianzhuang' (History and Contemporary Situation of Chinese Television Documentary), in San, Wanli (ed.) *Jilu dianying wenxian* (*Documentation and Fictionalisation*). Beijing: China Broadcasting Press.

—— (ed.) (2003) *Dianshi jilu pian jieshuo ci ji lunwen xuan* (A Collection of Narration and Essays of Television Documentaries). Beijing: China Broadcasting Press. Vols 1 and 2.

Chen, Li (2002a) 'Luetan jiaoyu dianshi jiemu xinwen fazhang zhanlue' (Notes on the Strategic Development of the CETV Educational News), in Li, Peng (ed.) *Zhongguo jiaoyu dianshi tai wenji* (Collection of Papers on the CETV), vol. 2. Beijing: National Broadcasting Television University Press: 141–3.

—— (2002b) 'Zhangwo lilun wuqi, shijian "sange daibiao" zhongyao shixiang' ('Three Representatives' in Practice), in Li, Peng (ed.) *Zhongguo jiaoyu dianshi tai wenji* (Collection of Papers on the CETV), vol. 2. Beijing: National Broadcasting Television University Press: 69–77.

Chen, Me (2001) *Dianshi wenhua xue* (Studies in Television Culture). Beijing: Beijing Normal University Press.

Chen, Qiguang (2004) *Dangdai Zhongguo yingshi wenhua yanjiu* (Research on Contemporary Chinese Film and Television Culture). Beijing: Beijing University Press.

Chen, Wu (1993) 'Zhongguo dianying zhi lu' (The Road of Chinese Cinema), Issues 1 and 2, vol. 1, *Mngxing Monthly*, May and June 1933, in Zhongguo dianying yishu yanjiu zhongxing (Chinese Film Art Research Centre) ed. *Zhongguo zuoyi dianying yundong* (The Chinese Left-Wing Film Movement). Beijing: China Film Publisher: 66–74.

Chen, Zhili (2002) 'Rushi hou de Zhongguo jiaoyu yu chelue' (Education and Strategies after China's Entry into the WTO), *Zhongguo Jiaoyu* (*China Education*), 9 January: 135–6.

Cheng, Bugao (1996) 'Xinwen yingpian tan' (Views on News Reel), Issue 5, Special Issue on *Mang gunü* (Blind Orphan Girl) 1925, in Zhongguo dianying zhiliao guan (China Film Archive) (ed.) *Zhongguo wusheng dianying* (Chinese Silent Movies). Beijing: China Film Publisher: 613–15.

Cheng, Jihua (1966) *Zhongguo dianying fazhan shi* (History of Chinese Cinema). Beijing: China Film Publisher.

China Film Association (ed.) (1997) *Lun Zhongguo shaoshu minzu dianying* (On Chinese Films of Minorities). Beijing: China Film Press.

China Statistical Yearbook (2002, 2003, 2004, 2005). Beijing: China Statistics Press.

ChinaKnowledge Press (2005) *Branding in China: The Media Platforms Reaching 1.3 Billion Consumers*. Singapore: ChinaKnowledge.

Chu, Yingchi (2003) *Hong Kong Cinema: Coloniser, Motherland and Self*. London: RoutledgeCurzon.

—— (2006) '*Legal Report:* Citizenship education through a television documentary' in V. Fong and R. Murphy (eds) *Chinese Citizenship: Views from the Margins*. London: Routledge: 68–95.

Clark, Paul (1987) 'Ethnic Minorities in China', *East-West Film Journal* 1, 2: 73–90.

Collier, John (1988) 'Visual Anthropology and the Future of Ethnographic Film' in J. Rollwagen (ed.) *Anthropological Filmmaking*. New York: Harwood Academic Publishers.

Corner, John (1996) *The Art of Record: A Critical Introduction to Documentary*. Manchester: Manchester University Press.

CSM (CVSC – Sofres Media) (2002) *Television in China: 2001 Overview*.

Cui, Baoguo (ed.) (2005) *2004–2005 nian: Zhongguo cuanmei canye fangzhan baogao* (Blue Book of China's Media: Report on Development of China's Media Industry 2004–2005), Beijing: Social Sciences Academic Press (China).

Cui, Wenhua (1998) *Quanneng yuyan de wenhua shidai: dianshi wenhua yanjiu* (Television Era). Beijing: Beijing Normal University Press.

Dahrendorf, Rolf (1994) 'Citizenship and Beyond: The Social Dynamics of an Idea', in B. Turner and P. Hamilton (eds) *Citizenship: Critical Concepts* vol. 2. London: Routledge: 292–308.

Davidson, Alastair (1999) 'Never the Twain Shall Meet? Europe, Asia and the Citizen', in A. Dividson and K. Weekley (eds) *Globalization and Citizenship in the Asia-Pacific.* London: Macmillan: 221–42.

Delanty, Gerard (2000) *Citizenship in a Global Age: Society, Culture, Politics.* Buckingham: Open University Press.

Deng, Qiyao (ed.) (2002) *Shijue biaoda* (Visual Representation: 2002). Kunming: Yunnan People's Publisher.

Derek, Paget (1998) *No Other Way to Tell It: Dramadoc/Docudrama on Television.* Manchester: Manchester University Press.

Derrida, Jacques (1980) 'The Law of Genre', trans. Avital Ronell, *Glyph*, 7: 202–232.

Devereux, L, and Hillman, R. (eds) (1989) *Fields of Vision: Essays in Film Studies, Visual Anthropology and Photography.* Berkeley: University of California Press.

Dittmer, Lowell (1994) 'The Politics of Publicity in Reform China' in Lee, Chin-Chuan (ed.) *China's Media, Media's China.* Boulder: Westview Press: 89–112.

—— (1994) *China Under Reform.* Boulder: Westview Press.

Ding, Ganlin (ed.) (2003) *Zhongguo xinwen shiye shi* (History of the Chinese Press) Third edition. Beijing: China Tertiary Education Press.

Ding, Yi (1979) 'Guanggao de zuoyong' (On the Functions of Advertising) *Wenhui Daily*, 14 January: 3.

Ding, Yaping (1998) *Yingxiang Zhongguo 1945–1949* (China in Film 1945–1949). Beijing: Culture and Art Publisher.

Documentary Handbook (from January 2003 to 2005, monthly journal). Beijing: CDAA: China Film and Television Documentary Academic Committee.

Donald, Stephanie Hemelryk and Kean, Michael (2002) 'Media in China: New Convergences, New Approaches' in S. Donald, M. Kean and Y. Hong (eds) *Media in China: Consumption, Content and Crisis.* London: RoutledgeCurzon: 3–17.

Dower, Nigel and Williams, John (eds) (2002) *Global Citizenship: A Critical Reader.* Edinburgh: Edinburgh University Press.

Dru, Gladney (1994) 'Tian Zhuangzhuang', *Public Culture*, 8, 1:161–175.

Du, Yunzhi (1986) *Zhongguo dianying shi* (History of Chinese Cinema). Third edition. Taibei: Commercial Publisher.

Editor Group of DV New Generation of Phoenix Television (2003) *DV Xinshi dai 01* (DV Era 01). Beijing: China Youth Publishing House.

Editorial 'Ba gongkuang nongcun zhong de dianying fangying gongzuo tigao yi bu' (Lift up Film Exhibition in Mines and Rural Areas), *Guangming Daily*, 14 July 1955.

Falk, Richard (2002) 'An Emergent Matrix of Citizenship' in N. Dower and J. Williams (eds) *Global Citizenship: A Critical Reader.* Edinburgh: Edinburgh University Press: 15–29.

Fang, Fang (2003) *Zhongguo jilu pian fazhang shi* (History of Chinese Documentary Film). Shanghai: China Drama Publisher.

Feng, Min (1992) *Zhongguo dianying yishu shigang* (An Outline of the History of Chinese Film Art). Tianjin: Nankai University Press.

Film Exhibition (Party journal) 1956–1965. Beijing.

Follesdal, Andreas (2002) 'Citizenship: European and Global' in N. Dower and J. Williams (eds) *Global Citizenship: A Critical Reader*. Edinburgh: Edinburgh University Press: 71–83.

Foucault, Michel (1980) *Power/Knowledge*. London: Harvester.

—— (1986) *The Archaelogy of Knowledge*. London: Tavistock.

—— (1988) *The Care of the Self: The History of Sexuality*, vol. 3. London: Allen Lane.

Friedman, Edward (1995) *National Identity and Democratic Prospects in Socialist China*. Armonk, NY: M.E. Sharpe.

Frow, John (2006) *Genre*. London: Routledge.

Fuchs, Peter (1988) 'Ethnographic Film in Germany: An Introduction' *Visual Anthropology*, I: 217–33.

Gao, Feng (2003) *China in Documentaries*. Guangzhou: Nanfang Publisher.

Gao, Guoan and Liu, Yongzheng (2002) *Yide zhiguo fangfa lun* (*Methods of Governing the Country by Morality*). Beijing: Economic Management Publishing House.

Gao, Jin and Zhang, Chaogang (2003) *Dianshi jishi zuoping chuangzuo* (Realist Television Film Production); *Dianshi lanmu jiemu cehua* (Television Programme Design). Beijing: Beijing Broadcasting Academy Press.

Gao, Weijin (2003) *Zhongguo xinwen jilu dianying shi* (History of Chinese Newsreel and Documentary Film). Beijing: The Central Communist Party Historical Materials Publisher.

Goldman, M. and Perry, E. (2002) *Changing Meanings of Citizenship in Modern China*. Cambridge: Harvard University Press.

Goldsmith, W. (1972) 'Ethnographic Film: Definition and Exegesis' in *PIEF Newsletter* 3(2) 1–3.

Gong, Jianong (1968) *Gong Jianong cong ying huiyi lu* (Robert Kung's Memoirs of His Silver Screen Life). Hong Kong: Culture Book House.

Gongmin daode jianshe shisi gangyao xuexi duben (Study Guide for the Outline in Carrying out Citizenship Moral Education) (eds) (2001). Beijing: Rural Reading Publisher.

Gongmin daode jiaoyu shouce (Handbook of Citizenship Moral Education) (eds) (2002) *Gongmin daode jiaoyu shouce* (*Handbook of Citizenship Moral Education*). Beijing: New China Publisher.

Gongmin daode keti zu (Citizen Moral Education Group) (ed.) (2002) *Zhongguo gongmin daode shou ce* (Handbook for Chinese Citizen Moral Education). Beijing: Red Flag Publisher.

Grant, Barry Keith and Sloniowski, Jeanette (1998) *Documenting the Documentary*. Detroit: Wayne State University Press.

Guo, Jianbin (2005) *Duxiang dianshi: xiandai chuanmei yu shaoshu minzu xiangcun richang shenhuo* (Television in the Remote Rural Area: Contemporary Media and Minorities' Daily Life). Jinan: Shandong People's Publisher.

Guo, Jing (ed.) (2003) *Yun zhi nan renlei xue yingxiang zhan shouce* (Yunnan Multicultural Visual Festival Brochure). Kunming: Yunnan People's Publishing.

—— (ed.) (2005) *Yun zhi nan jilun yingxiang luntan* (Yunnan Multicultural Visual Festival). Kunming: Yunnan Academy of Social Sciences.

Guojia guangdian ju (The State Administration of Radio, Film and Television) (December, 2003) *Guangyu chujin guangbo yinshi chanye fazhan de yijian* (Suggestions on Broadcasting Enterprises Development). Government document.

Guowu yuan (The State Council) (December, 2003) *Wenhua tizhi gaige shidian zhong zhichi wenhua chanye fazhan he jingyinxing wenhua shiye danwei zhuanwei qiye de liangge guandian de tongzhi* (In Support of the Transformation of Cultural Institutions into Cultural Enterprises). Beijing: Government Document.

Habermas, Jürgen (1974) 'The Public Sphere', *New German Critique*, vol. 3, 49–55.

—— (1989) *The Structural Transformation of the Public Sphere.* Cambridge, MA: MIT Press.

—— (1994) 'Citizenship and National Identity: Some Reflections on the Future of Europe' in B. Turner and P. Hamilton (eds) *Citizenship: Critical Concepts*, vol. 2: 341–58.

Hao, Shiyuan (2005) 'Foreword of the Series' in Luo, Xianyou (ed.) *Lishi yu minzu: Zhongguo bianjiang de zhenzhi, shehui he wenhua* (Ethnohistory: Politics, Society and Culture in China's Frontier). Beijing: Social Sciences Academic Press.

Hao, Tiechuang (2002) 'Dezhi he fazhi shuangguang qixia' (Working along both lines of governing country by morality and by law) in Shanghai Yanhuang Wenhua Yanjiu Hui (Shanghai Chinese Culture Research Association) (ed.) *Fazhi yu dezhi (Governing the Nation by Law and by Morality)* Shanghai: China Inspection Publisher: 13–18.

He, Shuliu (2005) *Zhongguo dianshi jilu pian shi lun* (History of Television Documentary in China). Beijing: China Media University Press.

He, Yuan (2003) 'Zhaoqi renlei dianying 1957–66' (Early Chinese Anthropological Filmmaking 1957–1966). *Art World Magazine*, March 2003, No. 154:14–15.

Heater, Derek (1990) *Citizenship: The Civic Ideal in World History, Politics and Education.* London and New York: Longman.

Heider, Karl G. (1990) *Ethnographic Film.* Austin: University of Texas Press.

Hong, Junhao (1994) 'The Resurrection of Advertising in China: Developments, Problems, and Trends'. *Asian Survey* 34.4:326–42.

—— (1998) *The Internationalization of Television in China: The Evolution of Ideology, Society, and Media Since the Reform.* London: Praeger Publishers.

Hong, She (1996) 'Wusheng de cunzai' (Existence of Silence) in Zhongguo dianying zhiliao guan (China Film Archive) (ed.) (1996) *Zhongguo wusheng dianying* (Chinese Silent Movies). Beijing: China Film Publisher, pp.1–18.

Hu, Jubin (1995) *Xin Zhongguo dianying yishi xingtai shi 1949–1976* (History of Ideology in Chinese Films 1949–1976). Beijing: China Broadcasting and Television Publisher.

Hu, Lide (2002) *Dianshi xinwen yu jilu pian sheying* (Photography of TV News and Documentary Films). Beijing: China Broadcasting Press.

Hu, Zhengrong (ed.) (2001) *Zhongguo chuanmei luntan: biandong zhong de quanquo guangbo dianshi* (China Communication Forum: Changes and Developments of the Electronic Media in the Twenty-first Century). Beijing: Beijing Broadcasting Academy.

—— (2003) *Zhongguo xibu guangbo dianshi fazhan zhanlue* (Strategies of Television Development in Western China). Beijing: Beijing Broadcasting Academy Publisher.

Hu, Zhifeng and Yin, Li (2003) *Dianshi fazhi jiemu: tezhi, chuangzuo, yu kaifa* (Television Law Programmes). Beijing: China Broadcasting and Television Publisher.

Hutchinson, John and Smith, Anthony D. (eds) (1996) *Ethnicity.* Oxford: Oxford University Press.

Jacobs, Lewis (1971) *The Documentary Tradition: from Nanook to Woodstock.* New York: Hopkinson & Blake.

Jia, Xiuqing (2004) *Jilu yu quanshe: dianshi yishu meixue benzhi* (Documenting and Interpretation: on the Essence of Television Art Aesthetics), Beijing: China Broadcasting Academy Press.

Jiang, Xiangyu (2001) 'Shilun yifa zhiguo yu yide zhiguo bingzhong de jige wenti' (Several Issues on Governing the Country by both Law and Morality), in Shanghai Chinese Cultural Research Association: *Fazhi yu dezhi* (*Governing the Country by Law and by Morality*). Shanghai: China Inspection Press: 241–50.

Jin, Xiumin (2005) *Jilu de mofang: Jilu pian xushu yishu yanjiu* (Research on Documentary Narratives). Beijing: Culture and Art Publishing House.

Kang, Ning (2003a) 'Zhongguo jiaoyu dianshi tai 2004 nian jiemu gaiban zongti qingkuang' (CETV Programme Reform 2004). Beijing: CETV.

—— (2003b) 'Zhongguo jiaoyu dianshi tai gaige yu fazhan baogao' (Report on CETV Reform and Development). Beijing: CETV.

—— (2004) 'Kang Ning tongzhi zai Zhongguo jiaoyu dianshi tai 2004 nian xinwen xuanchuan gongzuo huiyi shang de jianghua' (Comrade Kang Ning's Speech on the CETV Reform at a News Conference 2004). Beijing: CETV.

Kean, John (1991) *Media and Democracy.* Cambridge: Polity Press.

Keane, Michael (2005) 'A Revolution in Television and a Great Leap Forward for Innovation? China in the Global Television Format Business' in A. Moran and M. Keane (eds) *Television Across Asia: Television industries, programme formats and globalization.* London: RoutledgeCurzon: 88–104.

Kong, Deming (2002) *Dianshi wenti xiezuo* (Writing for Television). Beijing: Beijing Broadcasting Academy Press.

Kuehnast, Kathleen (1992) 'Visual Imperialism and the Export of Prejudice: An Exploration of Ethnographic Film', in P. Crawford and D. Turton (eds) *Film as Ethnography.* Manchester: Manchester University Press: 183–95.

Küng, Hans (2002) 'A Global Ethic for a New Global Order' In N. Dower and J. Williams (eds) *Global Citizenship: A Critical Reader.* Edinburgh: Edinburgh University Press: 133–45.

Lee, Chin-Chuan (ed.) (1994) *China's Media, Media's China.* Oxford: Westview Press.

—— (ed.) (2000) *Power, Money, and Media.* Illinois: Northwestern University Press.

—— (ed.) (2003) *Chinese Media, Global Context.* London: RoutledgeCurzon.

Leng, Yifu and Ma, Li (1998) *Dianshi jishi yu chuangzuo* (Making Television Documentaries). Beijing: People's Daily Press.

Leng, Yifu, and Zhang, Yaping (2002) *21 shiji de dianshi jingying linian* (Ideas on Television Operation in the Twenty-first Century). Beijing: Long March Publisher.

Li, Buyun and Wu, Yuzhang (1999) 'The Concept of Citizenship in the People's Republic of China' in A. Davidson and K. Weekly (eds) *Globalization and Citizenship in the Asia-Pacific.* New York: Macmillan Press: 157–68.

Li, Cunli (1999) 'Guanyu dangjin Zhongguo dianshi jilu pian de chuangzuo zuoxiang' (Creativity in Contemporary Documentary Film), in Li, Xianwen (ed.) *Guangbo Yingshi lun* (*Theory of Broadcasting and Television*). Beijing: China International Broadcasting Press: 281–94.

Li, Dehua and Xu, Xiaolin (2003) *Xinjiang, dui wai baodao de yizhi zhongyao liliang: Zhongguo xinwen she Xinjiang fengshe shi nian* (A Decade of the Xinjiang Branch of the China News Service). Hong Kong: Hong Kong China News Service.

Li, Peidong (2002) 'Dezhi gongneng lungang' (An Outline of the Function of Governing the Country by Morality), in Shanghai Chinese Culture Research Assocation (ed.) *Fazhi yu dezhi* (Governing the Nation by Law and by Morality), Shanghai: China Inspection Publish: 163–8.

Li, Peng (ed.) (1999) *Zhongguo jiaoyu dianshi tai wenji* (Collection of Papers on the CETV), vol. 1. Beijing: National Broadcasting Television University Press.

—— (ed.) (2002) *Zhongguo jiaoyu dianshi tai wenji* (Collection of Papers on the CETV), vol. 2. Beijing: National Broadcasting Television University Press.

Li, Xianwen (ed.) (1999) *Guangbo yingshi lun* (Theory of Broadcasting and Television). Beijing: China International Broadcasting Press.

Li, Yezhong (2002) '*Zhongguo jilu pian kua shiji sanda yanbian*' (Three Major Changes in Chinese Documentary Films from the Twentieth Century to the Present) in F. Zhang, S. Hung, Z. Hu (eds) *Quanqiu hua yu Zhongguo yingshi de mingyu* (Globalisation and the Destiny of Chinese Film and Television). Beijing: Beijing Broadcasting University Press: 260–71.

Li, Yiming (1997) ' "Shiqi nian" shaoshu minzu ticai dianying zhong de wenhua shidian yu zhuti' (Perspectives and Themes in Seventeen Years of Chinese Films on Minorities), in China Film Association (ed.) *Lun Zhongguo shaoshu minzu dianying (On Chinese Films of Minorities)*. Beijing: China Film Press: 172–85.

Li, Zhehou (1989) *Meixue, zheshi, ren* (Aesthetics, Philosophy and Human Being). Taiwan: Fengyun Shidan Publisher.

—— (2001) *Huaxia meixue* (Chinese Aesthetics). Tianjin: Tianjin Social Science Academy Press.

Li, Zhurun (1998) 'Popular journalism with Chinese characteristics'. *International Journal of Cultural Studies* 1(3), December.

Li, Zuofeng (2001) *Dianshi zhuanti pian shenghua yuyan jiegou* (Audio and Visual Structures in Special Topics of Television Documentary Series). Beijing: Beijing Broadcasting Academy.

Liang, Jian Zhen (2002) *Jiandian fangtan hongpi shu* (Red Book of *Focal Point*). Beijing: Culture and Art Publisher.

Liang, Jian Zhen, Sai, Na, and Zhang, Jie (2001) *Diaocha Zhongguo* (Investigating China) vols 1 and 2. Beijing: China Ethnic Art Publisher.

Lin, Qidong (2002) *Yingshi jilu pian chuanzuo* (Creativity in Film and Television Documentaries). Beijing: China Broadcasting Publisher.

Lin, Shaoxiong (ed.) (2003) *Duoyuan wenhua shihou zhong de jishi yingpian* (Realism Films in the Multicultural Era). Shanghai: Xuelin Publisher.

—— (2003) *Jishi yingpian de wenhua licheng* (Cultural History of Realism in Documentary). Shanghai: Shanghai University Press.

Lipkin, Steve (2002) *Real Emotional Logic: Film and Television Docudrama as Persuasive Practice*. Carbondale: Southern Illinois University Press.

Lister, M., Dovey, J., Giddings, S., Grant, I., and Kelly, K. (2003) *New Media: A Critical Introduction*. London: Routledge.

Liu, Deyuan (2001) 'Jilu dianying de xin shengming' (New Life of Documentary Films), in San, Wanli (ed.) *Jilu dianying wenxian* (Documentation and Fictionalisation). Beijing: China Broadcasting and Television Press.

Liu, Huishu (2001) Lun Zhongguo Lujia daode sixiang yu dezhi (On Confucian Morality and Governing the Country by Morality), in Shanghai Chinese Culture Research Association (ed.) *Fazhi yu dezhi* (Governing the Nation by Law and by Morality). Shanghai: China Inspection Press: 203–10.

Liu, Yannan (2003) *Dianshi chuanbo yanjiu fangfa* (Methodology on Television Research). Beijing: Beijing Normal University Press.

Liu, Xiaoli (ed.) (2004) *Dianshi jilun pian huojiang zuopin jieshuo ci ji lunwen xuan* (A Collection on Narration and Essays on Winning Television Documentaries). Beijing: Huawen Publisher.

Liu, Zhengxin (1999) 'Jiaoyu dianshi zhi wojian' (My View of the CETV) in Li, Peng (ed.) *Zhongguo jiaoyu dianshi tai wenji* (Collection of Papers on the CETV), vol. 1. Beijing: National Broadcasting Television University Press: 65–8.

Loizos, Peter (1993) *Innovation in Ethnographic Film: From Innocence to Self-Consciousness*. Manchester: Manchester University Press.

Lu, Di (2005) '2004 nian Zhongguo dianshi canye fazhan baogao' (A Report on the Television Industry in 2004), in Cui, Baoguo (ed.) *2004–2005 nian: Zhongguo cuanmei canye fangzhan baogao* (Blue Book of China's Media: Report on Development of China's Media Industry 2004–2005). Beijing: Social Sciences Academic Press (China), 221–41.

Lu, Hua, and Xia, Ning (2001) 'Qianquo hua beijing xia Zhongguo guangdian ye de sichang chongzhu: tezhen yu maodun' (Characteristics and Conflicts: the Reorganisation of China's Broadcasting Industry) in Hu, Zhengrong (ed.) *Zhongguo chuanmei luntan: biandong zhong de quanquo guangbo dianshi* (China Communication Forum: Changes and Developments of the Electronic Media in the Twenty-first Century). Beijing: Beijing Broadcasting Academy, pp.112–17.

Lu, Hua, and Zhao, Min (2002) *Dandai guangbo dianshi gailun* (Contemporary Broadcasting and Television). Shanghai: Fudan University Press

Lü, Xinyu (2003) *Jilu Zhongguo (Documenting China)*. Beijing: Sanlian Publishing.

Lull, James (1991) *China Turned On: Television, Reform and Resistance*. London: Routledge.

Luo, Xianyou (2005) *Lishi yu minzu: Zhongguo bianjiang de zhengzhi, shenhui he wenhua* (Ethnohistory: Politics, Society and Culture on China's Frontier). Beijing: Social Sciences Academic Press.

Luo, Yijun (ed.) (1992) *Zhongguo dianying lilun wenxuan* (Chinese Film Theory: An Anthology), vols 1 and 2. Beijing: Culture and Art Publisher.

Lyotard, Jean-Francois (1988) *The Differend: Phrases in Dispute*. Manchester: Manchester University Press.

McCormick, L. and Qing, Liu (2003) 'Globalisation and the Chinese Media: Technologies, Content, Commerce and the Project of the Public Sphere' in Lee, Chin-Chuan (ed.) (2003) *China's Media, Global Contexts*. Boulder: Westview Press: 129–58.

Macdonald, K. and Cousins, M. (1996) *Imagining Reality: The Faber Book of Documentary*. London and Boston: faber and faber.

Margulies, Ivone (ed.) (2002) *Rites of Realism: Essays on Corporeal Cinema*. Durham: Duke University Press.

Marshall, Thomas (1950) *Citizenship and Social Class*. Cambridge: Cambridge University Press.

Minogue, Kenneth (1995) 'Two Concepts of Citizenship' in A. Liebich and D. Warner (eds) *Citizenship East and West*. London: Kegan Paul: 9–22.

Moran, Albert and Keane, M. (2005) *Television Across Asia: Television Industries, Programmeme Formats and Globalisation*. London: Routledge Curzon.

Mulvey, Laura (1989) *Visual and Other Pleasures*. Bloomington: Indiana University Press.

Na, Ou (1996) 'Yingpian yishu lun' (Thoughts on Film Art), Issues 2, 3, 6, 7, 8, 9, 10, 15, *Film Weekly*, 1932, in China Film Archive (ed.) *Zhongguo wusheng dianying* (Chinese Silent Movies). Beijing: China Film Publisher: 489–97.

Ni, Zhen (1994) *Gaige yu Zhongguo dianying* (Reform and Chinese Cinema). Beijing: Beijing Film Publisher.

Nichols, Bill (1981) *Ideology and the Image*. Bloomington: Indiana University Press.

—— (1991) *Representing Reality: Issues and Concepts in Documentary*. Bloomington: Indiana University Press.

—— (1993) '"Getting to Know You . . .": Knowledge, Power, and the Body', in M. Renov (ed.) *Theorizing Documentary*. London: Routledge: 174–91.

—— (1994) *Blurred Boundaries: Questions of Meaning in Contemporary Culture*. Bloomington: Indiana University Press.

—— (2001) *Introduction to Documentary*. Bloomington: Indiana University Press.

—— (2005) 'The Voice of Documentary' in A. Rosenthal and J. Corner (eds) *New Challenges for Documentary*. Manchester: Manchester University Press: 17–33.

Nu, Xin, Lu, Xueyi, and Li, Peilin (eds) (2006) *2006 nian: Zhongguo shehui xingshi fengxi yu yuche* (Analysis and Forecast of China's Social Development 2006). Beijing: Beijing Academy of Social Sciences.

Ouyang, Hongshen (ed.) (2004) *Jilupian gailun* (Brief Introduction to Documentary). Chengdu: Sichuan University Press.

Paget, Derek (1998) *No Other Way to Tell It: Dramadoc/Docudrama on Television*. Manchester: Manchester University Press.

People's Daily, Editorial, 1 February 2001.

—— 6 December 1995 'Woguo guangbo yinshi shiye fazhan xunsu' (Rapid Development of Radio and Television in Our Country).

Plantinga, Carl (1997) *Rhetoric and Representation in Nonfiction Film*. New York and Cambridge: Cambridge University Press.

Qian, Xiaozhang and Gao, Weijin (1981) 'Zhongyang xinwen jilu dianying zhipian chang de lishi huigu' (Historical Review of the Central News Documentary Film Studio) in *Zhongguo dianying nianjian 1981* (China Film Annals 1981). Beijing: China Film Publisher: 143–62.

Qin, Hongwen (2005) *Dianshi yu shehui: Dianshi shehui xue yinlun* (Television and Society). Beijing: Xuelin Publishing.

Ren, Yifei and Zhou, Jinghong (2003) *Zhonghua renmin gongheguo minzu guanxi shi yanjiu* (History of Minorities' Relations in the People's Republic of China). Shenyang: Liaoning Minzu Publisher.

Ren, Yuan (ed.) (1997) *Dianshi jilu pian xinlun* (New Theorization of Television Documentary). Beijing: Beijing Broadcasting Publisher.

Ren, Yuan and Peng, Guoli (eds) (1999) *Shijie jilupian shilue* (Brief History of the World Documentary). Beijing: China Broadcasting Publisher.

Renov, Michael (ed.) (1993) *Theorizing Documentary*. New York: Routledge.

—— (1993) 'Towards a Poetics of Documentary' in M. Renov (ed.) *Theorizing Documentary*. London: Routledge: 12–36.

Roscoe, Jane and Craig Hight (2001) *Faking It: Mock-Documentary and the Subversion of Reality*. Manchester: Manchester University Press.

Rosen, P. (1993) 'Document and Documentary: On the Persistence of Historical Concepts' in M. Renov (ed.) *Theorizing Documentary*. London: Routledge: 58–89.

Rosenthal, Alan (ed.) (1988) *New Challenges for Documentary*. Berkeley: University of California Press.

—— (1995) *Writing Docudrama: Dramatising Reality for Film and TV*. Boston: Focal Press.

Rosenthal, Alan and John Corner (eds) (2005) *New Challenges for Documentary*. Manchester: Manchester University Press.

Rotha, Paul (1952) *Documentary Film*. London: faber and faber.

Rothman, William (1997) *Documentary Film Classics*. Cambridge: Cambridge University Press.

Ruby, Jay (2005) 'The Image Mirrored: Reflexivity and the Documentary Film' in A. Rosenthal and J. Corner (eds) (2005) *New Challenges for Documentary*. Manchester: Manchester University Press: 34–47.

San, Wanli (ed.) (2001) *Jilu dianying wenxian* (Documentation and Fictionalisation). Beijing: China Broadcasting Publisher.

—— (2005) *Zhongguo jilu dianying shi* (History of Chinese Documentary Film). Beijing: China Film Publisher.

Schreiber, Susan (1993) 'Constantly Performing the Documentary: the Seductive Promise of Lightening Over Water' in M. Renov (ed.) *Theorizing Documentary*. London: Routledge: 134–50.

Seldon, Mark (1993) *The Political Economy of Chinese Development*. New York: M.E. Sharp.

Shafir, Gershon (ed.) (1998) *The Citizenship Debates: A Reader*. Minneapolis: University of Minnesota Press.

Shanghai Yanhuang Wenhua Yanjiu Hui (Shanghai Chinese Culture Research Association) (ed.) (2002) *Fazhi yu dezhi* (*Governing the Nation by Law and by Morality*. Shanghai: China Inspection Press.

Shen, Guofang (2003) *Zhongguo chuanmei da qushi* (Tendencies of China's Mass Media). Chengdu: Sichuan People's Publisher.

Sherman, Sharon (1998) *Documenting Ourselves: Film, Video, and Culture*. The University Press of Kentucky.

Shi, Changshuan (2001) 'Woguo guangbo dianshi de jituan hua yunzuo yu shikao' (Operation and Thoughts on China Radio and TV Groups) in Hu, Zhengrong (ed.) *Zhongguo chuanmei luntan: biandong zhong de quanguo guangbo dianshi* (China Communication Forum: Changes and Developments of the Electronic Media in the Twenty-first Century). Beijing: Beijing Broadcasting Academy: 145–53.

Shi, Heng (1996) 'Woguo dianying je yinggai fuqi de shimin' (The Responsibility Our National Film Industry Should Take), Issue 9, *Yinxing*, 1927, in China Film Archive (ed.) *Zhongguo wusheng dianying* (Chinese Silent Movies). Beijing: China Film Publisher: 745–7.

Shi, Ning and Wang, Jie (eds) (2002) *Zhongguo gongmin suzhi xunlian 100 lie* (A Hundred Examples for Training Chinese Citizens in Quality). Beijing: New World Press.

Sinclair, J., Jacka, E., and Cunningham, S. (1996) (eds) *New Patterns in Global Television: Peripheral Vision*. Oxford: Oxford University Press.

Situ, Zhaodun (2001) 'Zhongguo jilu pian chuanzuo qianzhan' (The Future of Chinese Documentary Filmmaking) in San Wanli (ed.) *Jilu dianying wenxian* (Documentation and Fictionalisation), Beijing: China Broadcasting Publisher: 186–200.

Solinger, Dorothy (1999) *Contesting Citizenship in Urban China: Peasant Migrants, the State, and the Logic of the Market*. London: University of California Press.

Song, Zhuhua and Manduertu (eds) (2004) *Zhongguo minzu xue wushi nian 1949–1999* (Fifty years of Chinese Minority Studies). Beijing: People's Publisher.

Stan China Research Centre (2003) *Zhongguo chuanmei: Zhiben shichang yunyin* (China Media Forum). Guangzhou: Nanfang Daily Press.

Stan Culture International (2000) *Zhongguo chuanmei yu renwen kexue jiang xi lu* (Collection of Speeches of the Media and Humanities Seminar). Beijing: Stan Culture International.

Stella, Bruzzi (2000) *New Documentary: A Critical Introduction*. London: Routledge.

Stevenson, Nick (2003) *Understanding Media Cultures: Social Theory and Mass Communication*. London: Sage.

Su, Zhiwu (ed.) (2004) *Yazhou chuanmei luntan* (Asian Communication and Media Forum 2004) vol. 1. Beijing: Beijing Broadcasting Academy Press.

Su, Zhiwu and Ding, Junjie (eds) (2005) *Yazhou chuanmei yanjiu* (Asian Communication and Media Studies). Beijing: China Media University Press.

Sun, Xianghui, Huang, Wei, and Hu, Zhenrong (2005) '2004 nian Zhongguo guangdian canye fazhan baogao' (A Report on China's Broadcasting and Television Industry in 2004) in Cui, Baoguo (ed.) *2004–2005 nian: Zhongguo cuanmei canye fangzhan baogao* (Blue Book of China's Media: Report on Development of China's Media Industry 2004–2005). Beijing: Social Sciences Academic Press: 60–9.

Tao, Tao (2004) *Dianshi jilu pian chuangzuo* (Creativity in Television Documentaries). Beijing: China Film Publisher.

Theory Bureau of the Central Chinese Communist Ministry of Propaganda (2005) *2005 Lilun rendian mian dui mian* (Face to Face on Hot Topics in Theories). Beijing: People's Publisher.

—— (2006) *2006 Lilun rendian mian dui mian* (Face to Face on Hot Topics in Theories), Beijing: People's Publisher.

Thompson, John B. (1995) *The Media and Modernity: A Social Theory of the Media*. Cambridge: Polity Press.

Tomaselli, Keyan G. (1996) *Appropriating Images: The Semiotics of Visual Representation*. Hojbjerg: Intervention Press.

Tong, Gang (2004) 'Chanye zhence jie shuoguo, dianying kai chuang xin jiyuan – 2004 nian dianying gongzuo baogao' (Working Report on 2004 Film). *China Film Daily*, 31 December 2004.

Trinh T. Minh-ha (1993) 'The Totalising Quest of Meaning', in M. Renov (ed.) *Theorizing Documentary*. London: Routledge: 90–107.

Turner, Bryan (1994) 'Outline of a Theory of Human Rights', in B. Turner and P. Hamilton (eds) *Citizenship: Critical Concepts*, vol. 2. London: Routledge: 461–82.

—— (2000) 'Liberal Citizenship and Cosmopolitan Virtue'. in Andrew Vandenberg (ed.) *Citizenship and Democracy in a Global Era*. London: Macmillan: 18–32.

Turner, B. and Hamilton P. (eds) (1994) *Citizenship: Critical Concepts*, vol. 2. London: Routledge.

Vaughan, Dai (1999) *For Documentary*. Berkeley: University of California Press.

Wang, Hailong (2002) *Renle xue dianying* (Introduction to Anthropological Film). Shanghai: Shanghai Wenyi Publisher.

Wang, Jinhe (1999) 'Shilun jiaoyu dianshi zhuangti pian de xinwenxing' (Remarks on News Features of Documentary Series on CETV), in Li, Peng (ed.) *Zhongguo jiaoyu dianshi tai wenji* (Collection of Papers on the CETV), vol. 1. Beijing: National Broadcasting Television University Press: 62–4.

Warren, Charles (ed.) (1996) *Beyond Document: Essays on Nonfiction Film.* Middletown, Connecticut: Wesleyan University Press.

Wei, Yongzheng (2002) 'Falü he daode de qubie he lianxi' (Differences and Similarities between Law and Morality), in Shanghai Chinese Culture Research Association (ed.) *Fazhi yu dezhi (Governing the Nation by Law and by Morality).* Shanghai: China Inspection Publisher: 118–21.

Wei, Zhengshui (2002) 'Qiantan zhongguo jiaoyu dianshi fazhan zhi lu' (On the Development of the CETV), in Li, Peng (ed.) *Zhongguo jiaoyu dianshi tai wenji* (Collection of Papers on the CETV), vol. 2. Beijing: National Broadcasting Television University Press: 88–93.

Wenhua bu Dang zu guanyu dianying gongzuo de baogao (Report on Film by the Party Committee of the Ministry of Culture), July 1965.

Williams, L. (2005) 'Mirrors Without Memories: Truth, History, and the New Documentary', in A. Rosenthal, and J. Corner (eds) *New Challenges for Documentary.* Manchester: Manchester University Press: 59–75.

Winston, Brian (1993) 'Documentary as Scientific Inscription', in M. Renov (ed.) *Theorizing Documentary.* London: Routledge: 37–57.

—— (1995) *Claiming the Real: the Documentary Film Revisited.* London: British Film Institute.

Wittgenstein, Ludwig (1986) *Philosophical Investigations.* Oxford: Basil Blackwell.

Wu, Bingxin (2004) *Xinxing guizhu: Zhongguo dianshi* (New Middle Class: Chinese Television). Jinan: Shandong Art Publisher.

Wu, Keyu (2004) *Dianshi meijie jinji xue (Television Economy).* Beijing: Huaxia Publisher.

Wu, Wenguang (ed.) (2001) *Xianchang* (Document) vol. 2. Tianjin: Tianjin Academy of Social Sciences Press.

—— (ed.) (2005). *Xiangchang* (Document) vol. 3. Guilng: Guangxi Normal University Press.

Xi, Qiaojuan (2003) *Dianshi chuanmei yu chuanbo wenhua daqushi* (Television Media and Communication Culture). Beijing: China Book Publisher.

Xia, Hong (2003) '2003 meiti fazhan qushi: cong shuzi jiaodu fenxi chuanmei' (Media Development in 2003: Quantitative Analysis of Media in China' in Stan China Research Centre (ed.) *China Media Forum: Operation in the Capital Market.* Guangzhou: Nanfang Daily Press: 137–45.

Xiao, Ping (2003) *Jilu pian biandao shijian lilun* (Practice and Theory in Documentary Filmmaking). Shanghai: Shanghai University Press.

Xie, Beijian (2002) Daode, falü yu fanzui (Morality, Law and Crime). In Shanghai Culture Research Centre (ed.) *Fazhi yu dezhi (Governing the Nation by Law and by Morality).* Shanghai: China Inspection Publisher: 169–77.

Xinhua, Editorial, Daily, 13 February, 2001.

Xu, Guangchun (ed.) (2003) *Zhonghua renmin gonghe guo guangbo dianshi jianshi: 1949–2000* (A Brief History of Radio and Television in the People's Republic of China: 1949–2000). Beijing: China Radio and Television Publisher.

Yang, Weiguang (ed.) (1998) *Zhongguo dianshi lungang* (Chinese Television: Theory and Guiding Principle). Beijing: China Broadcasting and Television Publisher.

Yi, H. and Wang, Y. (2005) *Zhongguo dianying 2004* (Chinese Cinema in 2004) in Cui, Baoguo (ed.) *2004–2005 nian: Zhongguo cuanmei canye fangzhan baogao* (Blue Book of China's Media: Report on Development of China's Media Industry 2004–2005). Beijing: Social Sciences Academic Press (China).

Yin, Hong (2001) 'Zhongguo de jiaoyu dianshi yu shehui fazhan' (Educational Television and Social Development in China), in Li, Peng (ed.) *Zhongguo jiaoyu dianshi tai wenji* (Collection of Papers on the CETV), vol. 2: Beijing: National Broadcasting Television University Press: 51–55.

Yin, Li (ed.) (2001a) *Jiri shuofa* (*Legal Report*). Episodes 1999–2000: vols 1–4. Beijing: China People's Public Security University Press.

—— (ed.) (2001b) *Jiri shuofa* (*Legal Report*). Episodes 2001: vols 1–12. Beijing: China People's Public Security University Press.

You, Chun (2002) 'Zihao, gankai, qipan' (Proud Sigh of Emotion and Looking Forward), in Li, Peng (ed.) *Zhongguo jiaoyu dianshi tai wenji* (Collection of Papers on the CETV), vol. 2. Beijing: National Broadcasting Television University Press: 30–2.

You, Junyi (2002) 'Xuexi Jiang Zemin tongzhi dezhi sixiang, jianchi fade jiehe de zhiguo zhidao' (Study of Jiang Zemin's theory of governing the country by morality, and insisting on the combination of governing the country both by morality and law), in Shanghai Chinese Culture Research (ed.) *Fazhi yu dezhi* (Governing the Nation by Law and by Morality). Shanghai: China Inspection Press: 18–35.

Young, Iris Marion (1998) 'Polity and Group Difference: A Critique of the Ideal of Universal Citizenship' in Gershon Shafir (eds) *The Citizenship Debates: A Reader*. Minneapolis: University of Minnesota Press: 263–90.

Yu, Guomin (2002) *Jiexi chuanmei bianju* (Analysis of Media Change). Guangzhou: Nanfang Publisher.

Yu, Guoming (2001) 'Duiyu woguo meiti chanye xianshi fazhan zhuangkuang de jiben panduan' (Evaluation of the Contemporary Situation of the Chinese Media Industry) in Hu, Zhengrong (ed.) *Zhongguo chuanmei luntan: biandong zhong de quanquo guangbo dianshi* (China Communication Forum: Changes and Developments of the Electronic Media in the Twenty-first Century). Beijing: Beijing Broadcasting Academy: 118–22.

—— (2002) *Jiexi chuanmei bianju* (An Analysis of Changes in the Media). Guangzhou: Nanfang Daily Publisher.

—— (2003) *Chuanmei yinxiang li* (The Power of Media Influence). Guangzhou: Nanfang Daily Publisher.

Yu, Muyun (1985) *Xiangang dianying zhanggu* (*Historical Anecdotes of Hong Kong Cinema*). Hong Kong: Guangjiao Jing Publisher.

Yuan, Guiren (2002) 'Chengxian qihou, jiwang kailai, yushi jujin' (Speech on the Occasion of the Celebration of 15 Years of Satellite TV in China', in Li, Peng (ed.) *Zhongguo jiaoyu dianshi tai wenji* (Collection of Papers on the CETV), vol. 2. Beijing: National Broadcasting Television University Press: 1–11.

Zhang, Fengzhou (ed.) (1999) *Zhongguo dianshi wenyi xue* (Studies of Chinese Television Art). Beijing: Beijing Broadcasting Academy Press.

Zhang, Fengzhou, Huang, Shixian, and Hu, Zhifeng (eds) (2002) *Quanqiu hua yu Zhongguo yingshi de mingyu* (*Globalisation and the Destiny of Chinese Film and Television*). Beijing: Beijing Broadcasting University Press.

Zhang, Haichao (ed.) (2001) *Dianshi Zhongguo* (*Television China*). Beijing: Beijing Broadcasting University Press.

Zhang, Jianghua, Li, Dejun, Chen, Jinyuan, Yang, Guanghai, Pang, Tao, and Li, Tong (2000) *Yingshi renle xue geilu* (Brief Introduction to Ethnographic Film). Beijing: Social Science Academy Press.

Zhang, Xiaoming, Hu, Huilin, and Zhang, Jiangang (eds) (2006) *2006 nian: Zhongguo wenhua chanye fazhan baogao* (Report on the Development of China's Cultural Industry 2006). Beijing: Beijing Academy of Social Sciences.

Zhang, Yaxin (1999) *Zhongwai jilu pian bijiao* (A Comparative Study of Chinese and Non-Chinese Documentaries). Beijing: Beijing Normal University Press Press.

Zhang, Yingjing (1997) 'From Minority Film' to 'Minority Discourse', *Cinema Journal*, 36, 3:73–90.

Zhang, Zhijun (2003) *'Shilun 'san tiejin' de dazhong chuanbo xue yiyi* (The Siginficance of 'Three Proximities' in Mass Communication). *Dangdai dianshi*, vol. 1:34–8.

—— (2005) *'Rushi' yu Zhongguo guojia dianshi wenhua anquan* ('Joining the WTO and Cultural Security of the National Television in China'). Unpublished doctorial thesis from Beijing Media University.

Zhao, Yuezhi (1998) *Media, Market, and Democracy in China: Between the Party Line and the Bottom Line.* Urbana and Chicago: University of Illinois Press.

Zhao, Yushen (ed.) (2004) *Zhongguo guangbo dianshi tongshi* (General History of Chinese Radio and Television). Beijing: Beijing Broadcasting Academy.

Zhao, Wei (2003) 'Zhongguo jiaoyu dianshi tai: chuangjian quanquo zui da de xuexi pingtai' (Creating the Biggest Study Forum in the World: the CETV). 4 December, *Beijing Youth Daily*.

Zheng, Dachen (2002) *Dianshi meiti cehua* (*Schedule Television*). Beijing: China Broadcasting Publishing.

Zheng, Wei (1997) 'Zhong Xi jilupian yitong gaishuo' (General differences between Chinese and Western Documentaries), in Ren Yuan (ed.) *Dianshi jilu pian xinlun* (New Theorization of Television Documentary). Beijing: China Broadcasting Publisher: 167–210.

Zhong, Danian (2003) *Jilupian chuangzuo lungang* (Outlines of Documentary Film Making). Beijing: Beijing Broadcasting Academy Press.

Zhong, Dianfei (1956) 'Dianying de luogu' (Gongs and Drums of Film). *Wenyi Daily*, Issue 23.

Zhonggong zhongyang bangong shi (The Central Office of the Chinese Communist Party) (July 2003) *Zhonggong Zhongyang xuanchuan bu, wenhua bu, guojia guangdian zong ju, xinwen chuban zongshu guanyu wenhua tizhi gaige shidian gongzuo de yijian* (The Ministry of Propaganda, The Ministry of Culture, The State Administration of Radio, Film and Television, the Central News Publisher on Reforming Cultural Institutions). Government Document, Number 105. Beijing.

Zhongguo dianying nianjian 1980–2005 (China Film Year Book from 1980 to 2005). Beijing: China Film Publisher.

Zhongguo dianying yishu yanjiu zhongxing (Chinese Film Art Research Centre) (ed.) (1993) *Zhongguo zuoyi dianying yundong* (The Chinese Left-Wing Film Movement). Beijing: China Film Publisher.

Zhongguo dianying zhiliao guan (China Film Archive) (ed.) (1996) *Zhongguo wusheng dianying* (Chinese Silent Movies). Beijing: China Film Publisher.

Zhongguo guangbo dianshi xiehui dianshi shouzhong yanjiu weiyuan hui (Audience Research Committee of the China Broadcasting Association) (ed.) (2005) *Dianshi shouzhong tanxi* (Audience Research). Beijing: Central Compilation and Translation Press.

Zhongyang dianshi tai taiban bangongshi shiye fazhan diaoyan chu (CCTV Editorial) (2003) *Chuancheng wenming kaituo chuangxin – yushijujin de zhongyang dianshi tai* (*CCTV from 1958–2003*). Beijing: Dongfang chuban she.

Zhu, Jinghe (2002) *Jilun pian chuangzuo* (Creativity in Documentary Film). Beijing: People's University Press.

Zhu, Qingjiang and Mei, Bin (2004) *Zhongguo duli jilupian dang'an* (Files on the Chinese Independent Documentary Films). Shaanxi: Shaanxi Normal University Press.

Zhu, Yujun (2000) *Xiandai dianshi jishi* (Realism in Contemporary Television Documentaries). Beijing: Beijing Broadcasting Academy Press.

Zhu, Yujun and Yin, Le (1998) *Shenghuo de chongguo: xinshiqi dianshi jishi yuyan* (New Television Documentation of Language in the New Era). Beijing: Beijing Broadcasting Academy Press.

Filmography of Chinese Documentaries

Films

1966: Wo de hongweibing shidai / *Red Guards in 1966* / 1966 我的红卫兵时代
Ah Lu Xiongdi / *Ah Lu's Brothers* / 阿鲁兄弟
Aiguo dongya liangxiao yundong hui / *Sports Carnival of the Two Schools of Aiguo and Dongya* / 爱国东亚两校运动会
Aiguo yi jia / *Nation as One Family* / 爱国一家
Aizi fen / *Ancient Tomb in Nantong* / 矮子坟
Anhui jiuhuashan fengjing / *Sceneries of Jiuhua Mountain in Anhui* / 安徽九华山风景
Anshan he Anshan ren / *Anshan and Anshan People* / 鞍山和鞍山人
Aomen cangshang / *Suffering Macau* / 澳门沧伤
Babai zhuangshi / *800 Brave Soldiers* / 八百壮士
Bakuo nanjie shiliu hao / *No.16 Barkhor South Street* / 八廓南街16号
Baitai / *White Tower* / 白塔
Baiwan nongnu zhanqi lai / *Stand up, Million of Serfs* / 百万农奴站起来
Baiwan xiongshi xia jiangnan / *Hundreds of Thousands PLA Soldiers Cross the Yangzi River* / 百万雄师下江南
Bao rihuo hu ji / *Records of Violent Japanese Damage to Shanghai* / 暴日祸沪记
Baowei women de tudi / *Defend our Land* / 保卫我们的土地
Baowei Yan'an he baowei Shaan gan ning bianqu / *Protect Yan'an, Protect Shaanxi, Gansu and Ningxia* / 保卫延安和保卫陕甘宁边区
Beifa da zhanshi / *History of Northern Launch* / 北伐大战史
Beifa wancheng ji / *Northern Launch* / 北阀完成记
Beijing mingsheng / *Famous Places in Beijing* / 北京名胜
Beilou dianying yuan / *Cinema on the Back* / 背篓电影院
Beiping geyong dui / *Beijing Chore* / 北平歌咏队
Beiying / *In the Background* / 背影
Beiying / *On the Other Side of the Dam* / 背影
Bingchuan / *Glacier* / 冰川
Bingren / *Icemen* / 冰人
Biye qianxi / *Before Graduation* / 毕业前夕
Bu an ding de shenghuo / *An Unstable Life* / 不安定的生活
Budala gong / *The Potala Palace* / 布达拉宫
Buzai chan jiao / *No More Bound Feet* / 不再缠脚
Chama gudao / *Chama Road* / 茶马古道

Changcheng xuezhan shi / *History of Bloody War Near the Great Wall* / 长城血战史
Changjiang daqiao / *The Yangzi River Bridge* / 长江大桥
Changjiang mingsheng / *Famous Places along the Yangzi River* / 长江名胜
Chaoxian xixian jie bao / *Good News from Korea* / 朝鲜西线捷报
Chaozhou bajing / *Eight Sites in Chaozhou* / 潮洲八景
Chisheyingji de ren / *The Man with the Movie Camera* / 持摄影机的人
Chongfang huxian / *Revisiting Hu County* / 重访户县
Chongxiang taikong / *Flying towards the Universe*/ 冲向太空
Chuang / *Lost in the City* / 创
Chunfeng cong zheli chuiqi / *Spring Starts Here* / 春风从这里吹起
Chunjie yinxiang / *Spring Festival* / 春节印象
Cishan jiaoyu / *Charitable Education* / 慈善教育
Cizhong shengdan jie / *Christmas Eve in Cizhong* / 茨中圣诞节
Congfan Xizang de lianxiang / *Thoughts on Re-visiting Tibet* / 从返西藏的联想
Cuiren fenfa de shiye / *Inspiring Careers* / 摧人奋发的事业
Cun guan / *Village Cadre* / 村官
Da xinan kaige / *Victory in the Southwest* / 大西南凯歌
Daqing fangwen ji / *Visiting Daqing* / 大庆访问记
Daqing hongqi / *Daqing Red Flag* / 大庆红旗
Daqing Ren / *Daqing People* / 大庆人
Dazhai Ren / *Dazi People* / 大寨人
Dazhan Hainan dao / *Battles on Hainan Island* / 大战海南岛
Dengren / *The Deng Nationality* / 僜人
Dexing fang / *Dexing Lane* / 德兴坊
Diba jie yuandong yundong hui Zhongguo yuxuan hui / *The Eighth Far East Sports Carnival – China Preliminary* / 第八届远东运动会中国预选会
Dierci jiaofeng / *The Second Match – The Chinese Women's Volleyball Team and Japanese Women's Volleyball Team* / 第二次交锋
Diliu jie quanguo yundong hui / *The Sixth National Sports Carnival* / 第六届全国运动会
Ding Jun Shan / *Ding Jun Shan* / 定军山
Diwu ci yuandong yundong hui / *The Fifth Far East Sports Carnival* / 第五次远东运动会
Diyi liang qiche / *The First Vehicle* / 第一辆汽车
Dongbei yiyong jun kangri ji / *Record of Anti-Japanese Battles by Northeast Volunteer Army* / 东北义勇军抗日记
Dongbei yiyong jun kangri xuezhan shi / *History of Anti-Japanese Bloody Battles by Northeast Volunteer Army* / 东北义勇军抗日血战史
Dongfang liu daxue yundong hui / *Sports Carnival of Six Oriental Universities* / 东方六大学运动会
Doudong de 20 fenzhong / *Trembling for Twenty Minutes* / 抖动的20分钟
Dulong zu / *The Dulong Nationality* / 独龙族
Elun chun zu / *The Oroqen Nationality* / 鄂伦春族
E'er guna hepan de Ewenke ren / *The Ewenki Nationality near the E'er Guna River* / 额尔古纳河畔的鄂温克人
Fandui xijun zhan / *Against Chemical Warfare* / 反对细菌战
Feng Yuxiang / *Feng Yuxiang* / 冯玉祥
Fengqi huanji /*Fight Back* / 奋起还击
Fenyi Chenjisihan lingmu / *Moving Chenjishihan's Grave* / 奉移成吉思汗陵墓

Fudan daxue yiyong jun jianyue dianli / *Fudan University Volunteers Military Inspection* / 复旦大学义勇军检阅典礼

Fuzhou fengjing / *Fuzhou Sceneries* / 福州风景

Gaige kaifang 20 nian / *20 Years of Opening and Reform* / 改革开放20年

Gaige kaifang de Zhongguo / *China in the Era of Economic Reform and Open Door Policy* / 改革开放的中国

Gaishanxi he tade jiemei / *Gai Shanxi and her Sisters* / 盖山西和她的姐妹

Gangqing meng / *Piano Dream* / 钢琴梦

Gangtie yunshu xian / *Steel Transport* / 钢铁运输线

Gangtie zai jianshe zhong / *We Are Making Steel* / 钢铁在建设中

Gemingjun beifa ji / *Record of North Launch by the Revolutionary Army* / 革命军北阀记

Gemingjun zhanshi / *Fighting History of the Revolutionary Army* / 革命军战史

Gongbu de xingfu shenghuo / *Gongbu's Happy Life* / 贡布的幸福生活

Gongfei baoxing shilu / *True Records of Communist Violence* / 共匪暴行史录

Gongfei huoguo ji / *Records of Damage to the Country by the Communists* / 共匪祸国记

Guangdong quan sheng yundong hui / *Sports Carnival of Guangdong Province* / 广东全省运动会

Guanghui de licheng / *Glorious History* / 光辉的里程

Guanghui yeji / *Grand Contribution* / 光辉业绩

Guangming zhaoyao zuo Xizang / *Bright Sun Shining Over Tibet* / 光明照耀著西藏

Gudou Chang'an /*Ancient City of Chang'an* / 古都长安

Guirong xiyuan / *Guirong Theatre* / 桂容戏院

Gulu hu lian / *The Lake of Romance* / 沽泸湖恋

Guomin dahui / *National Congress* / 国民大会

Guomin waijiao youxing dahui / *Citizens March* / 国民外交游行大会

Guomindang geminjun hai, lu, kong dazhan ji / *Battles of the Navy, Land and Air Forces of the Nationalist Revolutionary Army* / 国民党革命军海, 陆, 空大战记

Haining chao / *Haining Wave* 海宁潮

Hairui baguan / *Hairui Dismissed from Office* / 海瑞罢官

Haixia qingsi / *Feelings Across the Taiwan Strait* / 海峡情思

Hanya / *Crow in Winter* / 寒鸦

Hao zai lishi shi renmin xie de / *Luckily, History Is Written by People* / 好在历史是人民写的

Heping wansui /*Long Live Peace* / 和平万岁

Hongqi manjuan xifeng / *Red Flag Sweeping the Western Region* / 红旗漫卷西风

Hongqi qu / *Red Flag Tunnel* / 红旗渠

Houjie / *Houjie Township* / 厚街

Huabei shi women de / *North China is Ours*/ 华北是我们的

Huaihai zhanbao /*Achievements of the Huaihai War* / 淮河战报

Huang Zhuanshi feng lin ru Zang zhi ji Dala Lama / *Special Envoy Huang Visits Tibet to Attend Dalai Lama's Funeral* / 黄专使奉令入藏致祭达赖喇嘛

Huanghai yumin / *Fishermen in the Yellow Sea* / 黄海渔民

Huanghe jubian / *Great Changes of the Yellow River* / 黄河巨变

Huanghua gang / *Huanghua Gang* / 黄花冈

Huangshan guanqi / *Spectacular Scenes in the Yellow Mountains* / 黄山观奇

Huanhu woguo fashe daodan hewuqi shiyan chenggong / *Welcome the Success of Our Country's Nuclear Weapon* / 欢呼我国发射导弹核武器试验成功

Huanle de Xinjiang / *Happy Xinjiang* / 欢乐的新疆
Huansong huiTai / *Farewell the Nationalist Soldiers Returning to Taiwan*/ 欢送回台
Huanying Zhou, Hu chu guo / *Farewell Zhou and Hu Visiting Overseas* / 欢迎周，胡出国
Huanying Zhou, Hu fanguo / *Welcome Zhou and Hu Returning Home* / 欢迎周，胡返国
Huanying Malaixiya xuanshou / *Welcome Sportsmen from Malaysia* / 欢迎马来西亚选手
Hunshi / *Marriage* / 婚事
Huo de kaoyan / *Fire in Helongjiang Forest* / 火的考验
Huoyao de xixian / *Western Frontier* / 活耀的西线
Ji Kong / *Paying Respect to Confucius* / 祭孔
Jiangsu tongzi jun lianhe hui / *Jiangsu Boy Scouts Association* / 江苏童子军联合会
Jianguo shi de yiye / *A Page on the Establishment of the Nation* / 建国史的一页
Jiaoji lu kehuo yunshu shebe ji yanxian fengjing / *Sceneries along Jiaoji Road* / 胶济路客货运输设备及沿线风景
Jiayuan / *Home* / 家园
Jiefang Shijiazhuang /*Liberating Shijiazhuang* / 解放石家庄
Jiefang Taiyuan /*Liberating Taiyuan* / 解放太原
Jiefang Xizang da jun xing / *Marching to Liberate Tibet* / 解放西藏大军行
Jiehun / *Marriage* / 结婚
Jietou tanfan / *Street Peddler* / 街头探访
Jiji daguan / *Skills Show* / 技击大观
Jinan can'an / *Jinan Tragedy* / 济南惨案
Jinan mingsheng / *Famous Places in Jinan* / 济南名胜
Jing'ai de Zhou Enlai zongli yongchui buxiu / *Forever our Beloved Premier Zhou Enlai* / 敬爱的周恩来总理永垂不朽
Jingzhong baoguo / *Loyality to the Nation* / 精忠报国
Jingpo zu / *The Jingpo Nationality* / 景颇族
Jinri Xizang / *Today's Tibet* / 今日西藏
Jinxiu heshan / *Beautiful Landscape of Sichuan* / 锦绣河山
Jinxiu Zhonghua / *Colourful China* / 锦绣中华
Jueding mingyun de shike / *The Moment Deciding Destiny* / 决定命运的时刻
Jungen zhange / *The Army's Victory* / 军耕战歌
Junjian xiashui / *Fleet Launch* / 军舰下水
Junmin tuanjie kang zhenzai / *Soldiers and People Unite to Fight Disasters* / 军民团结抗赈灾
Kaifang zhong de beifang chuangkou / *North China Under the Open Door Policy* / 开放中的北方窗口
Kaituo zhe you huanle / *Happiness of the Pioneers* / 开拓者有欢乐
Kang Mei yuan Chao / *Fight America, Support Korea* / 抗美援朝
Kangba de xinsheng / *New Life of Tibetans* / 康巴的新生
Kangri xuezhan / *Anti-Japanese Bloody War* / 抗日血战
Kaoshi / *Exams* / 考试
Keji de chuntian / *Spring for Science and Technology* / 科技的春天
Kong / *Empty* / 空
Kongzi guli / *Confuciusí Hometown* / 孔子故里
Kuangshan xuelei / *Tears and Blood of Miners* / 矿山血泪
Kucong ren / *The Kucong Nationality* / 苦聪人

Kuhun / *Crying the Bride* / 哭婚
Laizi nongcun de baogao / *Report from the Countryside* / 来自农村的报告
Lao Beijing de xushuo / *From Old Beijing Residencies* / 老北京的叙述
Lao Ren / *Old Men* / 老人
Laodong wansui / *Long Live Work* / 劳动万岁
Laoji jieji chou / *Remembering Class Hatred* / 牢记阶级仇
Laonian hunyin zixun suo jianwen / *Senior Citizen Dating Service* / 老年婚姻诸询所
Laoren men / *Elders* / 老人们
Liangshan yizu / *The Yi Nationality in Liangshan* / 凉山彝族
Liangzhong mingyun de juezhan / *Fighting Against Two Destinies* / 两种命运的决战
Lidui zhihou / *After Leaving the Team* / 离队之后
Ling de tupo / *Breaking Records from Zero* / 零的突破
Lingxiu he women tong laodong / *The Leaders Are with Us* / 领袖和我们同劳动
Lingxiu wansui / *Long Live Our Leaders* / 领袖万岁
Lishi de xuanzhe / *Historical Choice* / 历史的选折
Lishi xinfei yao / *New Leap in History* / 历史新飞耀
Liu Shaoqi tongzhi yongchui buxiu / *Comrade Liu Shaoqi Forever* / 刘少奇同志永垂不朽
Liu yi renmin de yizhi / *The Will of Six Hundred Million People* / 六亿人民的意志
Liulang Beijing / *Bumming in Beijing* / 流浪北京
Lizu / *The Li Nationality* / 黎族
Long Ji / *Long Ji* / 龙脊
Luoyang fengjing / *Luoyang Scenery* / 洛阳风景
Lüse de yuanye / *Green Grassland* / 绿色的原野
Lushan fengjing / *Lu Mountain Scenery* / 庐山风景
Luxun xiansheng shishi / *Death of Mr Luxun* / 鲁讯先生逝世
Luxun xiansheng shishi xinwen / *News of the Death of Mr Luxun* / 鲁讯先生逝世新闻
Maibao ren / *Qin, the Newspaper Man* / 卖报人
Mancheng hanmu / *Han Tomb Discovered in Man City* / 满城汉墓
Mangtong jiaoyu / *Blind Children's Education* / 盲童教育
Manyou jianwen lu / *Record of a Journey* / 漫游见闻录
Mao Zedong shixiang de weida shengli / *Great Victory of Mao Zedong's Thoughts* / 毛泽东思想的伟大胜利
Mao Zhuxi Zhu zong siling beiping yue bing / *Chairman Mao and General Zhu Inspecting the Army* / 毛主席朱总司令北平阅兵
Meiguo hongshizi hui Shanghai da youxing / *American Red Cross Marching in Shanghai* / 美国红十字会上海大游行
Meili de heichi / *The Beauty of Black* / 美丽的黑齿
Miao Zhongkai xiansheng wei Guangdong bing gongchang qingnian gongren xuexiao kaimu / *The Opening Ceremony of the Youth School in Guangdong Military Factory by Mr Miao Zhongkai* / 缪仲垲先生为广东兵工厂青年工人学校开幕
Miao zu / *The Miao Nationality* / 苗族
Miao zu de gongyi meishu / *Crafts of the Miao* / 苗族的工艺美术
Miao zu de wudao / *Miao Dances* / 苗族的舞蹈
Minnan shizhen jiaoyu / *Fujian Government Education* / 闽南市政教育
Minzu tiyu zhi hua / *Minorities Sports* / 民族体育之花
Minzu wansui / *Long Live the Chinese United Nation* / 民族万岁
Mou / *Moo* / 哞
Nanji, Women laile / *Here We Come, Antarctica* / 南极！我们来啦

Nanjing de jingzheng / *Nanjing Police* / 南京的警政
Nanjing mingsheng / *Famous Places in Nanjing* / 南京名胜
Nanjing Zhuan hao / *The Fall of Nanjing* / 南京专号
Nanlin cun de geshen / *Song of Nanlin* / 南林村的歌声
Nanren / *Men* / 男人
Nanyang daguan / *Views of Southeast Asia* / 南洋大观
Nikesong fang Hua / *Nixon Visiting China* / 尼克松访华
Nisu xinhua / *New Soil Characters* / 泥塑新话
Nongcun funu Yulan de wenhua shenghuo / *A Country Woman's Cultural Life* / 农村妇
　女玉兰的文化生活
Nongcun zai dayao jin / *The Countryside in the Great Leap Forward* / 农村在大耀进
Nongcun zhuanye hu fang Riben / *Rich Peasants Visiting Japan* / 农村专业户访日本
Nongren zhichun / *Spring for Farmers* / 农人之春
Nūzi tiyu guan / *Women Attitudes towards Sports* / 女子体育观
Ouzhan zhusheng youxing / *Celebration of European Victory of War* / 欧战祝胜游行
Piao / *Floating* / 飘
Pinbo – Zhongguo nüpai duo guan ji / *Fighting – The Chinese Women's Volleyball
　Team* / 拼博 – 中国女排夺冠记
Pingxi Xizang panluan / *Calming Down the Tibetan Riots* / 平息西藏叛乱
Pudong xin / *New Pudong District* / 埔东新
Putuo fengjing / *Putuo Scenery* / 普陀风景
Qingchun yuanmu / *Cemetery of Youth* / 青春圆墓
Qingguanlu shi hao / *Qingguan Road No.10* / 清关路10号
Qingshui jiang liuyu Miao zu de hunyin / *Miao Marriage in the Qingshui River Delta* /
　清水江流域苗族的婚姻
Qiyi zai Beiping / *July First in Beijing* / 起义在北平
Qiying yu tanmianhua jiang / *A Daughter for the Cotton Mat Maker* / 弃婴与弹棉
　花匠
Quanguo yundong dahui / *National Sports Carnival* / 全国运动大会
Qufeng / *Qufeng* / 欧风
Qufu mingsheng / *Famous Places in Qufu* / 曲阜名胜
Qumie wenyin / *Eradicating Mosquitoes and Flies* / 驱灭蚊蝇
Rehe xuezhan shi / *Bloody Battles in Rehe* / 热河血战史
Renmin de Nei Menggu / *People's Inner Mongolia* / 人民的内蒙古
Renmin gongshe hao / *The People's Commune Is Good* / 人民公社好
Renmin gongshe haochu duo / *Many Good Aspects of the People's Communes* / 人民公
　社好处多
Rexue Zhonghua / *Hotblooded Chinese* / 热血中华
Richan baiwan dun / *A Million Tons Production a Day* / 日产百万吨
Ruan Lingyu shishi xinwen / *News of the Death of Ruan Lingyu* / 阮玲玉逝世新闻
Sange mosuo nüzi de gushi / *A Documentary about Three Mosuo Women* / 三个摩梭
　女子的故事
Sanjiecao / *Sanjiecao* / 三节草
Shandong li de cunzhuang / *Village in the Cave* / 山洞里的村庄
Shandong minjian muban nianhua / *Woodcuts from Shandong* / 山东民间木板年画
Shangao shuichang / *High Mountains, Long Rivers* / 山高水长
Shanghai fengjing / *Shanghai Scenery* / 上海风景
Shanghai Fenhui chuntu / *Burning Opium in Shanghai* / 上海焚毁存土
Shanghai guangfu ji / *Records of Shanghai's Recovery* / 上海光复记

Shanghai haojie ji / *Shanghai Tragedy* / 上海浩劫记

Shanghai jiuhuo hui / *Shanghai Fire Brigade Association* / 上海救火会

Shanghai kangdi xue zhanshi / *Record of Shanghai's Anti-enemy History* / 上海抗地血战史

Shanghai kangzhan xuezhan shi / *Record of Shanghai's Bloody Anti-Japanese War* / 上海抗战血战史

Shanghai liangjiang nüzi tiyu shifan xuexiao yundong hui / *Sports Carnival of the Shanghai Liangjiang Female Teaching College* / 上海两江女子体育师范学校运动会

Shanghai wu sanshi shimin dahui / *Shanghai May 30th Citizen Conference* / 上海五三十市民大会

Shanghai yuandong saima chang kaimu / *Opening Ceremony of the Shanghai Race-course* / 上海远东赛马场开幕

Shanghai zhanzhen / *Shanghai War* / 上海战争

Shanghai zhizhan / *Shanghai Battle* / 上海之战

Shangwu yinshu guan fang gong / *Workers Leaving Commercial Press* / 商务印书馆放工

Shangwu yinshu guan yinshua shuo quanjing / *A View of the Commercial Press* / 商务印书馆印刷所全景

Shaoqi tongzhi renmin huainian nin / *People Remembering You, Comrade Shaoqi* / 少奇同志人民怀念您

Shekou mingzou qu / *Shekou Singing* / 蛇口鸣奏曲

Sheng Xinsun da chu sang / *Sheng Xinsun's Funeral* / 盛杏荪大出丧

Shengchan yu zhandou jiehe qilai: Nanni wan / *Production and Fighting Combine: Nanni Bay* / 生产与战斗结合起来: 南泥湾

Shenghuo de kaige / *Victory of Life* / 生活的凯歌

Shengli youtian / *Victory Oil Field* / 胜利油田

Shengli zhi lu / *The Road to Victory* / 胜利之路

Shenlu Ai! Women de Shenlu / *The Deer Story* / 神鹿啊! 我们的神鹿

Shenmi de xizang / *Mysterious Tibet* / 神秘的西藏

Shi shui pohuai liao tielu? / *Who Damaged the Railway?* / 是谁破坏了铁路?

Shidong Miao zu de longchuan jie / *Boat Festival of the Miao in Shidong* / 苗族的龙船节

Shije renmin gongdi / *The Enemy of the World* / 世界人民公敌

Shijie funü dahui / *The World Women's Conference* / 世界妇女大会

Shijie funü jie / *International Women's Festival* / 世界妇女节

Shijie nüpai mingxing sai / *The World Vollyball Match of the Women's Team* / 世界女排明星赛

Shijiu lu jun guangrong shi / *Glorious Record of No.19 Route* / 十九路军光荣史

Shijiu lu jun kangri zhanshi / *History of No.19 Route Army against the Japanese* / 十九路军抗日战史

Shijiu lu jun xuezhan kang ri- Shanghai zhandi xiezhen / *Real Images of the Bloody War against the Japanese by the No. 19 Route Army* / 十九路军血战抗日－上海战地写真

Shisan yingli changtu jingsai / *13 Miles of Long Distance Competition* / 十三英哩长途竞赛

Shisang / *Losing* / 失散

Siqing qu / *Homesick* / 思情曲

Siye nanxia ji / *Journey to the South by the Fourth Army* / 四野南下记

Songhu kangri jiangshi zhuidao hui / *Memorial for the Soldiers Who Died in the Shanghai Anti-Japanese War* / 淞沪抗日将士追悼会

Songhu xue / *Blood along the Songhu River* / 淞沪血

Suimeng qianxian / *Frontier between Shanxi Province and Inner Mongolia* / 绥蒙前线

Suiyuan qianxian xinwen / *News from the Frontier between Inner Mongolia and Shanxi Province* / 绥原前线新闻

Sun Chuanfang / *Sun Chuanfang* / 孙传芳

Sun dayuanchuai jianyue Guangdong quan sheng jingwei jun wu jingcha ji shangtuan / *Dr Sun's Inspection of Military, Police and the Business Community of Guangdong Province* / 孙大元帅检阅广东全省警卫军武警察及商团

Sun dayuanshuai chuxun Guangdong dongbei jiang ji / *Dr Sun's Inspection of the North River in Guangdong* / 孙大元帅出巡广东东北江记

Sun Zhongshan xiansheng beishang / *Dr Sun Marches North* / 孙中山先生北上

Sun Zhongsan xiansheng chubin ji zhuidao zhi dianli / *Dr Sun Yat-sen's Funeral* / 孙中山先生出殡及追悼之典礼

Sun Zhongsan xiansheng lingmu dianji ji / *Dr Sun Yat-sen Memorial Foundation* / 孙中山先生陵墓奠基记

Sun Zhongsan xiansheng wei dian jun ganbu xuexiao juxing kaimu li / *Dr Sun's Attendance of the Opening Ceremony of Yunnan Army Cadres School* / 孙中山先生为滇军干部学校举行开幕礼

Sun Zhongshan / *Dr Sun Yat-sen* / 孙中山

Sun Zhongshan lingmu dianji ji / *Foundation Stone for Dr Sun Yat-sen's Memorial* / 孙中山陵墓奠基记

Suzhou fengjing / *Suzhou Scenery* / 苏州风景

Taifeng erci xi hu / *Twice Typhoon Hits Shanghai* / 台风二次袭沪

Taishan mingsheng / *Famous Places in the Tai Mountains* / 泰山名胜

Taishan / *The Tai Mountains* / 泰山

Tamen shi zeyang fu qilai de / *How They Got Rich* / 他们是这样富起来的

Tianzhu jiao da misa / *Catherine Prays for Victory in the Anti-Japanese Battle* / 天主教大弥撒

Tie / *Iron* / 铁

Tielu Yanxian / *Along the Railway* / 铁路沿线

Tieren Wang Jinxi / *The Ironman Wang Jinxi* / 铁人王进喜

Tiexi qu / *District West of the Railways* / 铁西区

Tongxiang Lhasa de xingfu daolu / *The Road Brings Happiness to Lhasa* / 通向拉萨的幸福道路

Wanguo shangtui hui cao / *Gymnastics of a Thousand Business Associations* / 万国商团会操

Wanguo Zhonghua dui / *Chinese Teams* / 万国中华队

Wanxiang gengxin / *New Society* / 万象更新

Wazu / *The Kawa* / 瓦族

Weida de tudi gaige / *The Great Land Reform* / 伟大的土地改革

Weida de zhanshi / *A Great Soldier* / 伟大的战士

Wenhua dagemin qijian de chutu wenwu / *Artefacts Dug out During the Cultural Revolution* / 文化大革命其间出土文物

Wenhua xiu / *Culture Show* / 文化秀

Wo keai de jiaxiang / *My Lovely Home* / 我可爱的家乡

Wo shu she / *The Snake Boy* / 我属蛇

Wo yao shenghuo / *Mr Cool* / 我要生活

Wo zai Wangfujing penjiang liao yi wei laoren / *I bumped into an Old Man in Wangfujing on March 16, 2004* / 2004年3月我在王福井碰见了一位老人

Woguo diyike renzao diqiu weixing fashe chenggong / *Success of Our Nation's First Satellite Rocket* / 我国第一颗人造地球卫星发射成功

Women de dong / *Winter at 3000 Meters* / 我们的冬

Women de Nanjing / *Nanjing Is Ours* / 我们的南京

Women de wuyi nongmin de fangxiang / *The Direction of Our Five Hundred Million Peasants* / 我们的五亿农民的方向

Women zouguo de rizi / *Days We Have Experienced* / 我们走过的日子

Wu Peifu / *Wu Peifu* / 吴佩俘

Wugu / *Misty Village* / 雾谷

Wuhan zhanzheng / *Wuhan War* / 武汉战争

Wusanshi hu shao / *May 30th Tragedy in Shanghai* / 五三十沪潮

Wuxun zhuan / *Wuxun Biography* / 武训传

Wuyan meidian / *Blind Coal Store* / 无烟煤店

Xiang Mao zhuxi huibao / *Report to Chairman Mao* / 向毛主席汇报

Xianggang yibai tian / *One Hundred Days in Hong Kong* / 香港一百天

Xianqu ze zhi ge / *Song of the Pioneers* / 先驱者之歌

Xiao Shengming / *Small Lives* / 小生命

Xiaoqu / *Small Neighborhood* / 社区

Xiaoyuan baowei zhan / *Fight Against SARS on Campus* / 校园保卫战

Xibei fengjing / *Sceneries of the Northwest* / 西北风景

Xibu zai zhaohuan / *Calling from the West* / 西部在召唤

Xihu fengjing / *West Lake Scenery* / 西湖风景

Ximao jiawu chan jiashen yinyang jie / *Between Life and Death* / 细毛家务场甲申阴阳界

Xin de boji – ji Zhongguo nupai si lianguan / *Four Times Winners of the World Female Volleyball Competition* / 新的搏击: 记中国女排四连冠

Xin Guangzhou / *New Canton* / 新广州

Xin Shahuang fan Hua baoxin / *Anti-China Violence by the New Royals of Russia* / 新沙皇反华暴行

Xin zhengzhi xieshang huiyi choubei hui chengli / *Preparatory Meeting for New Political Consultative Conference* / 新政治协商会议筹备会成立

Xin Zhongguo de danshen / *The Birth of the New China* / 新中国的诞生

Xingfu de ertong / *Happy Children* / 幸福的儿童

Xingfu shenghuo / *Happy Life* / 幸福生活

Xinghua chunyu Jiangnan / *Jiangnan in Spring* / 杏花春雨江南

Xinghuo liaoyuan / *A Single Spark Can Start a Prairie Fire* / 星火燎原

Xinjiang fengguang / *Sceneries of Xinjiang* / 新疆风光

Xinjiang xiaheleke xiang nongnu zhi / *The Serf System in Xiaheleke County, Xinjiang* / 新疆夏合勒克乡农奴制

Xinling suixiang qu zhi yi / *Singing from the Heart* / 心灵随想曲之一

Xiongba Yazhou zhi da duohui – Shanghai / *Shanghai- the Great City in Asia* / 雄霸亚洲之大都会

Xishuangban na Daizu nongnu shehui / *The Serf Society of the Dai Nationality in Xishuangbanna* / 西双版纳傣族农奴社会

Xiu zixingche de ren / *The Man Who Repairs Bicycles* / 修自行车的人

Xiwang de chuangkou / *Window of Hope* / 希望的窗口

Xizang Nongnu zhidu / *The Serf System in Tibet* / 西藏农奴制度

Xizang wushi nian / *Fifty Years Tibet* / 西藏五十年
Xizang xunli / *Inspection of Tibet* / 西藏巡礼
Xu Guoliang chubin / *Xu Guoliang's Funeral* / 徐国梁出殡
Xu Shuzheng chu sang / *Xu Shuzheng's Funeral* / 徐树铮出丧
Xuanhua de chentu / *Floating Dust* / 喧哗的尘土
Xuelei de kongsu / *Tears of Bloody Stories* / 血泪的控诉
Xueluo yili / *Falling Snow in Yili* / 雪落伊梨
Xuesheng cun / *A Student Village* / 学生村
Xunye qianqiu / *Great Achievement Forever* / 勋业千秋
Ya, Taiwan / *Ah, Taiwan* / 呀，台湾
Yaba de zhengyue / *Last Spring Festival* / 哑巴的正月
Yafei huiyi / *Asia and African Conference* / 亚非会议
Yan'an shenghuo sanji / *A Few Clips of Yan'an Life* / 延安生活散记
Yang Hucheng yue bing / *General Yang Hucheng Inspecting his Army* / 杨虎成阅兵
Yangmei jian chu qiao / *Raise Your Eyebrows and Draw Your Sword* / 扬眉剑出鞘
Yangong xuelei chou / *The Salt Workers' Hatred of Exploitation* / 盐工血泪仇
Yangzhen youzhi yuan / *Yangzhen Kindergarten* / 养真幼稚园
Yanhai shisi cheng / *14 Cities along the Coast Line* / 沿海十四城
Yanmei / *Before the Flood* / 淹没
Yaoyuan de jia / *Home far Away* / 遥远的家
Yazhou fengbao / *Storms in Asia* / 亚洲风暴
Yemeng / *Nightdreams* / 夜梦
Yeying bushi weiyi de gehou / *Nightinggale, not the Only Voice* / 夜鹦不是唯一的歌喉
Yibu kuaguo jiuchongtian / *A Big Jump over Jiuchongtian* / 一步跨过九重天
Yiding yao ba Huaihe zhi hao / *We Must Control the Huai River* / 一定要把淮河治好
Yige ren he yizuo chengshi / *One City and One Person* / 一个人和一座城市
Yingxiong zhan zhen zai / *Heroes Overcoming an Earthquake* / 英雄战震灾
Yingxiong zhansheng beidahuang / *Heroes Win the Barren Land in the Northeast* /
　英雄战胜北大荒
Yishan tianhai / *Moving Mountains to Fill the Ocean* / 移山填海
Yishan zhaohai / *Moving Mountains and Building an Ocean* / 移山造海
Yongpan keji gaofeng / *Bravely Climbing the Mountain of Science* / 勇攀科技高峰
Youer yuan / *Kindergarten* / 幼儿园
Yuandong yundong hui / *Far East Sports Carnival* / 远东运动会
Yuanlin miaoguan / *Chinese Gardens* / 园林妙观
Yuanyuan / *Yuanyuan* / 元元
Yuanzheng shije gao feng / *Climbing the Highest Mountain in the World* / 远征世界
　高峰
Yuanzheng shamo / *Overcoming the Desert* / 远征沙漠
Yuehan tielu zhushao duan gongcheng / *Yuehan Railway Project* / 粤汉铁路主少段工程
Yuguan da xue zhan / *Bloody War at Yuguan* / 玉关大血战
Zai Ahzu de gutu / *On Grandpa's Homeland* / 在阿祖的故土
Zai Kunming / *In Kunming* / 在昆明
Zai lushang / *Migrant* / 在路上
Zai shengchan gaochao zhong / *At the High Tide of Production* / 在生产高潮中
Zai Xizang de rizi / *Days in Tibet* / 在西藏的日子
Zai yiqi de shiguang / *Wellspring* / 在一起的时光
Zai zong luxian guanghui zhaoyao xia / *Under the Light of the Great Policies* / 在总路
　线光辉照耀下

Zaici dengshang Zhumalangma fen / *Once More, On the Top of Mt. Everest* / 再次登上珠玛啦玛峰

Zhang Jizhi xiansheng de fengcai / *Mr Zhang Jizhi* / 张季直先生的风采

Zhang Zhuolin canan / *Tragedy of General Zhang Zuolin* / 张作林惨案

Zhanghua nirong chang / *Zhanghua Wool Fabric Factory* / 章华呢绒厂

Zhansheng Nujiang tianxian / *Overcoming the Nu River* / 战胜怒江天险

Zhejiang chao / *Zhejiang Waves* / 浙江潮

Zhenbao dao burong qinfan / *No Permission to Invade Zhenbao Island* / 珍宝岛不容侵犯

Zhenfu bingshan zhi fu / *The Hero Who Conquered Ice Mountain* / 征服冰山之父

Zhiye kuqi zhe / *Professional Mourner* / 职业哭泣者

Zhongguo Daojiao / *Chinese Daoism* / 中国道教

Zhongguo fojiao / *Chinese Buddhism* / 中国佛教

Zhongguo gongnong hongjun shenghuo pianduan / *Pictures of the Red Army* / 中国工农红军生活片段

Zhongguo gongyi meishu / *Chinese Art* / 中国工艺美术

Zhongguo guomindang quanguo daibiao dahui / *The Chinese National Guomindang Congress* / 中国国民党全国代表大会

Zhongguo hangtian cheng / *The City of Chinese Astronomy* / 中国航天城

Zhongguo hua / *Chinese Painting* / 中国画

Zhongguo jidu jiao / *Chinese Protestants* /中国基督教

Zhongguo jinji yuan fu riben di liu jie yuandong yundong hui / *Chinese Sportsmen Attending the Sixth Far East Sports Carnival in Japan* / 中国竞技员赴日本第六届远东运动会

Zhongguo mianxiang weilai / *China Faces Its Future* / 中国面向未来

Zhongguo minzu da tuanjie / *The Unity of Chinese Nations* / 中国民族大团结

Zhongguo Musilin / *Chinese Muslims* / 中国穆斯林

Zhongguo Tianzhu jiao / *Chinese Catholics* / 中国天主教

Zhongguo tiexue jun zhan shi / *History of China's Remarkably Brave Army* / 中国铁血军战史

Zhongguo yiliao dui zai Tanzanian / *Chinese Doctors in Tanzania* / 中国医疗队在坦桑尼亚

Zhonghua zhi sichou / *Chinese Silk* / 中华之丝绸

Zhongwai zuqiu bisai / *Sino and Foreign Football Matches* / 中外足球比赛

Zhongyang fangwen tuan zai xibei / *Delegation of the Central Government in the Northwest* / 中央访问团在西北

Zhongyin bianjie wenti zhenxiang / *The Truth of the Sino-India Border Dispute* / 中英边界问题真相

Zhou Fujiu da chusang / *Zhou Fujiu's Funeral* / 周扶九大出丧

Zhou zongli he women zai yiqi / *Premier Zhou Lives with Us* / 周总理和我们在一起

Zhu / *Bamboo* / 竹

Zhude weiyuan zhang huo zai women de xinli / *General Zhude Lives in Our Hearts Forever* / 朱德委员长活在我们的心理

Zhuhe / *Congratulations* / 祝贺

Zijin cheng / *Forbidden City* / 紫禁城

Zuie de dizhu zhuangyuan / *The Farm of Evil Landlords* / 罪恶的地主庄园

Zuihou de muxi shizu: guancha mosuo / *The Last Matrilineal Society: Observing the Mosuo* / 最后的母系氏族:观察摩梭

Newsreels

Budui shenghuo jianbao / *Brief News of Army Life* / 部队生活简报
Dianying xinwen / *News on Film* / 电影新闻
Guoji xinwen / *International News* / 国际新闻
Huabei xinwen / *Huabei News* / 华北新闻
Jianbao / *News Brief* / 简报
Jiefang jun xinwen / *News of the Liberation Army* / 解放军新闻
Jinri Zhongguo / *Today's China* / 今日中国
Kangzhan haowai / *Special Reports on the Anti-Japanese War* / 抗战号外
Kangzhan shilu / *Record of the Anti-Japanese War* / 抗战史录
Kangzhan teji / *Special Report on the Anti-Japanese War* / 抗战特辑
Minzhu de Dongbei / *Democratic Northeast* / 民主的东北
Renmin shijie / *People's World* / 人民世界
Shaoxian dui / *Young Pioneers* / 少先队
Tiyu jianbao / *Sports News* / 体育简报
Xin nongcun / *New Countryside* / 新农村
Xin Zhongguo jianbao / *Brief News of the New China* / 新中国简报
Zhongguo xinwen / *News of China* / 中国新闻

Television programmes and series

Aini meimei / *Aini Sisters* / 爱呢妹妹
Awa renmin chang xin'ge / *New Songs of the Va* / 阿瓦人民唱新歌
Baishou qijia / *From the Bottom* / 白手起家
Bangao shui zhai / *Shui Village* / 板告水寨
Baoxian Zhongguo / *Insurance in China* / 保险中国
Beimei yinxiang / *Impressions about Beimei* / 贝美印象
Chaoji banhui / *Super Classroom* / 超级班会
Daboji xiao banding / *Miao Stool Dance at Daboji* / 大簸箕小板凳
Diaoke shiguang / *Carving Time* / 雕刻时光
Dongfang shikong / *Oriental Horizon* / 东方时空
Du luo zhai xun meng / *Tujia Village* / 都罗寨寻梦
Duanqun Miao fengqing / *Miao Skirt* / 短裙苗风情
EPD zai xingdong / *EPD in Action* / EPD在行动
Falü yu diaode / *Law and Morality* / 法律与道德
Fanyue rili / *Looking Through Calendars* / 翻阅日历
Fazhi chuanzhen / *Court Alive* / 法制传真
Fazhi yuandi / *The Garden of Law* / 法制园地
Feichang diaocha / *Consumer Survey* / 非常调查
Fuxiang cai zhuxue bang / *Scholarship* / 福象彩助学榜
Ganbao Zang zhai / *Zang Village at Ganbao* / 甘堡藏寨
Guancha yu sikao / *Observation and Thinking* / 观察与思考
Guiju yu fangyuan / *Law and Harmony* / 规矩与方圆
Guoshi daohang / *Direction in Tertiary Education* / 国视导航
Guoshi guancha / *Observations* / 国视观察
Guoshi jiangtang / *Academic Seminar* / 国视讲堂
Guoshi xinwen / *Educational News* / 国视新闻

Guoshi zhishi / *Reporting* / 国视资视
Hainan / *Ocean Accident* / 海难
Haixuan / *Election* / 海选
Jiaodian fangtan / *Focal Point* / 焦点访谈
Jiaotong zongheng / *Traffic* / 交通纵横
Jiayao de laili / *The Origin of Fake Medicine* / 假药的来历
Jilu pian bianji shi / *Editorial Room for Documentary Film* / 纪录片编辑室
Jindai chunqiu / *Modern Chinese History* / 近代春秋
Jinri shuofa / *Legal Report* / 今日说法
Jintian wo zai jia / *Today I am at Home* / 今天我在家
Juanke chuan han / *Everlasting Wood Craft* / 镌刻传承
Kuche didai / *Car Knowledge* / 酷车地带
Luobo Yi xiang / *Yi Village* / 洛博彝乡
Manjiang Yao Zhai / *Yao Village* / 蛮降瑶寨
Meiren Xiang, Meiren Xiang / *Village of Beauties* / 美人乡，美人香
Ni Nu / *Zang Village* / 尼汝
Qianhu Miao zhai / *Miao Village with a Thousand Households* / 千户苗寨
Qiannian Baizhu cun nuo deng / *Bai Village in Dengruo* / 千年白族村诺邓
Qingchun Jia'nian hua / *Youth Party* / 青春嘉年华
Qingkou zhai san ji / *A Few Things about Qingkou Village* / 箐口寨散记
Ruili Daijia / *Dai Family* / 瑞丽傣家
Shehui jingwei / *Social Latitudes and Longitudes* / 社会经纬
Shisang chewan / *Trendy Vehicles* / 时尚车宛
Shitou zhai / *Village of Rock* / 石头寨
Taoping Qiang zai jishi / *Qiang Village at Taoping* / 桃平羌寨记事
Tunba cun chuanqi / *Legend in Tunba Village* / 吞巴村传奇
Wang Honger de bugui zhi lu / *Wang Honger's Road of No Return* / 王红儿的不归
之路
Wenming Zhonghua xing / *Journey of Chinese Civilization* / 文明中华行
Wo de taiyang / *My Sun* (2005 and 2006) / 我的太阳
Xibu jiaoyu / *West Education* / 西部教育
Xinwen diaocha / *News Probe* / 新闻调查
Yangguang huoban / *Sunshine* / 阳光伙伴
Yedao Li jia / *Li Village on Hainan Island* / 椰岛黎家
Zhengjuan da xuetang / *Stock Market* / 证券大学堂
Zhongguo mingzhai / *Famous Villages of China* / 中国名寨
Zhongguo minzu / *Chinese Ethnicities* / 中国民族
Zhonglu Zang jia / *Tibetan Households* / 中路藏家

Index

I have included in the Index only films that are given some detailed attention in the book. For a full list of films referred to see the **Filmography**.

Printed in the United Kingdom by
Lightning Source UK Ltd., Milton Keynes
140389UK00006BB/7/P